T0260670

**Stepping Through Cybersecurity
Risk Management**

Stepping Through Cybersecurity Risk Management

A Systems Thinking Approach

Jennifer L. Bayuk

For general information on our other products and services or for technical support, please contact our Customer Care Department within the United States at (800) 762-2974, outside the United States at (317) 572-3993 or fax (317) 572-4002.

Wiley also publishes its books in a variety of electronic formats. Some content that appears in print may not be available in electronic formats. For more information about Wiley products, visit our web site at www.wiley.com.

Library of Congress Cataloging-in-Publication Data applied for

Hardback ISBN 9781394213955

Cover Design: Wiley
Cover Images: © NicoElNino/Adobe Stock Photos; Courtesy of Jennifer Bayuk

Set in 9.5/12.5pt STIXTwoText by Straive, Pondicherry, India

Contents

Foreword *ix*
Preface *xiii*
Acknowledgements *xxv*
About the Companion Website *xxvii*

1   **Framework Elements** *1*
        References *16*

2   **Threats** *17*
2.1   Threat Actors *17*
2.1.1   Hackivists *22*
2.1.2   Insiders *23*
2.1.3   Hacker *26*
2.1.4   Competitors *29*
2.1.5   Lone Wolf *33*
2.2   Threat Networks *33*
2.2.1   Example: Identity Theft *34*
2.2.2   Zero-Day Threats *35*
2.3   Threat Vectors *37*
        References *44*

3   **Events** *47*
3.1   Event Classification *50*
3.2   Event Prevention *56*
3.3   Detection and Response *65*
3.4   Event Scenarios *77*
        References *87*

4   **Controls** *89*
4.1   Risk Appetite *91*
4.2   Policy *94*
4.2.1   Security Principles *96*
4.2.2   Formality *102*

4.3 Process *106*
4.4 Standards *114*
4.4.1 Internal Standards *114*
4.4.2 External Standards *116*
4.4.3 Security Architecture *123*
4.5 Procedures *130*
4.6 Guidelines *136*
References *140*

5 Assessments *143*
5.1 Standards Adherence *147*
5.2 Risk and Control Self Assessment *154*
5.3 Pentests and Vulnscans *160*
5.4 Audits *165*
5.5 Spot Checks *169*
References *172*

6 Issues *173*
6.1 Issue Identification *174*
6.2 Classification *177*
6.3 Criteria and Remediation *180*
References *183*

7 Metrics *185*
7.1 Measuring Cybersecurity *186*
7.2 From Measures to Metrics *189*
7.3 Key Risk Indicators *205*
References *216*

8 People *217*
8.1 Three Lines of Defense *217*
8.2 The Cybersecurity Team *224*
8.3 Enterprise Management *230*
8.4 Framework Element Owners *233*
References *235*

9 Risks *237*
9.1 Risk Categories *239*
9.2 Risk Treatment *242*
9.2.1 Controls *242*
9.2.2 Transfer *242*

9.2.3   Avoidance   *245*
9.2.4   Acceptance   *245*
9.3   Risk Appetite   *250*
9.4   Risk Tolerance   *255*
9.5   Probability Measurement   *260*
          References   *266*

10   Analysis   *269*
10.1   Reports and Studies   *269*
10.2   Safety Analogies   *275*
10.3   Decision Support   *278*
10.4   Conclusion   *280*
          References   *282*

          Appendix: Exercises in FrameCyber   *283*
          Index   *299*

Foreword

Humans have an affinity for determinism. Generally, we want to know cause and effect, and we want to know the outcomes of actions we take. Furthermore, many or most of us are not keen on surprises — especially surprises involving loss or extra work. These tendencies likely trace far back in time as evolutionary advantages. It helps survival if we know we should not eat that mushroom or wander into an unfamiliar, dark cave without a torch and thus might have an unexpected — and unpleasant — encounter.

The urge to have knowledge (and some control) of the flow of events led to the creation of myths, deities, rituals, and magic. Sometimes the consequences of these rituals were benign, such as performing a dance and a song at the solstice. But sometimes, the results were darker, as in ritual sacrifices to bring the rain. We have holdovers of many superstitions (to the detriment of black cats, for instance). We also see the creation of conspiracy theories to explain things we cannot understand. Too many people also think that changing one's mind based on new information is a weakness despite that being a fundamental component of the scientific process. The pull of determinism is strong.

As time passed, humans have seen the rise of science and the scientific method as we found ways to test and extend our knowledge. The results of that are all around us. For a long while, the belief was that science and technology could conquer all untoward occurrences. But we have repeatedly encountered failings where determinism does not rule. Global climate change and viral evolution are two classes of phenomena we cannot fully predict because of their intricacies and factors we do not yet fully understand. The more we learn about the world and its complex systems, the more we need to use stochastic methods to understand some likely behaviors. Loki and his brethren were random, and so too, it seems, are the probability distributions underlying the fabric of our quantum reality. Probability and its application to risk analysis and management have become accepted in most engineering disciplines.

In the early days of computing, we viewed digital computers as deterministic, modulo some uncommon malfunctions. However, as technology has advanced to interconnected global networks running dozens of virtualization layers, with access to petabytes of data and by millions of humans, we left determinism firmly in the dust along with rain gods and witches' curses. The combinatorics of interactions of all the variables coupled with the randomness and limitations of people means we can often only predict some trends and limited outcomes.

This is quite noticeable when we talk about cybersecurity. Our desire is for our systems to behave in predictable and constrained ways — to do our bidding with no harm and for us to be confident that we can engineer them accordingly. Once upon a time, the community thought that ***perfect*** security was achievable if only we followed some good practices in producing our code.[1] We now know that was naive, on the order of sacrificing small animals to the deities of intrusion and denial of service!

Practitioners of cybersecurity (and associated dark arts) have undergone an evolution in thinking about the protection of systems. We have evolved from strict security to the concept of trustworthy systems, then to measuring trustworthiness in context, then to resilience, and then to understand the context of risk. This is the journey that Dr. Jennifer Bayuk describes in the first chapter. We have reached the point of applying probability and statistics to attempt to divine the behavior of our computing artifacts. That does not mean determinism has no place, but we must understand its limitations. We need to embrace probability and risk analysis in computing to understand our systems' macro behaviors.

This book is a deep but understandable dive into the elements of cybersecurity and risk. The chapters examine the many aspects of reasoning about risk in a cybersecurity context and how to shape it. The book does not tell the reader how to build a type-safe program or how to put intrusion prevention systems into action — there are many other books available that do that. Instead, these chapters systematically examine the people, processes, events, and policies that compose the overall risk context of managing computing resources.

This book will be helpful to the newcomer as well as to the hierophants in the C-suite. The newcomer can read this to understand general principles and terms. The C-suite occupants can use the material as a guide to check that their understanding encompasses all it should. The text is accompanied by informative diagrams and illustrations that help elucidate the concepts. And each chapter has references to other insightful sources of information and enlightenment. This

---

1 This ignores that never had a common definition of what cybersecurity *is*. See *Cybersecurity Myths and Misconceptions* by Spafford, Mercalf, and Dystra, Pearson, 2023, for more details.

book is a carefully thought-out and well-researched text that belongs on the shelves of both apprentice and mage.

Set aside your beliefs about your control over your computing, and then read this book. Jennifer is a master of this topic area, and no matter how well you know the material already, you are likely to learn something new, no matter what your horoscope and tea leaves have already revealed. Oh, and be nice to black cats when you see them — they are not the ones who will be attempting to hack into your systems.

Eugene H. Spafford
July 2023

Preface

Throughout my career, I have been challenged to find ways to present the *computer security*, then the *information security*, and now the *cybersecurity* landscape to those outside the profession. Newcomers to the field of cybersecurity generally start in low-level positions where it is hard for them to see the ubiquitous reach of a cybersecurity program within the larger enterprise. One of my first attempts to explain this in a formal setting is illustrated in Figure 1 (Bayuk 1996). The outer circle of the figure depicts components that would be applicable to a variety of management domains holistically at the business process level, with the inner circle of cybersecurity operations support nested firmly within it. This diagram was adopted by the Information Systems Audit and Control Association (ISACA) when it developed the Certified Information Security Manager (CISM) program, and some form of it has been in ISACA CISM training materials ever since (Bayuk 2004).

As in any risk management discipline (credit risk, for example), a cybersecurity program composition starts with strategy. In consultation with business objectives, roles and responsibilities for accomplishing cybersecurity risk reduction will be assigned, and business leadership in those areas will formulate a strategy for making it happen. That strategy is communicated to stakeholders to formally enlist their cooperation, and, just as with any other risk management discipline, this ends up as management mandates in a cybersecurity policy. That policy is then supplemented with awareness activities (e.g., training) so that people who need to implement the policy, both cybersecurity staff and others, understand what they need to do to comply with the policy. Following the implementation of a policy, operations processes are developed to support the business with standards, automation, and procedures that accomplish risk reduction. Activities are monitored to make sure the cybersecurity operations have the desired effect of accomplishing cybersecurity policy and reducing cybersecurity risk.

If policies are monitored for gaps, such as blatant violations of policy and/or successful cybersecurity attacks, when gaps are discovered, the cybersecurity

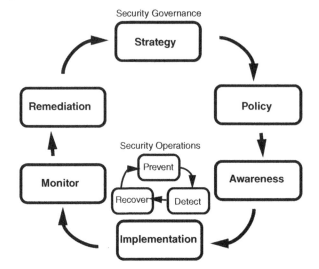

Figure 1 Cybersecurity Processes.

team should fall into a compliance mode or a remediation process. A remediation might entail a simple fix of broken software to ensure the enterprise is in compliance with policy and at lower risk for a security breach. In more serious cases, it may be that the policy adopted at the executive level did not result in a strategy that worked. So we may have to go back and look at our strategy. This iterative cycle is the same in any business operations, articulated by the familiar Drucker and Deming strategy taught in business schools, namely, plan-do-check-act management by observation, process, and controls. Cybersecurity uses all the same strategies common to any type of management activity. It is unique in that the domain is technically challenging and constantly changing, and the goal is to maintain cybersecurity and internet safety.

Of course, given that the discipline of cybersecurity is relatively historically new, decisions on cybersecurity strategy are not easy. However, steady increases in the number and breadth of cybersecurity attacks have placed increased focus on the process by which business management decides to implement security measures. Therefore, decision theorists often step in and try to help with cybersecurity problems. There is not as much debate on the actual process of decision analysis. A common method of analyzing decisions presents it as a five-step process (Keeney and Raiffa 1993):

1) Pre-analysis: decision-maker identification,
2) Structural analysis: the decision-maker structures the problem as a series of decisions and events, where the certainty level of events is affected by decisions,

3) Uncertainty analysis: event probabilities are assigned,
4) Utility or value analysis: consequences are identified for alternative decision/ event sequences, and the values of those consequences are estimated, and
5) Optimization analysis: the strategy that maximizes utility.

Though the cybersecurity field itself has yet to yield a standard on decision-making or even a set of preferred decision theories, decision theories tailored to other fields have been applied to computer security, information security, and cybersecurity for decades. A wide variety of academic papers have been devoted to applying the decision theory of the moment to information security. Virtually none have been adopted by experts in the field, but some that have been proposed are portfolio theory, value-focused thinking, prospect theory, game theory, marketplace models, utility theory, and Markov models. Though influential and to some degree successful in solving problems in domains other than cybersecurity, when applied to cybersecurity, the experiments varied widely with respect to (1) where the alternative decision choices should come from, (2) methods of reducing uncertainty, and (3) criteria for optimization analysis.

Through all this academic analysis of cybersecurity decision-making methods, the cybersecurity profession itself has held firm to a common approach, one based on the application of safety risk analysis to security risk (Bennett et al. 1975). This appears to be a straightforward reliance on probabilities of incidents based on historical data and seems to be the origin of the cost-benefit analysis equation so common in information security publications and standards. In this example (Endorf 2004), it is summarized in mathematical terms as follows:

F = expected frequency of attempts to produce an event that may cause damage
P = probability of success of the event if attempted
I = quantified consequences (i.e., cost) of a successful event

$$\text{Cybersecurity Risk} = F \times P \times I$$

Specifically, F is calculated by estimating the likelihood of a given type of security threat enactment in a given period of time; P is calculated by estimating the extent to which threat actors will achieve attack objectives, given the existing security measures; and I is calculated by estimating the monetary losses that could arise from that security event. Note that the resulting value is not actually a risk as defined in professional risk management standards. In that community, "risk" is defined as the probability that an event in a certain category may occur (positive or negative) and is measured in probability, not cost (COSO 2017). This cybersecurity equation, viewed in the light of risk management standards, refers instead to an estimate of the comparable *value* at risk.

In cybersecurity, the variables in this risk calculation are often renamed to reflect the nomenclature of the domain. Frequency is referred to as Threat; Probability is

Vulnerability; and Consequences as Impact. The result is an equation that looks like:

$$Risk = Threat \times Vulnerability \times Impact$$

The calculation is typically made in the context of annualized loss versus future return on investment in cybersecurity technology (Borg 2009). The resulting *Risk* value is then compared to the cost of a *countermeasure*. The *Vulnerability* is a subjective probability of the effectiveness of current security controls. Where vulnerability is sufficiently low, risk is deemed acceptable. If the estimated countermeasure costs are deemed to be more than the expected annual impact of a successful attack (the risk), then a decision-maker may instead decide to accept the risk. That is, a standard recommendation follows that:

$$If\ Cost\ of\ Countermeasure > Result\ of\ Risk\ Calculation, Then\ Accept\ Risk$$

This "traditional approach" to measuring cybersecurity risk is widely used and is still included as a correct answer on some cybersecurity certification examinations on how to make cybersecurity decisions. However, as a decision criteria, this value at risk calculation is extremely problematic. Even if the subjectivity of the vulnerability estimate was ignored, there is not one agreed-upon dollar amount that will stop a given cybersecurity breach. Any change to technology architecture has the potential to introduce risk even if intended to reduce it. Cybersecurity software solutions constantly evolve and are often incompatible with legacy technology architecture. Many changes have unintended operational consequences. Cybersecurity software, like all software, is plagued with bugs and design flaws.

Even if the minimum dollar amount for technology improvements was agreed upon between enterprise business and technology leaders, resisting attack is accomplished only through close collaboration among business and technology management, collaborating through changes in both business process and technology, in conjunction with collaborative continuous monitoring of adversaries, internal controls, and validation testing. It is very difficult to reduce such abstract oversight to a dollar amount without strategic analysis, which is absent from the equation. For a risk to be accepted based on estimated cost and impact alone would be suspect if the threat domain were fire or fraud. To trust it would be like buying a fire extinguisher without putting in a fire alarm or sprinkler system, checking on the capabilities of the local fire department, automating alerts to them, and/or installing fireproof insulation materials. In the absence of a well-planned cybersecurity governance and corresponding technology architecture, any single countermeasure is practically useless. Yet unfortunately, for many if not most cybersecurity professionals, the only education they have on risk is that extremely oversimplified equation.

The equation is the result of the cybersecurity community's desire to harmonize on an answer to an oversimplified "what do we need to invest?" question that is both common and appropriate coming from senior management. If the cost of the countermeasure is sufficiently low compared to the "risk" it would prevent, then deploying the countermeasure would be recommended as a result of the analysis. However, the simplification assumes that it is straightforward to match the risk of a given threat to the cost of some specific countermeasure(s) that would reduce the probability of the threat event's success. It is not that simple.

One example serves to present several problems with this approach. Consider a scenario where a decision-maker must decide how to secure a wire transfer system in a cloud environment. One method may be to deploy the system on an isolated network and allow anyone who is authenticated to the network to transfer wires. In this scenario, one threat would be that an internal user, someone with valid access to the network, would presumably find a way to send unauthorized wires. Another threat would be that an external user would find a way to break into the network to send wires.

Given multiple cultural deterrents such as background checks, electronic monitoring, and available sanctions, such as jail time, management may assess the probability that an internal user would abuse the check system at close to zero. However, given that all software is flawed and not all flaws are presently known, the probability that an external user would find a way to break into the network and elude detection may be assessed at something greater than zero, such as 25%. Management might predict the frequency with which an external attack may occur twice during some predefined time period, usually per year. The potential impact on the company from both threats would be on the balance of the bank account. Using $100,000 as a hypothetical bank account balance, the loss would be calculated in the risk equation: Risk = Threat × Vulnerability × Impact, as in:

$$\text{Risk}_{\text{Threat1}} = 0 \times 0 \times \$100,000 = 0$$
$$\text{Risk}_{\text{Threat2}} = 2 \times 0.25 \times \$100,000 = \$50,000$$

This analysis would be interpreted to mean that any countermeasure that has a budget of less than $50,000 should be implemented to mitigate the risk. This presents a problem. No matter how well-founded a risk probability assessment is, no manager is likely to spend half of the value at risk to mitigate a risk whose probability is not closer to 100%. This is because of the proverbial "elephant in the room" argument as illustrated in Figure 2, wherein "C" refers to an estimated cost of cyberattack and "T" refers to the technology cost of a countermeasure. The analogy of the elephant with the problem is that both are so large that no one can avoid them, and no one wants to talk about them because it makes them uncomfortable. The problem with the cybersecurity risk equation is that P is may be close

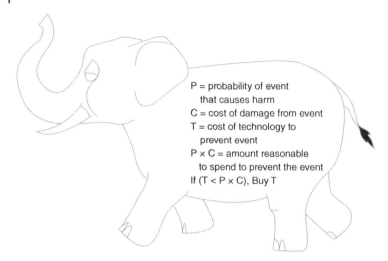

P = probability of event
   that causes harm
C = cost of damage from event
T = cost of technology to
   prevent event
P × C = amount reasonable
   to spend to prevent the event
If (T < P × C), Buy T

Figure 2 Elephant in the Room.

to 100% or unknown due to lack of historical data, T may not be the most appropriate method of reducing C, and simply spending once on T will not prevent harm because T needs to be maintained and there is an unaccounted for probability that it will not work. The equations assume there is data available that is very difficult to specify and collect. Moreover, although the method acknowledges the fact that risk is measured in probability, there is scarce guidance on justifying the probability estimates before or after spending T.

As Warren Buffet put it, "Our advice: Beware of geeks bearing formulas" (Segal 2009, p.16). It is obvious that an enterprise must take factors into consideration over and above preliminary estimates of control costs and losses.

Say the solution is to add an access control measure that requires a user to have their retina scanned, a fingerprint taken, or some other biometric identification check before they gain access to the wire transfer network. This would presumably reduce the probability that an external attacker would find a way to break into it, but due to the high probability of software containing bugs and flaws, the external attacker may find a way to bypass it. This observation leads to the recognition of another problem with the security risk calculation approach, that not all threats are anticipated. So, the probability of a successful attack after the security enhancement has been made is not zero, even if it reduces a known vulnerability. A typical fallback in such a case would be to *layer* security controls, that is, add a password or other type of software-enabled authentication to the wire transfer system in addition to the biometrics layer that protects the network. This would add incremental costs to an existing software deployment rather than the full cost of new cybersecurity-specific technology. Such costs would be considered additions to the existing system that already included biometric control, so the costs would still be compared to a risk equation that would appear as follows:

$$\text{Risk}_{\text{Threat2}} = 2 \times 0.25 \times \$100,000 = \$50,000$$

This back-to-the-drawing-board calculation is frequently recommended without corresponding advice to consider alternative architectures using existing security components and/or whether application software enhancements have been considered. This is yet another problem with the approach. Layers upon layers of security are added via decisions that assume some new technology will counter one new threat at a time, often without consideration of the total cost of ownership of the full set of security measures.

Texts containing this type of advice on security risk calculations typically ignore these obvious problems and also admit that the decisions will not be perfect. The method includes acknowledgement that a given countermeasure may not reduce a vulnerability to zero but still claim a substantial reduction of risk due to the countermeasure. Say that in this example, it is claimed to be reduced to 5%. Risk post-security-control-implementation is considered "residual" risk, as opposed to "inherent" risk, which assumes no controls are in place. In this case, even our first calculation was of residual risk because there is a network security control in our example. Adding in a software control that reduced the probability of exploit to 5% would make the new residual risk for threat 2:

$$\text{ResidualRisk}_{\text{Threat2}} = 2 \times 0.05 \times \$100,000 = \$10,000$$

The cost to deploy the solution would have to be \$40,000 (i.e., \$50,000−\$10,000) or less for it to compare favorably with the original estimate of risk. Methodical approaches to plugging in variables into both the risk equation and the calculation of the cost of security measures have been codified in a variety of toolsets designed for use by security managers.

Despite the obvious difficulties with the approach, the number of off-the-shelf products to assist the security professional in this type of risk analysis has been on the increase since the early 2000s (Schreider 2003). Other methods of calculating Return On Security Investment (ROSI) incorporated into such applications are Cost-Benefit Analysis (CBA), Return On Investment (ROI), Net Present Value (NPV), and Internal Rate of Return (IRR) (Gordon and Loeb 2016). All of these variations on the traditional approach assume that it is acceptable to make conclusions on how to invest in security in spite of obvious problems. They assume that it is possible to frame security purchase decisions in a context where benefits from security investment will be obvious, where the probability of a threat is calculable (even in cases where there is scant data available on similar occurrences), and where loss avoidance is guaranteed to at least some measurable extent. Yet as long as these decision support methods have been in use, critics have been noting that risk calculations designed for loss avoidance were created in fields where a history of events and corresponding loss data were available. As early as 1982, one observer admitted that all such efforts are compromised by a lack of actual case data, a tendency to overlook serious exposure to technology risks, and the excessive costs in the process of determining credible probability measures (Schweitzer 1982). These drawbacks remain true today.

In contrast, the cybersecurity decision support model in this book is based on risk analysis borrowed from the professional practice of operational risk management. Operational risk considers a business operation holistically and focuses on events and hypothetical events that may reduce business value. Controls to mitigate risk are not limited to any single domain, such as technology, but the entire business operation is in scope. Operational risk also considers any business process as a potential source of risk, even the technology control process itself. For example, security control professionals routinely accidentally cause system downtime when conducting cyberattack simulations called *penetration tests*.

Like cybersecurity risk management, operational risk management is inherently low on quantitative measures in comparison with its more mature risk industry counterparts: credit risk and market risk. However, in the past half century, professionals in the field have developed systematic data collection methods, control evaluation criteria, and risk analysis techniques that are directly applicable to cybersecurity decision support. Cybersecurity risk management can gain immediate value from adopting these techniques to support a wide variety of cybersecurity decisions.

Preparation for establishing a cybersecurity risk management program and tasks required to monitor risks have been the subject of several authoritative standards. Most if not all include a cycle that begins with governance and strategy, followed by policy and assessment, and finally by risk remediation through control implementation. The cycle is continuous and provides a feedback loop for the governance process. Figure 2 is a version published by the US National Institute of Standard and Technology Standard (NIST) (NIST 2018). The *Strategy* process in Figure 1 includes the same methods to establish governance that NIST describes in the *Prepare* process in Figure 3. The *Policy* process in Figure 1 includes the same advice to establish control standards as the *Categorize* and *Select* processes in Figure 3. The International Standards Organization also has separately designated processes for information security management (ISO/IEC 2022a) and controls (ISO/IEC 2022b). COBIT dedicates a domain called "Evaluate, Direct, and Support" to distinguish technology governance from management (ISACA 2019, p. 29). Governance mandates to minimize risk to a specified scope of digital assets is a preliminary step to any type of risk assessment and control implementation.

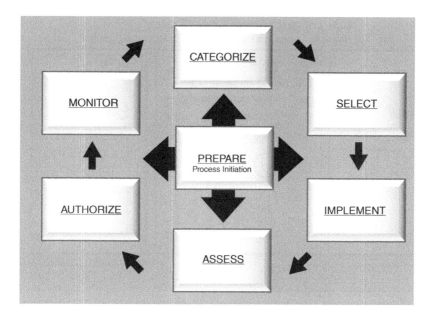

Figure 3 NIST Risk Management Process.

Cybersecurity framework preparation strategies and ongoing tasks provide the context necessary to demonstrate that risk assessment results are relevant to the decisions they are intended to support. NIST also observes that because organizational functions, supporting processes, information systems, and threats change over time, the validity and usefulness of any risk assessment are bound by time. Therefore, it is important that decisions based on cybersecurity risk assessment be continuously revisited as systems and associated threats evolve. Every enterprise will have to customize both strategy and tasks into their own cybersecurity risk management framework. This book utilizes a generic cybersecurity decision support model referred to as *FrameCyber*®. It is a tool that allows an enterprise to design and document its own cybersecurity risk management framework. FrameCyber® allows decisions on cybersecurity risk to be *framed* in a manner that both takes advantage of both operational risk management theory and technology industry standards while allowing for enterprise customization. It provides precise definitions for information relevant to decisions and a methodology for using that information in the context of cybersecurity risk management. It does this in full appreciation for the joke in Figure 4.

In contrast to the implication of the cartoon that standards need standards for consolidation, FrameCyber® is not a new standard and does not attempt to

Figure 4 FrameCyber® is not a Standard.

consolidate standards. It is merely a practical guide that a cybersecurity organization may use to document and communicate their own enterprise cybersecurity risk management framework. It respects, but does not replace, enterprise-selected cybersecurity standards. It is my expectation that up-and-coming cybersecurity professionals will find the guidance provided in this book invaluable as they design cybersecurity for systems of myriad complexity. The practical advice herein is founded in historical references, theoretical evolution, and current best practices presented in layman's terms. The aim is to make the book accessible not only to cybersecurity professional practitioners and would-be practitioners but also to their business and technology counterparts seeking a deeper understanding of the influence of cybersecurity on the evolution of the overall ever-evolving cyber landscape.

References

Bayuk, J. (1996). Security through process management. Paper presented at the National Information Systems Security Conference (NISSC), Washington, DC (22 October 1996,). https://www.bayuk.com/publications/BayukNISSC96.pdf (accessed 08 May 2023).

Bayuk, J. (2004). Delivery and Support. *Certified Information Security Manager Review Manual*: Chapter 5.

Borg, S. (2009). The economics of loss. In: *Enterprise Information Security and Privacy* (ed. C. W. Axelrod, J. Bayuk, and D. Schutzer), 103-114. Artech House.

Bennett, C. A., Murphey, W. M., and Sherr, T. S. (1975) *Societal Risk Approach to Safeguards Design and Evaluation*. Energy Research and Development Administration.

COSO (2017). *Enterprise risk management: Integrating with strategy and performance.* Committee of Sponsoring Organizations of the Treadway Commission.

Endorf, C. (2004). Measuring ROI on security. In: *Information Security Management Handbook,* Fifth Edition. (ed. H. Tipton and M. Krause) Auerbach.

Gordon L., and Loeb, M. (2016). Investing in Cybersecurity: Insights from the Gordon-Loeb Model, *Journal of Information Security, Volume 7, pp.* 49-59.

ISACA (2019). *COBIT 2019 Governance and Management Objectives*, ISACA, www.isaca.org.

ISO/IEC (2022a) *27001: Information Security, Cybersecurity and Privacy Protection — Information Security Management Systems — Requirements.* International Organization for Standardization/International Electrotechnical Commission, www.iso.org.

ISO/IEC (2022b) *27002: Information Security, Cybersecurity and Privacy Protection — Information Security Controls.* International Organization for Standardization/International Electrotechnical Commission, www.iso.org.

Keeney, R. L. and Raiffa, H. (1993). *Decisions with Multiple Objectives, Preferences and Value Tradeoffs.* Cambridge University Press.

NIST (2018). *Risk Management Framework for Information Systems and Organizations.* National Institute of Standards and Technology. https://nvlpubs.nist.gov/nistpubs/SpecialPublications/NIST.SP.800-37r2.pdf (accessed 08 May 2023).

Schreider, T. (2003). Risk assessment tools: A primer. *Information Systems Control Journal, Volume 2, pp.* 20-23.

Schweitzer, J. A. (1982). *Managing Information Security, A Program for the Electronic Age.* Butterworth Publishers Inc.

Segal, D. (2009). In Letter, Buffet Accepts Blame and Faults Others, *NY Times,* March 1, 2009, p. 16.

Acknowledgements

I started my career in cybersecurity when it was called Computer Security, lived through its transition to Information Security, and emerged as one of the small minority of Cybersecurity Risk Management professionals who have been in the field since before its recognition as a promising career choice. At first, I referred to the members of our profession, including myself, as "jacks of all trades, masters of none." But now I recognize that that we who practice cybersecurity have a very specific expertise: the instinct to recognize patterns of potential misuse of technology. While most people appreciate technology for the convenience it offers, cybersecurity professionals recognize its inherent potential to cause harm. For this expertise, I am indebted to the camaraderie of that *entire* community, as well as the leadership and coaching of computer security expert Ed Amoroso in my days at Bell Laboratories, information security expert Pat Ripley in my days at Bear Stearns, and risk management experts Mike Donahue and John Davidson in my days at Price Waterhouse and Citi, respectively. I am also indebted to those who contributed to this work via proofreading, questioning, and other invaluable support: Jeanne Apryaz, Rachel Chernati, Andy McCool and my editor at Wiley: Brett Kurzman. Thank you all for your time and patience. Notwithstanding, my deepest debt is to my husband Michael for his loving patience throughout the endeavor.

About the Companion Website

This book is accompanied by a companion website.

www.wiley.com/go/STCRM

This website includes:

- Professor Guide
- Color Figures

1

Framework Elements

In the realm of risk, cybersecurity is a fairly new idea. Most people currently entering the cybersecurity profession do not remember a time when cybersecurity was not a major concern. Yet, at the time of this writing, reliance on computers to run business operations is less than a century old. Prior to this time, operational risk was more concerned with natural disasters than human-induced disasters. Fraud and staff mistakes are also part of operational risk, so as dependency on computers steadily increased from the 1960s through the 1980s, a then-new joke surfaced: *To err is human, but if you really want to screw things up, use a computer.*

Foundational technology risk management concepts have been in place since the 1970s, but the tuning and application of these concepts to cybersecurity were slow to evolve. The principles are the same, but they have been applied differently over the years to adapt to changing technology. There is no doubt that cybersecurity risk management tools and techniques have continuously improved. While in the 1980s, an inspection of system capabilities to restrict access to data was enough to earn a system a gold star, in the 1990s, full data inspection of user records and comparison with job functions augmented the inspection of the system's capabilities. That is, even a well-defined system can be misused by unauthorized or unintentional entry of data that allows excessive privileges. In the 2000s, the assumption that a system could maintain data integrity by separating operating system and database access was challenged by viruses and hacks targeting networked databases. In the 2010s, the assumption that a system could maintain data availability by well-tested backup and fail-over procedures was shattered by distributed denial of service attacks. In all cases, the technology industry stepped in to provide a new set of automated security controls to be integrated into existing systems and built into new systems going forward. Although the consequences of cybersecurity incidents have become dramatically more profound over the decades, available controls have also become more comprehensive, more ubiquitous, and more effective.

Stepping Through Cybersecurity Risk Management: A Systems Thinking Approach,
First Edition. Jennifer L. Bayuk.
© 2024 John Wiley & Sons, Inc. Published 2024 by John Wiley & Sons, Inc.
Companion website: www.wiley.com/go/STCRM

This book shares that perspective. It is intended to help anyone who works in cybersecurity understand how their own cybersecurity job function helps contribute to that continuous lifecycle of improvement. It should also help those considering working in cybersecurity decide in which cybersecurity functions they are most interested. FrameCyber® is intended to make cybersecurity risk management visible to those who are contributing to it and comprehensible to those looking in from the outside. Like any effort to increase visibility, increasing transparency in cybersecurity requires clearing out some clouds first. Like any effort to increasing visibility, increasing transparency in cybersecurity requires clearing out some clouds first. Unfortunately, there are a plethora of myths that currently cloud management thinking about cybersecurity (Spafford et al. 2022).

The first myth is that people who work in cybersecurity risk analysis are less influential in solving hard cybersecurity problems. Because they are not contributing to cyber defense tools and techniques with technology operations and engineering teams, sometimes they are dismissed as paper-pushers. The truth is that it is not technology implementation, but rather constant analysis that makes cybersecurity risk management most effective, specifically the analysis of aggregate cybersecurity events, cybersecurity issues, and cybersecurity assessments. Data gleaned from these analyses are consolidated into a framework for decision-making. This framework in turn prompts decisions on defensive tactics and technologies that allow the profession of cybersecurity risk management to evolve. To borrow a phrase from the DevOps community, starting with technology and then backing into analysis is to *shift right*, a derogatory term for building technology before knowing what its validation test looks like. In the cybersecurity analogy, to *shift left* means to populate the defense team with people who are capable of testing whether the control objective of being resilient to cyberattack is met. This exposes another myth about cybersecurity, namely, that cybersecurity risk is a pure technology problem.

In any risk discipline, it is appropriate to be guided by the expectations of management from an enterprise perspective, i.e., what executives expect cybersecurity risk managers to actually produce. A lot of people working in cybersecurity risk management are producing risk assessment reports intended to be consumed by executive management. The topics on these reports range from assessment of regulatory compliance to assessment of enterprise ability to thwart the latest attack to hit the headlines. Thus, the paper-pusher analogy. This reporting activity sometimes takes place in the absence of answers to basic questions, such as:

- What do executives do with the reports?
- In what operational process, if any, are the reports expected to be utilized?
- What behavior should be influenced by information in the reports, and does it differ from what is actually done?
- Are the reports the most effective way to communicate the results of cybersecurity risk analysis?

Such reports produced in the absence of a process designed to produce a continuous cycle of improvement in decision-making are headed for the recycle bin, or worse, retaliation against their authors for exposing vulnerabilities without offering solutions.

It is easy to forget that the role of Chief Information Officer (CIO) has only been around for less than half a century and the role of a Chief Information Security Officer (CISO) for a few decades. (*Note, herein, we refer to the highest-ranking person whose sole job is information security as the CISO, although of course the title may differ depending on the organization*). The pace of technology change has been skyrocketing within that timeframe. The likelihood that any cybersecurity risk management process is fully mature cannot conceivably be high, and the likelihood that cybersecurity continuous improvement processes are mature is even lower. Admittedly, progress has been made in maturing security operations, investigation, and forensics. However, these processes have evolved in *response* to successful cyberattacks, that is to *realized risk*, then been adopted as industry best practices. We are not yet ahead of the game.

It is revealing that cybersecurity professionals have labeled many of their operational activities as "cybersecurity risk management" activities. For example, it is obvious that running an antivirus (AV) system is a risk management activity, as it is meant to reduce the risk of a specific risk category of events, namely, harm to systems *from malicious software*. However, this narrow usage is limited to specific risk categories and does not address the aggregation issue. Questions at the aggregate level are:

- Do cybersecurity management activities cover the full spectrum of cybersecurity risks within business process?
- If cybersecurity management activities cover the technology environment, does this cover all cybersecurity risks to business process?

Risk management concepts are much older than technology. Risk management is the art, not the science, of identifying potentially negatively impacting events and avoiding them. It also includes an interpretation, popular in gambling and investing, which involves opportunity. That is, the term "risk" is not always used to characterize events that have negative impact but may also be applied to events that have a positive impact. In this sense, risk means opportunity, or the flip side of the probability of a negative event. However, that interpretation draws gasps of disbelief from cybersecurity professionals because in the domain of cybersecurity, the use of the term risk ubiquitously applies to negative events, so herein, we safely let that opportunity concept go. As cybersecurity risk management professionals, we are expected to estimate the probability of negative impacts due to cybersecurity events.

To do that, we need data that we can gather on these events that we can analyze. A famous example of how to estimate the probability of negative impacts was provided by Peter Bernstein in his book: "Against the Gods, The Remarkable

Story of Risk." Bernstein described how Edward Lloyd, the owner of a coffee house in London in the late 1600s, started recording the arrivals and departures of ships in combination with observations of conditions abroad, major ship auctions, and marine route hazards (Bernstein 1996). Lloyd's coffee house became a gathering place for marine insurance underwriters, and his list was eventually expanded to provide news on foreign stock markets, ship accidents, and sinkings. One hundred years later, this brand of risk analysis became the Society of Lloyd's and eventually the insurance company we know today as Lloyd's of London. They were trying to gather data about the past to predict the future. That is what risk management is all about.

Today, it is a fundamental principle of risk management that the ability to successfully predict the future based on past events requires historical data. Unfortunately, we do not have a lot of historical data on cybersecurity, and technology changes so rapidly that by the time we collect it, it may be obsolete. Nevertheless, we experience events, and recording them adds to our ability to recognize patterns of activity that may increase cybersecurity risk.

However, even when the risks of dependency on computers became blatantly obvious in the 1980s, computer security was largely a technology control exercise, not one populated with risk management professionals. Controls adequate to reduce risk to an acceptable level were almost nonexistent. Computer security professionals hopelessly stood by as Microsoft Windows allowed access to data through networks without logins, as the Internet allowed software to be downloaded onto people's personal computers without their knowledge, and as viruses had cascading effects on business processes. Only after 9/11 was computer risk management elevated to executive levels, and then although it became more and more obvious, the control side still failed to catch up.

More recent events, however, have elevated cybersecurity risk management concerns even higher. For example, the massive organized criminal industry that feeds on identity theft, the devastating impact of cyberwarfare attacks against Estonia and Sony Corporation, and the post-9/11 escalation of cyber espionage to cyberwar made cybersecurity risk management a Board-level conversation. However, some methods by which cybersecurity risk is managed still lag far behind the best practices in the broader field of operational risk management. It is often seen as a technical exercise whose professionals are not required to have insight into business process supported by the technology in scope. There has been a lot of effort to normalize and standardize cybersecurity tools and techniques, when in reality the controls required by different businesses can be very diverse. This situation calls for a hard look at how we make cybersecurity decisions at both the enterprise and the organization level.

For a start, it is helpful to acknowledge that cybersecurity decisions are indeed made at multiple levels within an enterprise, where enterprise refers to an entity, whether corporate, government, or nonprofit. Enterprises may comprise a wide variety of organizations, from holding companies and business units to corporate support functions and financial services. A key element of the definition for the purposes of risk management is that enterprises are bound by due diligence obligations, whether legal or ethical, to provide oversight to ensure the strength and stability of the organizations of which they are composed. To this end, an enterprise will often establish a risk management framework to be shared across and within its constituent organizations. These include suppliers, service providers, affiliates, newly acquired companies, regulators, and media outlets. The framework is intended to provide transparency at the enterprise level to the activities and decisions made within each organization. Where such activities and decisions concern the use of technology, the framework extends to transparency of systems support for business activities.

The International Standards Organization considers information security management itself a system, *Information Security Management System*, or *ISMS* (ISO 2022). The word *system* is used in the context of the field of systems engineering, wherein a system is an arrangement of parts or elements that together exhibit behavior or meaning that the individual constituents do not (INCOSE 2023). The systems engineering profession has also produced a tool used for defining systems called a *systemigram*, merging the terms "system" and "diagram" (Boardman and Sauser 2008). In a systemigram, even complex systems are defined in one simple sentence focused on the system mission. This is called the *mainstay*. Considering FrameCyber®, a cybersecurity risk system in the same manner as an ISMS, its definition in a single sentence might be "FrameCyber® empowers enterprises to oversee organizations that evaluate cybersecurity risk to support decisions." This is the mainstay of the systemigram in Figure 1.1. A systemigram places the system to be defined at the top left and the system's value proposition at the bottom right. The mainstay connects system components (nouns) with activities (verbs) that define relationships between them. A sentence formed by the mainstay is the system mission of statement. The idea is that the system is defined by its purpose, and the purpose should be clear by demonstrating how its main components contribute to its expected deliverable. Figure 1.1 therefore defines a tool for creating a cybersecurity risk framework. Nonetheless, just as in any complex system, there are many other perspectives that people understand about it.

A systemigram allows for multiple threads connecting to its mainstay to flesh out the context in which the system is expected to work. The most obvious context, depicted in Figure 1.2, is that cybersecurity risk is concerned with the activities of bad actors who threaten the enterprise. The full set of cyber actors that threaten an organization is often referred to as its "Threat Catalog." Threats are of primary importance because without a clear understanding of who will probably attack and what the methods they are likely to use to enact cyber threats, it is highly unlikely that an enterprise will be prepared to thwart the attack. Notice that the who and what of a threat are different. The existence of a bad actor does

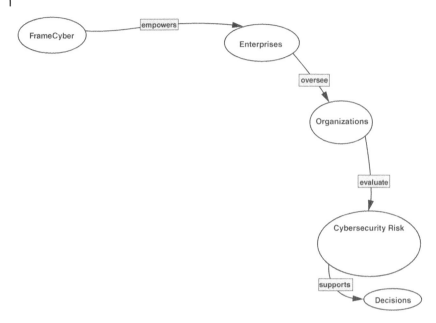

Figure 1.1 Cybersecurity Framework Systemigram Mainstay

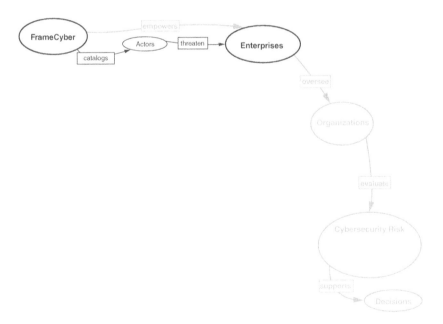

Figure 1.2 Cybersecurity Risk Framework Threat Perspective

not imply that the threat will be enacted or that it will succeed. So although threat is of primary importance in analyzing risk, it is nevertheless a small piece of a larger puzzle.

Cybersecurity attack events, of course, trump all assumptions based on probability. Successful cyberattacks are realized risk – actual examples of events producing negative impact. The probability of a past cyberattack event's occurrence is 100%; hence, the probability of an event in its risk category is 100%. Note that we focus here on attack events because, although some may argue that not all negatively impacting cybersecurity incidents are attacks, unintentional negatively impacting accidents have long been classified as operational risk as business environment and internal control factors (BEICFs) whether or not they are technology related. When an accident exposes a cybersecurity vulnerability, the event may be an operational loss event, but is not considered a cybersecurity incident.

Figure 1.3 illustrates how a risk framework focuses on events. Events may be internal to the enterprise, external in that they occurred elsewhere, and/or hypothetical activities of threat actors (*scenarios*). They may have common root causes. They may cause monetary losses. Classified into categories, negatively impacting events may form the basis of a *risk register*. Where controls are not sufficient to prevent damaging events, vulnerability *issues* are identified. While the word *issue*

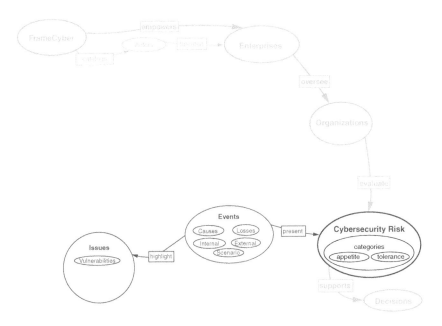

Figure 1.3 Cybersecurity Risk Framework Event Perspective

simply means an important topic for discussion, in risk management generally the word refers to situations that present evidence that a risk is highly probable. In cybersecurity specifically, the word *issue* is reserved for system weaknesses that increase the probability that enacted threats will result in successful cybersecurity attacks. Issues are typically prioritized for remediation based on this probability.

Where issues indicate high probability of successful cyberattack, the perspective of the technology controls community should be brought to bear on cybersecurity risk. As previously mentioned, the cybersecurity operations community is mature compared to the cybersecurity risk analysis community, and there is a great deal of information on how to reduce vulnerabilities exposed by events. As with any formal enterprise initiative, it starts with executive management establishing policy mandates for reducing risk with management controls. Policy mandates are strengthened by the publication of management "controls" designed to establish policy compliance. These controls may be in the form of processes, standards, and procedures, and are designed to reduce risk to acceptable levels. Where controls are well designed and managed, they also provide the basis for assurance that management mandates for risk reduction are adequately met. Figure 1.4 adds a control perspective to the system definition.

Even organizations with relatively mature controls may succumb to cyberattack when issues identified in the course of responding to cybersecurity events are identified too late to act upon them. Therefore, sound cybersecurity risk

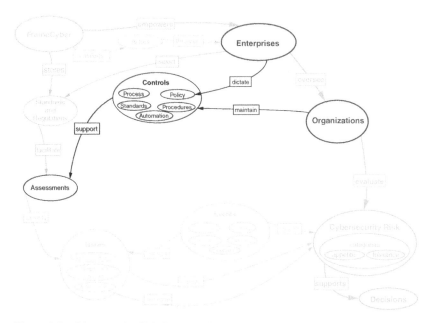

Figure 1.4 Cybersecurity Risk Framework Control Perspective

management also involves identifying vulnerabilities before they are exploited by cyber threat actors. To do this, enterprises typically adopt standards of best practices and regulatory guidance that list technology controls recommended (*in the latter case, required*) for minimizing cybersecurity risk. An enterprise may even publish custom internal Risk and Control Matrix (RCM) for this purpose. It allows management to compare the enterprise's cybersecurity posture to the set of published requirements to "assess" its own cybersecurity risk. The term is in quotes because what is meant by assessment varies widely. Synonyms are evaluation, judgment, gauging, rating, estimation, appraisal, opinion, and analysis. While standards and regulations are not exactly yardsticks that can be held up to an organization to measure cybersecurity risk, comparison of a standard with organizational practices does yield information that can be used to identify vulnerabilities and other potential cybersecurity risk issues. Cybersecurity risk management as a profession has produced a wide variety of such assessment tools. They are not equally useful, and even the most thorough are not always 100% germane to their targeted audience. What they have in common is that they are tools used to identify situations that foster recognition that the probability of a cybersecurity event with negative impact on an organization may be high. Note that one of the most popular of these tools, the NIST Cybersecurity Framework (NIST CSF 2024), itself states that the tool should not be used as a compliance checklist, but to guide your analysis of your own organization, and see if there are issues. Figure 1.5 illustrates the basic concept of cybersecurity risk assessment.

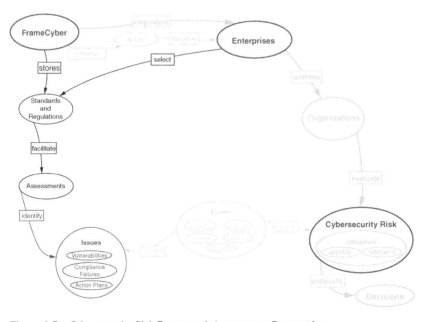

Figure 1.5 Cybersecurity Risk Framework Assessment Perspective

The issues identified in an assessment are often referred to as "risk issues" because they reflect a situation that may or may not reflect high probability of suc-cumbing to cyberattack. But, in reality, noncompliance with a standard may not indicate a high probability of successful cyberattack. For example, an enterprise may have implemented custom controls to compensate for the lack of compliance with an industry standard requirement. There may also be an issue remediation "action plan" underway that will eliminate the issue in a very short timeframe. That is, a known issue with a planned solution in combination with a compensating control will be a lower priority as a "risk" issue even if the risk of exploit is still high. All issues are often stored in an issue-tracking system to ensure they are not dismissed before being properly evaluated. Figure 1.6 highlights the influence of issue tracking and its influence on cybersecurity risk management.

Of course, logging issues is only productive if they are actually remediated, so an issue-tracking system will typically be accompanied by management trend metrics. Moreover, organizations that manage technology routinely collect data points on uptime and storage capacity, and automated cybersecurity controls are similarly monitored to ensure they are operating as designed. Such measurement data is assembled into performance and risk metrics. Trends in risk metrics may demonstrate that controls are either implemented incorrectly or improving over time, that is, trending negatively or positively, indicating increasing or decreasing

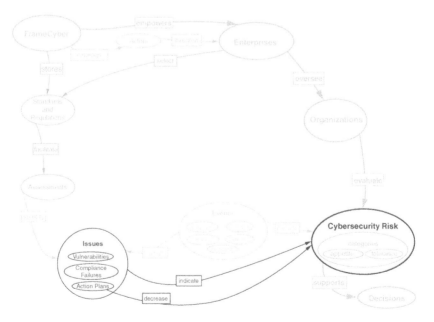

Figure 1.6 Cybersecurity Risk Framework Issue Perspective

vulnerability to probable cybersecurity attacks. In this manner, issue and control metrics may also be combined to produce "key" risk indicators.

Negatively impacting events are also risk indicators. Those that are similar are classified into risk categories. Some events are prohibited by policy, such as customer data breaches, and the enterprise risk appetite for those events will be low. However, just as enterprises are willing to tolerate monetary losses in the pursuit of potential profit gains, they may have a higher tolerance for events in other cybersecurity risk categories, such as disruption of cafeteria menu systems. Events may be measured and tracked to produce trends on threats and root causes. That data, like that collected by Lloyd on ship hazards, may serve as a risk indicator. Figure 1.7 illustrates the perspective on risk that focuses on metrics.

Of course, all statisticians know that even metrics can be subjective. At the end of the day, it is important to remember that a framework is only as good as the people who operate it. Figure 1.8 shows the interaction of enterprise staff within the FrameCyber® framework. Without being specific with reference to any given organization chart, it includes key roles for managers, risk analysts, and security operations. They decide whether risk remains within appetite and whether tolerance measures are adequate to alert them to risk. This aspect of cybersecurity, the governance aspect, relies on a wide variety of people, in different enterprise job functions, all contributing actively to the risk management process. These people

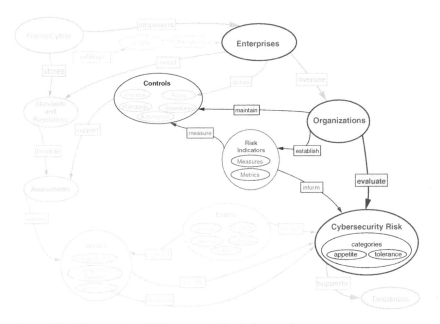

Figure 1.7 Cybersecurity Risk Framework Metric Perspective

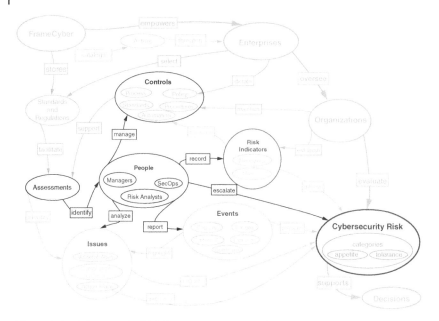

Figure 1.8   Cybersecurity Risk Framework Focus on People

perform assessments, manage controls, make observations, report events, analyze issues, and engage in a host of other activities intended to fortify the enterprise against cybersecurity risk.

Many organizations that establish formal roles and responsibilities for enterprise risk management segregate responsibility for day-to-day decisions on implementing strategy from evaluating the extent to which remaining, or *residual*, risk is below risk appetite. Many also segregate responsibility for such strategic decision-making from responsibility for evaluating the efficacy of that strategy in reducing risk. In an enterprise with legal requirements for due diligence, decisions made based on risk analysis are routinely challenged by the enterprise via oversight processes such as audit and investigation.

Note as well that audits may cover both the efficacy of the risk management practices and their correct execution by both line managers and risk managers. In an enterprise where line management, risk management, and audit share information on respective findings, they often share a risk register to ensure that they are all aware of each other's perspectives. The transparency of a shared risk management framework allows the Board of Directors and/or other external oversight functions to leverage the independent opinions of the risk managers that are not part of business management to gain assurance that the information they receive from business management is both accurate and comprehensive. Figure 1.9

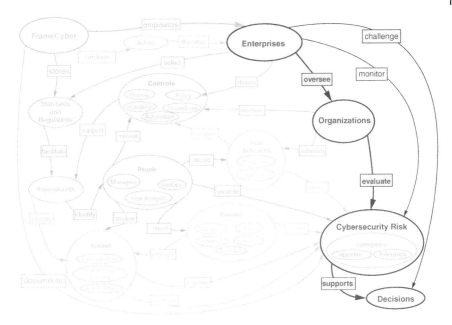

Figure 1.9 Cybersecurity Risk Framework Focus on Risk

illustrates the capability for a cybersecurity framework to produce information relevant to management decisions with respect to cybersecurity. Information on other framework elements is systematically collected and linked to risk categories to facilitate monitoring and reporting required to support decisions on whether or how to *treat* each risk. That is, *treatment* is a risk industry way to refer to the process of selecting and implementing measures to reduce, or *treat*, risk. The aggregate information is also required to facilitate oversight of the risk management framework itself.

Bringing it all together, Figure 1.10 defines a framework for organizing information for the purpose of enhancing communication with respect to cybersecurity risk management. The object of FrameCyber® is to facilitate a shared understanding of cybersecurity risk so that risk-related decisions made at the organization level are well understood at the enterprise level. Cybersecurity risk, like any category of risk events, is defined as a set of events that may be feasibly classified as a cybersecurity incident. Cybersecurity risk inherits that definition of risk from the larger discipline of the professional practice of risk management, wherein risk is defined as an event or set of similar events and measured in probability. Hence, a cybersecurity framework is constructed to shed light on the probability that cybersecurity event will have a negative impact on the organization. The scope of the environment in which cybersecurity risk is probable is a key element of the

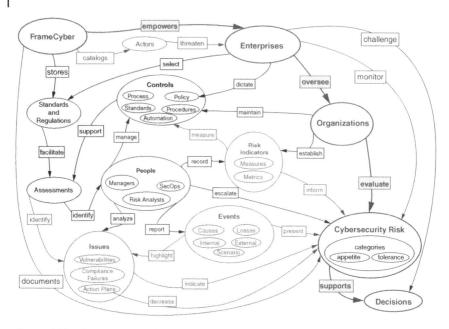

Figure 1.10 Cybersecurity Risk Framework

framework, that is, the enterprise. As the enterprise is ultimately responsible for decisions made at the organization level, the level of transparency should allow the enterprise to credibly challenge those decisions.

Business management generally defines its activities in terms of processes or workflows that communicate how business activities should be performed. Risk managers aggregate this basic business documentation across the enterprise and use it as the first building block of a shared communications framework. That is, they will start with business process and identify the set of events that could occur that would negatively impact steps in the process, or the process as a whole. After linking the events (or event categories) to the processes, risk managers research and identify existing or potential controls, that is, measures designed to reduce the probability of the events of negative impact. Both the business process managers and risk managers then establish joint risk monitoring using such a shared risk management framework. Business management processes thus grow to include control artifacts such as policies, technology architecture frameworks, and implementation standards. These are included as artifacts in the management risk and control self-assessments and provide not only risk managers but also internal and external auditors with a starting point for risk assessment activities.

Because such a framework can establish how technology supports business objectives, it makes it possible to identify technology devices and data that are relevant to the assessment of whether business processes may be impacted by cybersecurity events. Thus, even independent risk management activities rely on technology underlying business processes to collect data, and use that data in risk analysis, risk articulation, and risk profiling of the business objectives at stake. Where comprehensive risk management activities can be anticipated, as in business processes that use large amounts of data about people, or personally identifiable information (PII), it should be part of the business technology development activity to ensure the availability of information for use in cybersecurity risk management. As the Committee on Sponsoring Organizations of the Treadway Commission (COSO) describes in its Enterprise Risk Management Framework, *"when making necessary investments in technology or other infrastructure, management considers the tools required to enable enterprise risk management activities"* (COSO 2017).

FrameCyber connects assessments, controls, events, issues, metrics and people together in a manner that enables enterprises to manage cybersecurity risk. Figure 1.11 is a simplified illustration of how framework elements are connected. *Issues* are situations that indicate inherent risk. *Assessments* facilitate issue identification. *Events* are evidence of risk. *Controls* are used to reduce risk to an acceptable residual level. *Metrics* facilitate oversight and support management decisions concerning cybersecurity risk. *Risks* related to cybersecurity are made visible via FrameCyber and such comprehension supports sound decisions.

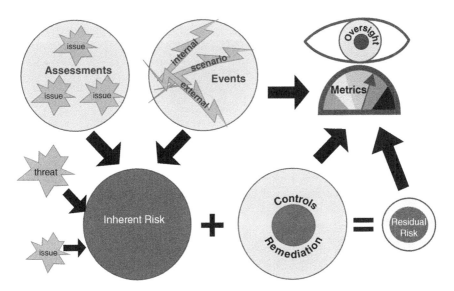

Figure 1.11 Cybersecurity Risk Framework in a Nutshell

References

Bernstein, P. (1996). *Against the Gods, The Remarkable Story of Risk*. Wiley.

Boardman, J. and Sauser, B. (2008). *Systems Thinking: Coping with 21st Century Problems*. Taylor and Francis.

COSO (2017). *Enterprise Risk Management: Integrating with Strategy and Performance*. Committee of Sponsoring Organizations of the Treadway Commission.

INCOSE (2023). "Most General 'System' Definition," International Council On Systems Engineering, 2023, https://www.incose.org/about-systems-engineering/system-and-se-definitions (accessed 14 February 2024).

ISO/IEC 27001 (2022). *Information Security, Cybersecurity and Privacy Protection – Information Security Management Systems — Requirements*. International Organization for Standardization/International Electrotechnical Commission. www.iso.org.

NIST-CSF (2024). Framework for Improving Critical Infrastructure Cybersecurity, version 2.0. National Institute of Standards and Technology. https://csrc.nist.gov/publications (accessed 15 January 2024).

Smith, L., "Shift-Left Testing," Dr. Dobb's Journal. 26 (9): 56, 62, September 2001, https://www.drdobbs.com/shift-left-testing/184404768 (accessed 14 January 2024).

Spafford, G., Metcalf, L. and Dykstra, J. (2022). *Cybersecurity Myths and Misconceptions, Avoiding the Hazards and Pitfalls that Derail Us*. Addison-Wesley.

2

Threats

The National Institute of Standards and Technology defines a threat as:

> Any circumstance or event with the potential to adversely impact organizational operations (including mission, functions, image, or reputation), organizational assets, individuals, other organizations, or the Nation through an information system via unauthorized access, destruction, disclosure, or modification of information, and/or denial of service (NIST 2012).

The systemigram in Figure 2.1 narrows this definition to cyber threats. The mainstay declares that threats embolden adversaries who exploit vulnerabilities which expose assets that enable adversary objectives. That is the basic idea behind a cyber threat. The threat itself is a circumstance or event that the adversary believes will enable objectives to be achieved.

2.1 Threat Actors

The most important thing to know about cybersecurity threats is that the actors who enact them may be dangerous adversaries. The second most important thing to know is that there is an interaction between an adversary and its target whether or not the target chooses to actively participate. A corollary is that: *if the target is not actively combatting the adversary, then the adversary has an advantage.* In the "Art of War," Sun Tzu brought transparency to this situation by saying:

> *If you know the enemy and you know yourself*
> *you need not fear the result of 100 battles.*
> *If you know yourself but not the enemy*
> *for every victory gained you will also suffer a defeat.*
> *If you know neither the enemy nor yourself*
> *you will succumb in every battle.*

Stepping Through Cybersecurity Risk Management: A Systems Thinking Approach,
First Edition. Jennifer L. Bayuk.
© 2024 John Wiley & Sons, Inc. Published 2024 by John Wiley & Sons, Inc.
Companion website: www.wiley.com/go/STCRM

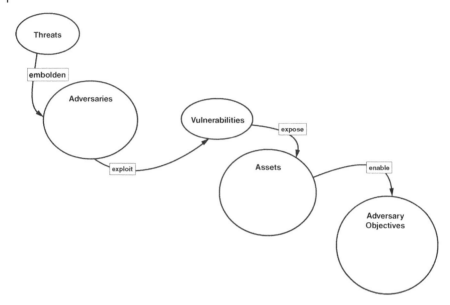

Figure 2.1 Threats

It seems like common sense that cyber threat preparedness cannot just come with knowing yourself. Sun Tzu may have been assuming that once vulnerability to the adversary is understood, a threat target would of course fortify itself against known adversaries, and that is why it would not fear the battles. His point was you need to know not only your own capabilities but those of your adversary to have assurance that your capabilities will keep you from defeat.

In the FrameCyber® system definition, the first context added to the mainstay is that it *catalogs actors who threaten enterprises*. Following Sun Tzu's advice, the study of cybersecurity adversaries starts with the list of bad actors that target the enterprise. A well-known example of such a *threat catalog* is the ATT&CK platform (MITRE 2015–2023). MITRE is a company that is not an acronym (the MIT in MITRE does not stand for MIT, the Massachusetts Institute of Technology). MITRE's ATT&CK framework classifies cybersecurity threat actors into groups based on clusters of activity associated with a common source. Cybersecurity threat analysts track these groups of threat actors and contribute their observations to the platform. Of course, due to the ephemeral nature of cyber threats, different organizations' threat actor definitions may partially overlap or partially contradict those designated by other organizations. Some groups accrue multiple aliases due to various organizations tracking the same group under different names. Nevertheless, the point of sharing this type of information, this *threat intelligence*, is to gain full appreciation of the actors known to be actively targeting

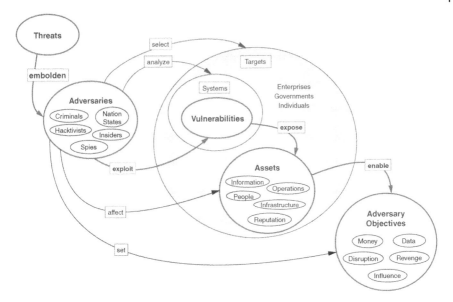

Figure 2.2 Adversaries

your enterprise or those similar in markets or technology. The first step in knowing your adversary is to understand which actors are targeting you and others in your industry.

Just as we need to understand our own cybersecurity framework to know the adversary, we must also understand systems within which threat actors targeting us operate. Drilling down into the threat system definition of Figures 2.1 and 2.2 fleshes out the context in which adversaries operate. Categories of adversaries include (though are not limited to) criminals, hacktivists, nation-states, sadists, and terrorists. Adversary objectives are also diverse. Criminals are typically after money. Hacktivists want influence. Terrorists typically want disruption. Nation-states typically seek information/data, but a growing number are also seeking disruption, money, and influence. Sadists are commonly associated with revenge, but revenge may take the form of other more tangible objectives like disruption or money. What these diverse adversaries have in common is that they focus on targets that have assets they can use to enable achievement of their objectives. Enterprises, governments, and individuals have information, operations, people, infrastructure, and reputations to uphold. Threats produce negative effects on these organizations and perhaps others in their community through theft and/or misuse of these assets.

The idea of classifying threat actors by motive and links to their objectives is a high-level expression of an industry standard threat classification taxonomy, the *Structured Threat Information Expression* (STIX™) (OASIS 2020). The standard

Threat Actor Type	Objective
Activist/Hacktivist	Make a political statement (Anonymous); voting systems
Competitor	Trade secrets, competitive analysis, or disruption of service
Criminal	Profit; anything they can monetize for cash
Crime-syndicate	Organized crime as a technology business
Hacker	Hacking for thrill or challenge
Insider-accidental	Unintentionally exposes the organization to harm
Insider-disgruntled	Financial gain; personal benefits for retaliation or revenge
Nation-state	World supremacy
Sensationalist	Embarrassment and brand damage
Spy	Cyber espionage
Terrorist	Telecom, energy grid, government defenses
Other, e.g. Lone Wolf	Cybercrime-as-a-service model is furthering the reach of solo actors.

Figure 2.3   Threat Actor Types

was created to make it easy to describe and share information about threat actors in a systematic, automated manner. The full list of actor types in STIX is displayed in Figure 2.3. STIX further classifies actors by motive, capabilities, goals, sophistication level, past activities, resources to which they have access, and their role in an organization (if any). To fully characterize a threat actor in a manner where others can benefit from your research, you need to capture more than just what they are after, but what drives them, what skills they can bring to bear on an attack, how well they can sustain attacks, and what software or equipment they have at their disposal.

One way for an enterprise to produce a custom threat catalog is to ingest a threat data feed from a place like MITRE and start reading through the list. Although there are commercial products with that feature, there have been too many hundreds of threat actors cataloged over the years to make that approach efficient or effective. Nevertheless, shared public and private information on threat actor attributes can be used to filter the wide range of all threat actors down to those that are most probably targeting the enterprise in a process such as that displayed in Figure 2.4. If a threat actor's objectives may be met using the assets of an enterprise, then the actor passes the first filter. If the threat actor's capabilities, i.e., skills and expertise in system software, match the systems that are used by the enterprise, the actor passes the second filter. If the actor has enough resources to present a feasible challenge to the enterprise cybersecurity defenses, then this passes the third filter. Other filters include, but are not limited to, the level of activity currently observed from the threat actor and the level to which the threat actor is

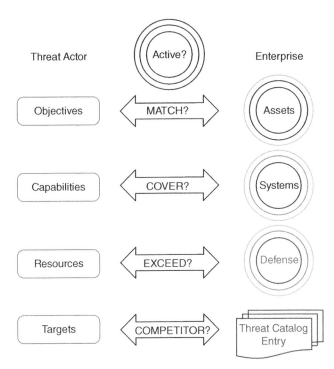

Figure 2.4 Threat Catalog Filter

affiliated with other organizations that may already be included in the enterprise threat catalog. In this manner, an enterprise can focus on protecting itself from the threats that it judges to have the most potential to negatively impact it.

Figure 2.4 illustrates how such a filter would be applied to threat actor attributes to arrive at a decision on whether to include the actor in a local threat actor catalog. First, it narrows the full set of possible candidates to those who are known to be active. This does not necessarily mean we take the list of all active candidates and then keep asking questions about them. Rather, we put ourselves in the position of the threat actor and review our assets to see how others might benefit from compromising them. The visual in the diagram is intended to emphasize that we are not analyzing the actor itself at this high level, but the extent to which threat actors generally see us as a target. Then we look at our systems. Is the capability to find exploits in our systems widely known or does that take special expertise? If the answer is "widely known," we may want to change something about our systems at this point to make our enterprise less of an easy target. The next question is about resources. Are the resources required to overcome our defenses readily available or obtained only at high cost. If it is easy for a threat actor to obtain resources in excess of those needed to successfully penetrate our defense, then this may also be cause for changing our systems, this time to bolster defenses in order to minimize the number of adversaries that can pass this filter. Finally, the diagram includes reference to the adversary's current targets. If these look like us, then there is a high probability we are targets as well.

The "objectives match assets" filter may look easy to pass because any organization with a lot of money could feasibly have assets that would enable some threat actor goals. But note that in the case of a hacktivist, the money alone would be an intermediate step toward achieving their objective. For example, the objective of the group Cyber Partisans is to overthrow the government in Belarus. Although money may be useful in funding their organization, they can achieve their objective much more quickly by attacking the Belarusian government and its supporters directly. So enterprises with no affiliation with Belarus would use this filter to screen out the Cyber Partisans. An organization that provides military supplies to Belarus, on the other hand, would match that filter.

2.1.1 Hackivists

This word hacktivist is an amalgam of "hacking" and "activist." "Hacktivist" refers to groups that have specific political agendas and design cyberattacks that call attention to their causes to gain public support and/or actually achieve political advantage by weakening opposing systems.

An example threat catalog entry for the cybersecurity hacktivist group *Cyber Partisans* appears in Figure 2.5. The data in the threat catalog entry could have come from an information-sharing site or been collected locally based on observations by cybersecurity staff. Either way, the choice of whether to include a threat actor is dependent on attributes of the actor that identify the enterprise as

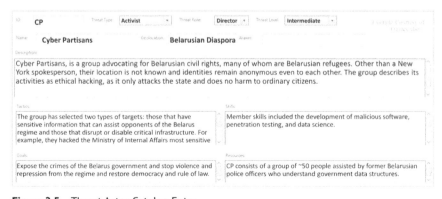

Figure 2.5 Threat Actor Catalog Entry

a probable target. Obviously, Cyber Partisans is not a threat actor that will make everyone's catalog. It does not even appear on MITRE's ATT&CK platform. Nevertheless, the information in its threat catalog entry is useful in quickly assimilating the essence and purpose of its activities.

2.1.2 Insiders

On the opposite spectrum from hacktivists on the threat actor applicability scale are *insider threats*. Insider threat is the potential for an insider to use their authorized access or understanding of an organization to harm that organization. This harm can include malicious, complacent, or unintentional acts that negatively affect the integrity, confidentiality, and availability of the organization, its data, personnel, or facilities (CISAa 2023).

Every enterprise is subject to insider threat, so the "Active?" filter question is assumed to be true. Even in organizations that believe all insiders are trustworthy, an insider threat can be accidental rather than intentional. Figure 2.6 displays the difference between an unintentional and an intentional insider threat. Any current or former staff member, contractor, or other business partner who at any time had authorized access to an organization's network, system, or data could have *exfiltrated* this data in a manner that exposed it to other threat actors and/or used their access to negatively impact system integrity or availability. Note that "exfiltrate" is a military term for stealthy withdrawal that is commonly used by cybersecurity professionals to refer to unauthorized data transfer. The source of the study that produced Figure 2.6 refers to the people who do it unwittingly due to inattention or ignorance as "people bugs," an analogy with a software bug that creates a security vulnerability. Although their activity may reveal vulnerabilities with which the CISO must deal, once an

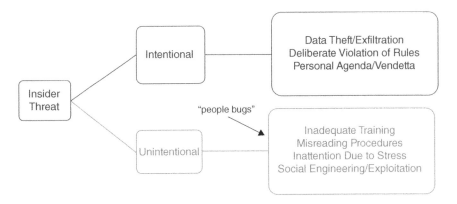

Figure 2.6 Type of Insider Threat

incident has been determined to be an accident, these are not treated with the same adversarial intensity as a threat actor cyberattack.

Insider threat is also ubiquitous because people who work within the organizations that they attack are often motivated by money and they know where it is stored and/or have responsibility for maintaining cash balances as part of their job function. There are many cases where people intentionally get jobs in places where there are a lot of money transfers knowing that they can probably figure out how to manipulate them and quit fast before they get caught. That said, studies of intentional insider threat do not cite money as the top motivating factor. There are also cases where employees are blackmailed into stealing enterprise intellectual property or committing fraud, as well as cases of nation-state espionage agents intentionally getting jobs that place them in positions of access to intellectual property and trade secrets (Brumfield, 2022). Moreover, in the technology industry, a significant source of insider threat activity is revenge (Cummings, 2012). Where a revengeful insider has access to money, they often take it not out of need, but because they feel they deserve it, given the manner in which they have been treated.

A common profile for technology worker insider threat includes holding grudges. They typically work in a high-stress environment and spend so many hours building large-scale systems that feel pride of ownership. But, of course, they do not own the systems they built; the organization owns the systems. One day, they may get a new boss and a negative performance review and are told their skills do not fit their job function anymore and they are not as well valued as they used to be. But the system they built is still humming along, and they still are the resident experts. They prove that *they are really* the system owners by bringing the system to its knees. Insider threats that reach national news read like a hostage crises. An exemplar insider threat actor was a disgruntled network administrator for the city of San Francisco. The administrator actually held the city of San Francisco hostage while he disabled network access and refused to give up the passwords (Singel, 2008).

There is a well-researched insider threat profile of which people who manage technology should definitely be aware. The most common types of Information Technology (IT) sabotage involve someone developing a program that monitors for a certain situation and when it detects the situation, it wreaks havoc. For example, a lot of disgruntled IT people think they might get fired and if that happens, they want to retaliate effectively. Many of these people independently come to the same idea of creating a computer program in some kind of automated scheduling system that downloads the current list of employees every day and checks to see if they are on it. If the program cannot find their own name on the employee list, then the program will delete all the files on the network. Another variant of that tactic is installing remote system administration tools that have trivial security so if they did get dismissed and they were no longer authorized to be on the network, they could still come back and wreak havoc through these hidden "backdoors." Unfortunately, the trends in insider threat show that this type of technology system admin threat is on the rise. The insider threat will not have a specific name because if malicious insiders were identified they would quickly become outsiders. Nevertheless, "insider threat" has a permanent entry in an enterprise threat catalog to ensure that the checks and balances necessary to prevent insiders from causing damage are systematically developed.

That said, not all insiders that threaten the organization have a lot of technical knowledge. Sometimes they just have access to highly functional systems and they know how transactions are monitored on those systems; so they can make unauthorized changes and fly under the radar. Sometimes they change job functions and their access to the systems in their old department is not removed so they can still do transactions in their old job function while the people who replace them may not know the systems as well as they did, so it takes them a while to get caught. These insider fraudsters depend on a *low and slow* approach, that is, low dollars at infrequent intervals, which is something that is common in any kind of fraud, even stealing petty cash. People commit a small crime first and then sit around and see if they get caught. If they do not get caught right away, they start taking more and more money until the theft becomes visible. They do not get caught very soon because the organization is not obviously adversely impacted. If the insider just stayed low and slow they would probably be able to commit that fraud for a much longer period of time, maybe forever, but it is far more likely they get greedy for quick rewards and they get caught. If these people are in management positions, then they are more likely to steal a greater amount possibly because they feel a sense of entitlement to their gains. Statistically, managers commit fraud for longer periods of time than the average insider threat because they can evade detection as they are part of the management control system.

These threats are rarely detected by management, but typically by an independent auditor whose job is to tick and tie all the transactions looking at the cash in the bank and making sure it matches what the computer says it should be. That is, a very common way to commit fraud is to take money out of the bank and not update the computers internally and if you are the one who checks the balance in the bank account for the company that is how you can evade detection for a very long period of time. Another way that organizations commonly detect fraud is that customers complain about maybe not getting a product or service they ordered and the customer service team finds out that the manager of the shipping department has been stealing customer orders. Sometimes a coworker will notice some insider threat; whether it be that hidden program in a job scheduling system or debits in the company's books that do not match what is in the bank account, or a customer complaint. The coworker's suspicion is just as likely to catch an insider threat as a deliberate audit looking for it.

Currently, it is not possible to reliably estimate the true extent of insider threat cases as a percentage of cyberattacks because organizations sometimes deal with insider threat as a Human Resource (HR) issue and their investigations may be classified as such. Reliable studies of aggregated cyberattack statistics place insider threat actors as involved in only 18% of total cyberattacks (Verizon 2022).

Figure 2.7 shows an example of an insider threat attack. In this case, the threat actor was a disgruntled employee. A network administrator was given a poor performance review by a supervisor. He went back to his desk and started erasing the configuration of the routers that delivered enterprise network traffic. His work was systematic. He took the routers down one by one until, luckily for the enterprise, he took down the router which carried his own network connection to the others. By that time, ten routers were compromised and 90% of enterprise network connectivity in North America was disrupted.

It may seem surprising that one relatively low-level employee has the power to cause this type of havoc. Indeed, it was a surprise to non-technology management of the enterprise at the time and that vulnerability has since been rectified with technology controls. But, generally, if an administrator can fix a system problem, they can also create it. The only real solution is to minimize the number of staff who have such power and do your best to make sure they are happy at work.

2.1.3 Hacker

The word "hacker" used to mean someone who spent long hours writing computer code with a single purpose and through intense concentration over long periods of time, was successful in achieving their goals. Good hackers could take any problem capable of being solved by a computer and write a program to solve it. It was only after some people got good at programming destructive technology that the word "hacker" took on the negative connotation of an adversary achieving an objective. Now "hacker" is commonly understood to refer to any unauthorized user who attempts to or gains access to an information system. The STIX standard defines hacker as "an individual that tends to break into networks for the thrill or the challenge of doing so; hackers may use advanced skills or simple attack scripts they have downloaded."

The most comprehensive study of confirmed cyberattacks in 2022 showed that website hackers played a role in over 70% of all cyberattacks. That study defined hacking as "attempts to intentionally access or harm information assets without (or exceeding) authorization by circumventing or thwarting logical security mechanisms" (Verizon 2022). If you consider the website of an organization to be their "front door" on the Internet, then adding hacks on the "back door" means trying to bypass security that employees use for remote access, or that businesses use to automatically share data. Backdoor hacking adds a few percentage points to

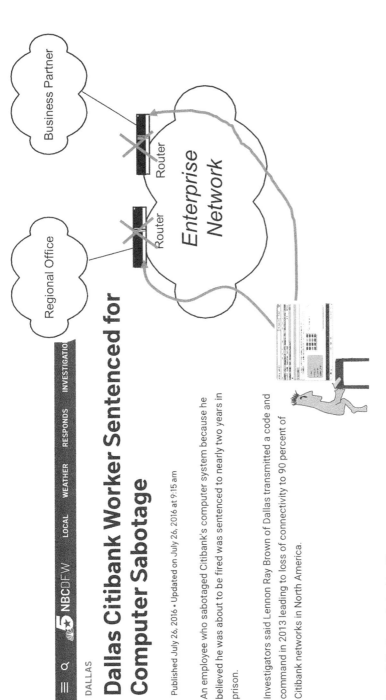

Figure 2.7 Example Insider Threat

the number of incidents that are attributable to hackers, as does scanning for and exploiting known system-level vulnerabilities exposed to the internet.

In 2021, there was a massive web application vulnerability that indicated thousands of companies were highly vulnerable to their data being visible to threat actors via a backdoor vulnerability (NIST-CVE 2021). The software is named "log4j" because it provides logging capabilities for Java applications. Due to the nature of its purpose, it was able to inspect any aspect of the operating system to which the web application had access and to write files to the operating system disk. It was so insidious that the US Federal Trade Commission (FTC) issued this warning (FTC 2022):

> Log4j is a ubiquitous piece of software used to record activities in a wide range of systems found in consumer-facing products and services. Recently, a serious vulnerability in the popular Java logging package, log4j (CVE-2021-44228) was disclosed, posing a severe risk to millions of consumer products to enterprise software and web applications. This vulnerability is being widely exploited by a growing set of attackers.

Note that the "CVE" in the FTC warning refers to the MITRE Common Vulnerability Enumeration, which had published in the National Vulnerability Database (NVD) in August 2021. It was so widely exploited in November 2021 that researchers hastily converged on a few updates to the NVD in December 2021 before the FTC warning appeared in January 2022.

It is very important to understand that this vulnerability was discovered by a hacker. It is a typical web hack in that it exploits vulnerabilities in a popular web server (note, the technology is referred to as "web server" because it delivers website content to internet users). The hacker exploited this vulnerability and the exploit was reported publicly. The public report provided all sorts of less experienced threat actors with knowledge that enabled them to take advantage of the hacker's findings and exploit the vulnerability on their own. Figure 2.8 is a message sequence of a log4j attack. It shows how a threat actor can exploit website functionality to resolve variables it expects to process while creating a log entry to send the webserver commands. In this first message, it sends a command to add its own internet-connected database to the list of trusted code sources in the website's code library. This plants malicious software ("malware") on the web server. Figure 2.8, shows that after the threat actor plants the malware, they can send standard web queries to the compromised website that contain variables that resolve to malicious commands and thereby to scan the internal system and collect any data to which the webserver has access. Where the network allows outbound access, the threat actor can also exfiltrate data back to its own server.

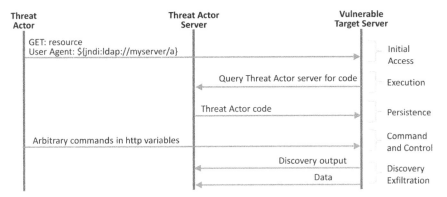

Figure 2.8 Log4j Attack Explained

The ability to execute arbitrary commands on a target system is referred to as "command and control" or "C&C." It provides the same capability to the hacker as the authorized users of the compromised system. Log4j was a hacker jackpot.

2.1.4 Competitors

A competitor threat is someone who seeks to gain advantage in business. Even before computers, competitors were known to steal intellectual property, trade secrets, strategic plans, or other business data from a rival organization. They have also been known to orchestrate denial-of-service attacks on each other. Competitors rarely personally engage in hacking but rely on criminal networks with the skills to achieve their objectives. A famous example is that of the online gambling industry routinely engaging in Distributed Denial of Service (DDoS) attacks during high-profile sports events to knock users off competitor sites so theirs would be the only place open to place a bet (Menn, 2010).

On the Internet, one device connects to another with a simple request to "synchronize" on a network session, referred to by computer scientists as a "SYN" network "packet" of information. The receiver replies with an acknowledgement, a "SYN ACK" packet. The first device must send an "ACK" back to complete the session. After this "handshake," the two devices then begin exchanging information. The diagram on the left of Figure 2.9 illustrates the concept. The connecting device is labeled "CLIENT" and the device that accepts the connection is labeled "SERVER." The first three arrows in the diagram on the left of Figure 2.9 illustrate the connection, which happens before any actual communication can happen between them. The arrows labeled "FIN" illustrate the protocol's graceful disconnect handshake.

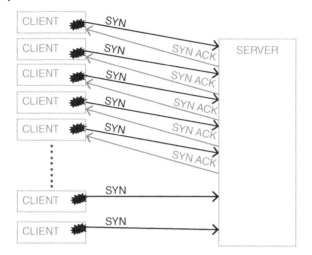

Figure 2.9 Distributed Denial of Service Attack

A DDoS attack starts out with a hacker compromising thousands of internet-connected computers and installing command and control malware on them designed to send "SYN" packets to the target. The right side of Figure 2.9 represents the malware as spiked splotches. Once enough compromised machines are assembled, the hacker automates communication with the command and control malware to start sending SYN packets. The target receives the SYN and replies with SYN ACK, and waits for an ACK from the client, but none comes. Eventually the session times out, but not before all the network resources of the targeted server have been occupied by packets that are not valid connections. Any other machine on the internet attempting to communicate with the server is effectively blocked by the onslaught of connections from the malware.

The utility of DDoS attacks to close competitor websites is obvious, and DDoS has also been used by nation-states to weaken or humiliate their adversaries. In that sense, nation-state cybercriminal activity is now a special case of competitor threat. Although "competitor" and "nation-state" are both on the STIX list of threat actor types, in the context of intellectual property theft, it has become increasingly difficult to tell them apart. That is, nation-states hack the organizations serving other nations looking for information that can benefit their own global economic profile. They do not stop at government agencies, but also routinely hack their domestic business' foreign competitors. Intellectual property and trade secrets stolen in these attacks are turned over to a domestic business for exploit and development. At first, this activity was not widely reported in part due to the attack target's reluctance to admit their own vulnerability (Epstein and Elgin 2008). But as the sophistication of nation-state attacks increases, so too does the probability of harm to the target's global economic standing (Perlroth 2021).

In a bold move in 2010, Google announced that it was a target of such an attack. Hackers lurked in their network for months, collecting and storing data on algorithms and other intellectual property, then exfiltrated it out of the Google network in large batches. In 2009, Google installed new network security software and the activity suddenly became visible. Still, it took months to eradicate the threat. That year, the term "Advanced Persistent Threat" (APT) was coined to describe systematic continuous targeted espionage, and subsequently has been used to label such actors as they are identified (e.g., APT1) (Mandiant 2013).

A typical competitor attack will focus on customer data and/or intellectual property that are typically stored in database management systems (DBMS). One of the earliest such attacks which is still quite common exploits a vulnerability in the way a webserver handles a programming language called Structured Query Language (SQL). The attack is called "SQL Injection" because the threat actor is able to "inject" SQL commands into the webserver.

A website "form" is designed to collect data and put it into a database. It presents a blank "form field" for the user to type, then takes what is typed and stores it in computer memory, then sends the memory field to the database for storage. The diagram in Figure 2.10 illustrates this simple concept in an oversimplified manner. A user types a name and password in a website login form and the computer sends those fields to the database so it can collect and display the user's data on the browser. The first two login and password fields in Figure 2.10 show data that would typically be entered by a user. The two on the right show something a hacker may try to type into the fields to see if the webserver will pass the field content directly to the database without checking that the fields were free of

```
login = username_field_contents
pwd = password_field_contents
user_data = select user from CustomerData where (user.name = login) and (user.password = pwd)
display user_data
```

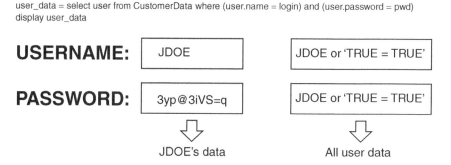

USERNAME: JDOE | JDOE or 'TRUE = TRUE'

PASSWORD: 3yp@3iVS=q | JDOE or 'TRUE = TRUE'

JDOE's data | All user data

Figure 2.10 SQL Injection Fields

computer code. If so, it gives the hacker a way to take data from the DMBS directly without even having to login.

While intellectual property is usually not available from a public-facing webserver, it is often stored in a DBMS accessible from internal webservers. If the competitor can get to the internal webserver via some other means, the SQL Injection attack could still work. Figure 2.11 shows two different attack paths that a hacker can take to attempt SQL Injection attacks. The first targets the public-facing, or external, webserver. The sequence of events comprising the attack are labeled with numbered circles and the data in solid lines. The second targets the internal webserver. The sequence of events comprising the attack are labeled with numbered triangles and the data in dashed lines.

The hacker is pictured at the lower left of Figure 2.11. The Universal Resource Locator (URL) used in the internal attack is: *https://www.acme.com/ innocuousurl?field="select ALL from table"*. The browser connects to the www. acme.com website and the website's code incorporates that code in its query for data, causing the DBMS to respond with more data than the website would under normal circumstances.

In the external attack, the initial access starts with phishing, which phonetically sounds like "fishing" and is so called because it uses a lure to bait its targets. The "ph" is a throwback to the earliest days of hacking when computer abuse mostly consisted of telephone fraud. The lure of a phishing attack is a website link designed to appear interesting or useful to the victim. In step 2, the user clicks on the link and it downloads malicious C&C software onto the user's vulnerable desktop. This malware allows the hacker to enter commands on the user's home

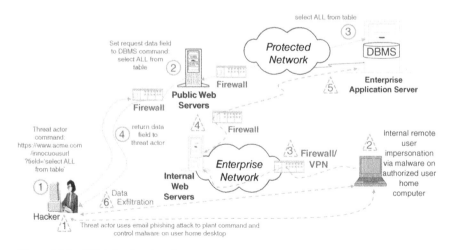

Figure 2.11 SQL Injection Attack

desktop in a similar manner as described in phase 1 of the log4j attack on web servers, by having the malware on the desktop query the hacker server for the malicious commands. The hacker uses this interactive C&C capability to record the user's keystrokes and read processor memory to obtain the user's credentials on internal web servers. The hacker then piggybacks on the home user's access to the Virtual Private Network (VPN) of their employer who is the threat actor's true target. The threat actor impersonates the user on the internal network (step 4) and uses an SQL injection attack (step 5) on an internal website to access trade secrets and intellectual property. To the enterprise, this would look like an insider threat because the stolen data is exfiltrated to the home user's desktop. The hacker would then use the C&C capability to retrieve the data from the user's home desktop.

SQL Injection may seem like a simple programming error to avoid. However, new programmers entering the field of web application design typically make this mistake. Only software development teams who know enough to routinely scan code for such mistakes can completely avoid them. The Open Web Application Security Project (OWASP) and the SysAdmin, Audit, Network and Security (SANS) are two organizations that maintain lists of the most common mistakes that programmers and administrators (admins) make that leave systems vulnerable to hackers. Some form of this SQL Injection attack has been on both lists for decades (OWASP 2021).

2.1.5 Lone Wolf

Another class of cyber threat actors is a group that the news media refers to as "lone wolves." The expression is an analogy because wolves are known to hunt in packs, so a lone wolf can be viewed as a gangster without a gang. A lone wolf has all the criminal association of a gang, but no external support. (The term is not cyber-specific. Plenty of mass shooters have been referred to as lone wolves.) A lone wolf may be motivated by money or revenge and can produce negative impact. A classic cyber threat actor lone wolf example is an Eastern European hacker named Igor, whose hacking focused narrowly on car diagnostic software that he then sold online. He appeared to have worked alone and was caught because he used his real name by mistake in some online forum. The threat of lone wolves seems small, but as online cybercrime marketplaces mature, it is increasingly easy for these types to get access to more sophisticated hacking tools and techniques.

2.2 Threat Networks

The opposite of a lone wolf is a threat network. In the threat actor landscape, actors with diverse objectives often find kindred spirits in organized crime syndicates that are similar to legitimate technology businesses. The difference is that the software and services they provide are designed to make it easy to commit criminal acts. Threat networks include malware development shops, service providers, and customers for stolen data. Although it is possible for hackers to independently commit fraud, data theft, and denial of service attacks, they also take advantage of criminal networks to lower their personal risk of prosecution. A hacker that uses SQL Injection to steal consumer credit card data may not be interested in the tedious task of impersonating consumers to make purchases using their cards. Instead, it is possible to use threat actor networks to sell the data to others who will.

2.2.1 Example: Identity Theft

Figure 2.12 steps through the activities of a threat actor network whose objective is to obtain personally identifiable data to misuse for financial gain. The activity labeled "1" is the hacker compromising some online data repository where a lot of personally identifiable information has been exposed, typically thousands of customer records from popular online retailer that include name, address, login, password, and credit card information (*if this scenario appears implausible to you, check out: https://haveibeenpwned.com*). The second activity in Figure 2.12 is the hacker offering the stolen data for sale to other cyber

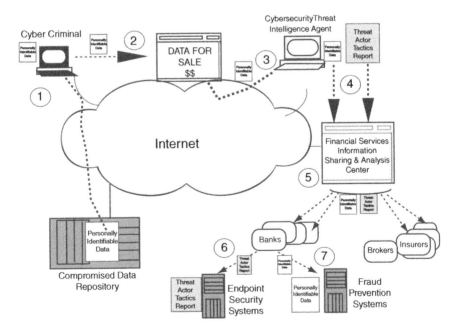

Figure 2.12 Identity Theft Network Operations

criminals, who will actually be the ones to use the data. They use the credit card data to buy things. They use the credentials to log into bank accounts and move the funds to offshore accounts that have no regulations requiring returning unauthorized money transfers. Recall that the cybercriminal who steals the data is not necessarily the one who uses it. A hacker may find it more profitable and possibly safer to sell the data in pieces, for example, 10 credit card data sets for $10. A less technical cybercriminal may not have the skills to hack to get data, so it is easier for them to buy it. The hacker will set up a website on which to sell the data utilizing networks that are not accessible by commercial browsers. The buyer is the one who commits that actual crime of identity theft, albeit aided and abetted by the hacker. The networks on which these sales take place are heavily encrypted and configured to allow anonymous access to avoid attribution of the activity to identifiable people. Collectively, these networks are called the "dark web."

Fortunately, the successful operation of a data-selling site on the dark web requires that it be visible to potential identity theft threat actors, and this allows law enforcement to create cybersecurity surveillance operations, which is depicted as activity number 3 in Figure 2.12. Ironically, law enforcement impersonates cyber criminals to establish themselves as part of this threat actor network so they can witness and record criminal transfer of personally identifiable data. Banking security operations staff and cybersecurity vendors who market "threat intelligence" also scan the dark web looking out for this type of activity. If a bank or bank threat intelligence vendor finds personally identifiable data for sale, they will typically write up a report that will be shared throughout the financial industry. The Department of Homeland Security in the US has set up information sharing and analysis centers by industry so that people can share information about cybercrime without attribution and combine their forces to combat it. In this example, the information is shared with the Financial Services Information Sharing and Analysis Center so all the banks, broker dealers, and insurers that may be victimized along with the consumer can use that data to create filters in their security systems to try to weed out highly probable unauthorized fund movement in the wake of a data breach. Although the threat network had made its money, the systematic identification and response made possible by surveilling threat networks helps the financial industry to mitigate damage by enabling some (though by no means all) victimized consumers to be compensated.

2.2.2 Zero-Day Threats

Another cybercrime marketplace revolves around zero-day vulnerabilities. Figure 2.2 shows threat actors analyzing their target's systems looking for vulnerabilities that they can exploit to access target assets. The day a hacker finds a vulnerability that no other person has made public is day zero in the life of that vulnerability. So these hitherto unknown vulnerabilities have the nickname *zero-day threat*. But as with the personal information thief hacker, vulnerability exploits should not be assumed to be operated by the people who discovered the vulnerability. Many hackers simply find vulnerabilities and sell them because it is perfectly legal to find a vulnerability but usually not legal to exploit it. The dark web is not totally anonymous. Another way in which threat actors try to hide their trails is by using crypto-currency transactions that are advertised as "anonymous." But international police forces are getting increasingly better at tracing those supposedly anonymous currency exchanges.

Nation-state threat actors have historically been the main customers for zero-day threats and have the resources to build exploits for them (Perlroth 2021). Another opportunity to sell a vulnerability is to sell it to the software company that created the vulnerability through a bug bounty program; that is, many companies actually set aside budgets to pay hackers who find security loopholes in their products so they can fix them before too many other people find out. People hacking in search of vulnerabilities include threat actors who are going to use the vulnerability maliciously and corporate security staff who are trying to find them so that they can get them fixed. There are countless commercial and underground vulnerability scanning products designed to reveal software vulnerabilities.

The software vulnerability industry includes many professional and criminal functions for different aspects of the workflow are done by different groups of people. Figure 2.13 shows the lifecycle of a vulnerability in the zero-day marketplace. If a person who finds or buys a vulnerability decides not to be the one to launch a cyberattack with it, it can be sold to software developers in the exploit marketplace who in turn will sell the exploit software they create to more commercial malicious software providers who will incorporate the exploit code into nice, easy to use "exploit kits" with windows and drop-down boxes all sorts of features for storing the results. The exploit kit maker may in turn sell the exploit kits to someone who will host them in a cloud just like any other business will host a software as a service (SaaS) operation. Or they may supplement the kit with instructions and deliver the product to customers directly, and this configuration may be customized for a given buyer.

Where the kit includes obviously malicious use cases such as ransomware and DDoS, cybercrime market makers contact potential customers via e-mail and chat on the dark web to agree on prices and sell not just software but crimeware services. They engage in market delivery services to operate malware on behalf of buyers like the gambling site operators who contract for DDoS. Where the software simply scans for vulnerabilities, its customers will be both cybersecurity defenders and threat actors.

Figure 2.13 Zero-Day Marketplace

2.3 Threat Vectors

Although some threats are relatively easy to execute, it takes a lot of research and planning to figure out how to successfully attack a prepared target. Threat actors spend considerable time and energy in *reconnaissance* to identify vulnerabilities in their target's systems. Even if they find vulnerabilities, it may take months or years to figure out how those vulnerabilities expose the target's assets in such a way that they can manipulate. Then they need to devise tactics, techniques, and procedures (TTPs) to exploit the vulnerabilities to affect or manipulate the assets to enable their objectives. The methods by which threat actors set about achieving their goals vary widely. Cybersecurity professionals call this situation the "attacker's advantage and the defender's dilemma." A defender needs to be vigilant on all battle fronts. The threat actors need just one vulnerability to breach the defender's lines. Nevertheless, although there are a wide variety of activities in which threat networks engage to launch cyberattacks, there are also distinct attack patterns that are recognizable to experienced cybersecurity analysts.

Figure 2.14 is a list of threat actor tactics, including reconnaissance, listed in the order they typically appear in an attack (MITRE 2015–2023). These tactics are

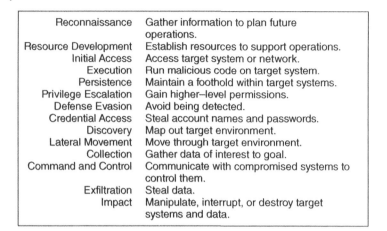

Reconnaissance	Gather information to plan future operations.
Resource Development	Establish resources to support operations.
Initial Access	Access target system or network.
Execution	Run malicious code on target system.
Persistence	Maintain a foothold within target systems.
Privilege Escalation	Gain higher–level permissions.
Defense Evasion	Avoid being detected.
Credential Access	Steal account names and passwords.
Discovery	Map out target environment.
Lateral Movement	Move through target environment.
Collection	Gather data of interest to goal.
Command and Control	Communicate with compromised systems to control them.
Exfiltration	Steal data.
Impact	Manipulate, interrupt, or destroy target systems and data.

Figure 2.14 Threat Actor Tactics

mostly progressive. For example, you must access a target system or network before being able to execute code on its systems. The series of activities sequentially performed in the course of a cyberattack is called a "threat vector."

It is common to display simple cybersecurity threat vectors as sequential chevrons, and more complicated ones can be drawn using any process flow methodology. Figure 2.15 displays a threat vector corresponding to the attack paths drawn in Figure 2.9. The attack on the public-facing website has four steps, and only one is activity performed by the hacker. The rest are executed by the victim. The attack on the internal website has six steps, and two are executed (unwittingly) by the victim. However, the numbers are not as important as the explanatory power of the step breakdown. The idea is that these vectors may be used to train stakeholders to comprehend their vulnerability to attacker's activities. Also note that the internal attack vector separates the activity of the *DBMS* returning data to the hacker and the *web server* returning data from the DBMS to the hacker, merging the two steps of the external hack into one step in the internal hack and designating the web server and the DBMS as a business application. Although the portrayal may be perfectly reasonable for the intended audience and analysis of enterprise vulnerability, it also makes it hard to compare the vulnerability of the same attack across different environments. For example, one environment may have more safeguards than another on how websites should verify that data requested from the database confirmed to that which is expected.

The observation that different organizations may present the same attack paths using different levels of technology granularity is a common occurrence in the field of cybersecurity operations. Because technologies emerge so quickly, it is

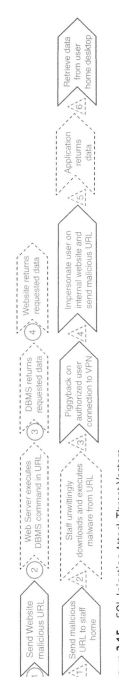

Figure 2.15 SQL Injection Attack Threat Vectors

Table 1 - Vulnerability Tower of Babel, 1998

Organization	Name referring to vulnerability
AXENT (now Symantec)	phf CGI allows remote command execution
BindView	#107—cgi-phf
Bugtraq	PHF Attacks—fun and games for the whole family
CERIAS	http_escshellcmd
CERT	CA-96.06.cgi_example_code
Cisco Systems	HTTP—cgi-phf
CyberSafe	Network: HTTP 'phf' attack
DARPA	0x00000025 = HTTP PHF attack
IBM ERS	ERS-SVA-E01-1996:002.1
ISS	http—cgi-phf
Symantec	#180 HTTP server CGI example code compromises http server
SecurityFocus	#629—phf Remote Command Execution Vulnerability

Figure 2.16 Vulnerability Tower of Babel

difficult to converge on common patterns. This phenomenon dates back to the first days of computer viruses. At that time, companies that marketed security software would individually find new attacks simultaneously and each publish them under different names, the vendors all seemed to be antistandard, each claiming that their product was unique and thwarting efforts by cybersecurity analysts to put them in well-defined categories. Antivirus vendors gave different names to the same virus and each claimed to have discovered it first. A famous paper called the situation the "Vulnerability Tower of Babel" (see Figure 2.16) (Martin 2001).

In response to this confusion, the US Defense Advanced Research Products Agency, together with NIST, sponsored a conference to discuss setting standards for vulnerability labeling. The effort was merged with the Common Vulnerabilities and Exposures (CVE) initiative started by MITRE around the same time. Ongoing efforts flowing from this initiative led to the creation of the NVD which also standardized product names Common Platform Enumeration (CPE) and created the Common Vulnerability Scoring System (CVSS) to help communicate the threat level associated with the vulnerability. The US Department of Homeland Security's Cyber and Infrastructure Security Agency (CISA) also leveraged the CVE to warn the public when exploits for the vulnerabilities are currently known to be actively sought and exploited. They broadcast the existence of Known Exploited Vulnerabilities (KEV). A parallel effort was launched within the software development community to try to avoid creating vulnerabilities to begin with, which is the Common Weakness Enumeration (CWE), a shared list of software and hardware weakness created by developer's mistakes like not checking web input fields for SQL code. This data helps inform research in Common Attack Pattern Enumeration and Classification (CAPEC), which catalogs common attacker techniques such as SQL Injection. These repositories are frequently cross-referenced to collectively produce a common vocabulary for cybersecurity professionals working independently on various aspects of threat analysis, detection, response, and mitigation. They have reduced the Tower of Babel problem by making it possible for vendors

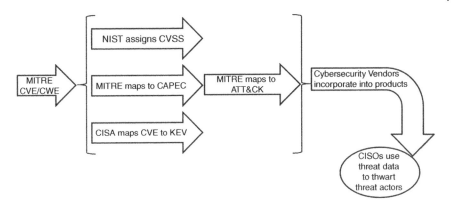

Figure 2.17 From CVE to Cyber Defense

to incorporate diverse threat intelligence using standard terminology into their products. Figure 2.17 shows the relationship between these standards.

The job of a cyber-threat analyst is to decide whether your adversary can exploit your vulnerabilities. This is a solemn task. A consensus approach is necessary to provide comfort in good judgment. Over time, the methodology has been to dissect the attack vector into TTPs with which a given threat actor has expertise. Threat vector TTP components correspond generically to common technology components and allow an enterprise to assess enterprise vulnerability at every step in combinations of threat vectors that contain them. The result is a cybersecurity industry standard for representing steps in an attack path that is a key component of MITRE's ATT&CK data. Figure 2.18 is a snapshot of the ATT&CK knowledge base of cyber adversary behavior and taxonomy for adversarial actions across their lifecycle (MITRE 2015–2023). Readers who wish to explore MITRE's ATT&CK threat vector matrix will find an interactive version at the link below the figure. The threat actor tactics listed in Figure 2.18 are the column headings. Specific alternative techniques that enact activities representing the tactic are listed below them. An attack can be described in a standard manner by selecting the activity of the tactic that best represents what transpired within the attack. Not every tactic needs to be used in describing an attack, but by connecting the selections, you can complete a chevron that describes the attack in an industry standard method. The idea is to recognize patterns used by actors who target the enterprise so that a defender can ensure that there are adequate defenses.

For example, the tactic of "Initial Access" may be enacted by exploiting a public-facing application like Apache log4j or it may be done via phishing. Looking back on previous descriptions of hacker activities that compromise desktops, it may seem to some improbable that it is so easy to commandeer other people's

Initial Access → Execution → Persistence → Escalation → Evasion → Access → Discovery → Movement → Data → Commands → Exfiltration

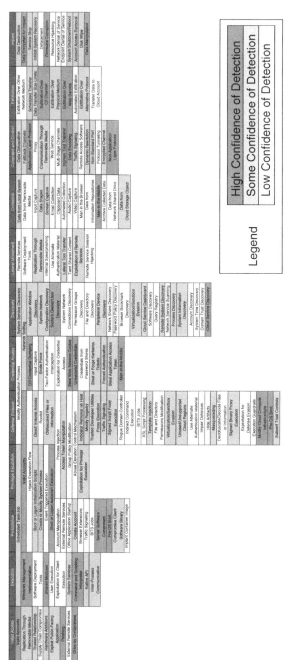

Figure 2.18 An ATT&CK Threat Vector Matrix

computers in the quantity required for successful attack. For example, the 500,000 machines that may be required to conduct a successful denial of service attack. But the "Initial Access" column also includes a very insidious and often overlooked initial access tactic referred to as "Drive-by Compromise." In this instantiation of the tactic, the threat actor is not targeting any specific company or person. An example of drive-by compromise is the distribution of malware through paid advertising, a practice called "malvertising" an amalgam of "malicious" and "advertising." This is also an example of cybersecurity criminal networks utilizing commercial ecommerce services to execute attacks. Other such examples include business email compromise (BEC), wherein the attacker impersonates an online business partner. These examples of online fraud have historically has been propagated via postal mail and telephone but have since moved to email and other easily exploited online services.

The fact that attacks like DDoS and SQL Injection are sometimes aided and abetted by malvertising is startling and alarming. When hackers can plant malware on user's computer simply because they visited a newspaper's website, it becomes very obvious that they have the ability to fully capture all of the personal profile data for that user accessible via a browser, and if there is an exploitable desktop vulnerability, C&C malware can be installed on the user's desktop. Threat networks harvest information gleaned from malvertising and make it available on the internet's most sinister web marketplaces, namely, the dark web.

A more recent alarming development in the capabilities of threat networks is aided and abetted by Artificial Intelligence (AI). Note, AI has long been a trusted tool in the cybersecurity toolkit to sift through logs and identify patterns of suspicious behavior. But AI evolved into more of an active helping hand in a wider variety of tasks, and as naïve users attempt to make their lives easier by relying on AI, hackers are weaponizing it to their advantage. Just as malvertising may lead a user astray from the shopping experience they are pursuing, AI can deliver false results, called "AI hallucinations" (Coker 2023). For example, hackers have employed AI hallucinations to target software developers known to be querying the internet for help in specific configuration or coding problems. Rather than deliver practical and useful assistance, AI hallucinations instead deliver a "cuckoo's egg" to the software repositories of its victims. The false result is called a cuckoo's egg because the cuckoo lays her eggs in the unattended nests of birds with similar-looking eggs and the mother bird to whom the nest belongs raises the cuckoo chick. A cuckoo has a shorter incubation period than the victim species. It hatches, is fed by the mother, then attacks the other eggs. The cybersecurity analogy is that security vulnerabilities are like the unattended nests and the cuckoo's egg is the vulnerability nestling inside: unauthorized, undetected, but lying in wait to spring (Stoll 1989). Because AI hallucinations are often customized for the target and were actually requested by the end user, their widespread use is especially dangerous.

It is important for every organization to understand the extent to which it is the target of a sophisticated adversary. If a threat actor in your catalog is only skilled on the Windows operating system and you are a Linux shop, you probably could set aside that attack profile and look for one that more specifically matched your environment. A systematic study of threat actors should classify their TTPs into vector patterns that you can compare to your own systems. If you systematically collect TTP information about every threat actor targeting the enterprise and map those TTP patterns to your own environment, then you can use that pattern to create requirements for detecting specific tools and techniques of the threat actors.

That is, knowledge of the TTPs enables you to design pseudo attacks against your own enterprise that can be executed by a "red team," a term for penetration testers hired by an enterprise to emulate the activities of real threat actors in order to test defenses. Colloquially referred to as "red-teaming," observation of the impact of red team activities can be can be used to perform defensive gap assessment. TTP patterns gleaned from a threat catalog become a *threat model*, which historically has been referred to as a *design-basis threat* (DBT) (Garcia, 2008).

A DBT describes characteristics of the most powerful and innovative adversary that it is realistic to expect security to protect against. In New York City, it may be a terrorist cell equipped with sophisticated communications and explosive devices. In Idaho, it may be a 20-strong posse of vigilantes carrying machine guns on motorcycles. Adopting a DBT approach to security implies that the strength of security protection required by a system should be calculated with respect to a technical specification of how it is likely to be attacked. In physical security, this process is straightforward. If the DBT is a force of 20 people with access to explosives of a given type, then the strength of the physical barriers to unauthorized entry must withstand the ton of force that these twenty people could physically bring into system contact. Barrier protection materials are specified, threat delay and response systems are designed, and validation tests are conducted accordingly. In cyber security, potential attacks are the aggregated set of all publicly documented cyber attacks to date.

Just as owners of nuclear power plants must build barricades to thwart tanks and helicopters, cybersecurity defenses must plan for known TTPs and enterprise mitigations should be sufficient to thwart attack pattern likely to be used against it.

References

Brumfield, C. (2022). Recent Cases Highlight Need for Insider Threat Awareness and Action, CSO Online (29 September 2022). https://www.csoonline.com/article/3675348/recent-cases-highlight-need-for-insider-threat-awareness-and-action.html (accessed 08 May 2023).

Coker, J. (2023). Generative AI A Boon for Organizations Despite the Risks, Experts Say, InfoSecurity Magazine, October 27, 2023. https://www.infosecurity-magazine.com/news/generative-ai-a-boon-for/ (accessed 08 November 2023).

Cummings, A., Lewellen, T., McIntire, D., Moore, A.P., Trzeciak, R. (2012). Insider Threat Study: Illicit Cyber Activity Involving Fraud in the U.S. Financial Services Sector. CMU/SEI-2012-SR-004.

Epstein, K. and Elgin, B. (2008). The taking of NASA's secrets. *Business Week* (1 December), pp. 73–79.

Federal Trade Commission (2022). FTC Warns Companies to Remediate Log4j Security Vulnerability. https://www.ftc.gov/policy/advocacy-research/tech-at-ftc/2022/01/ftc-warns-companies-remediate-log4j-security-vulnerability (accessed 08 May 2023).

Garcia, M. (2008). *The Design and Analysis of Physical Protection Systems*, Second Edition, Butterworth-Heinemann.

Jaiswal, A. (2022). Log4j2 Vulnerability Explained in Details. https://cybermeteoroid.com/log4j2-vulnerability-explained-in-details (accessed 08 May 2023).

Mandiant (2013). APT1 Exposing one of China's Cyber Espionage Units. https://www.mandiant.com/resources/reports/apt1-exposing-one-chinas-cyber-espionage-units (accessed 08 May 2023).

Martin, R. (2001). Managing Vulnerabilities in Networked Systems. https://www.researchgate.net/figure/Vulnerability-Tower-of-Babel-1998_tbl1_2955531 (accessed 08 May 2023).

Menn, J. (2010). *Fatal System Error*. Public Affairs.

MITRE (2023). Enterprise Matrix. https://attack.mitre.org/matrices/enterprise/ (accessed 08 May 2023).

NIST-CVE (2021). Apache Log4j Vulnerability. National Institute of Standards and Technology. https://nvd.nist.gov/vuln/detail/CVE-2021-44228 (accessed 08 May 2023).

NIST 800-30 (2012). Guide for Conducting Risk Assessments. National Institute of Standards and Technology. https://nvlpubs.nist.gov/nistpubs/Legacy/SP/nistspecialpublication800-30r1.pdf (accessed 08 May 2023).

OASIS (2020). STIX, version 2.1. http://docs.oasis-open.org/cti/stix/v2.0/stix-v2.0-part1-stix-core.html (accessed 08 May 2023).

OWASP (2021). Open Web Application Security Project® Top Ten. https://owasp.org/Top10/ (accessed 08 May 2023).

Perlroth, N. (2021). *This Is How They Tell Me the World Ends: The Cyberweapons Arms Race*. Bloomsbury.

Singel, R. (2008). San Francisco held cyber-hostage? Disgruntled techies have wreaked worse havoc. *Wired* (16 July). https://www.wired.com/2008/07/insider-tech-at/

Stoll, C. (1989). *The Cuckoo's Egg, Tracking a Spy Through the Maze of Computer Espionage,* Doubleday.

Verizon (2022). Data Breach Investigations Report. http://www.verizon.com/business/resources/reports/dbir/ (accessed 08 May 2023).

3

Events

In the days before computers, adversaries used physical measures to attack targets. In the physical realm, targets defend not just against crime and war, but also natural disasters. Understanding the foundations of our response to physical threat events makes it easier to understand the evolution of cybersecurity event response. For example, lightning is a significant threat, but it only causes harm if it actually makes contact, so there are physical methods to *prevent* that contact from occurring. The lightning rod in Figure 3.1 is one such method. However, lightning rods do not always work. If lightning bypasses the rod and a fire starts, then the target can at least *detect* that a fire has started. A fire alarm is one such detection method. Perhaps the community also has a fire station that detects the smoke and alarms the fire department. These capabilities provide information that the fire is occurring. Of course the building is still burning, so just detecting that smoke and knowing there is a fire does not actually help us thwart the lightning. So the target also needs some kind of mechanism with which to *respond* to the fire alarms. Figure 3.1 includes all three elements of the *prevent, detect, respond* triad. Unfortunately, regardless of how soon a lightening fire is caught, it is very likely that the fire will cause damage. For a physical security incident, the best that can be done is to try to prevent; if you cannot prevent, at least detect; and once detected, respond. By the time the first responders (as we still call them, even in cyber) get to the scene of the fire, the accident, the murder, or other physical security events, these emergency response teams know that there could be damage and they may not be able to prevent or even recover anything that was damaged or destroyed.

In the early days of computer security, this *prevent, detect, respond* process was adopted for computer incident response. However, back then, instead of saying *prevent, detect, respond* security management models have been labeled with variations on that theme, including, but not limited to (Bayuk 2010b, p. 21):

Stepping Through Cybersecurity Risk Management: A Systems Thinking Approach,
First Edition. Jennifer L. Bayuk.
© 2024 John Wiley & Sons, Inc. Published 2024 by John Wiley & Sons, Inc.
Companion website: www.wiley.com/go/STCRM

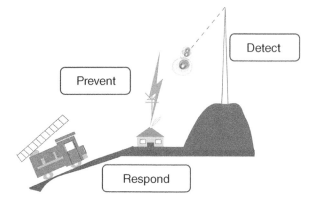

Figure 3.1 Prevent Detect Respond

- *Plan-Do-Check-Correct*
- *Plan-Secure-Confirm-Remediate*
- *Prepare-Detect-Respond-Improve*
- *Restrict-Run-Recover*

These all boil down to:

- Have a response plan.
- Act according to the plan.
- Make observations to see the plan is working.
- Make changes to the plan based on the observations.

This strategy reflected the opinion of the first cyber first responders that, unlike human life or property damage, a target could always get back what it had lost when a computer was damaged because it had backup. Prudent targets set backup intervals to an achievable recovery point objective, allowing them to recreate the computer and put enough data back to maintain operations. Recovery meant achieving the recovery point objective. Lessons learned from the harmful event were used to shore up your prevention processes so that it should not happen again, and through the 1980s and the 1990s computer security management happily executed and continually improved computer security *prevent, detect, recover* cycles.

However, as cyberattacks became more prevalent, recovery was not always possible. Like a fireman or an emergency management technician, sometimes all that can be done in the face of an attack is respond. In appreciation of the need for clarification of the capabilities cybersecurity can bring to risk management, NIST coordinated an international collaboration to produce a twenty-first century cybersecurity version of Figure 3.1. It is depicted in Figure 3.2 (NIST-CSF 2024). Pragmatic wisdom that has evolved over the last half century has changed the cycle from *prevent, detect, recover* to *identify, protect, detect, respond, recover*. Note the inclusion of a preliminary step to the event response cycle: *identify*. In the physical world, it may seem easy to set the scope for detection and response functions by physical location. But in cybersecurity, one of the hardest problems cyber defenders face is defining the boundaries of the enterprise digital environment. *Identify* calls attention to hard problems in asset management and supply chain management that need to be solved to even understand what needs to be protected. The NIST CSF *Identify* function at first included a *Governance* category similar

Figure 3.2 NIST-CSF Functions

to the *Strategy* step in Figure 3.1 and the *Prepare* step in Figure 3.2. In version 2 of the CSF, this has rightly matured to become a parallel process that crosses all other functions. It calls attention to the necessity of clearly defined strategy for an enterprise cybersecurity program as a whole, as opposed to its component parts.

To complete the analogy with physical security, the identify function helps cyber defenders place the lightning rods (detect measures) effectively. Most of the time, those lightning rods work. Similarly in cybersecurity, the fact that a threat actor is targeting an organization does not necessarily mean that it will be able to exploit systems to gain access to assets. Without a threat actor inspired and capable of enacting a threat, a threat is just a plan. Even if the targeted system has vulnerabilities, it does not necessarily follow that the adversary has the skills to perform an exploit or will select the vulnerable system within its target. Therefore, threats together with vulnerabilities do not equal exploits. Figure 3.3 illustrates this concept that lightning does not equal fire.

The combination of threats and vulnerabilities may allow exploits, but there is still a probability that those exploits may not occur. Nevertheless, threat intelligence may provide evidence that threat actors have exploited the vulnerability in similar organizations, and a CISO should interpret this evidence to indicate that

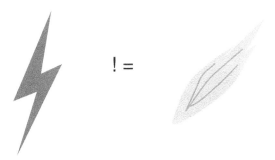

Figure 3.3 Threats Don't Equal Exploits

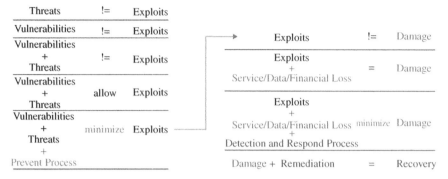

Figure 3.4 The CISO Equation

the probability is high that exploits might occur. In that case, a CISO should implement more effective prevention mechanisms to minimize the probability that an adversary will accomplish an exploit despite prevention mechanisms. The first column of a theorem called "The CISO Equation," depicted in Figure 3.4, codifies the logic in this line of reasoning.

Even if the prevention mechanisms fail and an exploit does occur, this still does not necessarily mean that damage will be caused. Breaking into the cafeteria menu system rarely damages an organization. It is only when harm occurs as a result of that exploit that there is damage, such as information confidentiality, integrity, or availability breaches. To detect whether vulnerabilities have been exploited to cause harm, a CISO should implement detection capability. Predefined response procedures should be in place to contain and mitigate damage. For example, patching software vulnerabilities is like upgrading the lightning rods after a fire. Full recovery may require more time to achieve, just as a fire victim may take time to recover in the hospital. These concepts are codified in the column on the right of Figure 3.4. They are so well ingrained in the minds of today's CISOs that the CISO Equation depicted in Figure 3.4 is common knowledge.

3.1 Event Classification

When cyber threat actors attack, the cybersecurity professional calls that a cybersecurity incident, successful cyberattack, or realized cyber risk. If the event has resulted in quantifiable monetary loss to the enterprise, it will also be called a loss event. The first three terms refer to the same event type from different perspectives. Technology management commonly refers to any event that detracts from the performance of technology services as an incident, and to distinguish the events where incidents are caused by deliberate attempts to harm, they use the adjective "cybersecurity" for the incident. However, not all cybersecurity incidents would routinely be classified as a successful cyberattack. If a threat actor exploits vulnerabilities in an enterprise network only to break into the cafeteria menu system, then the threat actor has not met objectives. (Note: the term actor is often used as a *modifier* for *objective*, omitting a term, such as "their," as in "their objectives," because the reference to the attacker is obvious.) The attack was not successful. Even in a successful cyberattack, the attacker's objective may be met, but the impact does not negatively impact the company. This is the case wherein a hacktivist may temporarily replace the website of a government agency with their own political message, but other than bad publicity, there is no negative impact on the victim because they do not have customers or investors to lose due to the event, so the agency may not even consider the event significant enough to catalog hacktivism as a risk.

The term "realized" as applied to risk is meaningful because it is not just a probability that some hypothetical thing may happen anymore; it actually did happen. After things happen we suddenly know there is a 100% probability of it happening. Before it happened, we may not have thought so, but once it has occurred there is no longer a doubt about whether or not it will occur. That debate is over. Even the government agency that denies they are at any risk over the event will likely classify the event as such and incorporate it in its to-do list to prevent it going forward.

The term "loss event" is applied to a cybersecurity event when it results in a quantifiable monetary loss. That loss will be aggregated with the losses of all events that result in monetary loss, and it is common to see that sum presented in executive and board presentations as "Losses due to Cybersecurity Risk" side by side with losses due to other operational risk categories.

That is, a cyberattack is not necessarily successful or a realized cyber risk, but a loss event that has a cyber-related root cause is considered a cybersecurity incident, a successful cybersecurity attack, and a realized cyber risk. Figure 3.5 illustrates the relationship between the four sets of events.

Considered from the perspective of an enterprise Chief Risk Officer (CRO), enterprise risk encompasses credit, market, and operational risk, along with any others more specific to its mission. Cybersecurity risk falls into the operational risk category, that is risks that disrupt business operation. At the enterprise level, negatively impacting events are divided into event categories and newly identified events are classified into those categories. This is helpful in estimating the resources necessary to assess the extent to which events in each category may cause negative impact on the enterprise. It also helps narrow the potential set of mitigating controls that may reduce the risk of event

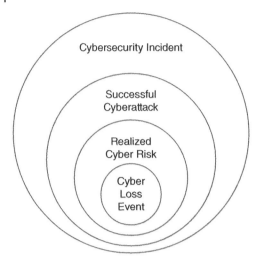

Figure 3.5 Cybersecurity Event Attributes

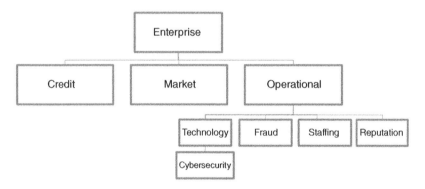

Figure 3.6 Enterprise Risk Hierarchy Example

recurrence to an acceptable level. These events are a subset of enterprise risk as in the example of Figure 3.6.

Where such classification is done at the enterprise risk level, the same type of classification will typically be applied to event subcategories within the category of cybersecurity. Figure 3.7 shows two alternative cybersecurity risk subcategories in the form of a taxonomy hierarchy. In the first, events are classified according to their outcome. In the second, they are classified according to threat actor tactics.

In the first example, the enterprise classifies events using a triad of cyberattack outcomes invented in the early days of computer security that was used to ensure completeness when evaluating information security requirements. Although the triad has often been dismissed as simplistic and dated, it is still

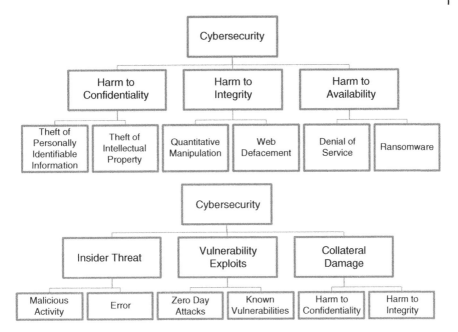

Figure 3.7 Alternative Cybersecurity Event Subcategories

difficult to come up with an example where a threat to information does not fall under one or more of these categories:

- *Harm to Confidentiality*: access to information by someone not authorized to view it,
- *Harm to Integrity*: manipulation of data that changes information to misinformation, and
- *Harm to Availability*: data corruption and/or deletion that makes information unusable.

Within each cybersecurity event category, subcategories further differentiate events for which the enterprise has different risk appetites and/or requires different management controls to reduce the risk to an acceptable level. Controls in this context are often called risk "treatments." In the case of the harm to confidentiality risk in the top left of Figure 3.7, its subcategories, theft of PII and theft of Intellectual Property, may have similar risk appetites (usually low). However, the treatment to reduce risk of attacks on PII versus Intellectual Property will typically be different. This is because PII is a byproduct of customer interaction and Intellectual Property is the enterprise's most closely held secrets. Therefore, depending on the enterprise business model, the percentage of staff who interact with customer information may be much higher or lower than the percentage of staff who interact with company secrets, or vice versa. In a company that closely interacts with the general public, requirements for automated management control over PII must be ubiquitous to treat the risk of PII theft. In a company where the only PII data resides in HR databases, it may be that the treatments for theft of Intellectual Property are more demanding than those required to manage theft of PII risk. Either way, the risk reduction control distinction has led to the separation of the two types of events into separate risk subcategories.

In the second example, the enterprise has decided that cybersecurity events should be classified into these categories:

- *Insider Threat*: cybersecurity incidents in which the threat actor is an insider,
- *External Exploits*: events in which enterprise vulnerabilities were exploited by outsiders, and
- *Collateral Damage*: events that occur outside the enterprise and result in negative impact on enterprise operations.

As in the first example, further analysis into threat actors in each subcategory reveals tactics that are thwartable using different sets of controls. Figure 3.8 shows the control mapping from the *Insider Threat* event subcategories to two control functions: protect in the form of Identity and Access Management (IAM) and detect in the form of Zero Trust Architecture (ZTA) respectively. These approaches utilize overlapping control technologies, but the design and architecture of technology controls differ when utilized in the service of different *control objectives*, which is a generic term for the goals that management intends to achieve through implementation of actual controls. In this case, thwarting accidental insider threat is one control objective and thwarting intentional insider threat is another. IAM controls support the former control objective by focusing on the authorized user and supporting their ability to use system resources in accordance with the

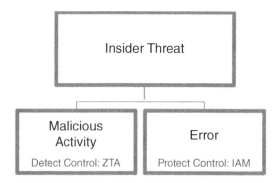

Figure 3.8 Risk Subcategories Mapped to Control Strategies

requirements of their job function. ZTA leverages IAM controls but has an additional control objective to prevent access by unauthorized users. Achieving this objective requires detection of unauthorized activities. Controls in support of this objective include alerts when users perform unexpected activities and may enforce thresholds on such behavior as an additional level of access control (NIST 800-207, 2020). That is, the accidental insider event and malicious insider event are different subcategories because they have a different probability of occurrence and different controls that minimize the risk of occurrence of an event in each subset.

These differences drive the choice of different treatments for insider accidental information compromise versus insider malicious activity. To understand why, it is helpful to think of the events in the context of the enterprise systems. Insiders have authorized access, so limits on authorized access can limit the damage of any mistake they may make. Where a mistake is made, transaction logs should contain all user activities, hopefully enabling a transaction rollback at the application level. However, if an insider intentionally tries to bypass such established controls, their activities will likely deviate from normal authorized user behavior. Such deviations are more likely to be detected by User Behavioral Analysis (UBA) monitoring systems at the infrastructure level than audit trails at the business application level.

A UBA system works by extracting user identities from activity logs and storing a historical abstract pattern of activities for each user. These may include the normal work hours, the application and file shares accessed, the people with whom they communicate via email or chat, and even keystroke patterns and other biometric attributes of the person. When enough information is collected to establish a pattern, the UBA system will start comparing the user's new activity to the historical pattern and alert when the user identity engages in system activity that deviates from the pattern. Though prone to false positives as people engage in new projects, UBA is very good at detecting abuse of *service accounts.* Service accounts are credentials used not by humans, but by unattended software processes. These accounts are often sometimes referred to as *generic IDs* or *privileged accounts* because they are not associated with a single individual but with an automated process like a backup that occurs when no user is logged into the system. Because these accounts are typically created for a single purpose, it is easier to create a rule based to detect when they are used for something other than the purpose for which they are designed. There is no need to have the UBA system create a historical pattern because they should only be used for one or two commands, so an administrator who creates the account can also create the UBA pattern. Service accounts are frequent targets of both insider and external threats, but an effective ZTA control should be able to detect unusual activity and either alert on it or block it.

3.2 Event Prevention

IAM is the most fundamental protect control. Its basic principles were born out of logical theorems in the mid-twentieth century, which combined properties of subjects (computer users) and objects (programs or data) with methods of specifying attributes of subjects that indicated they should have access to objects. The simplest of these classified both subjects and objects into hierarchical levels, such as public, secret, and top secret, then only let subjects have access to objects if the subject was the same level or higher. For example:

Define Object Labels: $A > B > C$
Define Subject Levels: $A > B > C$
Rule: **Access** (Subject, Object) **if and only if** Level(Subject) $>=$ Label(Object)

These rules only worked if there could be a mediator between a subject's request for the object and the object itself that would consult the access rules before allowing the subject to access the object. Hence the creation of the security principle called "complete mediation," which specified that computer operating systems must contain a "reference monitor" capable of intercepting all subject access requests and consulting rule bases in order to determine whether a subject was authorized to access an object before granting such access. Figure 3.9 is an example of complete mediation using a reference monitor. This concept is the basis for all modern identity and access management systems.

Imagine yourself in the position of a manager responsible for maintaining control over financial data that is routinely manipulated by staff under your supervision, like a business application that transfers money between bank accounts, colloquially called a "wire transfer" system. You begin by hiring people whom you consider trustworthy, and you verify this by doing background checks on new hires to ensure they have no known history of committing fraud. You work with Legal to ensure

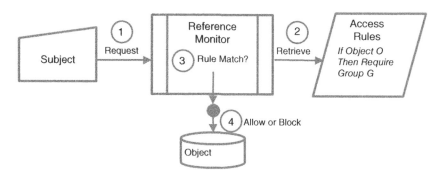

Figure 3.9 Reference Monitor

that there is a policy whereby staff will be fired and prosecuted if they commit fraud and publish that policy in the enterprise "Code of Conduct" document. You work with HR to ensure that all staff are trained on that code of conduct and must formally agree to it with a signature as a condition of employment. The code of conduct will include intellectual property and nondisclosure clauses. You work with IT to ensure that your staff has no authorized access to perform any system or application function that is not specifically assigned to their job role and absolutely necessary for them to accomplish the business activity that is specified by their job function. You also tell them that you require an audit trail of all information accessed and functions performed by anyone with access to the wire transfer system.

Of the due diligence efforts you have initiated, the third will undoubtedly prove the most difficult to accomplish. The first thing IT will do is make sure that your staff members do not have "administrative" system privileges. Administrative privilege is a generic term to refer to a computer user who configures access for all other users. Someone has to do this, and this privilege has the side effect of enabling the "administrator" to impersonate other system users. Hence, the number of users with administrative privileges is typically kept to a minimum and admins themselves are rarely granted access to the business applications they are responsible for securing.

This is enabled via a technical control called "separation of privilege" which dictates that a system should require multiple parameters to be set to enable special privileges not granted to every system user. For example, for administrative access, a user must first be configured as a normal user, then also be added to a group. This keeps the number of users capable of impersonating other users to a minimum. This also creates a hierarchy of power to operate system functions where the admins have the ability to allow or deny system functionality to users who do not themselves have that power. This power can extend to the device integrated circuit level, where operating systems reserve electronic memory space for admins that cannot be accessed by normal users. This is to ensure that they cannot perform administrative functions like granting permissions to other users.

The separation of user space from administration space is not always observed in computer systems engineering but as hacking increased in the late 1990s, it became obvious to systems engineers that this was a necessary, though insufficient, feature to prevent hackers from running roughshod over publicly available systems. Although it is now more generally accepted that systems integrity requires the separation of user space from administrative space, the extent to which users can be limited to data sets by operating systems is still not very granular. An operating system typically only enforces controls at the level of a file or database or folder, not at the individual set of numbers, such as bank accounts and currency fields, within a file or database.

The example of financial transactions has been introduced to emphasize that without doubt there are cases where it is not appropriate to default permissions to an entire database or file using an operating system reference monitor alone. Instead, application service accounts are granted broad access to data and transactions and the application software restricts individual users to those transactions to which their job role requires them to be entitled. These more "fine-grained entitlements," as they are called, are integrated into a reference monitoring written into the code of the business applications. Unfortunately, business application developers are rarely interested in limiting functionality, they focus on enabling it. They prefer to rely on operating system reference monitors to make access control decisions. But if every wire transfer user had the same permissions as the application service account to change any data in a wire transfer file, then it would be very difficult to hold any one staff member accountable for the money they transferred. Business application developers have to (i) create distinct data fields in files that represent transaction-level user permissions, (ii) correctly retrieve them to dynamically create rules that work for different types of transactions, and (iii) create informative error messages for users who attempt to use features for which their access is denied.

Unfortunately, the systems engineering profession has been slow to consider such security functionality as a feature of the business application software. The software "feature" is wire transfer. Security is referred to as an "ility," an adjective that systems engineers reserve for attributes that they do consider to be functions of a system, like performance, something to be anticipated in final deployment but not at the level of an architectural decision. When security is not considered a function of the system, technology developers do not typically get positive feedback from their customer-focused business managers for adding features that enhance only internal staff security functionality. In fact, security features that limit user activity to very specific authorized use cases run the risk of user frustration due to the inability to easily facilitate client expectations for quick and easy cash transfers. When they are not part of system design, it can be very complicated to "bolt-on" effective security capability (Ricci et al. 2014).

The core security principle that defines identity and access management is "least privilege," which is a cyber security shorthand for "everyone should have exactly the permissions they need to perform their assigned role, and no more." Therefore, permissions need to be carefully crafted to correspond to staff who need to use the system to accomplish their job function. This is done by defining a label for the job function in an access management system and mapping the job function permissions to the label, then assigning the label (typically called a "role") to a user. Where the user requires only a subset of the data accessible via the functions, they will also be assigned a label called a "group." The group is then mapped to some data indices that restrict the individual from seeing any data set that does not contain the assigned indices.

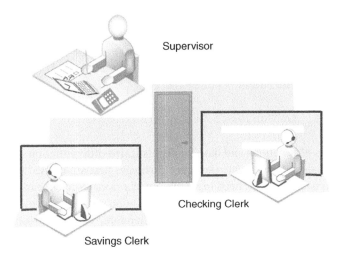

Figure 3.10 Least Privilege Example

For example, say that the wire transfer system has two roles and two groups. The groups are clerk and supervisor as in Figure 3.10. The clerk role is to answer the phone, authenticate the customer via caller ID and secret code, and enter the transaction requested by the customer. The supervisor role is to review the call recording and approve the transaction for release of funds. The two groups are checking and savings. Depending on the caller selection of account type, the call will be routed to a clerk who is a member of the checking group or savings group. Each has a different set of data that it can access, the checking accounts and savings accounts, respectively.

The supervisor will be a member of both groups. Expressed in the same form as the simple hierarchical access control example from the mid-twentieth century, role-based and group-based access rules look like this:

```
Define Object Labels:
  Checking = Checking Account Table
  Savings = Savings Account Table
Define Subject Roles:
  Checking Clerk = {View Balance, Enter amount, Enter
Account, Save Transaction}
  Savings Clerk = {View Balance, Enter amount, Enter
Account, Save Transaction}
  Supervisor = {View Transaction, Enter Approval}
Define Object Groups:
  Checking Clerk = {Checking}
```

```
Savings Clerk = {Savings}
Supervisor = {Checking, Savings}
Rule: Execute <Function> for (Subject, Object) if
and only if
    Role(Subject) includes <Function>
    and
    Label(Object) in Subject(<Group List>)
```

Various permutations of functions and data for sophisticated differentiation of permissions allow managers to segregate the set of privileges that are needed to perform activities on a need to know, need to modify, and/or need to delete basis, according to the responsibilities of that individual. Application entitlement rules are created to correspond to sets of responsibilities. Therefore, when a person comes into a new role, it does not take an inordinate amount of time to figure out what permissions they need because the role is predefined. It may need to be redefined when job functions change. But no matter how many employees you have and no matter how many times that job function rotates between individuals, the role is only created once. Least privilege is very important, and having processes to control these privileges is even more important, especially in operations that require a high degree of trust, such as wire transfer between the enterprise treasury and those of clients or business partners.

Least privilege is important, but not enough by itself to prevent accidental misuse of systems that have a high risk of negative consequences. These systems should have some kind of check and balance function as in the clerk/supervisor example above. In some companies they call this the "doer" and the "checker." Someone performs activity, but it does not actually complete its function until another person looks at it, agrees it is acceptable for the system to do, and signs on with their own credentials, checks the same transaction data that has already been set up by the doer, and creates a log to the effect of: "yes, I've checked this." This type of access control is called "segregation of duties." It requires that a single operation within the computer cannot be accomplished without complete authentication and cooperation of two or more individuals. If someone does perform an unauthorized wire transfer, then there would be two people within the system that would both have to deny having done it to avoid culpability, and the probability of collusion with two people is lower than the probability of one person doing something unauthorized. The probability of a single individual being a fraudster is combined. If the probability of one person being a fraudster is 10%, the probability of two is mathematically squared, or 1%, so segregation of duties is a very common user-level cyber security principle that reduces the risk of accidental cybersecurity incidents.

A more common example of doer/checker happens in grocery stores when a clerk enters a price change, but needs a manager to enter some kind of unique code that allows the system to override the default price. Even in this IAM scenario, separation of privilege must be implemented first before least privilege and segregation of duties can be accomplished.

Since before the internet, firewalls have been the go-to control of choice in preventing intruders from accessing enterprise assets, despite the fact that data theft has historically been committed using authorized insider credentials to both breach network security and access data (Bayuk et al. 2012, Chapter 2). Diagrams like the one in Figure 3.11 have long been used to illustrate network attack vectors. The diagram on the left of Figure 3.11 shows where firewalls control access via concentric circles and the thicker line represents the network "perimeter," the outmost boundary of an enterprise network where it touches the internet. That line must have a way for authorized users to cross, such as staff working remotely and internet users accessing web applications. The diagram on the right shows where both the perimeter and firewalls must be left open to allow that authorized access. Small circles on the lines indicate where a user must authenticate to some device to reach the part of the internal network for which the circle is labeled. A bridge on the line shows that users on one side of the line can cross it based on the location of the circle to which they authenticated. To summarize the diagram, firewalls protect the enterprise perimeter, authorized users skip right through the firewalls to perform their job functions, and hackers simply piggy-back on the authorized access paths from the user's workstation or steal the user's credentials to do so. That is why there is a question mark on the "Perimeter" label at the left of the diagram. The analogy with a physical perimeter is not justified when it comes to networks. There are too many options for traversing a network in comparison with a guarded gate.

This situation has been obvious to cybersecurity professionals for decades. In 2004, a group calling themselves the "Jericho Forum" brought widespread attention to misplaced faith in what they called "perimeterization." They promoted a new approach to cybersecurity that they called "de-perimeterization" and issued "Commandments" (Jericho Forum, 2007). The commandments were common sense approaches to avoiding reliance on firewalls to prevent unauthorized access. Nevertheless, the cybersecurity community had unwarranted faith in the effectiveness of passwords as access control and was so focused on network security that – except in high-risk areas like bank operations or trade secrets – Jericho's warnings went largely unheeded. Figure 3.12 summarizes the Jericho message. It warns of the dangers of trusting perimeters like the one in Figure 3.9 to keep malicious actors out of the network. It emphasizes that data is exposed due to the permissive nature of network connections that are assumed to be utilized only by authorized users. Of course, the high prevalence of identity theft and phishing attacks on desktops have made it obvious that many authorized connections cannot be trusted. Multiple labels for new types of control, "Data Centric Security"

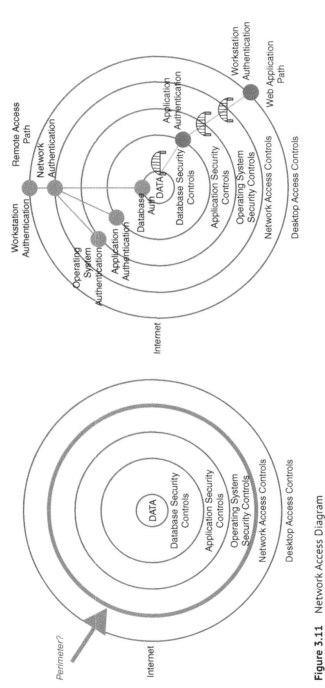

Figure 3.11 Network Access Diagram

"De-perimeterization is happening, and is inevitable; central protection is decreasing in effectiveness"

Surviving in a Hostile World.

Whereas boundary firewalls may continue to provide basic network protection, individual systems and data will need to be capable of protecting themselves.

- In general, it's easier to protect an asset the closer protection is provided.
- Assume context at your peril.
- Devices and applications must communicate using open, secure protocols.
- Any implementation must be capable of surviving on the raw Internet; e.g., will not break on any input.
- Authentication, authorization, and accountability must interoperate/exchange outside of your locus/area of control.
- Access to data should be controlled by security attributes of the data itself.

Figure 3.12 Summary of Jericho Forum Commandments

and "User Centric Security," for example, were approaches that focused away from network as the main tool for cybersecurity risk reduction.

In late 2009, cybersecurity staff at Google detected anomalous activity on internal networks that had no explanation other than deep-rooted occupation by an advanced persistent threat. In the decade prior, nation-state attacks on the US government had been steadily escalating and data theft had spiraled completely out of control. With this backdrop, a cybersecurity industry analyst noticed that "almost every security device, such as a firewall, comes with at least one port labeled 'untrusted' and another labeled 'trusted'." He suddenly realized that network controls were designed to form a fence around authorized users, but that once inside the fence, all users were considered "trusted," that is, authorized. Only then did he fully grasp that threat actors who were able to breach externally facing network controls took maximum advantage of this situation by disguising their activity as that of authorized insiders to remain undetected for years. The analyst made his living studying cybersecurity and this fact had not until then occurred to him, so he understood that he was not the only one to whom this idea had not yet occurred. He sounded an alarm in an article: "No More Chewy Centers!" (Kindervag, 2010). The article began with an old saying in information security: "We want our network to be like an M&M, with a hard crunchy outside and a soft chewy center." He went on to summarize a new model for network security, which he called "Zero Trust" model, that basically echoed Jericho Forum's commandments.

Zero Trust was much more catchy than "commandments," and the audience for such advice was growing more receptive. Zero Trust Architecture (ZTA) became the label for a new technology model for cybersecurity. In the network access model of Figure 3.11, the source network address, or internet protocol

(IP) address, is how user traffic gets routed through network to back and forth devices to which they login or otherwise access. A user starting out on the internet will be assigned an IP address from a local internet service provider (ISP). However, once a user logs in to an internal network, the user's original address is typically "translated" to an internal one, and so appears to any applications and servers as somehow more "trustworthy." Figure 3.13 illustrates a Zero Trust model wherein both the end user's source address and identity on the device to which they are physically operating is maintained throughout each network layer that brings the user closer to the requested resource. In contrast to Figure 3.11's network access path allowing anyone on the network level to access a resource at that level or those below it, ZTA requires multiple layers of network access control that progressively narrow a user's access to only a small set of resources that are segmented from each other at the network level and individually authenticated. The approach is known as "microsegmentation," and has also colloquially been called the "honeycomb" model of network security (Sherwood et al. 2005, pp. 270–272).

Although designed to deter and thwart malicious outsiders, ZTA also makes it more difficult to enact accidental insider threats by limiting the network connectivity afforded to authorized insiders. Conversely, segregation of duties and separation of privilege controls targeted at accidental insider threats make it more difficult for intentionally malicious insiders, as well as external threats to accomplish escalation of privilege within a ZTA.

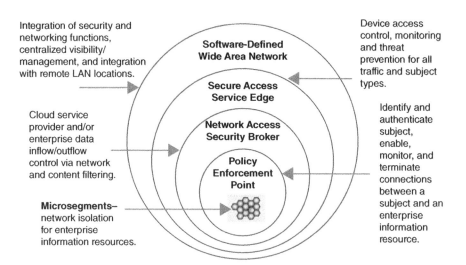

Figure 3.13 Zero Trust Extended Perimeter

3.3   Detection and Response

When Sun Tzu called attention to the didactic nature of the interaction between adversary activities and enterprise defenses, his point was that only if you understand how your adversary could possibly negatively impact the enterprise can you be in a position to adequately protect yourself. Figure 3.14 is a diagram from more recent military advice on adversary analysis. It was drawn by John Boyd, a fighter pilot once charged with training others. Boyd emphasized that one must be constantly aware of what is going on around you when you are in a small plane. Situational awareness is key to survival. Your current observations must be detailed enough to combine them with what you know from experience about your allies and your plane, knowledge about the adversary's background and mission, and recently observed patterns in your environment. Quick analysis of this information provides you with the situational awareness required to orient yourself and understand whether you are in the direct target of a capable threat actor and/or whether you are in a position to successfully counter-attack or defend yourself. Thus oriented, you can make decisions to change your position to one that provides you better advantage. You can fly up, down, circle, or whatever action you can take while continuing to observe to see if your hypothesis that action would improve your situation was correct. Observe, Orient, Decide, Act (OODA) is an open loop in that it is an iterative process, allowing for constant new information and feedback. It is a pattern that has been successfully adopted for cybersecurity operations, which also often require this type of situational awareness analysis to support quick decisions.

OODA is cybersecurity's version of Drucker and Deming's Plan-Do-Check-Act (PDCA) management strategy. The difference is that the OODA loop was developed by a fighter pilot and emphasizes the need to assimilate both expected and unexpected observations and make time-sensitive decisions to change operation to thwart an adversary, while PDCA loops span the timeframe of manufacturing cycles. Cybersecurity does not have the luxury of waiting for a new product version to manufacture before altering workflow to avoid negative consequences. Figure 3.15 illustrates the cybersecurity's adoption of the OODA loop.

The first responder in a cybersecurity incident is typically security operations, (affectionately known as *SecOps*). In any cybersecurity program, there are four major operational areas that need to operate as a single OODA Loop: Cyber Incident Response, Identity and Access Management, Network Security, and Vulnerability Management. Viewed holistically, the Cybersecurity Program simultaneously operates them all to build the program level OODA loop. Some organizations reserve the slang SecOps for Cyber Defense and others consider all four organizations collectively, otherwise known as Cybersecurity Operations. In many

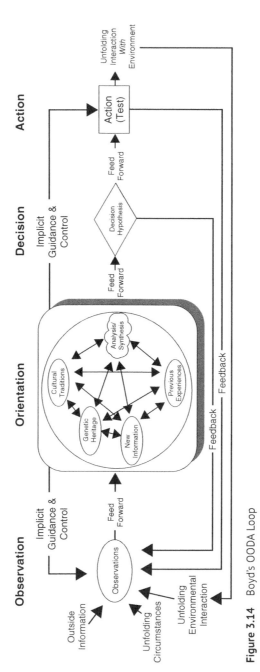

Figure 3.14 Boyd's OODA Loop

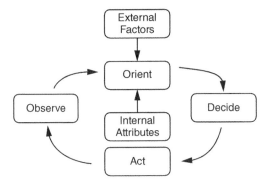

Figure 3.15 Cybersecurity's Version of OODA

organizations, methods by which security and technology quickly and accurately communicate with business application owners, legal, public relations, and executive management (e.g., Enterprise Crisis Management) leverage emergency communication procedures managed by a Chief Information Officer (CIO), which could be considered an extension of SecOps.

Cybersecurity incident may seem like a generic term but there are industry standards that describe IT incidents generally and cyber security incidents as a subcategory. When system operation is disrupted, it is expected that a technology operations team will detect and investigate the event, record event details in a centralized incident management system of record, and label the event as either an incident or a problem. This vocabulary follows the nomenclature of the Information Technology Infrastructure Library (ITIL) that many companies use as a roadmap for IT Service Management (SkillSoft 2007). Following ITIL, there are three terms that describe the effect and root causes of unexpected events in an information system, and they have slightly different meanings:

Incident: any unplanned result in the operation of an information system that interrupts or reduces the quality of IT services that users receive.
Problem: any incident whose cause is unknown.
Known Error: a subsequent event matching the symptoms of an existing problem and has been established to be from the same root cause. The incident is considered another occurrence of that problem, as opposed to a new one.

In any technology management process, no matter what vocabulary is used, an incident is a record created from details received from a service desk or help center, an automated network notification, or a notification from IT (either manual or automated). Examples include the following: the internet is not working, a user has been locked out of their account; a computer screen shows a virus alert; or computers are rebooting for no planned reason. Where the

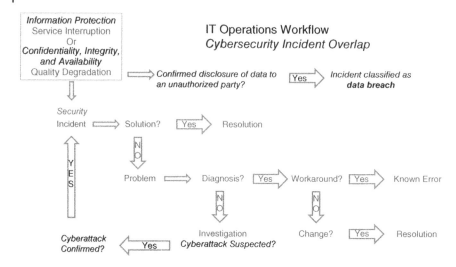

Figure 3.16 Technology Workflow/Cybersecurity Overlay

cause of an incident has been determined to be malicious, the incident should be classified as a security incident.

Figure 3.16 provides an example workflow wherein technology operations steps are listed in plain text and cybersecurity incidents that are identified via the technology operations workflow include supplemental workflow steps in italics. Any service disruption may cause an incident. If the root cause of the incident is known and can be addressed, the incident is easily resolved. An example of this would be a user unable to work due to a forgotten password. A password reset procedure does the trick. If the source of the problem is quickly identified and a solution is developed, this will take more time than a situation for which a procedure exists, but still not a cause for concern. If there is no diagnosis and no known solution, there will be an incident triage effort, some identification and sifting of attributes to determine which fall though the sieve to be declared "security" incidents. Depending on the size and threat profile of an organization, there could be several "incidents" for which there is no quick diagnosis in a day, week, month, or year. Of those, some small percentage might be declared "security" incidents worthy of response, qualified as a bona fide enacted threat. In this case, a lead SecOps analyst will typically be appointed to ensure the investigation follows a preestablished cybersecurity response playbook.

Just as in an Emergency Medical Technician (EMT) triage, a technology incident triage relies heavily on industry standard measures and subsequent incident classification. There is an order to EMT response activities based on a patient's observable symptoms. For example, if there is evidence of gurgling in the throat of a completely unresponsive patient, an EMT may as a priority investigate the airway and take steps to diagnose and eliminate damage to the airway as an issue before moving forward. Similarly, if there is evidence of a potential malware intrusion, SecOps should classify the incident as malware and remediate or dismiss malware as a symptom before moving forward. Yet as in the EMT situation, simple remediation of the most obvious risk indicator often does not preclude damage from a coincident symptom. An obstructed airway may be remedied only to uncover evidence of breathing irregularities related to a lung injury, just as malware processes may be killed only to discover that the malware has reconfigured access control in a manner that is significantly more dangerous than the initial threat actor footprint.

Where a realized cybersecurity risk happens to the enterprise, it often generates logs of adversary activity or its aftermath. The expectation is that the people responsible for systems security within the target organization will have instrumented the environment with unauthorized access alerts and will be alerted to the event and see some evidence of incident before it is formally declared to be related to cybersecurity. Regardless, the workflow will follow some aspects of ITIL merged with some aspects of the NIST standards for cybersecurity incident handling (NIST 800-61r2 2012, p. 42). Figure 3.17 shows common steps in the approach.

It is often a great challenge for security teams to be nimble enough to execute this loop quickly to deflect threats because they rarely have the full authority to make the necessary updates to IT and network systems to recover. Recovery procedures themselves may cause collateral damage. There are also Advanced Persistent Threat (APT) incidents, as described in Chapter 2, that are more like a tree falling in the forest where no one hears it when it happens. It is an incident, it is just not recorded and the triage does not begin until it is reported to a service desk or otherwise comes across a tripwire in the technology environment that triggers an incident that gets classified as a problem.

Such challenges are typically met with well-defined escalation procedures that ensure that the most knowledgeable engineers and business stakeholders are readily available and equipped to assist SecOps as they move through the investigation stages. Figure 3.18 illustrates the process by which information about an incident is typically identified and escalated as it moves along the path from analysis through mitigation containment, eradication, and recovery. The center of the circle in Figure 3.18 shows the incident appearing in a centralized incident management system that consolidates information from a variety of sources.

Figure 3.17 Incident Response Sequence

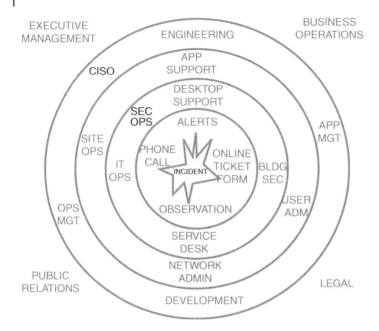

EXECUTIVE
MANAGEMENT

ENGINEERING

BUSINESS
OPERATIONS

CISO

APP
SUPPORT

DESKTOP
SUPPORT

SEC
OPS   ALERTS

APP
MGT

SITE
OPS

IT
OPS

PHONE
CALL

ONLINE
TICKET
FORM

INCIDENT

BLDG
SEC

OPS
MGT

OBSERVATION

USER
ADM

SERVICE
DESK

NETWORK
ADMIN

PUBLIC
RELATIONS

DEVELOPMENT

LEGAL

Figure 3.18   Incident Escalation

There could be an automated system-down alert that goes to the technology operation center, such as an internal user enters a ticket through an online form to report that their data appears corrupted. It may be a direct observation by someone who works within the IT environment. Once that incident is recorded (typically in an incident "ticket"), it is routed through the workflow like the one in Figure 3.16 depending on its source. The initial assigned group (typically called a "Level 1" support group) may be desktop, service ("help") desk, or even physical security. As mentioned in the context of ITIL, if there is a procedure that can resolve the incident, then it can usually be handled by Level 1 support. But if that group determines that the incident is unknown, then it will likely automatically be added to the SecOps queue for awareness and potential insight based on threat intelligence that it may have readily available. Level 1 will have also forwarded the incident to the application or administration team who would escalate again to the group who is more skilled in system configuration and log analysis. The escalation would result in a thorough analysis of activity logs and specification of the system(s) that are suspected to be the source of the incident. That is, groups at all levels will escalate sideways for support to answer questions about the incident in areas of the investigation that are outside the bounds of their own expertise.

Most technology operations teams have a timer threshold on investigation analysis prior to declaring a conference call with all engineers and developers in the scope of the technology impacted. When that threshold is reached, everyone within the outer circle of the diagram in Figure 3.18 will join a call while they are diagnosing the problem on their own workstations and listening to the observations of other people working on the incident and sharing logs and screenshots online. This group will either contain or develop a plan for analysis and mitigation. A network administrator may suggest isolating all outbound traffic from an impacted server and the CISO would have to approve this. Typically, there will be someone from SecOps or a service desk monitoring that call and making sure that everything is documented and there is at least one person responsible for every part of the diagnosis and mitigation as the incident progresses.

At the end of the initial conference call, an incident analyst will be assigned to summarize the situation in an email to executive management, business operations, public relations, and legal (or a formal crisis management team if there is one). It will inform them of the current negative system impact (if any) and whether the cause has been diagnosed as a threat actor, thus presenting the immediate need to move to stage *contain,* which may present additional negative impact. If the incident has been declared a security incident, there will typically be another set of data fields in the incident response system created to record security-specific details and linked to the original incident ticket, a security incident response ticket (SIRT). Also during the response call, the group will typically form a committee of specialists in the event risk category wherein status reports are heard and resources allocated in the form of additional staff, consultants, forensic investigators, equipment, and/or other resources to help with whatever system configuration, monitoring, control enhancements, and/or forensics may be required to resolve the incident.

For example, consider the SQL Injection attack that is the second vector in Figure 2.15, wherein the staff member unwittingly downloads and executes malware from a URL sent to a user's home email. Consider that this simple threat vector may not be noticed by either the user or anyone else in the enterprise until long after its occurrence. The vector shows a data theft by one threat actor that may be part of a much larger criminal network. Figure 3.19 illustrates the environment within which this typical data theft frequently operates. It starts with the threat vector within a financial system. The numbers in Figure 3.19 correspond to an event activity sequence as follows:

1) Cyber criminals steal personally identifiable data, such as SSN, date of birth, credit card, etc., from a compromised financial institution (second threat vector in Figure 2.15).
2) Criminal sells the data to other criminals who presumably will use it to defraud financial institutions and their customers.

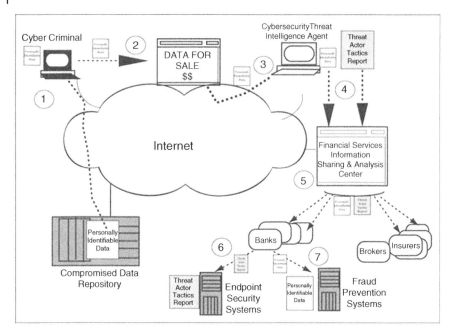

Figure 3.19 Common Scenario Event

3) A cybersecurity threat intelligence vendor analyst discovers the data for sale, investigates the criminal, and publishes a report of the criminal's activity as a cyber "threat actor."

4) The threat analyst forwards both the report and the data to the US Department of Homeland Security (DHS) sponsored Financial Industry Information Sharing and Analysis Centers (FS-ISAC).

5) FS-ISAC shares both threat and fraud data with members. The targeted enterprise discovers that data was exfiltrated from their systems, but does not know which one.

6) The targeted enterprise uses information in the threat intelligence vendor actor report information to tune cybersecurity protection systems to automatically detect and alert on the threat actor tactics in the intelligence report.

7) The compromised data is incorporated into fraud analysis and prevention systems of all banks, with the result that competitors realize from whom the data was stolen.

Only after the activity sequence in Figure 3.19 is completed does the response depicted in Figure 3.18 begin. In this case, the targeted enterprise finds threat actor tactics in its activity logs via observation or alert and Level 1 would have confirmation that public-facing sites must be compromised. Then they would immediately escalate to admins for confirmation, who would escalate to the engineers, a conference call would be convened, and a containment decision made. For example, a containment decision might be to shut down the website while the application and infrastructure engineering and operations work over-time to secure their environment. The crisis committee is then convened. At the meeting of the crisis committee, several other enterprise actions may be taken. For example:

- The enterprise Help Desk sets up a special task force to deal with customer complaints,
- A forensics specialist is brought in to identify the point of intrusion,
- Public relations issues a press release, and
- Legal makes arrangements for identity theft protection services for impacted customers and writes letters to them with the details.

While the crisis steps are being taken, SecOps works closely with the technology groups. While the application groups focus on the SQL Injection vulnerability, SecOps and the VPN engineers and admins study the initial threat vector (the second row in Figure 2.15) to look for ways to disrupt it. Obviously, threat actors cannot be stopped from sending malicious URLs to staff homes. Perhaps more obviously, trying to train the user community to stop clicking on email does not work. Even if enterprise controls reinforced the training, staff cannot be prevented from falling prey to accidental or malicious malware installs on their home devices. So more network and desktop specialists are brought in to help to examine the next step in the threat vector, and ask "Is it possible to prevent a threat actor from piggybacking on an authorized user connection to the enterprise VPN?" Zero trust technology may provide some way to disallow multiple simultaneous TCP/IP sessions from the same user. If enterprise users can be limited to one session without negative impact, this could thwart a piggy-back rider. The VPN desktop client could be configured to prevent local network traffic flow on the home machine while it is running, thus disconnecting the threat actor. Perhaps an auto-termination of sessions left idle for more than a few minutes will help as well. Those controls can be quickly configured and be tested by skilled penetration testers to see if they can figure out a way to exploit the staff's home computer access even with these new controls in place. If the fix can be implemented and successfully tested, the root cause is determined, and the risk of event recurrence is likely reduced.

For some cyber-defenders, this is not where the incident ends, but where it begins. This is often the case for the cyber forensics specialist (who may be generically referred to as *CyberForensics* or *cyberforensics*), especially when they have been hired only after the time of crisis has passed. There may still be a significant amount of technology activity in event cleanup, so it is important for them to establish the facts of the case as soon as possible before audit trails or potential malware samples may inadvertently be destroyed or disturbed. Like police at a murder scene, their first task is to make sure no evidence is destroyed. That said, cyberforensics investigators do not necessary collect all the evidence personally. They will know what they are looking for, but need to rely on local standards and procedures to figure out how to find it. CyberForensics itself refers to the set of tools, techniques, activity, and goals of the investigation process (Bayuk 2010a, pp. 1–5). Figure 3.20 depicts the CyberForensics mainstay: CyberForensics facilitates investigation by preserving evidence that strengthens cases.

Of course, a lead investigator plays a major role, but like all cybersecurity processes, there will be a lot of people involved in various directing and supporting roles. Figure 3.21 enriches the definition from the investigator's perspective. Investigators support the CISO or another executive, such as legal or technology management, who may have ordered the investigation. They examine systems in the initial scope of the event and determine what data is available that may be useful in identifying the full extent of the intrusion and its source. From that analysis comes an initial list of system components from which various types of forensic data are harvested and assembled for preservation and analysis. Any unexpected files found on the system are suspected to be malware and subjected to reverse engineering, that is reading the code if it is visible or automatically decoding compiled binary programs to see what commands the malware may have executed at the operating system level.

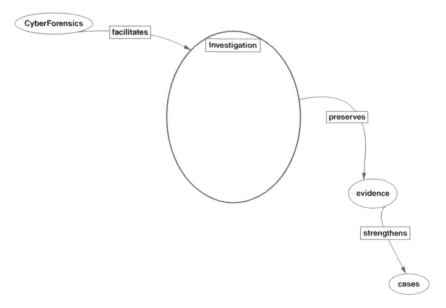

Figure 3.20 Cyber Forensics Mainstay

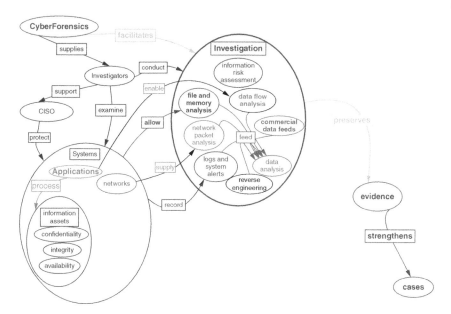

Figure 3.21 Cyber Forensics Investigation

This initial data gathering data step is typically repeated as data from the systems initially identified is likely to include activity logs that highlight additional steps in the threat vector and thereby expand the scope of the investigation. Figure 3.22 shows the desired output of the iterative analysis. In the best case, a tool like reverse engineering malware will help an investigator understand how the malware threat vector works and that shows them where to look to additional malware that may have been used in the attack. Reverse engineering may also lead to clues in the code that, in combination with threat intelligence, can help identify the threat actor as well. Application data flow analysis may uncover crimes like fraud. Of course, the major output is evidence preservation and chain of custody that can be used in court to prove that the evidence presented therein is the same as that collected at the time of investigation.

Of course, enterprise investigations have no weight in the courts, so it is never too early to enlist the support of law enforcement. CISOs should make it a point to identify and meet their local cybersecurity law enforcement specialists as well as any who have the enterprise within their jurisdiction at a regional or nation state level. This saves time in trying to figure out who to call in the event of a cyberattack and the law enforcement contact will then at least be familiar with the business mission in advance of an urgent call to arms. Figure 3.23 adds the perspective of law enforcement. They will be the primary users of the collected evidence in the short term and be able to testify to its contents should the need arise.

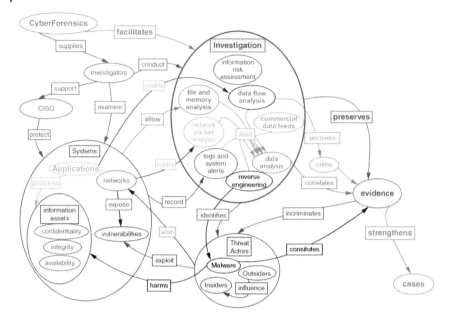

Figure 3.22 Cyber Forensics Output

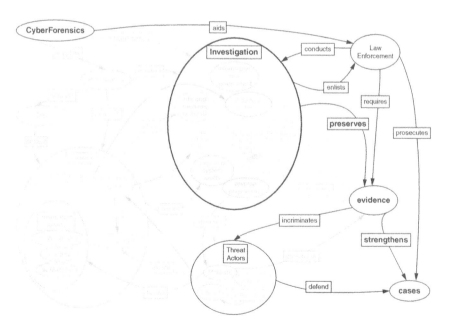

Figure 3.23 Cyber Forensics Use Case

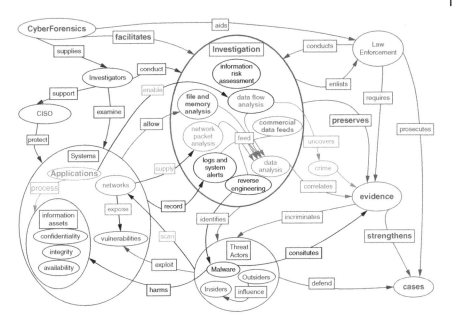

Figure 3.24 Cyber Forensics Systemigram

Figure 3.24 shows that putting it all together reveals a complicated process, but not one so complex that it cannot be understood by a person who does not work in technology. If and when the case goes to court, a skilled investigator or cybersecurity expert witness will be called upon to describe the evidence and the process used for evidence collection in layman's terms, so a judge and jury can decide for themselves whether a crime occurred.

3.4 Event Scenarios

In order for nontechnical staff in organizations such as public relations, legal, business operations, and executive management to react appropriately to news that there may be a security incident in progress, they should have had some kind of cybersecurity awareness training. At the very least, they should be made aware that once an internal cybersecurity event is reported to them the levels of escalation in Figure 3.17 have already occurred. They should have confidence that the support groups, engineers, and admins are working on the incident. They should understand that the service desk is recording information that will answer the questions that this nontechnical group will have about the incident. Their questions may include, but not be limited to:

- How many users are impacted?
- Are there any product features or services that are unavailable?
- For how long have they been unavailable?
- Are there connections to external systems or internal systems that are degraded in integrity?
- Does this mean we cannot trust the information that is coming through those connections?

Awareness training should help these groups understand what decisions they may need to make, and what processes they need to establish within their own organizations to prepare for responding to a cybersecurity event. For example, a public relations office writing a press release must be able to provide some explanation of expected impact on customers, or why a system may be unavailable for some period of time. A legal office may need to report a data breach to regulators and state government agencies. They will need to understand the incident not from the perspective on the admins, but from the perspective of customers. It is rare for a technology infrastructure group to predict this impact without some awareness training themselves on the business process underlying the application.

A highly effective type of cybersecurity event awareness training is a community enactment of a hypothetical event in a category known to be a high risk, called *scenario analysis*. The awareness starts with the recognition that there are three basic types of environments from which an enterprise's set of risk events is collected: internal, external, and scenario. Internal events are attacks on the enterprise. External events are attacks on organizations that have processes and technology footprints similar to our own. Scenario events are hypothetical exercises in threat and response awareness.

These event types acknowledge that a cybersecurity incident is not composed solely of adversary activity. They are composed of the interaction between adversary activities and enterprise defenses. It is not possible to analyze and classify events in the absence of the control environment in which they occur. The term "realized risk" refers to an event that negatively impacted the enterprise, but it does not mean the enterprise was the threat actor target. Where the enterprise is the target *and* there is realized risk, it is an *internal* cybersecurity event.

Where an internal event reaches a postmortem stage, the postmortem often turns into a scenario event because people ask questions about possible variations of the attack such as, "What if the attack had been more damaging than it was?" or "What if the attack had happened during business hours?" Scenario analysis is the process of answering those types of questions. Scenarios do not have to originate in an internal event. Where successful attacks happen to a competitor using the same business processes and same technology operating in the same cyber ecosystem, a cybersecurity risk organization may systematically collect information about external events from news reports and threat intelligence vendor data feeds. Another resource for collecting external events is the annual Verizon Data Breach Report, which consolidates events from a wide variety of global law enforcement and large corporations and publishes them by industry (Verizon 2022). There are also data exchanges based on membership wherein member companies in a given industry will contribute their risk events to have access to details of those of their industry peers (e.g., ORX 2022).

An external event may not drive the estimate of probability of internal occurrence of an event in that category to 100% in every comparable enterprise, but in the absence of identifiable mitigating controls, it certainly should bring it into the high range. Where probabilities are high that an external event of a certain category may occur, the event earns the classification of cybersecurity risk (i.e., cybersecurity risk is measured in probability by event classification).

It is best practice for a cybersecurity risk organization to take a deep dive into the circumstances of self-identified, well-defined cybersecurity risks, at least on a category level, whether they present as internal, external, or hypothetical events. The goal is to arrive at a justifiable loss estimate for internal and external event occurrence. Regardless of the event's original source, once it is inducted for internal analysis, the event is called a *scenario* event. Scenario analysis is performed on events that are thought to score high on the risk scale, as measured in probability.

The "scenario" in "scenario analysis" refers to a script corresponding to a very specific cybersecurity event. To develop a scenario, cybersecurity risk analysts hypothesize conditions wherein all or part of the threat vector from the event is attempted by a highly qualified adversary targeting the enterprise. The vector may also be extended with TTPs known to be associated with a given threat actor or group. The scenario is a description of the likely activities leading up to, during, and after a probable risk event.

Scenario analysis is an exercise with all the players identified in Figure 3.17 to step through the scenario together. When this type of community enactment is performed as a *reenactment* of a real event, it may be coincident with a postmortem, but the analysis delves much deeper into business impact than a typical technology postmortem. Stakeholders and experts in the target business process and technology will be enlisted to participate in the group examination. The objective of scenario analysis is to determine to what extent the situation that results from the hypothetical attack has the potential to negatively impact business processes and/or cause other downstream losses that can be measured in monetary value, such as theft, lawsuits, or regulatory fines (BASEL 2011, p. 21). A secondary objective is to strengthen effective collaboration among all stakeholders.

Figure 3.25 Cybersecurity Event Record

Figure 3.25 shows an example of a documented internal cybersecurity event on which a scenario may be based. Like any other computer record, it has a unique identifier. Right next to the identifier is a drop-down field used to indicate what priority should be given to the incident in cases where multiple incidents vie for SecOps staff's attention. These are followed by summary and description fields so that information on it can be immediately shared. The event type will be *internal, external,* or *scenario.* The status will be *open* or *closed.* An enterprise will typically also track the organization wherein the event occurred, the state of the investigation, the source that reported it, whether it be an automated alerting system, a customer report, or any other avenue from which the event was derived, and the risk category to which the event belongs. The contact field may be automatically populated with the person who creates an incident record, or in the case of an automated record (as in one delivered by an autonomous alert monitor) it may be filled in with a staff member or group who specializes in the given alerts type, risk category, or source.

As in any type of investigation record, some fields will be easier to fill in than others. Even something that seems as simple as the event date may change often in the course of the investigation. The date of an event is of course the date on which it occurred. But note that the event record in Figure 3.25 also includes two other dates: "Report date" and "Date ended." Because many cybersecurity incidents span several days, even months and years, the "Date ended" is used to calculate an event duration, and trends in event duration can be a significant risk indicator. Moreover, unless the event source is an automated alert, the date on which the impacted enterprise becomes aware of the event, the report date, is often much closer to the ended date as opposed to the event date. So the trend in the duration between event date and report date could also be a significant risk indicator. Where an enterprise tracks post-mortem and remediation timeframes, the event end date may not be recorded until the investigation and/or recovery is completed. Also, only after an investigation is completed can a risk analyst record with some certainty who was the threat actor and what vector they used to enact the threat.

Though the scenario script is written by cybersecurity, the exercise itself may be moderated by any qualified and experienced facilitator. It should be a clearly defined and repeatable process (BASEL 2011, p. 51). That is, consistency in moderating discussion is a more important criterion than cybersecurity experience for a facilitator of scenario analysis sessions. The moderator must communicate well enough to keep the group focused and make sure that all voices are heard, while also reigning in potentially biased opinions on the effectiveness of their own organization's defenses. The session typically starts out with a presentation of the event using the subset of standard field definitions that are available in Figure 3.25. For example, scenario event participants may be presented with event information that includes only the report date, the event source, initial contact, summary, report date, and threat vector initial access tactic. This is the same information that would be available to SecOps only after the event was reported. This enables the participants to identify what activities would happen next, given their knowledge of standard procedure and problem management strategies. Other event details that are part of the script may be revealed only as they pertain to discussions by the scenario participants.

The session will begin with reactions from the person or group who has been identified as the initial contact for the reported incident. That participant will describe what actions would be taken and what systems consulted. Control strategies like IAM and ZTA are included in this chapter on events because of the instructive nature of a cybersecurity event. Participants will be expected to identify when and where the adversary must bypass existing authentication and/or adversary activity may be expected to be captured by logs or alerts. The cybersecurity analyst author would infer from the script what new information the consulted systems could be expected to reveal about the event. As actions include escalations, the group to whom the event was escalated would in turn offer information about their expected actions and systems interactions. A scribe would document the sequence of activities and a cybersecurity threat analyst would build and modify the likely threat vector in response to the information revealed. Figure 3.26 shows typical players gathered for the exercise.

For example, if the scenario is a ransomware attack, the initial access and execution portion of the threat vector may look like that in Figure 3.27. The IT operations participant would be the event's first point of contact. The first thing that person may do is try to access the file share themselves, or it might be to run a diagnosis that displays who is currently connected to the file share and each user's corresponding level of activity. The first action would reveal simply that the file share is unavailable. The second would be more likely to reveal the event's cause.

As the escalations continue, at some point, the cybersecurity analyst will not be the authority on what happens next. Participants will learn from each other how previous activities may cause the event to cascade through the enterprise

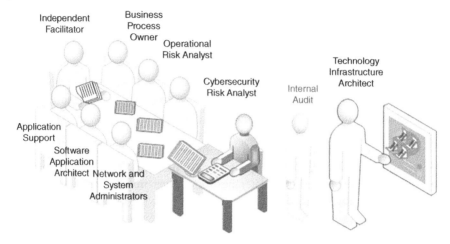

Independent Facilitator

Business Process Owner

Operational Risk Analyst

Cybersecurity Risk Analyst

Internal Audit

Technology Infrastructure Architect

Application Support

Software Application Architect

Network and System Administrators

Figure 3.26 Scenario Workshop

infrastructure. Though the proximate cause may be quickly pinpointed to activity on the compromised user's workstation, it may not yet reveal the root cause of the negative impact.

That is, another item in an event data record that may take some time to ascertain is the event *root cause*. In operational risk analysis, "root cause" is a term of art. It refers to a situation in which, in comparison with a specific risk event, if the root cause had not occurred, the event also would have not occurred. There is a difference between a *root* cause and a *proximate* cause. In a legal environment, the definition of proximate cause is an event so close to the crime that it undoubtedly caused it. In the scenario depicted in Figure 3.27, the phishing link may be decided to be the proximate cause, because the event occurred when the threat actor sent the email. In operational risk, however, the situation of the victim is also considered. For example, if a murderer stabbed a victim in a dark alley, then the stabbing would be a proximate cause of the victim's injury, that is, the cause closest in proximity to the event. However, if the victim should have been prevented from entering the dark alley, then the absence of a prevention method could also be considered a cause of the injury. That is, if there is a way that the enterprise can prevent the victim from being in that alley, that control weakness may be considered a cause as well. This example illustrates the difference between a proximate cause and a root cause. A root cause is a situation without which the event would not happen, and if that situation were eliminated, it would drastically reduce the probability of the event's recurrence, if not prevent the event entirely. In this example, it is not possible to prevent the stabbing, because that is activity performed by a threat actor. But it is theoretically possible to prevent your own staff from being alone in a dark alley. This is why traveling executives in countries with

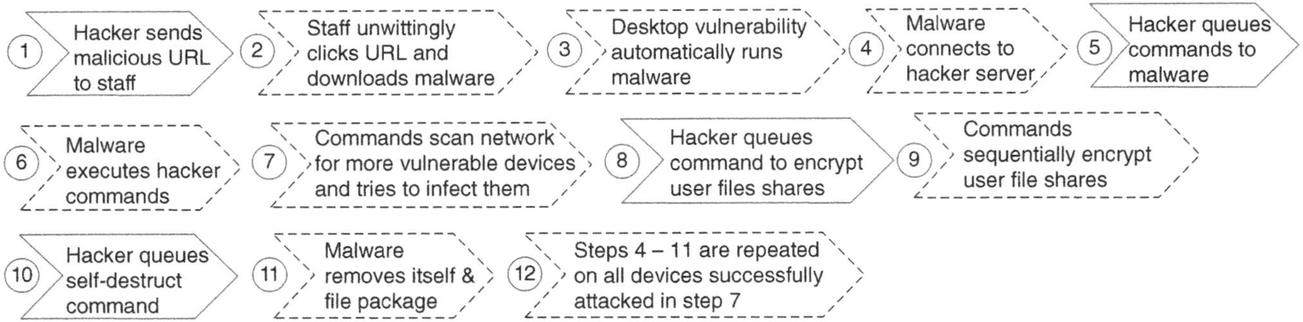

Figure 3.27 Example Ransomware Initial Threat Vector

rampant crime are often provided with corporate physical protection services. Though it sounds like blaming the victim, it is actually closer to a practical method in which to reduce the risk of the event's harmful consequences. In operational risk, the focus is on the instructive characteristics of the event, namely the cyber defender lessons learned from interaction between the adversary and the target. If something that would lower the risk to an acceptable level can be accomplished, then the confidence that the root cause has been identified increases and eliminating that root cause situation may prevent the incident's recurrence. With an eye toward identifying the root cause, the cybersecurity threat analyst will therefore carefully document the steps in the threat vector that are necessary for the actor to act on objectives, these more proximate causes will link back to the root.

Key to successful scenario analysis is a structured process for mapping threat vector components to data used in developing loss estimates. Where data or computing processes are impacted, there must be a unit of measurement to provide a feasible estimate of that impact. Examples include, but are not limited to, the number of data records, lost CPU cycles, and hours spent in investigation. The scenario aggregate loss estimate will depend on calculations based on those units. It is impossible to add up negative impact unless it is clear what that data includes and why it should be a factor in computing scenario impact. Moreover, the connection between threat vector activity and these units of measurement should be well documented using fact-based evidence and clear reasoning supporting the scenario output. These units should make it possible to document the situation resulting from the scenario in quantitative terms including, but not limited to, time spent investigating threat actor activity, expected data exfiltration, malware or ransomware damage to data integrity and/or systems availability, data restoration or repair, lost productivity, lost business, incurred liability, insurance penalties, regulatory violations, and technology control restoration (Rohmeyer and Bayuk 2019, pp. 62–71).

To fully calculate losses, it may sometimes be necessary to bring in an external forensics team or similar consultant to opine on estimated costs of an outsourced investigation. Many companies do not have internal forensics experts because security incidents are infrequent, but may have external forensics teams on call. Scenario analysis is an opportunity to rehearse how quickly they may respond and how they can help contain an incident.

To ensure all potential sources of loss are covered, well-run scenario analysis includes an element of *challenge* by a person independent of the business process under scrutiny. Typically, this role will be played by internal audit or independent risk management. The "challenger" is necessary to ensure that no one is deliberately overlooking a critical function that is in the scope of the cyberattack. In addition, a well-run scenario analysis process will change and evolve as the environment evolves to make sure that threat intelligence is fresh and that the experts are selected not because they were good in the last scenario analysis, but because they really are the experts for the current scenario under scrutiny.

Though scenario analysis may be expected to produce a description of losses in the form of data and units, it is not likely that the actual loss numbers will be available at the end of the exercise itself. Once all the loss data is accumulated, a financial analyst is often engaged to retrieve the actual costs of the units identified and calculate the loss estimates that appear in the final report.

During the scenario workshop, it is helpful to analyze activities in a timeline. A shared workspace is typically employed for this purpose. It typically starts with the report date, but may be extended in either direction to show the intervals between activities that occurred within the event. For any given cybersecurity attack, there are at least three timestamps of significance and possibly others: the timestamp the threat actor commenced the attack, the timestamp that the attack was reported, and the timestamp the enterprise fully recovered. The further apart the attack start date and its recovery date, the longer the potential damaging impact from that event. If intervals like the time to identify, the time to respond, and the time to recover are measured in days rather than hours or minutes, that in itself is cause for a recommendation for improvement in threat intelligence and response.

In the ransomware example in Figure 3.26, it was acknowledged that the first thing the IT Operations participant may do is choose between trying to access the file share themselves or run a diagnosis that displays who is currently connected to the file share and each user's corresponding level of activity. Considering the goal is to minimize the timeline of potential damaging impact, it is obvious that the latter choice is the best. Whether the participant can access the file share, the full diagnosis is likely to be required anyway. This is just one of countless basic examples of procedural efficiencies that are a byproduct of scenario analysis. Figure 3.28 is an example of a timeline based on a hypothetical attack based on the threat vector in Figure 3.27. The scenario calls for the target user to have access to multiple file shares, one of which is a payment application accessed by customers. The timeline in Figure 3.28 shows the phish email delivery, the malware launch on the user desktop, and three of the file shares being encrypted sequentially. It shows that IT Operations receives an alert that the first file share is disabled a few minutes after the malware launch. It shows that encryption begins on the second file share before IT Operations has finished diagnosing the issue with the first one. The second file share supports a payment processing application, so the failure of that application produces another alert. IT Operations diagnoses the user desktop as the cause of the disruption and escalates to network administration to disable it from the network before it can finish encrypting the third file share. The remainder of the timeline enumerates recovery and forensic activity.

An example loss calculation corresponding to the timeline in Figure 3.28 is shown in Figure 3.29. Of course, every enterprise will have its own nomenclature and

Activity	Timestamp	Activity	Timestamp
Desktop Phish Email Received	12/12/23 8:13 AM	Payment Processing Backup Activated	12/12/23 8:57 AM
Desktop Malware Install	12/12/23 8:27 AM	Crisis Management Group Convenes	12/12/23 9:15 AM
File Share 1 Encrypt Start	12/12/23 8:27 AM	IT Ops End Phish Email Eradication	12/12/23 9:45 AM
File Share 1 Connect Alert	12/12/23 8:31 AM	Payment Processing Backlog Recovered	12/12/23 9:57 AM
File Share 1 Encrypt End	12/12/23 8:35 AM	Missing Payments Identified	12/12/23 10:22 AM
File Share 2 Encrypt Start	12/12/23 8:35 AM	File Share 2 Rebuilt	12/12/23 11:39 AM
IT Operations Diagnosed File Share 1	12/12/23 8:35 AM	Payment Processing Application Recovered	12/12/23 11:39 AM
File Share 2 Connect Alert	12/12/23 8:38 AM	Shift Change	12/12/23 4:00 PM
Payment Processing Application Fails	12/12/23 8:38 AM	Missing Payments Applied	12/12/23 4:01 PM
File Share 2 Encrypt End	12/12/23 8:40 AM	CISO Reports Incident to Law Enforcement	12/12/23 4:26 PM
File Share 3 Encrypt Start	12/12/23 8:40 AM	Legal Files Regulatory Report	12/12/23 4:56 PM
IT Ops Escalate to Network Admin	12/12/23 8:41 AM	General Ledger Server Rebuilt	12/12/23 10:18 PM
File Share 3 Connect Alert	12/12/23 8:43 AM	Incident Contained	12/12/23 10:18 PM
General Ledger Application Fails	12/12/23 8:38 AM	Overtime Ended	12/12/23 11:00 PM
Network Admin Disconnect Desktop	12/12/23 8:44 AM	File Share 1 Recovered	12/12/23 11:00 PM
IT Ops Triggers Outage Call	12/12/23 8:45 AM	Forensics Team Work Begins on Desktop	12/13/23 10:31 AM
SecOps Declares Security Incident	12/12/23 8:47 AM	Forensics Team Sends to EDR Vendor	12/13/23 11:06 AM
SecOps Alerts all Staff of Phishing Attack	12/12/23 8:49 AM	EDR Vendor Provides AV Update	12/13/23 6:17 PM
Crisis Management Group Informed	12/12/23 8:55 AM	IT Ops Runs AV Update for Enterprise	12/13/23 7:00 PM
IT Ops Begin Phish Email Eradication	12/12/23 8:56 AM	Recovery Complete	12/13/23 11:00 PM

Figure 3.28   Example Ransomware Timeline

Outages	Minutes	Hour	Min	Avg Payment Fee	#Waived	Goodwill Loss
File Share 1-Storage Only	21	0	21			
Payment Processing	22	0	22	$34.00	684	$23,256.00
General Ledger	823	13	43			
Payment Processing Full Recovery	184	3	4			
Lost Payments Recovered	446	7	26			
Technology Staff Expense				**Rate**	**# Staff**	**IT Expense**
Overtime Level 1	419	6	59	$50	2	$698.33
Overtime Level 2	42	0	42	$100	3	$210.00
Overtime Level 3	420	7	0	$200	2	$2,800.00
Forensics Team	35	0	35	$600		$350.00
						$4,058.33
					Total Loss:	**$27,314.33**

Figure 3.29   Example Ransomware Loss Calculation

method for performing this type of calculation. In this example, technology outages are displayed, but not necessarily the source of monetary losses. This reflects a choice by the target enterprise to restrict loss calculations to dollars spent, as opposed to business opportunity lost due to employee lack of productivity or lost business due to application outages. Nevertheless, this calculation is possible and the outage numbers are often presented to decide if it makes sense to pursue that type of presentation. This enterprise has chosen not to represent technology's actual time working on the event, but only the difference between the hours covered by their salaries and the expense of paying for extra help to address the event. This loss is quite minor for a ransomware event, and the reason for that is the quick work by IT Operations in diagnosing proximate cause as that is the path to containing the damage.

Note that the timeline includes items that are not visible in the loss calculations, but nevertheless important outcomes of scenario analysis. The CISO reports the incident to law enforcement and legal files a regulatory report. The event is too minor for public relations to have issued a public statement, but it is evident that some customers had delayed transactions, and the losses show that fees on those transactions were waived. This indicates that the crisis management team weighed options for customer communication and decided to communicate only with those who were negatively impacted. When customers are compensated for service interruptions without requesting compensation, this is referred to as "goodwill" in financial circles. It shows that public relations had a hand in minimizing the possibility that this event would generate hostility toward the enterprise on social media.

At the end of the scenario exercise, there will be enough information to produce an end-to-end threat vector produced by the exercise. It is possible that some details will not be available at the time of the community enactment, but they will be tracked down later and a report produced that contains both the estimated losses and an end-to-end threat vector produced by the exercise. That vector will be carefully examined and a root cause specified. As indicated by the threat vector diagrams, some vector activities are performed by the threat actor, some are automated, and some are performed by enterprise staff. For the automated activities or those performed by staff, the scenario participant who offered a given activity will be noted but not considered either the root or the proximate cause. Of threat actor activities, individually, no *single* act would likely be the root cause of the successful attack. For the threat actor activities to be successful, they have to occur in a sequence that includes the target. That is, one of the outcomes of scenario analysis is the identification of an activity within the event that, if disrupted, would disrupt and disable the entire threat vector sequence. Where losses are high, there will at least be some recommendation that a remediation should be proposed in the form of some activity that is (i) controlled by the target and (ii) would disrupt future events in the same risk category.

However, just because the root cause is identified does not mean that the scenario exercise has also identified an appropriate set of controls that will work to disrupt the vector. It is enough to fully document the threat vector and the business impact of the event. This information would then be used to create one or more "risk issues" that will be formally tracked until remediated. Both the scenario event and the issue(s) are linked to the risk and available for historical references by those charged with calculating the probability of the risk's recurrence.

References

BASEL (2011). *Operational Risk – Supervisory Guidelines for the Advanced Measurement Approaches.* Basel Committee on Banking Supervision. bis.org.

Bayuk, J. (2010a). *CyberForensics, Understanding Information Security Investigations.* Springer.

Bayuk, J. (2010b). *Enterprise Security for the Executive: Setting the Tone at the Top.* Praeger.

Bayuk, J., Healy, J., Rohmeyer, P. et al. (2012). *Cyber Security Policy Guidebook.* Wiley.

Jericho Forum (2007). Commandments version 1.2. https://collaboration.opengroup. org/jericho/commandments_v1.2.pdf (accessed 08 May 2023).

Kindervag, J. (2010). No More Chewy Centers, Introducing the Zero Trust Model of Information Security. https://media.paloaltonetworks.com/documents/Forrester-No-More-Chewy-Centers.pdf (accessed 08 May 2023).

NIST-CSF (2018). Framework for Improving Critical Infrastructure Cybersecurity, version 1.1. National Institute of Standards and Technology. https://nvlpubs.nist. gov/nistpubs/cswp/nist.cswp.04162018.pdf (accessed 08 May 2023).

NIST 800-61r2 (2012). Computer Security Incident Handling Guide. National Institute of Standards and Technology. https://nvlpubs.nist.gov/nistpubs/ SpecialPublications/NIST.SP.800-61r2.pdf (accessed 08 May 2023).

NIST 800-207 (2020). Zero Trust Architecture Standard. SP800-207. National Institute of Standards and Technology. https://nvlpubs.nist.gov/nistpubs/ SpecialPublications/NIST.SP.800-207.pdf (accessed 08 May 2023).

NIST-CSF (2024). Framework for Improving Critical Infrastructure Cybersecurity, version 2.0. National Institute of Standards and Technology, https://www.nist.gov/ sites/default/files/images/2023/08/07/CSF-wheel-revamp-final-white.png (accessed 15 January 2024).

ORX (2022). Operational Risk Exchange. https://managingrisktogether.orx.org (accessed 08 May 2023).

Ricci, N., Fitzgerald, M., Ross, A. et al. (2014). Architecting Systems of Systems with Ilities: An Overview of the SAI Method. Conference on Systems Engineering Research, Massachusetts Institute of Technology. http://seari.mit.edu/documents/ presentations/CSER14_RicciSAI_MIT.pdf (accessed 08 May 2023).

Rohmeyer, P. and Bayuk, J. (2019). *Financial Cybersecurity Risk Management.* Springer Apress.

Sherwood, J., Clark, A., and Lynas, D. (2005). *Enterprise Security Architecture.* CMP Books.

SkillSoft (2007). Course: ITIL: The Service Desk and Incident Management. SkillSoft Corporation. www.skillsoft.com/ (accessed 08 May 2023).

Verizon (2022). Data Breach Investigations Report. https://www.verizon.com/ business/resources/reports/dbir/ (accessed 08 May 2023).

4

Controls

Controls are risk reduction measures. They may be manual, automated, or both. Controls may be directly enumerated, but are often documented as an interrelated set of risk management instructions that include strategic assertions, delegation of security roles and responsibilities, workflow, automation configurations, step-by-step procedures, and general advice. These documents are classified into risk appetite, policies, processes, standards, procedures, or guidelines, respectively.

Controls are not effective in isolation. Figure 4.1 depicts controls as a hierarchy composed of multiple control methods that comprise enterprise cybersecurity risk reduction measures. Specifically for cybersecurity, management controls are established with cybersecurity risk appetite, and extend into cybersecurity policy, cybersecurity processes, internally developed cybersecurity standards, cybersecurity procedures, and cybersecurity guidelines. For the remainder of this chapter, we will forgo the adjective *cybersecurity* from these control methods on the assumption that all the controls to which they refer are directed at minimizing cybersecurity risk.

Controls are interactive by design. They are composed at different levels of enterprise organizational structure and addressed to different organizational constituents whose interactions render the controls effective. The risk appetite comes from the top and is colloquially referred to as "tone at the top." It is the executive management articulation of the extent to which a risk may be deemed acceptable. It is then the responsibility of the CISO to create a process by which senior management can negotiate and agree on an enterprise cybersecurity policy that reflects that appetite. Each business leader, including the CISO, creates processes for their own organizational operations, and aligns with each other's processes to create cross-organizational workflow. Typically, one of a CISO's processes is to select cybersecurity industry standards that align well with enterprise goals for cybersecurity risk management and use them to create methods to demonstrate cybersecurity

Stepping Through Cybersecurity Risk Management: A Systems Thinking Approach, First Edition. Jennifer L. Bayuk.
© 2024 John Wiley & Sons, Inc. Published 2024 by John Wiley & Sons, Inc.
Companion website: www.wiley.com/go/STCRM

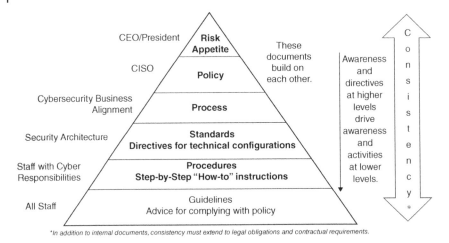

In addition to internal documents, consistency must extend to legal obligations and contractual requirements.

Figure 4.1 From Risk Appetite to Controls

regulatory compliance. Those standards are supplemented with enterprise cybersecurity architecture and engineering standards comprised of technology configurations. The staff responsible for maintaining those standards create operational procedures to maintain, measure, and monitor the standard's correct implementation. At the bottom of the hierarchy are enterprise stakeholders who do not create the cybersecurity framework, but operate within it. Nevertheless, they are executing the enterprise mission. They are performing their own job function in a way that is constrained by the policy, process, standards, and procedures that are created to establish management control. To help them understand how to operate within these constraints, they typically are also supplied with guidelines.

Documentation of each control method builds on those prior in the hierarchy. All leverage the tone at the top and policy for authority and awareness. Directives at higher levels focus on the activity of the lower levels. If there is pushback, it must go back up the chain as far as the feedback loop, but while someone may be lobbying for change to some procedure, staff should still be executing the one that is in place. There should be total reliance on the government structure and flexible communication mechanisms to make sure that there is both consistency across the board and opportunity for people to provide feedback. It is not just a tone at the top feeding down, it is enterprise's consistency with the mission. Figure 4.2 spells out these definitions for quick reference.

Cybersecurity risk is thus reduced via chains of controls woven across document subjects and types. One policy statement concerning the existence of standards in multiple technology domains may refer to multiple standards documents, and this set of standards documents may contain a common procedure, such as that executed by a help desk for managing technology change requests. Therefore, control documents are often stored electronically at a level of granularity that allows for links to cross-reference at both the document and control level. If there is an effective

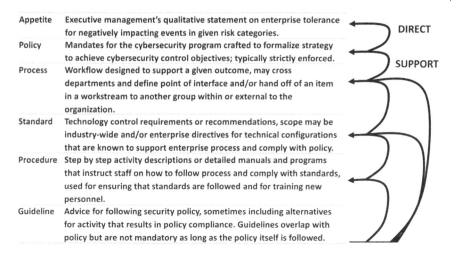

Appetite	Executive management's qualitative statement on enterprise tolerance for negatively impacting events in given risk categories.
Policy	Mandates for the cybersecurity program crafted to formalize strategy to achieve cybersecurity control objectives; typically strictly enforced.
Process	Workflow designed to support a given outcome, may cross departments and define point of interface and/or hand off of an item in a workstream to another group within or external to the organization.
Standard	Technology control requirements or recommendations, scope may be industry-wide and/or enterprise directives for technical configurations that are known to support enterprise process and comply with policy.
Procedure	Step by step activity descriptions or detailed manuals and programs that instruct staff on how to follow process and comply with standards, used for ensuring that standards are followed and for training new personnel.
Guideline	Advice for following security policy, sometimes including alternatives for activity that results in policy compliance. Guidelines overlap with policy but are not mandatory as long as the policy itself is followed.

DIRECT

SUPPORT

Figure 4.2 Control Method Definitions

control upon which a business process depends to control the operation of technology, then it should be documented and the document record stored in a repository that is either part of or connected to the enterprise risk management framework. The repository should allow the controls to be accessed by those who operate it and linked to evidence of correct implementation and/or effectiveness.

4.1 Risk Appetite

Appetite in any field is hunger, or craving. It is generally acknowledged as a good thing to have a healthy appetite and that is the basis for risk appetite in a business context. Typically, one does not have a successful business without some worthwhile risk-taking. An entrepreneur must make an investment to set up shop, create a product, and obtain inventory to sell. An entrepreneur who takes a chance that a new product launch will be successful may hedge their bet using various techniques, such as surveys and demographic studies of potential customers. That type of chance is called *market risk*, which is measured in the probability that people will buy the product.

Another ubiquitous business risk appetite concerns credit. When credit is extended to a consumer, business, or government entity, some financial manager must estimate the odds (i.e., the *probability*) that the balance will be repaid, and make business decisions accordingly. Where there is a market for a new product, an entrepreneur may be tempted to extend credit to customers to make a sale. However, if delivered inventory remains unpaid, then that is a negatively impacting credit risk. On the other hand, if the customers must resell a vendor's products and they cannot get the money to pay for them until after the vendor has shipped them some inventory on credit, then that vendor must have a healthy appetite for credit risk to stay in business.

A third major risk category is less transparently managed, and that is operational risk. This includes any event that may disrupt business operations or cause financial expenditures unnecessary to operate the business: employee errors, natural disasters, systems failures, fraud or other criminal activity, cybersecurity attacks, and data breaches. It is the role of management to reduce the probability that these negative risk events will occur and the first step in that journey is to confront the possibility that they may occur and form an opinion about whether the benefits of inattention to the risk are worth the potential negative impact.

Cybersecurity risk appetite is generally not as healthy as market or credit risk appetite. The trade-offs for market and credit risk are fairly easily quantifiable. But cybersecurity risk appetite is a judgement call on how much flexibility there is in business requirements to use software without risking too much of the safety and stability of the enterprise technology environment. Cybersecurity risk appetite is management's way of articulating how much uncertainty about degraded performance due to cyber threat actors may be acceptable. Despite its inherent differences from market risk or credit risk, its advent follows convention for other risk appetite statements. That is, risk appetite is a strategic assertion at the executive management level, such as a statement issued by a Chief Executive Officer (CEO) or other individuals at the highest level of authority for enterprise management.

Figure 4.3 is an example cybersecurity risk appetite statement. In this case, management deems it to be unacceptable to not act to prevent damage from publicly announced software vulnerabilities (i.e., unpatched systems are unacceptable). However, in acknowledgement that *unknown* vulnerabilities cannot be guaranteed to be avoided, some damage due to those types of cybersecurity events is accepted as a possibility. The fact that the unknown vulnerabilities may occur is itself an acknowledgement of the need for technology controls to minimize damage, but if that damage does occur due to zero-day threats, probably no one will get fired over it.

A risk appetite statement is synonymous with tone at the top. It is the opinion of the highest level of management on the extent to which cybersecurity plays a role in achieving enterprise mission. It is most effective when devised to establish

CYBERSECURITY IS A MAJOR CONCERN.

THE ENTERPRISE HAS **NO TOLERANCE** FOR KNOWN VULNERABILITIES IN ITS SYSTEMS, **NO TOLERANCE** FOR DATA BREACHES, AND **LOW TOLERANCE** FOR UNKNOWN VULNERABILITIES.

Figure 4.3 Succinct Risk Appetite Statement

a legal and regulatory compliance foundation for taking into account cybersecurity considerations when executing the enterprise mission. Once internally declared, the statement serves as a guiding light for internal programs designed to mitigate cybersecurity risk.

Of course, such a high-level statement may be dismissed as spurious unless it is accompanied by a strategy to hold management accountable for compliance. So any such risk appetite statement should be supplemented with an narrative of how that statement maps to enterprise policies for corporate governance. This level of detail may only be privy to Board and Executive level communication, but if it does not exist, it is a red flag that management does not appreciate its potential to support management control over technology.

Moreover, once careful consideration is given to how best to communicate to get people to share enterprise values with respect to cybersecurity risk, a risk appetite will likely be more detailed than the example risk appetite in Figure 4.3. Although it states that cybersecurity is of major concern and sets a tone at the top, it is generic in that it treats all systems and data equally. For example, "no tolerance for known vulnerabilities" means all publicly known vulnerabilities in all of our systems should be fixed. However, if enterprise systems that pose no security risks are identified, such as a cafeteria menu kiosk with no network connectivity, then the risk appetite seems like overkill and is therefore likely to be ignored with respect to the kiosk. No tolerance for data breaches implies high levels of data protected and limited authorized access paths. Acknowledgement that there is one system to which the rules do not apply calls into question where the line is drawn. Therefore, it is helpful for the risk appetite to help draw the line. Figure 4.4 is an example of a risk appetite statement that provides more guidance. It is specific to the enterprise business, in this case a financial services firm. It sets the stage by calling attention to the products it wants to protect and the fact that dependence on technology is an inherent vulnerability. It asserts that the firm

Electronic commerce relies on digital technology to connect customers to products and services.

The enterprise maintains state of the art cybersecurity tools and techniques, which it continuously improves to ensure customer information security and online safety.

***Therefore, the enterprise has no appetite* for cybersecurity risks that negatively impact customer information or experience on our electronic commerce platforms.**

Due to inherent risks in maintaining an adequate pace of change, the firm has a *low tolerance for disruptions in availability* of online services. We are dedicated to maintaining a six-sigma approach to platform stability.

Figure 4.4 Specific Risk Appetite Statement

takes pride in its ability to continuously innovate and improve technology, and in so doing it maintains control over customer identification, authorization, data integrity, and availability.

4.2 Policy

Like risk appetite, policy is a ubiquitous control issued by the most senior management in the enterprise. The subject of policies ranges widely across business and technical management domains. Also like appetite, policy is intended to be understood by the layman. It is composed of principles derived from the risk appetite statement, legal and regulatory requirements, and industry best practices in reducing cybersecurity risk to an acceptable residual level.

Note that the risk appetite statement addresses only the business function and not obligations the enterprise may include in its cybersecurity requirements due to legal and regulatory requirements. This is because compliance risk is not the same as cybersecurity risk. The two are often confused because there are so many cybersecurity requirements imposed by legal and regulatory obligations that cybersecurity staff is often dedicated to such compliance activities. However, the risk of noncompliance with legal obligations is an existential risk. The government can close an enterprise for noncompliance with regulatory requirements without a successful cyberattack even occurring. Noncompliance with legal obligations can result in cancelled contracts even in the absence of any known vulnerability exploits. Hence, compliance requirements are often assumed to be incorporated into policy requirements rather than overtly stated. A CISO's policy process should incorporate compliance requirements by routine, rather than via an outcome of risk analysis.

To see how policy is derived from risk appetite, consider the example risk appetite statement in Figure 4.4. The statement is meant to inspire people to minimize cybersecurity risk. It is short and succinct but may be misinterpreted. Although it makes the point that cybersecurity, (i.e., customer privacy, the integrity of financial records, or the ownership of financial assets) is a priority, it also emphasizes that client access to information must not be disrupted. However, one would be wrong to assume that client access to information and experience supersedes cybersecurity. The message is to implement a "fail safe." Although the statement is a high-level management directive to maintain client access to information and experience, an engineer should think "if we have to take a hit for innovation, then it should not be on confidentiality, but instead on availability, so I should deny access, shut down the connection, and send the user to customer service."

The very simplest example of a fail safe mechanism is the reference monitor embedded in an average network firewall, illustrated in Figure 4.5. The figure

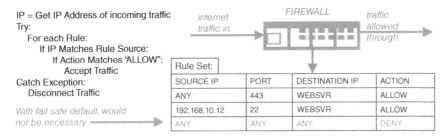

```
IP = Get IP Address of incoming traffic
Try:
    For each Rule:
        If IP Matches Rule Source:
            If Action Matches "ALLOW":
                Accept Traffic
Catch Exception:
    Disconnect Traffic

With fail safe default, would
not be necessary
```

Rule Set:			
SOURCE IP	PORT	DESTINATION IP	ACTION
ANY	443	WEBSVR	ALLOW
192.168.10.12	22	WEBSVR	ALLOW
ANY	ANY	ANY	DENY

Figure 4.5 Example Firewall Rule Set

includes a high-level rule processing algorithm on the left and two access "allow" rules on the right. The first rule allows any device on the internet to access web servers. The second rule allows only one very specific IP address on the internet to connect to server operating system login prompts. This was a typical ruleset in the early days of firewalls: one rule for users, another much narrower rule for specific admins. No other access was intended to be allowed. In the past, to prevent any other network traffic, some firewalls actually required an administrator to write the third rule in the example explicitly into the rule set, namely, if any traffic on the outside does not match a rule above, then it is not allowed to pass through. Therefore, those who understood reference monitors, but were not sophisticated with firewalls would often write rules for traffic that was allowed through and did not realize that if you did not write the third rule, then any traffic would be allowed in. This common vulnerability was soon identified, and now virtually all firewall manufacturers observe the principle of fail safe defaults. If there is not an explicit match with an allowed rule, then an access attempt will fail. Thus, a corresponding directive in a cybersecurity policy document would be:

> By default, no access shall be granted to customer data. Under no circumstances should any request for customer data be granted without clear identification of the user, strong authentication, and a check for authorization to the resource.

While on the topic of rule sets and their compliance with policy, it is important to observe that the word "policy" is often used by cybersecurity professionals, especially vendors, to refer to technical configurations like a firewall rule set. For example, firewall vendor documentation will refer to rules like the ones in Figure 4.5 as a "firewall policy." This is a misnomer from an enterprise perspective because there are multiple ways you can implement policy. It does not have to be a specific ruleset on a specific brand of firewall. Policy is a management dictate for controls at the principle level, and often includes dictates establishing responsibility for design and maintenance of the controls. The actual choice of technology to implement the dictates is left to the person responsible for control implementation. So when you hear a set of rules within a security tool referred to as *policy* or a *policy configuration*, know that is not the same as enterprise policy, which, if violated, could get the culprit fired. At its most strict, a rule-set level of technical configuration can be described as an enterprise standard. At the level that management typically establishes cybersecurity policy, those who issue the policy are not even cognizant of what those configuration parameters might be. Therefore, when you hear the word policy used in a governance of risk management context, it means management directive. If you hear the word policy while sitting with the engineers who are executing operating system security commands, then it probably means a set of system parameters. Moreover, there may be more than one management policy that addresses cybersecurity. A very large enterprise may have multiple policies that address cybersecurity, such as separate policy documents for information security, compliance, legal, and privacy.

4.2.1   Security Principles

Like segregation of duties and segregation of privilege principles introduced in Chapter 3, *fail safe* is a foundational security principle, sometimes referred to as the principle of *fail safe defaults*. It is a requirement to deny any and all access that is not explicitly authorized. It means that when a system is delivered, it should be configured to do nothing unless there is a security configuration that authorizes an authenticated user to perform some function. Fail safe defaults is an excellent example of the expressive power security principles that can be understood in layman's terms. In a few short words, a CISO can compose a management directive that a CEO will fully understand and at the same time will require all technology staff in the enterprise never to deploy a system without a reference monitor that does not explicitly check for authorization before granting access to data of a given type. In this chapter, many security principles are enumerated. However, the complete set of security principles upon which policy is based constantly evolves and CISOs often develop their own principles to help shape their security policy.

To accomplish more reliable security, the identity check made by a reference monitor could solicit more proof of identification before allowing access. This follows the principle of *multifactor authentication*. The original factors of multifactor authentication were very clearly separated into three categories: something only the user knows, something only the user possesses, and something that is unique to the user's physical being. Each factor was clearly a stronger authenticator than the previous one. As depicted in the examples of Figure 4.6, allowing users to choose passwords and requiring them to keep them secret was the first method of trying to make sure that only the person granted access was the person using it.

However, passwords are easy to steal and share. So those with requirements for strong security began providing users with various types of hand-held devices.

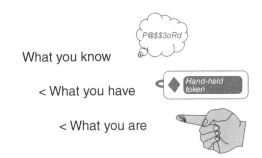

Figure 4.6 Authentication Factors

The first ones were the size of a small calculator and gradually became smaller. Some were designed to fit on a key chain so the user could easily keep track of where they were. These devices are still in use in a high-security environment, but most users' second factor is now either an app or a message on their phone. No matter what the device, a hand-held token typically displays a string that changes so often a person has to have the device in their possession to use it. This considerably cut down on threats that exploited passwords, but token devices themselves can be shared and may be vulnerable to eavesdropping threats.

The third factor, biometrics, *what you are*, seems empirically to be stronger than what you have in your possession because there is only one you. Implementation of checking a body part to produce a security feature has proved difficult to accomplish in a way that can never be spoofed. That is, some abstract digital representation of the body part must be collected and stored in the computer access control system for comparison with future collection of the same abstract and the software used for the collection and comparison itself may have security flaws. Nevertheless, the three factors taught us that some forms of identification are certainly less reliable than others. So multifactor authentication has evolved from a prescriptive standard to more of a guiding security principle that a password is not enough to prevent spoofing identity. Hence, effort should be taken to make it harder to bypass authentication, commensurate with the risk of the unauthorized access.

Figure 4.7 summarizes the types of authentication factors, or *credentials*, that have been incorporated into identification and authentication mechanisms, although the technology industry is continuously inventing new ones. Each has their advantages and disadvantages. However, the basic principle is to use multiple types of factors in a combination that is hard to imitate. When multiple factors of credentials are required to access a resource, the term *authentication sequence* refers to the order in which the credentials are presented and processed.

It is important to recognize that authentication sequences cannot be so difficult that the authorized user finds it difficult to prove their own identity, which would defeat the purpose. If people recognize why it is necessary to go through an

Strings you can Know

password   +g00D+B4g0TN

passphrase   Too good to be forgotten

PIN   262846

encryption key
1364f4e838740580cf03cb49a8735af2

Things you can Have

certificate   MIGHAgEAMBMGByqGSM49AgEGCCqGSM49AwEHBG0wa
wIBAQQgxxpBtON79qtjJkVUIB9+LHxUQ58mfvSqJpaNYt6kki
m1+hRANCAATrdPkWpROsF46maK7pHLUNskoNHjTI+i2dtu+kj
E95uWeZy+Oq6Tge2jNYWVVqP1zHBbKeAB6+pd1NzzSVT8C

handheld token

phone

MAC address | 00 | D0 | 59 | C1 | 8B | 3A |

smart card

USB dongle

Attributes that you Are

eye scan

face recognition

fingerprint

handwriting   *My Signature*

keystroke pattern

voice print

Figure 4.7   Authentication Alternatives

authentication sequence to be able to execute a system command, then they will gladly follow given instructions and identify themselves. But if the instructions are hard to follow, or if they do not work, then the users will dismiss the security procedure as a waste of time and energy and find some other way to get their job done. So when designing user-facing security procedures, systems security engineers strive for them to be easy to operate. Hence, a very important security principle to observe is *psychological acceptability*.

For example, in a setting where a user is assigned to a desk in a secured office, it makes sense for a few authentication factors to be recognized automatically without much effort on behalf of the user. For example, they could enter their password (something they know), and then the system can automatically scan a badge hanging around their neck (something they have), as well as their face (something they are). This allows strong authentication because it prevents someone who knows the user's password from sitting down at their desk and logging in. It also cuts down on the number of operations the user has to perform that stand between them and their work. However, in an unsecured office setting, additional authentication factors would be implemented, such as one-time strings, or *tokens*, delivered handheld device or phone app (something they have, the device or phone).

The difficulty in passing authentication (i.e., the *work factor* involved) should be commensurate with the capabilities of enterprise-identified threat actors and the probable negative impact of user impersonation to enterprise mission. That is, if there is a process that requires people to research public information about your company, and the user is accessing the same public information that anyone out on the web can access on your website, and all they have the ability to do is read it, just as any external user would, then you do not need to make them log in on three factors of authentication when they are sitting at their desk at work to get to that same information. You can leave them logged into the network with a connection only to the internet and an isolated network that keeps all of their traffic out of enterprise systems so they cannot hurt anyone else on your network (a.k.a., *a sandbox*). This allows them to get their job done without spending a lot of time fighting an unnecessary security battle. Where a user's ability to perform well at their job is negatively impacted by cybersecurity measures, the probability that they will take their entire work product out of the enterprise network is increased. This increases the probability that the results of their research, which the enterprise may highly value, will end up on a publicly accessible desktop, and subsequently on the dark web.

Users want to be productive, and any authentication sequence with a work factor of more than three minutes is going to be viewed as a hindrance on the job function. Figure 4.8 is a famous example of how users feel about security and how tempted they are to look for bypasses. In the image, there is a very small road leading to an important-looking building and the road is blocked by a gate, the kind of gate that you drive up to, insert your identity card, and the gate opens. The image

Figure 4.8 Psychological Acceptability

shows a picture of that gate in the snow and what you see at the side of the picture is car tracks bypassing the gate. Many cybersecurity professionals have this picture framed in their office as a reminder that, if you install a gate and your users, either individually or as a group, find it quicker to get around it than to go through it, especially when that gate looks too small and ridiculous to hold back an obvious threat, then the users themselves will feel comfortable going around it because they will rationalize that you did not really care that much about security anyway.

A security principle related to the idea of simplicity is *economy of mechanism*. When designing system features, find the easiest mechanism that can accomplish the goal in as simple and small a function as possible. This helps to limit the number of ways that it could get hacked. Consider that if multiple security experts read the code looking for vulnerabilities and the code is very simple, it should be difficult to avoid that fail safe default. But if the code is very complicated, then that makes it less obvious, even to its developer, whether there is a security bug or flaw that only an expert could find. Moreover, when security is too complicated, people have trouble executing it. Instead, they are tempted to find ways to bypass it altogether, which is another reason to keep it simple.

Another security principle that addresses the need for code transparency is the principle of *open design*. An example is found in the work of the Internet Engineering Task Force (IETF). A precursor to the now ubiquitous open source communities, the IETF has managed an open and collaborative software engineering process since 1969. Its mission is to produce relevant, high-quality technical engineering documents that influence the way people design, use, and manage the internet in such a way so as to make the internet work better (IETF, n.d.). Its volunteer members (most paid by their employers to help influence standards) work together to establish rough consensus on which features should be implemented. They also collaborate on writing and testing proof of concept code that then is typically shared. The standards that specify code features and functions are publicly distributed via a process called "request for comments." If they were to keep their protocols secret, then only a few people would be looking at them, and the probability that someone would find a bug before that protocol was released would be very high. The attitude is that, if you cannot tell your friends how the security works, then the only people who will figure it out are the people who are trying to find your vulnerabilities. In cybersecurity, the mantra for that is "when you are keeping your friends out, it is your enemies who get in."

As we know from the *prevent, detect, respond* triad, if you cannot prevent, you should try to be able to detect. Where system confidentiality, integrity, or availability is compromised, whether maliciously or accidentally, the first question is whether authorized users created the event or understand how the unauthorized users were able to bypass controls in order to do so. The answer to these questions is often found in system activity logs. Every mechanism or activity that is part of a system algorithm that leads to access to a valuable resource should create a log of its activation and the result of any of its access control checks or reference monitor operations. For example, where a request is made for a resource, its reference monitor records all the input, queries its rule list, checks and records the result, and then records the response it sent back to the requester. That way, if assets do get compromised, then there is a place to look to see when and what actually happened. If this logging activity is not created upon system deployment, then in the event of a cybersecurity incident, typically there will be no log data available when SecOps goes looking for it.

Moreover, it is not enough to turn on standard logging. There must also be enough information to be correlated with data produced by other systems in an end-to-end threat vector. In many cases a threat actor will first access the network via a remote access system, then pass through an internal network gateway, then login to a server or workstation, then use a database login to extract data. Each of those devices' reference monitors should be collecting all data available from the source connection. For example, both the source and destination IP address could be collected for each connection a user makes on those devices. It may also be possible to query the authentication logs from the device with the source IP address to identify the name of the user who was in possession of the IP address at the time of that prior login. Forensic investigators will attempt this type of query to collect the data they need to find out who really did what and when it was done. These techniques are not only for forensics after the fact, but in real time when looking for bypass. The IP address trail could be used by a reference monitor rule to deny access to requests where the user name did not match one used in a prior authentication on the same network connection. Where at least one of the authentications in the trail makes use of authorized multifactor authentication, there should be records of the first login, the second factor of authentication, and the internal resource authorization. Then and only then should the system consider the user authorized and allow transactions to be processed. If you have a record of an end-to-end transaction that is missing a record of the middle step, i.e., the second factor of authentication, then you know that someone was able to send a message all the way into the third level of depth bypassing the required authentication sequence. Given the existence of this broken message sequence in the logs, it is clear that you have a security issue in your network and it is possible to identify an issue even though you have not yet declared a security incident.

This concept is encapsulated in another security principle, namely *comprehensive accountability*. This is a requirement to keep complete audit logs of all significant system activities and store them in an untampered manner both for future investigation and for automated analysis by intrusion detection algorithms. The name for security databases with these features is Security Information and Event Management (SIEM). SecOps will typically configure all devices to automatically copy every command executed by an administrator and all application security logs to a SIEM for safekeeping in the event a forensic investigation is necessary to determine the root cause of a cybersecurity incident. Administrative and business functional and data access is monitored, audited, and automatically analyzed as appropriate to identify and alert SecOps on probable misuse of system resources.

Used in combination, security principals are thus a very handy vocabulary to have when establishing policy to maintain risk appetite to an acceptable level. Table 4.1 provides a summary of the security principles introduced so far as well as other security principles upon which policy is routinely based.

4.2.2 Formality

Policies are high-level management directives based on security principles that correlate with risk appetite. They are often created without reference to any implementation, but minimally should specify who in the enterprise is primarily responsible for ensuring compliance with directives. Hence, the document may be formally organized around roles and responsibilities at the organizational level.

The most critical function of policy is to maintain strategic alignment of the enterprise cybersecurity program and the business processes that it supports.

Table 4.1   Security Principles

Security Principles	
Complete Mediation	All access requests are intercepted by a reference monitor to verify authentication and authorization.
Comprehensive Accountability	All *administrative* and *business functional* and *data* access is monitored, audited, and automatically analyzed as appropriate to identify and alert on probable misuse of system resources.
Defense in Depth	All access to resources requires authorization through multiple layers of separately configured controls.
Economy of Mechanism	Keep the design as simple and small as possible.
Fail Safe	Deny access unless it is explicitly authorized.
Least Common Mechanism	Minimize the resources allocated to each user when multiple users share the same system mechanism.
Least Privilege	Users have exactly the permissions they need to perform their responsibilities, and no more.
Multifactor Authentication	Authentication sequence work factors are commensurate with risk of compromise.
Open Design	Never assume that design secrecy will enhance security.
Psychological Acceptability	Requirements for identification, authentication, and authorization features include ease of use and operation.
Recovery Point Objective	System requirements must include archive and availability of a known good state from which system operation may safely resume after an outage.
Recovery Time Objective	System requirements must include the length of time a system outage can be tolerated without breaching risk appetite.
Segregation of Duties	Ensure that functionality to complete high-risk tasks is divided and access to all required subtasks cannot be performed by a single user.
Separation of Privilege	Do not grant special system privileges based on a single technical configuration.
Verification and Validation	Critical controls are tested for compliance with design requirements as well as functional ability to achieve intended control objectives in a production environment.
Zero Trust	Enforce per-request identification and authorization mechanisms that do not rely on an assumption that it is possible to secure a network.

That is, policy must maintain its relevance as changes in both threat environment and business environment evolve. Hence there must be open lines of communication between those who run the cybersecurity programs and those who operate the enterprise in general. This is important not just to have an appropriate policy, but also to ensure that those whose job functions are impacted by policy directives are empowered to execute their responsibilities in compliance with those directives.

A cybersecurity program must therefore have an *awareness* arm that broadly communicates how the enterprise is expected to maintain cybersecurity risk below appetite. But it does not extend to training every single person impacted by policy on every job function. It simply provides enough resources to ensure that policy is readily available as well as to assist people who need to implement technology according to policy in their own scope of work. For example, in areas like desktop management, a security engineer may be assigned to conduct a review process in coordination with the people who are selecting desktop technology to be deployed throughout the firm. The security engineer will work side-by-side with the desktop engineers and contribute their knowledge and expertise on secure architecture and software. They will focus on critical configurations and plans to maintain metrics and logs that can be used to demonstrate policy compliance.

A policy establishes its credibility by designating authority for implementing and/or monitoring its mandates and being "signed off" by enterprise management at the highest level (i.e., the CEO). It also gains credibility via the existence of cybersecurity program resources designed to help others follow it.

Policy also gains credibility when other departments, especially technology, design processes that comply with it. For example, a policy could delegate network security to the CIO and the CIO could then establish a network engineering and administration group that manages all network connectivity in compliance with policy. In that situation, if an individual from any department other than that networking group tries to procure an internet connection from an internet service provider directly to their office, that should be recognized as a policy violation, and the procurement should fail. In this manner, people may become aware of policy constraints and be directed to the proper resource, in this case, network engineering, via basic guardrails on a variety of standard business functions.

In this manner, it becomes obvious that policy carries the full weight of executive management. It is a mandate that must be followed. Failure to follow a policy, or attempting to bypass or otherwise violate it, could result in termination, and rightfully so. The only reason one would not follow policy would be an extremely unusual extenuating circumstance, which would make it impossible for someone to follow the policy. In the internet connection example, it may be that an office procures an emergency internet line after being hit with a tornado (and even then, they should get network engineering to configure it). Policy is meant to be followed. It is a mandate for methods with which to comply with management and regulatory objectives for managing risk, information security risk, and cybersecurity risk.

Although effective policy is issued and signed off by the Chief Executive officer, a CISO will generally have a policy writing arm. This group works closely with all organizations responsible for technology implementation to ensure that policy directives are feasible to implement with generally available resources. A common mistake people make in policy documentation is to delegate responsibility without providing the expertise and resources necessary for compliance. Sometimes a policy is written using words like "should" or "will," instead of "is" or "shall." *Should* implies a directive is optional. *Will* implies that it is ok to comply with a plan for the future instead of now. If these words are used in policy, it should be with full appreciation for their correct interpretation. Any use of "will" should be accompanied by a future date when the planned policy will be fully in effect.

Figure 4.9 is an example policy excerpt relating to authorized system use. It begins with the directive to observe security principles of least privilege and multifactor authentication. It then directs the organization to classify all users into one of four categories: employees, contractors, vendors, and customers. Responsibility for onboarding and establishing least privilege access policies is allocated to specific departments based on user category. Responsibility for oversight of the process is delegated to legal and information security departments.

The policy is the first management level control that takes the risk appetite of the firm and attempts to codify it in a way that it can form the basis of access to systems. In the context of the risk appetite statement in Figure 4.4, the requirements that are specific to the customer user category reflect the importance of maintaining customer data in very tightly controlled application profiles. The time-limited access for non-employees reflects commitment to least privilege, and this reflects lack of appetite for any unnecessary data exposure. Though these excerpts are far from complete, it assigns organizational accountability for designing processes, standards and procedures for implementation of controls that conform to this policy and should reduce risk of unauthorized access to a level below appetite. This policy provides solid direction from which more detailed control documents may evolve.

Maintaining accountability for policy implementation therefore relies heavily on collaboration between the CISO and HR to use standard organization designations and job titles. It is also common for HR that an enterprise staff to create a code of conduct to refer to a policy document for a new employee to learn more details about their roles and responsibilities for implementing elements of the cybersecurity program. In addition, it will refer all staff members to consult the code of conduct for responsibilities related to following the cybersecurity program.

Section B: Authorized Use

B.1: Business Purpose
All information technology at Firm shall be associated with an "Application." The application is the business purpose of the technology that is recorded in Application Inventory.

B.2: Least Privilege
Where individuals require access to an organization's facilities, operational processes, technology systems, and information ("resources") in order to ensure the success of the enterprise mission, this access shall be:
(i) limited to least privilege with respect to the individual's function; and
(ii) provisioned only after receipt of a successful background check approved by Legal that may be customized for that function.

B.2.1: User Classification
Responsibility for determining the minimum possible access requirements for an individual's function is allocated based on user classification. Individuals who do not have a business relationship with the enterprise that falls into a defined user classes shall have no authorized access and all individuals who are granted systems access shall endeavor to ensure that such unclassified individuals are unable to access enterprise resources that are not declared by Legal to be publicly accessible (e.g. advertising and corporate investor websites).

B.2.2: Departmental Responsibility
The table below lists the business relationships that form the basis of user classification and designates the department responsible for fully onboarding each member of the class prior to an individual in that class being provisioned with authorized systems access. That organization is also be responsible for specifying minimum possible access requirements for an individual's function, subject to the review and approve of Information Security.

Category	Department	Requirements specific to Category
Employees	Human Resources	Access shall be disabled during authorized leaves of absense including medical leave and extended vacations.
Contractors	Service Risk Management	Access is justified only for the duration of an active Statement of Work.
Vendors	Supplier Management	Access is justified only where contractually requirements specify what functions will be performed and access controls are configured to restrict access.
Customers	Customer Care	Access may never be customized but granted only in the form of application entitlement profiles approved by Information Security.

Figure 4.9 Example Policy

4.3 Process

To some it may seem arbitrary that policy is put before process in the control pyramid. This establishment of the policy itself is a process, as a process is a workflow designed to support a given outcome. The argument goes that, for different areas of the enterprise, strategic statements on risk appetite may require different workflow with unique goals to be articulated in policy. Consequently, each organization within the enterprise should have control over its own policy. But this argument does not go far because to decide on process without first clearly articulating the expected outcome of the workflow is essentially premature. If it is difficult for process to achieve risk appetite below an acceptable level, then it is the process that should change, not the policy that established that outcome as a process goal.

The key to harmony between policy and process is for policy to strictly avoid dictating how a goal should be accomplished and instead focus on roles, responsibilities, and measurable outcomes. The difference between these policies and processes is that processes get down to workflow. Connected to the workflow will be standards. To support standards, there will be procedures. But at the policy level it is just what shall be at the control objective level. It is not "how" it works. It is a process that lays the groundwork for how it will be accomplished, at least at a high level.

Processes may cross departments and define points of interface and/or hand-off of an item in a workstream to another department either within, or external to, the organization. Security program processes often have touch points with business processes that have requirements, such as identifying authorized users or deploying business applications. These will vary with the size and nature of the organization, as well as the diversity in roles and responsibilities.

Chapter 3 includes a detailed description of a cyber security operations process wherein technology incidents identified as problems were escalated through multiple technology support organizations including SecOps. That process may be owned by the CISO, but there are numerous people across a dozen organizations executing it. There are also security processes in the realm of IAM wherein the security group itself acts as a helpdesk for people requesting or having problems with user login credentials. ITIL refers to this type of security process as "security management" and emphasizes that it cannot work in isolation. Rather, it is critical that security processes be integrated with each of the other IT process management teams to meet both internal and external (i.e., customer and regulatory) security requirements. The idea that an IAM or a SecOps process may be performed in a manner completely internal to a cybersecurity department is not coherent. Cybersecurity processes are enterprise-wide workflows designed to achieve the outcomes of information confidentiality, data integrity, and systems availability. This is not possible without cybersecurity roles and responsibilities crossing multiple organizations.

An easy and flexible way to approach cross-organizational process definition is with a Responsible, Accountable, Consulted, Informed (RACI) matrix. While policy specifies organizational roles and responsibilities for executing the mission of the cybersecurity program, a RACI matrix specifies who does what in a more granular view. It can be used for any process or task that requires cooperation for coordinated activity. Like policy authority designations, a process RACI matrix is designed to establish unquestioned accountability and to function through individual staff role changes. While policy typically refers to responsibility at the organization level by department name or department head title, a process may refer to individuals by job title within organizations instead of by name. Maintaining accountability and responsibility for process execution therefore relies heavily on the role of HR to use standard job titles across organizations, just as it does for policy compliance at the organizational level. It does this by assigning roles to individuals or groups for these aspects of process:

R – Responsible: The designated role performs activity specified by the process.

A – Accountable: The designated role is the authority and decision-maker responsible for the design and quality of process performance, and also to provide oversight.

C – Consulted: The designated role contributes knowledge and participates in two-way communication with those responsible and accountable as the activity is planned and executed.

I – Informed: The designated role receives one-way communication on the details of the activity, typically from those responsible, and is expected to act on it responsibly.

Figure 4.10 is a high-level RACI matrix for enterprise processes that are typically managed by a CISO.

In a RACI matrix, it is important to establish sole accountability, so it is clear to whom the ultimate decisions belong. But it is also perfectly fine to distribute responsibility broadly where that makes sense. In most organizations, security monitoring is delegated to the CISO or the CIO, the person who is accountable for accomplishing it. This example lists the CIO as being accountable for "Security Monitoring" because in the SecOps example in Chapter 3, security monitoring was depicted as integrated with technology monitoring. Typically, the CIO owns most of the technology resources that are being monitored and it is very difficult to do monitoring unless you can hold the CIO accountable for the technology asset inventory and associated monitoring configuration. Several organizations like the Service Desk and SecOps may be responsible for actually monitoring technology,

Participant: Process:	CIO	CISO	SecOps	Admins	Application Teams	Human Resources	Legal
Identity and Access Management	Responsible	**Accountable**	Informed	Responsible	Consulted	Responsible	Consulted
Cybersecurity Metrics	Consulted	**Accountable**	Responsible	Informed	Informed	Informed	Informed
Security Architecture	**Accountable**	Consulted	Consulted	Responsible	Consulted	Informed	Informed
Cybersecurity Response	Responsible	**Accountable**	Responsible	Responsible	Responsible	Consulted	Consulted
Security Monitoring	**Accountable**	Consulted	Responsible	Responsible	Consulted	Informed	Informed
Vulnerability Management	Responsible	**Accountable**	Responsible	Responsible	Responsible	Informed	Informed

Figure 4.10 Cybersecurity Process RACI Matrix

but SecOps is primarily responsible for the security part. Some Administration teams may be assigned responsibility for monitoring security-related alerts in the context of other alerts for which they are responsible in their administrative domain.

In this example, the CISO and Application Teams have enough stake in the outcome of the security monitoring to be consulted in the course of process development and execution. HR and Legal do not participate in the monitoring itself, but will be informed of its results. Depending on how enterprise security responsibilities are allocated, these assignments may differ widely. A RACI matrix is simply a documentation tool that very clearly articulates how responsibilities have been assigned.

Another cross-organizational process typically managed by cybersecurity is IAM, and colloquially referred to as the Joiners, Movers, and Leavers (JML) process. JML is a reference to the people who come in and out of the enterprise and need access to systems, defined as follows (Canavan, 2014):

Join: A user begins a business relationship with the organization.

Move: A "joined" user's access requirements change in correspondence with a change in job role, a move from one job to another.

Leave: A user ends a business relationship with the organization.

Access Request: A "joined" user's access requirements change in correspondence with new responsibilities or changes in assigned tasks within the same job.

JMLs have access to resources in the form of credentials to systems needed to perform an assigned job function. To support this requirement, someone has got to decide exactly what access is needed for the job function, specifically, what is the least amount of data and functionality that must be provided to enable them to help make the enterprise successful no matter what their job role or responsibility. Note that JMLs are not just employees. They may be contractors, third parties, customers, or business partners that require access to enterprise systems to assist with its mission.

Another term for joining is *onboarding*. This was the term used in the example policy excerpt of Figure 4.9. Note that the delegation of onboarding to the various departments in that policy provides the opportunity for those departments to design their own processes to execute their assigned responsibilities. These processes are routinely designed to introduce significant financial and legal obligations on their designated users for compliance with security and other company policies via contracts that they have established for that purpose.

Many users will join, transfer, and leave the same enterprise several times in their career history. In order to maintain their identity correctly, an enterprise needs to track the history of how that person interacted with its systems. From an efficiency perspective, it is tempting to treat all joiners equitably, to provide them with building access, email, and default department file shares. However, where the tone at the top has established multifactor authentication and least privilege principles by policy, each individual's access should be more specifically questioned. These people could be espionage agents. They could be advanced persistent threat actors seeking to infiltrate the organization. Just because they may have passed routine background checks required for any staff member does not mean that they are not capable of exploiting whatever access they are granted to try to gain unauthorized access to other enterprise systems.

The secondary objectives are to make sure that those staff members are accountable for those IT assets issued to them and there is a loss theft process to report a missing asset. If the assets assigned to an individual are in any way in jeopardy, personal devices should be wiped and perhaps repurposed or even destroyed to make sure that they no longer contain enterprise data or the ability to access it remotely, and this also applies to staff member whose employment has come to an end. Moreover, any file shares in which they participated that are no longer needed should be wiped as well. That requires some kind of an IAM system capable of storing information on assets and file shares allocated to an individual, a trigger from that system to a device operations team, and an automated method to wipe storage that is no longer required.

The RACI in Figure 4.10 shows only HR as the sole organization responsible for the notification part of the IAM process. That is because HR is typically the department that records changes in employee status in an IAM system, or the IAM system is automatically fed by an HR system. But this responsibility may differ in organizations that split administrative duties by user type. For example, HR may administer employees, vendor management may administer contractors, and supplier risk management may administer maintenance vendors.

There may be one IAM system that is shared by all organizations that are responsible for some form of staff onboarding and offboarding or they may each have their own. But there has to be some way to clearly specify the authoritative source of identity, credential, and entitlement data resides and know that all access to it is audited. Where an IAM system is the sole authoritative source for a user in a given category, if someone requests systems access for an individual not identified in that system, it will be refused. Otherwise, the process will be easily exploitable and at high risk of insider threat.

Processes are often documented only by workflow wherein activities are communicated via annotated illustration as in Figure 4.11. The illustration provides a high-level description of the cross-organizational workflow that may be established to support movers in the employee user category. In this process, an existing employee who had previously joined in one job function is now moving to another. Activities are assigned to groups or job titles within a group as labeled in bold font. The actual activity performed by each group within their own process stages is left to be documented as step-by-step procedures.

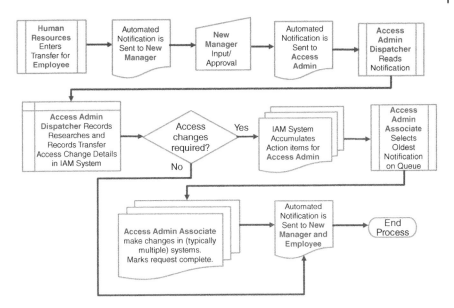

Figure 4.11 Movers Process Documentation

The process begins when HR enters the transfer record into the IAM system. The system automatically sends an access change order request notification to the employee's new manager. That new manager enters the access needed for the new job function. That request is forwarded to an Access Admin Dispatcher. The dispatcher retrieves the new manager's request and verifies that it is possible to execute, given the entitlements that must be modified and the manager's authority. The dispatcher provides specific instructions for executing the changes. For example, if a login is needed on an SSO system for access to new applications, then the employee may keep the same SSO login string, and that login would be granted access to the new applications. In some cases, they will not need applications that they had access to their old job anymore, so those entitlements would be terminated.

Once the required changes are specified, they are placed in a queue monitored by Access Admin. An associate picks up the request, makes the required changes, and marks the request completed. Note that this shows a three-way segregation of duties, the manager approves the request, the dispatcher translates the approval into technical configurations, and the associate enters the technical configurations. The process enables each to perform their role in an efficient and effective manner.

Figure 4.11 uses a simple workflow documentation format and is clear and suitable for small organizations. Where processes are very complicated, a simple process flow may span several pages and have cross-page links. To reduce the

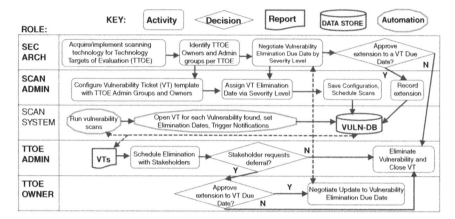

Figure 4.12 Vulnerability Management Process

possibility of confusion in process interpretation, there are specialized tools that represent processes in standard formats. Larger organizations will typically collaborate on process documentation using such tools so that people can quickly grasp who does what at a glance.

Figure 4.12 is an example of such process documentation in a grid format. Tools will add and store rows and labels for quick retrieval and facilitate quick links and distribution methods. Each organization that participates in the process is represented by one row in the grid, and may participate in document preparation as required. The example illustrates a vulnerability identification and elimination process, often referred to as vulnerability management. The row labels on the left show that the process spans four organizations (in bold) and one automated vulnerability scanning system. Roles are listed in order of their appearance in the process. Activity expected from the role also appears in order of execution sequence. Unidirectional arrows show the flow of activities both with the role and points of handoff to another role. Bidirectional arrows on dashed lines refer to communication required to complete one or more activities. Decision diamonds branch in a given direction is based on the answer to a question.

The diagram is typical of a process established by a CISO wherein a security architecture team selects and implements a system for scanning enterprise technology for known vulnerabilities (and potentially corrects security configuration as well). The SCAN ADMIN row refers to the administrator team responsible for the scanning system itself. The administrators configure and operate the scanning system using information provided by the security architects. This includes the technical targets of evaluation (TTOE), the set of devices that must be scanned to see whether they are vulnerable to known threats. It also includes the administrative teams responsible for eliminating any vulnerabilities found on devices, typically a specific group for different types of devices. For example, eliminating a desktop vulnerability might be a task assigned to the IT service desk, while eliminating a Linux vulnerability would typically be a task assigned to the server administrators.

The configuration parameters would also include some method by which to automatically estimate the potential impact on the enterprise, should the vulnerability be exploited. It would be a nominal measure of vulnerability severity level. For each TTOE type and severity level, an architect would specify the timeframe in which vulnerabilities in predefined severity levels should be completed. Severity parameters would be based on the cybersecurity policy statements about minimizing risks associated with known vulnerabilities. For example, if the vulnerability is classified as low severity and there is low tolerance for known vulnerabilities, it may be a month. However, if there is no tolerance for known vulnerabilities and the severity is critical, it may be a day.

Once this setup is complete, the system scanner runs on a schedule input by the administrators and delivers any vulnerabilities found in the form of a "ticket" to those responsible for configuring the vulnerable device. The ticket includes the device identifier, vulnerability, any information available about how to eliminate the vulnerability, and the date on which the vulnerability is expected to be eliminated. An administrator would treat this just as any other system maintenance task, something to be scheduled with developers, users, and/or other stakeholders associated with the targeted device.

If for any reason, a stakeholder associated with the vulnerability claims the vulnerability cannot be eliminated by the due date, the stakeholder would request a deferral. The reasons for this will be reviewed with the business owner of the device in question. This is typically a business person responsible for the application running on the device. If this person approves the deferral, the request will be escalated to a security architect. The architect would presumably review the reasons for deferral and may recommend *compensating controls* in the interim before the vulnerability eradication. The result of that discussion would trigger a decision by the security architect on whether to also approve the deferral. Either way, the vulnerability ticket will remain open until the vulnerability is eliminated.

Note that the term *compensating control* is a term of art in risk management. It means that a control requirement is not fully met, but there is some control in place that either partially or fully meets the legislative intent behind the requirement. In this example, the requirement is to eliminate known vulnerabilities and a compensating control may be network isolation for the device that is vulnerable. The vulnerability is still there, but the attack surface is reduced. An example of a compensating control that fully meets a requirement is a technology standard that dictates that all devices install a specific EDR tool, but one device has an operating system that is not supported by the EDR vendor and so uses another EDR tool with the same feature set as the one dictated by the standard.

Based on the wordy process explanations above, the picture in Figure 4.11 is worth 394 words and the picture in Figure 4.12 is worth 775 words. Yet the process descriptions provided by the figures are concise and complete. That is why people use diagrams to explain processes and reinforces the adage, "A picture is worth 1,000 words."

Although every enterprise has its own method of establishing accountability for cybersecurity control processes, a CISO will typically establish processes for areas including, but not limited to:

1) Identity and Access Management
2) Intrusion Detection and Prevention
3) Digital Forensics
4) Metrics and Reporting
5) Policy and Program Management
6) Privacy
7) Regulatory and Legal Compliance
8) Resilience
9) Risk Assessment
10) Security Architecture and Engineering
11) Security Operations
12) Secure Software Development Lifecycle
13) Third-Party Oversight
14) Threat Intelligence
15) Vulnerability Management

4.4 Standards

4.4.1 Internal Standards

Systems that are shared across organizations, such as the IAM system described in the JML process in Section 4.3, are instances of enterprise technology standards. Standards describe how an enterprise has decided to automate rote activities for the humans who are executing processes like JML. Typically, where all groups executing a cross organizational process use the same system, the process is more efficient and effective than it would be if every group had their own automation tools that had to be either manually or technically integrated. This is the primary reason why enterprises adopt technology standards. Because everyone in the enterprise is subject to the same cybersecurity policy, the efficiency is especially apparent for cybersecurity standards. Even when responsibility for technology configuration does not lie with the CISO, as in the technology monitoring RACI in Figure 4.10, the CISO is often consulted to help make certain that the technology selected is compliant with policy, or as we say colloquially in cybersecurity: *policy-compliant.*

In addition to reference to common systems, RACI matrices and work flows developed for processes provide critical input required to develop standards for access to data. For example, the matrix at the top of Figure 4.13 is a simplified RACI matrix corresponding to enterprise business application support process. In it, the CIO is accountable for tasks related to application operation (i.e., security monitoring and infrastructure change), while the Application Manager is accountable for tasks related to application deployment and operations (i.e., software update and report distribution). Technology operations is responsible for making changes to the environment and shares responsibility for monitoring it. The application manager is informed of security and infrastructure operations, consulted on software updates, and responsible for application report distribution.

The matrix at the bottom of Figure 4.13 is a corresponding Access Control Matrix (ACM) that identifies the least amount of information each role needs to effectively perform their function, phrased in data access control language. Only those whose functional roles include responsibility for reading or writing the information specified in the first column of the row are granted write access to it. For example, the Technology Operations team is responsible for Infrastructure Change and Software Update. Therefore, it must have write access to configurations and software, while the Application Manager may have to help troubleshoot any software issues in production and would be granted only read access. The Application Owner may have access to the application itself, and be able to read

RACI TASK:	CIO	Technology Operations	Security Operations	Application Manager	Application Owner
Security Monitoring	Accountable	Responsible	Responsible	Informed	Informed
Infrastructure Change	Accountable	Responsible	Consulted	Informed	Informed
Software update	Consulted	Responsible	Consulted	Accountable	Consulted
Report Distribution	Consulted	Consulted	Consulted	Accountable	Responsible

ACM Information:	CIO	Technology Operations	Security Operations	Application Manager	Application Owner
Application Software	Read	Read, write	Read	Read	None
Security Configuraiton	Read	Read, write	Read offline	Read offline	None
Security Metrics	Read	Read	Read, write	Read offline	Read offline
Application data	Read encrypted data flow	Read encrypted data flow	Read encrypted data flow	Read encrypted data flow	Read

Figure 4.13 Access Control Matrix Derived from RACI

Application Data, but otherwise has no access to the software or configuration. The absence of responsibility for write access to Application Data may indicate that only application users, such as customers, should be allowed to change that data. Similarly, only those whose functional roles require read access to the data are allowed to see it in an unencrypted version. For those responsible for application updates and monitoring, it is enough to be able to read the flow of the information through the system, not the actual data content.

Where detailed technical configurations and protocols are to be mandated, a policy will typically include reference to one or more standards documents, and appoint accountability for the establishment of standards. Standards are thus enterprise directives for technical configurations that comply with policy. The scope of a standard may be enterprise-wide for a given technology or apply only to technology within a single department. Standards may be device specific, architectural, and/or warranted in any case where potential data exposure warrants economic and effective oversight of control strategy execution.

In organizations that develop software, it is common to have a standard that governs the stages of the software build, deploy, test, and maintenance activity, referred to as a software development lifecycle (SDLC) standards. It may specify which programming languages to use for different types of software modules, in what software code repository to store the code while it is under development, and what are the approved methods for delivering code from that development environment to a quality assurance or testing platform where it will be tested. If security requirements for building secure code are included in a SDLC, it may be referred to as a Secure SDLC (SSDLC) (NIST SP 800-218, 2022). In this case, it would likely include static and dynamic code vulnerability scanning such as those described in Section 2.2. Figure 4.14 shows the variety of cybersecurity tool choices there are to make in establishing an SSDLC (Synopsis, n.d., p. 6). Although some SSDLC products may combine several of these tool functions into one product, it is often necessary that the enterprise security standard include specifications for small code modules to transfer software from one stage in the lifecycle to the next. Note that SSDLC is just one process of those listed at the end of Section 4.3, and is of the number of systems that may be required to be identified, purchased, configured, monitored, and maintained in support of cybersecurity processes.

4.4.2 External Standards

The word *standard* is very common in cybersecurity to refer to many different documents that are published by many organizations. It refers to industry and

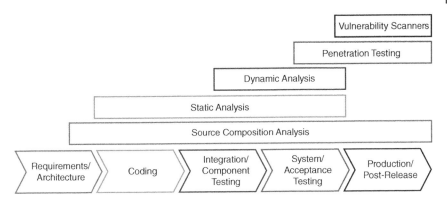

Figure 4.14 Secure Software Development Lifecycle Systems

regulatory standards as well as enterprise standards. One of the first cybersecurity industry standards was the Trusted Computer System Evaluation Criteria (NCSC, 1985), also known as *The Orange Book*, nicknamed for its color in a larger set of technology publications called "The Rainbow Series." It was the source of the consensus on the properties of subject and objects described in Section 3.2, a precursor to today's NIST standards.

One of the first legal standards was the US Computer Fraud and Abuse Act (Department of Justice, 1986) that made it unlawful to access a computer without authorization. It was quickly followed by regulation in the form of the Computer Security Act of 1987, which directed The National Bureau of Standards (NBS, now NIST) to develop standards of minimum acceptable practices for securing federal government systems. Since that time, nearly every industry regulator has established minimum security requirements for safeguarding systems and information for the businesses in their scope of authority.

Nevertheless, as appropriately put in a design guide that accompanies ISACA's COBIT: "There is no unique, one-size-fits-all governance system for enterprise I&T. Every enterprise has its own distinct character and profile, and will differ from other organizations in several critical respects: size of the enterprise, industry sector, regulatory landscape, threat landscape, role of IT for the organization and tactical technology-related choices, among others." (ISACA, 2019, p. 15).

Figure 4.15 is a systemigram that illustrates how these industry and regulatory standards are used by an enterprise to develop their own custom cybersecurity standards. The mainstay reads: *Cybersecurity standards include requirements that guide management who operate the system security architecture that controls*

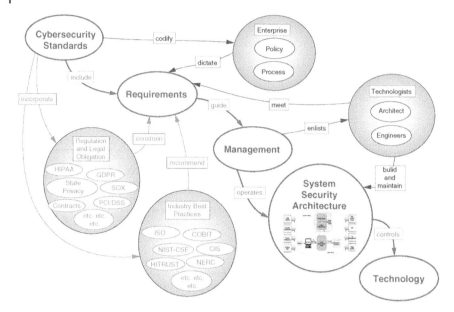

Figure 4.15 Cybersecurity Standards Systemigram

technology. Regulations and Legal Obligations on the far left of the figure shows the influence of legal contracts, regulatory requirements, and industry best practice standards on the requirements process. The legal and regulatory standards present obligations, which constrain requirements. The industry standards do not have the same weight, so they are incorporated as recommendations. *Enterprise* in the upper right of the figure acknowledges that cybersecurity standards are intended to codify enterprise policy and processes; therefore, those documents are incorporated as dictates. Once the requirements are established, they guide management who enlist technologists to build security architecture that both meets the requirements and enables them to control enterprise technology.

The small diagram in the "System Security Architecture" concept of the systemigram is sourced from the NIST Zero Trust Architecture standard (NIST, 2020). It is there as a reminder that industry and regulatory standards are not checklists to be observed in the course of composing internal standards. Rather they are guidance for creating requirements for technology architecture that must be designed and built within the enterprise in order to achieve its mission. At base, it is a set of hardware and software components configured to communicate on selected network protocols to facilitate business operations. Technology architecture is more generic than security architecture. Within technology architecture, there are components that allow certain subjects to access certain objects, and be able to read, manipulate, or remove them from the enterprise systems environment. The set of components that control security within a technology architecture exists whether or not they are planned by management. But if they are not planned, it is almost certain that they do not enforce access as specified in management's policy (if there is one).

Regulatory standards are government requirements to protect information. The people in government who are charged with making industries like financial services safe from corruption and fraud are also charged with considering the appropriate way to reduce the risk of data breaches in the industry. Examples of regulators are the US Department of Health and Human Services (HHS) and the European Data Protection Board (EDPB). Regulatory standards are often named for the law that gave the regulator the charge to protect information, like the Health Insurance Portability and Accountability Act's Security Rule (HIPAA) and the European Union's General Data Protection Regulation (EU GDPR) supported by HHS and the EDPB, respectively. These are not technical standards that are straightforward to just read and implement. They are descriptions of controls for which there are a wide variety of implementation options. They have to be mapped to enterprise data and applied to the systems that house the regulated data elements.

Note that although HIPAA and GDPR are similar in that they are both standards, they have very different constituents. HIPAA requires security controls for personal health information while GDPR is far more broadly applicable to many more companies because it classifies a far wider set of information as personally identifiable. This extends to internet activity.

Another example more broadly applicable regulation are requirements created to support the US Sarbanes-Oxley Act section on financial reporting integrity requirements, specifically SOX Section 404. In a few paragraphs SOX 404 requires public companies to assess and attest to the ability of their financial reporting systems to maintain data integrity. The paragraphs are deceptively simple, but when codified, require tight controls on data processing that are typically managed using Enterprise Resource Planning (ERP) systems.

There are perhaps as many regulatory cybersecurity standards as there are regulators. Different business situations require attention to specialized data classification and handling processes. These sometime extend to specific security mechanisms with which data must be securely shared with the regulator. However, except where technology mechanisms are supplied by the regulator, this does not imply that all business in the scope of that regulation will find it straightforward to comply. There is typically some aspect of internal systems that have to be customized to accomplish compliance with standards.

Also in the obligatory standards side, there are legal and contractual requirements. Legal requirements tend to be more high level than regulations and contractual requirements tend to be much more specific. An example standard that is the basis for a *contractual* requirement is the Payment Card Industry Security Standards Council's Data Security Standard (PCI DSS) (PCI, 2022). PCI DSS lists technical security requirements imposed by contracts that allow financial institutions to participate in credit card processing networks. Such association-driven contractual requirements are more straightforward to implement than others because they are more prescriptive. Data definitions and technology to be secured are sometimes imposed by the operational requirements of processing the financial transactions to be secured, and these can be leveraged to create very specific security requirements.

Another example is the Society for Worldwide Interbank Financial Telecommunications (SWIFT) Customer Security Framework. It not only specifies control requirements but directly identifies the cybersecurity risk that the control is meant to reduce (SWIFT, 2022). SWIFT can do this because it is not only a standards body, but an industry participant, and every organization that uses their assessment is running a similar, if not the exact same, business process, namely, money transfers between banks. The categories of events that have negative impact on those processes are well understood, and the technology environments at SWIFT member banks are similar enough to state with confidence that very specific sets of technology controls will reduce business risk.

Unlike the legal and regulatory obligations just described, standards that are based on industry best practices are sought out by cybersecurity professionals charged with securing information. They are naturally curious about what other people are doing to secure a similar environment, to gain some assurance their own control plans are on the right track. There are a variety of cybersecurity best practice standards publications. At one extreme with respect to detail is the Center for Internet Security (CIS). CIS compiles highly technical standards for operating system configurations. For example, it proscribes how to establish least privilege and comprehensive accountability on specific versions of Linux. At the other extreme is the International Organization for Standardization (ISO) standard for security management requirements (ISO/IEC 27001, 2022) and a companion set of reference technology controls (ISO/IEC 27002, 2022). The recommendation is to use the first standard to establish management policy and process for security, and the second to fortify them with control standards and procedures. ISO also publishes a plethora of standards for a wide range of technologies spanning intellectual, scientific, technical, and economic needs for standardization. Hence, a large global enterprise may select an ISO standard simply because of its reputation for bringing together global expertise.

Some regulations may also be best practices, but best practices are not legally binding unless they are also regulation. NIST CSF is a special case of industry best practice that is also a regulatory standard. Like ISO, its full set of documentation encompasses a wide range of technology not specific to security. But unlike ISO, US Federal government agencies and contractors are obligated to incorporate NIST standards into their own. For those agencies, NIST standards are regulation and for a more general audience, they are a source of best industry practice.

Regulatory and industry standards have in common that they are not customized for any specific enterprise environment. They are either requirements or advice for a professional in creating internal standards. These documents *inform* enterprise cybersecurity standards. Enterprise cyber security standards are, by definition, customized specifications for how to configure and deploy cybersecurity technology controls within the enterprise infrastructure.

An enterprise security standard is the set of detailed technology configurations that control the behavior of the security components of the technology architecture. In contrast to the regulatory and industry standards that may be a source of some requirements, the enterprise version provides the detail on exactly what is implemented.

The NIST Special Publication SP800-53 (NIST SP 800-53, 2013) is an industry best practice standard that also is regulatory required for the protection of US federal systems. Like all industry and regulatory standards, it is intended to be customized by its target audience. It makes a great example of an industry standard because it is clearly intended to be customized. This is evident in the document's extensive use of brackets that indicate a reader should replace the description in them with something that makes sense for their environment. Figure 4.16 is an excerpt from NIST SP 800-53 that shows exactly how a required control should be customized by the reader. The layout of each control is identical and the organization-defined parameters are clearly identified. The base control definition is offered, while the optional enhancements are determined by the audience.

Figure 4.17 shows how the NIST SP 800-53 Access Control requirement number 6 (AC-6) might be customized by its audience. The figure shows that *least privilege* is defined as "Employ the principle of least privilege, allowing only authorized accesses for users, or processes acting on behalf of users, that are necessary to accomplish assigned organizational tasks." Presumably, a customization of this sentence would be included in an enterprise policy reference to the expected handling of sensitive data by type. The standard includes ten (10) control enhancements with fill-in-the blank values demonstrating how its audience can meet requirements for least privilege. Figure 4.16 contains just part of the first, but should suffice to show how the NIST language is adopted by its audience to specify exactly how it complies with the control requirements. In this case, it starts by establishing complete authority for executing standard security and technology processes using very specific technology platforms. It would continue through the other least privilege requirements by specifying technical configurations that would enable the NIST-specified access control enhancements to be implemented.

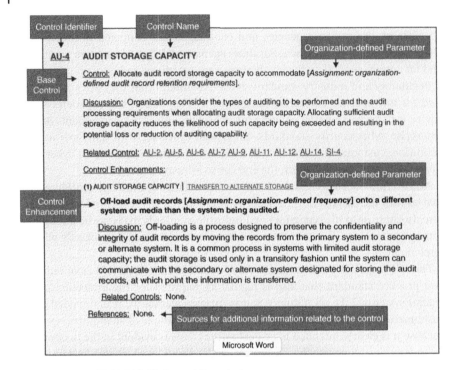

Figure 4.16 NIST SP 800-53 Control Description

NIST SP 800-53 Version:
LEAST PRIVILEGE | AUTHORIZE ACCESS TO SECURITY FUNCTIONS
Authorize access for [Assignment: organization-defined individuals or roles] to:
(a) [Assignment: organization-defined security functions (deployed in hardware, software, and firmware)];

Enterprise Custom Version:
Access to security functions is limited to designated individuals within the Chief Information Security Office and the Technology Administration Engineering Office to:
(a) The Chief Information Security Office maintains the Identity Manager System and the Single Login System (SLS) for the purpose of establishing and maintaining user identity through the Joiners Movers Leavers process. All enterprise access controls must exclusively utilize these systems.
(b) The Technology Administration Engineering Office is responsible for centrally receiving all cyber equipment using the Technology Asset Management System (TAMS). Through TAMS, administrators are assigned to customizing access controls in all enterprise hardware, operating systems software and cloud platform as a service administrative services.

Figure 4.17 Enterprise Standard Derived from Industry Standard Guidance

Although the example shows wording designed to call attention to the language of the standard, the map from an internal standard to an external standard does not have to be such an exact match. As long as the internal standard does not conflict with the external requirement and an argument can be made that some internal control maps to the requirement, and there is evidence the control is operating effectively, the internal standard can achieve compliance with an external standard.

4.4.3   Security Architecture

A prerequisite to standards is an enterprise systems architecture. A systems architecture is composed of the technology that has been acquired to support the enterprise mission. Like physical building architecture, there are common patterns. Also like building architecture, it is always better to have completed an architecture document before breaking ground. However, unlike building architecture, the symbols and icons used to depict systems architecture patterns vary widely, even within the same industry. Commonly used diagraming tools will supply a variety of template choices and even allow custom imports. Architects may select icons from multiple templates to include in the same document. Large cloud service providers publish dictionaries of customized symbols to make it easier to communicate with customers about the multiple cloud use cases that vary in architectural complexity, or *cloud workloads.* Cloud workloads vary from relatively uncomplicated SaaS accounting systems to cross organizational data flows between multiple enterprise-wide applications, and a systems architecture diagram uses the cloud-specific icons when representing cloud workloads while utilizing simpler templates to represent architecture housed in private data centers.

That is, same device may be represented using different icons, even in the same document, depending on who creates the diagram. For example, the top row of icons in Figure 4.18 shows four different symbols for a server and the bottom row shows four different symbols for a database server. In very large organizations, it makes sense to adopt internal standards for a technology icon library. That said, technology service providers with branded icons are not likely to observe them, so technology engineers and architects (including cybersecurity ones) may have to be fluent in several icon languages. There is no "right" choice, although like languages, business communication is always easier if staff is fluent in the languages that are prevalent in the region in which the enterprise operates.

What is the same about systems diagrams is that they represent networks, computers, users, and expected communication between them. The diagram in Figure 4.19 is an example of a common technology architecture pattern. The example includes technology devices housed in enterprise data centers and cloud

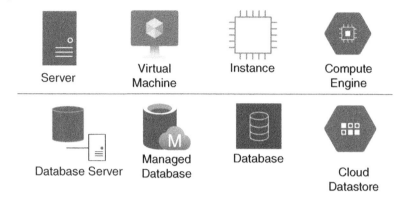

Figure 4.18   Alternative Technology Architecture Icons

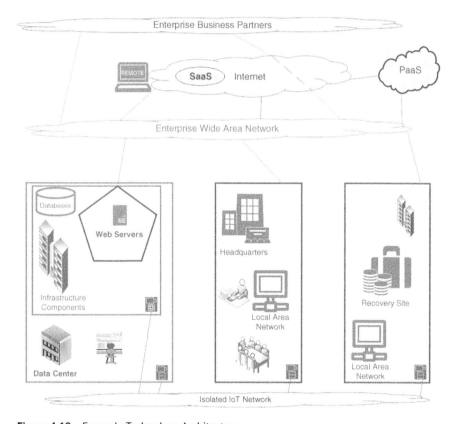

Figure 4.19   Example Technology Architecture

infrastructure, both hosting commercial off the shelf software (COTS) and internally developed applications. The diagram also shows an enterprise owned and operated network that is segmented to limit access to critical applications to well-defined data flows and *fails over* to a backup location in the event of a local disturbance. This is the sort of diagram maintained by a Chief Technology Architect to be used in high-level presentations, as well as to provide a resource for new employees or auditors who need to orient themselves to an unfamiliar environment. It does not contain the level of detail needed by network or server engineers tasked with installation and maintenance of these technologies. Those would typically specify additional details, such as make and model of critical network components, communications protocols for major network links and private connections leased from telecommunications vendors.

The diagram also includes Software as a Service (SaaS) vendors used by the enterprise, and some of these may connect to the data center and cloud workloads in support of business application data flow. These connections will typically traverse the internet. This reflects a situation where the internet is used as a conduit between partners, but most of information processing is conducted within each enterprise's private networks, whether in data centers or virtual private clouds. There are even methods where business partners may bypass the internet and connect directly to the enterprise. This type of connection is typically reserved for highly critical functions that must work in the face of major disasters. It may be that the telecommunication provider is impacted by the same event that impacts a local internet provider; hence, significant effort is spent ensuring that the physical path of lines leased from telecommunications suppliers is sufficiently diverse, so that no single tornado or hurricane could completely sever required connections.

Note that these high availability architectures were not motivated by the possibility of threat actors launching denial-of-service attacks, but by the inherent risk of lack of connectivity due to natural and human-made disasters. Though not motivated by cybersecurity risk, cybersecurity risk management fully leverages them to also deter or deflect an intentional subversive attack on enterprise architecture. That is, the technology architecture includes controls constructed in response to requirements to support legal and contractual requirements for reliability. In an enterprise that takes those requirements seriously, features to support stipulated reliability features may be expected to be implemented without invoking the governance process established to minimize cybersecurity risk. Although it is expected that the CISO will collaborate with the CIO on establishing a baseline for cybersecurity architecture, as long as the CIO is dedicated to supporting business mission, resiliency due to diligence is typically the responsibility of the technology infrastructure team. The CISO should have an oversight and testing function from the perspective of cybersecurity, but would not be expected to design high availability architecture.

The example of resilience calls attention to the fact that every technology architecture contains within it a security architecture. Availability is one of the security triad of requirements: confidentiality, integrity, and availability. It follows that a security architecture exists whether or not it is planned. But if a security architecture is planned, the casualty is less likely to be availability than confidentiality or integrity. Diligent attention to security control design will produce better management controls than waiting to see what capabilities emerged from technology's efforts to meet business requirements. Where enterprise technology is architected and designed to be secure, it is possible to publish technical security configuration standards that allow engineers to make sure that they are in lock-step with policy in their every day job function. Where this link is lacking, engineers often comment that they feel like they work in the wild west, constantly haunted by both real and potential ambushes at every turn on the trail.

Figure 4.20 demonstrates an exemplar security architecture illustrated as an overlay on the technology architecture in Figure 4.19. It follows terminology

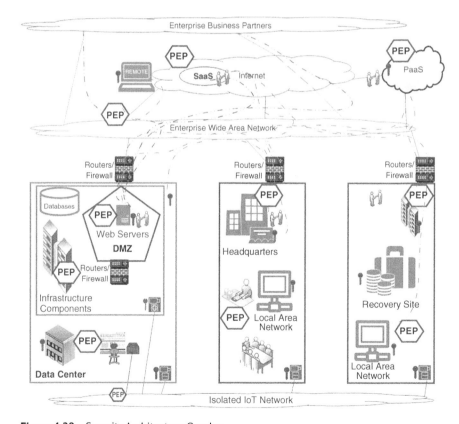

Figure 4.20 Security Architecture Overlay

published in the NIST Zero Trust Standard (NIST SP 800-207, 2020). It shows that the enterprise has established basic network connectivity that is controlled at each location by firewall technology to limit the data transfer protocols in both internal and external data flow. Over the years, technologies marketed under the term *firewall* have incorporated policies that examine not only IP addresses, but attributes of both the source and destination devices. So the *Routers/Firewalls* objects in the diagram should also be interpreted to provide the ability for network operations to monitor that data flow through these devices, albeit not the ability to read it. Note that some networks have more security controls than others. The network at the bottom is secured not by firewalls, but by not being accessible from any physical location other than the data center and backup site. This control choice is based on the fact that the network is only used to access physical equipment at those locations, such as doors and ventilation systems. That equipment is protected with physical badges and monitored with cameras, also hosted on that isolated network.

Dot-dashed lines in the security diagram indicate that the information within the data flow is encrypted. Handshake icons indicate that the network destination is authenticated upon connection, and potentially also the source. Key icons indicate that the connection requires authentication of the device as belonging to an authorized enterprise asset group and also may be used to facilitate data encryption. Security configuration on these devices is typically managed with security software agents that also detect and alert on known malware and vulnerabilities.

The level of network security thus far described is a *control plane*, required for enforcing standards for network traffic flow. A control plane routes all network connections to a given location to *policy enforcement points* wherein users are required to present at least two factors of authentication and be checked for entitlements before being allowed to connect to an actual resource, such as a business application or a file share. The network is configured to prevent these resources from connecting to each other unless they have an established preauthorized path on a virtual *data plane*. Network monitoring tools are capable of detecting traffic that deviates from such established paths and should be configured to alert where deviations are identified.

Standards thus dictate very specific technology requirements to protect resources with multiple controls of varying strength, depending on the risk appetite associated with the underlying data. Note that some resources in the diagram reside in cloud environments, such as SaaS vendors, and some of these may connect to the enterprise data center and cloud workloads in support of business application data flow. These connections will typically traverse the internet and rely on handshakes and keys for authentication and encryption, and may also be supplemented with device authentication.

By contrast, data planes are implemented by software. The zero trust architecture plus fine-grained application entitlements protects the data confidentiality integrity, but security architectures must also be engineering for availability. Redundant network connections can help guarantee access to data, but cannot guarantee that the data itself will be available and resilient to software-based attacks. Data planes are designs for software resilience. They chart how data moves around the network and typically have requirements for:

1) Resilience thresholds
2) Static analysis of resilience capabilities and flaws
3) Dynamic analysis of system behavior under realistic disruptive conditions (Curtis, 2019, p. 5)

Resilience thresholds rely on a scope target and a time target. The scope is a specification of the systems that support transactions or services that are critical to sustain the enterprise mission, and for each system, the set of components and data that need to be available to resume operation after an outage. This is the recovery point objective. The time target is the maximum time a system can be unavailable before the outage impacts enterprise mission, namely the recovery time objective. Where recovery point and time objective can be reliably specified, these provide adequate resilience thresholds. Static analysis of the recovery point supports verification of control correctness, whereas dynamic analysis of the system under stress supports validation of control effectiveness.

The idea is to make sure the recovery point is archived often enough not to lose data and that the recovery time be as minimal as possible. These requirements have driven the development of architectures that maintain two copies of the same database that are synchronized to within milliseconds. The availability of a complete data copy, in combination with multiple redundant software servers and dynamic routing of users to ensure network bandwidth availability, is called a high availability architecture because the backup is not a standby, but also is actively serving users, earning it the label *hot-hot*.

Figure 4.21 is a diagram of a high availability architecture. It provides a solution for system availability in the face of multiple types of negatively impacting events. The dynamic network routing has features to detect rapidly fired packets that are not user traffic patterns and thereby protects against network denial of service. There is synchronous replication from one database to the other, and the complete copy of the database ensures that if either database goes down, the other will have all but a few milliseconds worth of transactions. The redundant web servers ensure that regional disasters like floods and fires will not impact availability. The recovery time objective is a few milliseconds. The recovery point objective may seem to be the same, because if the primary database goes down, the standby database that survives will hold all the data except that which is a few milliseconds old. However, this architecture is an availability control only for access to the data, not the data itself. If a threat actor attack is able to compromise data in

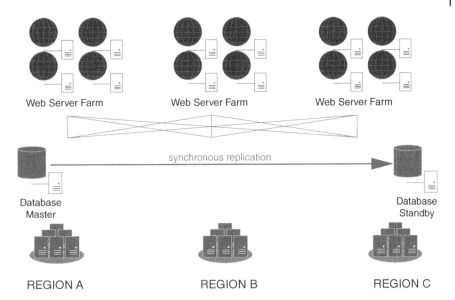

Figure 4.21 High Availability Architecture

the primary database (e.g., changing all account balances at the database level), the data corruption would of course be automatically replicated to its standby and both data sets would be equally inaccurate. Therefore even this type of availability architecture should have a backup plan.

One way to think about data plane resilience is to understand that software security is a small part of a much larger global problem of poor software quality (Krasner, 2022). If data flow is part of the software requirements in a secure software development lifecycle standard and not bolted on just prior to or after deployment, then it would be tested in quality assurance and validated once it moved to production. Any resilience implemented and tested in the service of cybersecurity will have a positive impact on software quality and vice versa. The extent to which an application support team can fully specify how its data flows around the network is also the extent to which zero trust network monitoring can be tuned to identify and disconnect unauthorized data access by an application service account.

Like the technology architecture diagram of Figure 4.19, security architecture diagrams like Figures 4.20 and 4.21 are used by new staff and/or assessment evaluators to orient themselves to an unfamiliar technology landscape. They also function as a quick reference for all technology staff engaged in updating infrastructure or software. Technology staff need this reference because if any of the security standard configurations are not observed, the environment undergoing change may be compromised and used as a launch point for threat vectors comprised of unauthorized data flow. Where a security architecture diagram does not exist, it can be a mystery for even experienced technology staff to attempt to operate within even well-defined security constraints. Social media catering to software engineers often contain remarks like they have to *hack away at the security with a machete* in order to get their jobs done.

4.5 Procedures

Once standards are established, those responsible for implementation are held to them. Just as standards support both the policy and process levels of the control hierarchy above them, procedures support not just standards, but may directly support policy and process as well.

However, given all the technologies that comprise security architecture and the data and network integrations between them, it can be very difficult to know how to comply with standards. Even if it seems conceptually obvious how to comply, it can be difficult to create corresponding technical configurations with a high level of confidence. Success is not just reliant on training and skill. It takes years of practical experience to navigate through ever-changing technology products and tuning them to perform the functions for which they were acquired, and nothing else. For those who have worked in technology for more than a year, it is very obvious that a new hire previously unfamiliar with the enterprise security architecture cannot be immediately effective in its operation. To remediate this issue, the same engineers who created the standards are often tasked to write procedures to fill in the gap between the standards and the experience necessary to implement them correctly and effectively.

Procedures are step-by-step activity descriptions in the form of detailed manuals and programs that instruct staff on how to fulfill the control responsibilities within their job function. A person executing a cybersecurity procedure is operating a control. By the fact that their role includes a procedure, their activity is integrated into the governance structure of the enterprise. Procedures maintain stable and secure configuration through change. They are used for ensuring that standards are followed and for training new personnel.

Procedures should be documented at a level of detail so granular that staff who are new to the enterprise can follow them without asking any questions. This is difficult to do in all cases, so procedures are often accompanied by videos that demonstrate how to perform the task. Of course, stopping in the middle of a task to watch a video increases the time it takes to execute the procedure, so that is why it is preferable that they stand on their own.

Procedures may also include the configuration and operation of automated workflow identified within process documents. In some cases, procedure is even built into a system, so that the person executing the procedure is given instruction one step at a time as they make their way through it. In that sense, they can be like an online form one uses to pay with a credit card. You do not have to learn it to follow it, you just read as you go along. They can also be hybrid, where there are easy-to-follow instructions supported with automation that minimizes the chance a person will make a mistake in data entry.

For example, security monitoring is typically performed by a SecOps analyst following a step-by-step instruction to review and respond to security alerts. Procedures are needed because a new cybersecurity analyst may not know very much about the environment and might be distracted by the variety of data and the number of buttons with options to view different screens. Moreover, it may not be possible to directly supervise a person 24 hours a day, so starting them on an easy procedure is a productive way for them to learn while unattended.

Figure 4.10 includes reference to security monitoring at the process level. Figure 4.22 provides an example of a security monitoring procedure that supports the associated process. The procedure instructs the analyst to be very focused, just to look at a screen and select the highest priority alert in the queue at the top of the screen. The selection results in display of detail corresponding to the alert. There may be a lot of detail, but again, they are instructed to be narrowly focused. It says to ascertain just two data items, specifically, the application it concerns and the alert source (i.e., device or network IP address). The next instruction is to search an application registry for the application data owner and asset inventory for the device or the network owner of that alert source. It labels that data "the alert context." The next step is to extract the priority that was automatically assigned to the alert from its context. If the priority

The Security Operations Center Analyst:
1. Select the highest priority alert in the queue
2. Ascertain context:
   2.a. app or data in alert, search application registry for app/data owner
   2.b. device or IP in alert, search asset inventory for device and/or network owner
3. If the priority is "critical", convene call with supervisor and app/data/device/net owners
4. Use data in alert to distinguish between anomaly and intrusion:
   3.a. if intrusion or cannot tell, make a note in the log asking supervisor for instruction
   3.b. anomaly, place alert on list for end-of-shift call with app/data/device/net owners

Figure 4.22 New SecOps Staff Monitoring Procedure

is "critical," then even a new person is empowered immediately to convene a call with the application data device owners that they have identified in the context to learn from the experts about why this anomaly is happening in the environment in the impacted technology; this allows the supervisor to deal only with alerts that have not been classified as anomalies in an obvious way. A new person could figure it out from the data on the screen presented by their systems without worrying about missing a critical alert. In this example, because the new analyst is quickly picking up the high priority alerts from the queue, the remaining ones are lower priority and can be scanned periodically by more experienced operators that will more easily pick up on the difference between anomaly and intrusion. A new analyst will also get a chance to analyze these lower priority alerts when no high alerts are above it in the queue. Further procedure steps would assist the new analyst in learning how to use additional data fields and communications to try to distinguish between anomaly and intrusion.

Just as the Security Operations Center analyst is screening for threat actors coming into internal systems, there are physical guards at the gate screening unauthorized people accessing the building. It is common for them to follow a procedure that requires them to ask every potential visitor who comes to the gate for identification as well as the reason for their visit. Visitors may be required to identify which staff member they intend to visit, so the guard can use that information to search for a visitor appointment. If the visit is expected, the guard would ask for identification, take a photo of the individual, and the staff should be ready to either show up at the gate and escort the visitor in, or maybe the guard is authorized to give the visitor a pass to get to the elevator for the floor where that staff member is located. Figure 4.23 shows an example of such a procedure. In the example, if the visitor is not expected, then the guard is instructed to explain to the visitor that they cannot get in the building unless some staff member authorizes them to access the building for a specific reason in advance of the visit. If that visitor goes away without staff authorization, then that guard still has procedure steps to follow. The procedure contains instruction on how to save a photo of the individual's failed physical access attempt in case there emerges a pattern of similar threats in the

The guard at the gate:
1. Ask visitor for identification and staff they are visiting
2. Search building access system for visitor appointment
   2.a. If visit is expected, notify staff in appointment
   2.b. If not, explain to the visitor that staff must call security to authorize admission
3. If no staff authorization, save visitor ID and photo in log

Figure 4.23 Gate Guard Procedure

future. So the guard at the gate is the physical equivalent of the Security Operations Center analyst, with the intruder at the doorstep of the network.

Procedures are the most ubiquitous type of management control. Everywhere you look in any kind of enterprise, you see people operating controls. Frequently, these include procedures in organizations other than security that are critical to effective cybersecurity risk management. An example is found in most user service desks. The procedure in Figure 4.24 is an example service desk procedure. The service desk individual following the procedure is instructed to ask the caller to identify themselves. The procedure is facilitated by an online system wherein the service desk can look up the person. A system form provides a few alternatives for the lookup. The procedure includes very specific questions to ask in a specific order and corresponding form data entry using the answers to the questions. The questions are ordered to obtain the identity of the caller in the smallest number of steps possible, which ensures the timeliness and quality of the authentication process. Once the identity provided is confirmed to be a valid user, a verification code is sent to the email or phone user contact information associated with the identity and previously stored in the online system. The same code is displayed to the service desk and the service desk asks the caller to recite the code.

Notice how step 7 refers to the user record in the system (i.e., "user first name"), but it continues the practice established in steps 1–6 of referring to the person on the phone as "caller." Procedures must always be worded carefully, so that the service desk can distinguish between someone who has not been properly identified and someone who is authorized. The caller cannot be referred to as a user

Service Desk personnel will follow these instructions:
1. Receive phone call for assistance. Request caller's first and last name. Ask the caller if they are a customer.
2. Type caller's first and last names into the corresponding search screen fields on the Department Identity and Access Security System (DIASS). If the caller is a customer, select the button to the right of the word "CUSTOMER." Select "SEARCH".
3. Matching records will appear in a search result table under the search form. If more than one record is in the table, ask the caller for more information with which to select the correct record.
    a. If the caller is a customer, ask: "What service do you use?"
    b. If the caller is not a customer, ask: "What department do you work for?"
4. Select the answer to question 3 from the "Department" dropdown list.
5. The list of matching records will again appear in the table below. If there are still multiple, ask the caller their middle name or address to find a unique record.
6. If no record in the identity management system corresponds to the caller, refer the caller to their sales associate or supervisor and politely end the call. STOP HERE
7. Select the **SEND** button under the user first name, then ask the caller to recite the code sent.
8. If the caller cannot recite the code, refer the caller to their sales associate or supervisor and politely end the call. STOP HERE

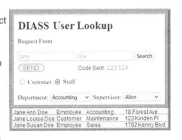

Figure 4.24 Service Desk Procedure

unless and until the authentication has successfully been completed. Receipt of the correct verification code allows the procedure to continue and otherwise it ends. Either way, all activity executed in the procedure is recorded and logged by the system. Such procedures help ensure that customer information is not unintentionally provided to imposters, as well as provides an audit trail to be used in the event of a report of identity theft.

Even highly skilled people often need procedures. For example, when the activity is not performed very often and the person most familiar with it may be unavailable when it is required, such as during routine annual refresh of certificate or encryption keys (i.e., a control meant to ensure that, if an APT had accessed them undetected, then at least after some point in time, they would no longer work). Such procedures are often critical controls in cases wherein successful outcome is predicated on the procedure being followed to the letter, such as in creating a chain of custody for cyberforensic evidence.

Procedures are invaluable in situations where the task is not performed often enough for people to memorize it. For example, consider that the *Technology Workflow/Cybersecurity Overlay* in Figure 3.16 represents a process that is routinely followed by technology operations and only occasionally supplemented with the SecOps activities in the Cybersecurity Overlay that appears in lighter lines and fonts. That is, the *Investigation* step at the lower center of the figure is often the same at the start of a cyberattack detection as any other technology problem with no apparent solution. As described in Section 3.3, engineers and administrators skilled in system configuration and log analysis would look at activity logs and examine the system(s) that are suspected to be the source. The disturbance may present itself in different forms depending on its source.

In any such investigation, engineers would be expected to run standard diagnostics, or system "health checks," that could reveal a malfunctioning component or a runaway process consuming scarce resources. These may include but are not limited to:

- Analysis of network traffic to identify patterns in dropped data packets or ports unexpectedly blocked.
- Application data flow tests that may reveal failing network handshakes where encryption keys must be compatible to complete a connection.
- Operating system resource consumption, such as disk full conditions or inability to allocate memory.
- Web server, application server, and database server error log messages or unexpectedly idle server processes.
- Recent modification of resource permissions, such as file permissions, encryption keys, or database connection strings used by unattended application processes.
- Comparison of hash values of critical files to a known benign version previously archived for this purpose.

In the absence of standard diagnostic procedures like these assigned to specific job roles, it is very difficult to know that they have all been simultaneously checked. Even where the procedures exist, if the person who was assigned one of these roles did not write the procedure and was assigned to perform it and had not performed it before, then it would likely not be performed quickly without access to the step-by-step documentation for the procedure.

Moreover, if in the process of such an investigation, a cybersecurity incident was confirmed, then those logs and configurations would have to be immediately preserved for fear a threat actor's next steps would be to try to remove evidence of the incident. It is now common for logs to be copied to secure locations automatically, but there are quicker ways to check for negative system impact than to utilize activity logs. As highlighted in the last item of the list above, there should also be a procedure to check which of the critical files in a system has been modified within the duration of an incident. There may be thousands of logs, but because a threat actor typically impersonates an existing user, the traces of threat actor activity in logs may appear normal. Without identification of which data may have been modified, it will be difficult to trace the threat actor's vector or assess the potential impact.

Therefore, once the health checks confirm that the problem is likely to be a security incident, a procedure to preserve forensic evidence related to the event should be executed immediately. These will include activities such as identifying, assembling, and preserving evidence in a manner that can be verified to have taken place at the time of the incident.

Such near real-time preservation of that evidence is an essential component of any cybersecurity risk management strategy. It should include, but not be limited to:

- Which witnesses to assemble to observe and/or participate in the evidence preservation process. For example, one may supplement technology team with a legal and/or cyberforensics firm to be on retainer for this purpose, so they can testify to the integrity of the data if needed at a future date.
- How to digitally fingerprint data using a cryptographic hash value that can later be used to verify that it is the same set of data present on the systems that were compromised in the cyberattack.
- On what storage medium to copy both the fingerprinted data and its hash value in such a manner that the integrity of both files will be retrievable at some unknown future date (i.e., a technology device that is expected to be in production operation for decades).
- Where to duplicate the storage medium onto an isolated environment where it is safe for investigators to continue to examine the copy while the original is safely archived.
- How to demonstrate the storage medium chain of custody from the incident to some future need to produce it, while preventing the storage medium from damage, tampering, or theft. For example, place the storage medium in escrow or an auditable safe deposit box.

1. Assemble Investigation Team
   Who: SecOps   *How:*
   a. Call Forensics Partner at 555-1212, provide Customer #528453, request investigator dispatch to war room
   b. Start online meeting with crisis management team, service desk, and war room, record session
   c. Login to <u>Crisis Management System</u>, at top left of dashboard, select "Convene Team." A pop-up window will prompt for meeting location, paste online meeting link into meeting location, followed by address of war room. Select "Send."
   d. Order 100 GB USB drive and send service desk to retrieve and deliver to war room
   e. Create new site in secure cloud storage
   f. Send representative to war room.
2. Collect Data
   Who: OS Admin *How:*
   a. Join online meeting with service desk and war room, start screen share
   b. Stop the operating system(s) of impacted machine(s).
   c. Unmount the disk drives from the machine(s)
   d. Create new virtual machine in isolated network with elastic disk capacity. For each disk drive from step c:
      • Mount the disk drive on new VM
      • Create archive in most commonly compatible operating system format, e.g. tar –cf DiskA. tar DiskA
      • Create hash sum of archive file, e.g. sha256sum --b Disk-A.tar >Disk-A.hash
      • Copy both archive and hash file from the VM to SecOps share
3. Preserve Evidence
   Who: SecOps   *How:*
   a. Copy all files provided by Admin to SecOps in step 2.b. to USB Drive and to secure cloud storage site.
   b. Login to <u>Crisis Management System</u>, at bottom left of dashboard, select "Print Escrow Label" and print to label printer.
   c. Wrap USB device in tamper-proof materials and securely affix two labels.
   d. Arrange pickup from war room by Delivery Vendor, insure and provide detailed package tracking and certification of delivery.
4. Manage Investigation

Figure 4.25   First Steps of a Forensics Procedure

Figure 4.25 provides example initial steps for an evidence preservation procedure. It includes exact references to systems procured and preconfigured for the purpose of crisis management. It includes specific technology tasks and commands to be executed to preserve evidence. It also includes references to stocks of resources like USB drives and secure packaging materials required to establish a chain of custody once evidence has been collected. It also ensures that the same evidence is simultaneously delivered to the incident investigation team to support efficient analysis of available evidence.

Figure 4.25 also indicates that after the evidence is preserved, the process of managing the investigation continues. The investigation will include activities related to examining and interpreting the evidence with confidence, so if the same examination is done at a later date from the preserved version, then the later investigation will reach the same conclusions with respect to evidence.

4.6   Guidelines

At the bottom of the control hierarchy are guidelines. *Guidelines* are suggestions for following security policy, sometimes including several alternatives for activity that will result in compliance. They are not mandatory even within a department. Although optional, they are often furnished to provide the target audience with options on how to comply with process, policies, standards, and/or procedures.

Guidelines are in some sense admissions that there is one thing a governance process cannot predict and control human behavior. Although the behavior of computing devices is generally predictable (with the exception of generative artificial intelligence), humans left to their own devices may miss the point of a control and devise a behavior for compliance that inadvertently neglects its legislative intent.

For example, many organizations allow users to choose any password they like that meets complexity standards, so users may devise any method they like when they are actually creating a new password. However, to influence this behavior, there may be established guidelines for how to choose a secure password. For example, suppose the standard for passwords is set to 10 characters that include at least one upper case, one lower case, one number, and one special character. The number of combinations of possible strings to use for a password limits these requirements to those that are very hard to guess. However, users persist in very predictable methodologies for choosing passwords based on parameters that they think are known only to them, such as their pet's names or favorite color. A threat actor who targets a specific user will quickly assemble the data on these proclivities and use them to create string combinations that are highly probable to be selected as passwords by the target user. Although there may be compensating controls like multifactor authentication that reduce the risk of password guessing attacks, where users are targeted, there are espionage capabilities that will defeat those as well. So choosing a hard password is still a baseline control worth establishing guidelines to strengthen authentication controls.

Figure 4.26 is an example guideline for choosing a secure password. It reflects the enterprise standards to use a required 12-character password composed of numbers, special characters, and both upper and lowercase letters. It instructs the user to think of a phrase that is private, readily recognizable only to themselves and that they will remember with pleasure. Using that phrase as a base, the guidance is to use the words in the phrase to turn the phrase into a string of characters that meets the length requirement. With that accomplished, it instructs the user to substitute numbers or special characters for some of the letters in the nonsense string. The result is a password that is easy for the user to remember, but difficult for others to guess.

Publishing such guidelines raises user awareness of their own thought process in making decisions on how to comply with security policy. While guidelines are not a reliable management control, they are an attempt to provide some control coverage in the gray area where automated controls cannot constrain user behavior. Therefore, guidelines are often included in mandatory training and also published on posters and other awareness reminders, so that users cannot deny that they know if they follow them, they will be more likely to be compliant with policy than not.

Choose Strong Passwords!

- For accounts at work and wherever you use your credit card or other financial data online, use different passwords for each site and choose passwords based on phrases that (i) remind you of the account and (ii) make you smile:

```
I like to swim in the summer
```

- Condense the phrase to 12 or more characters:

```
Iltsitsummer
```

- Substitute at least 2 of the or more characters with uppercase characters, numbers, and symbols that remind you of the originals:

```
|12$i+SU33e&
```

- The resulting password is easy to remember but very hard to guess!

Figure 4.26 Password Selection Guideline

Where policy dictates that all staff are required to follow policy and standards and procedures, making correct choices with respect to secure behavior is typically emphasized in a legally binding employee code of conduct or contractor agreement. The reason guidelines are important is because most staff do not understand the technical details of how cybersecurity policy is implemented. So even if they agree with high-level risk appetite statements and try to abide by the code of conduct in their day-to-day activities, they often do not have the capacity to make conscious decisions on how their actions influence risk. Potential insider threats can sometimes be distinguished from those who are willing participants in the security program by monitoring their behavior with respect to such choices.

In contrast, what enterprise cybersecurity guidelines *are not* is *popular* advice on complying with a control. They are not duplicating information in industry practices or trying to get users to understand how the security program should be managed and how all information should be protected. They are not the same as advice from industry standards or regulations on compliance. Enterprise guidelines may cover some aspects of these topics, such as advising users on how to spot email phishing attempts, but they do not just republish the exact same language downloaded from some authoritative source like CISA Cybersecurity Best Practices (CISA, 2023). These sites inform those who write the guidelines, but they typically customize them in a manner that connects them to the enterprise and to their obligations to contribute to enterprise security. In the case of phishing training, a guideline would typically contain a screenshot of what a phish email would look like if it appeared in their own accounts. It would not be presented as

How Enterprise Cybersecurity Guidelines Help

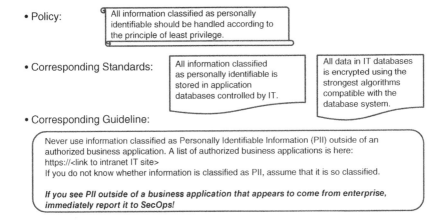

- Policy: All information classified as personally identifiable should be handled according to the principle of least privilege.

- Corresponding Standards: All information classified as personally identifiable is stored in application databases controlled by IT. / All data in IT databases is encrypted using the strongest algorithms compatible with the database system.

- Corresponding Guideline:

Never use information classified as Personally Identifiable Information (PII) outside of an authorized business application. A list of authorized business applications is here: https://<link to intranet IT site>
If you do not know whether information is classified as PII, assume that it is so classified.

If you see PII outside of a business application that appears to come from enterprise, immediately report it to SecOps!

Figure 4.27 Data Protection Guideline

selected examples of professional advice on in general how to follow best practices and security.

Figure 4.27 shows an example of how a guideline is used to support policies and standards. The policy is that all information classified as Personally Identifiable Information (PII) should be handled according to the principle of least privilege. The corresponding standards are requirements for infrastructure configuration required to restrict data access to business application technology. All information classified as personally identifiable is stored in application databases controlled by IT, and all of those databases store data in an encrypted format. Combined with least privilege entitlements to application data by job function, these standards should ensure that no one see the data in an unencrypted format other than application users. So the requirement for least privilege access to PII becomes a task for the database administrators and the application administrators to implement and enforce with automation. The corresponding guideline then advises the users never to use information classified as PII outside of an authorized business application. A list of authorized business applications is included by reference. The guideline further stipulates that if a user does not know whether some information is classified, then they should just assume it is PII.

The bottom of Figure 4.27 further advises users that, if they see enterprise PII in a context other than an authorized business application, they should report this immediately as a security incident. Such advice typically accompanies guidelines and creates a force multiplier for detecting security policy violations.

Another potential force multiplier that often accompanies guidelines is to *fail safe*. In this case fail safe advice might be to delete data if you think that is the right thing to do to protect it from misuse. However, this is not as common as the *report an incident* addendum because if there was an actual cybersecurity incident wherein a threat actor intentionally exposed the PII observed by the user, then deleting it could destroy valuable forensic evidence.

Regardless of the type, control documents should be organized so that references between them are transparent, and someone engaged in a control activity understands their place in the hierarchy. Though some degree of confidentially should be applied to the more detailed security configuration information, generally, compliance with policy is easier for everyone where the principle of open design should be applied to the control environment at all levels.

References

Canavan, R. (2014). Process of the Month – Joiners, Movers and Leavers. IT Asset Management Review (26 March). https://www.itassetmanagement.net/2014/03/26/process-month-joiners-movers-leavers-process/ (accessed 08 May 2023).

CISA (2023). Cybersecurity Best Practices. Cybersecurity & Infrastructure Security Agency. https://www.cisa.gov/topics/cybersecurity-best-practices (accessed 09 May 2023).

Curtis, B. (2019). How do You Measure Software Resilience? Consortium for Information & Software Quality™ (CISQ™). https://www.it-cisq.org/cisq-files/pdf/How-Do-You-Measure-Software-Resilience-CISQ.pdf (accessed 08 May 2023).

Department of Justice (1986). Computer Fraud and Abuse Act 1986, 9-48.000. US Department of Justice. https://www.justice.gov/jm/jm-9-48000-computer-fraud (accessed 08 May 2023).

IETF (n.d.). Mission Statement. Internet Engineering Task Force. https://www.ietf.org/about/introduction/ (accessed 08 May 2023).

ISACA (2019). *COBIT 2019 Design Guide, Designing an Information and Technology Governance Solution*, ISACA, www.isaca.org.

ISO/IEC 27001 (2022). *Information Security, Cybersecurity and Privacy Protection – Information Security Management Systems – Requirements*. International Organization for Standardization/International Electrotechnical Commission. www.iso.org.

ISO/IEC 27002 (2022*). Information Security, Cybersecurity and Privacy Protection – Information Security Controls*. International Organization for Standardization/International Electrotechnical Commission. www.iso.org.

Krasner, H. (2022). The Cost of Poor Software Quality in the US. Consortium for Information & Software Quality™ (CISQ™). https://www.it-cisq.org/wp-content/uploads/sites/6/2022/11/CPSQ-Report-Nov-22-2.pdf (accessed 08 May 2023).

NCSC (1985). Trusted Computer System Evaluation Criteria, US Department of Defense, 5200.28-STD. National Computer Security Center. https://csrc.nist.gov/csrc/media/publications/conference-paper/1998/10/08/proceedings-of-the-21st-nissc-1998/documents/early-cs-papers/dod85.pdf (accessed 08 May 2023).

NIST (2013). Security and Privacy Controls for Federal Information Systems and Organizations. NIST Special Publication 800-53, Revision 5, April 2013. National Institute of Standards and Technology.https://nvlpubs.nist.gov/nistpubs/SpecialPublications/NIST.SP.800-53r4.pdf (accessed 08 May 2023).

NIST SP 800-207 (2020). Zero Trust Architecture Standard. National Institute of Standards and Technology. https://nvlpubs.nist.gov/nistpubs/SpecialPublications/NIST.SP.800-207.pdf (accessed 08 May 2023).

NIST SP 800-218 (2022). Secure Software Development Framework (SSDF) version 1.1: Recommendations for Mitigating the Risk of Software Vulnerabilities. National Institute of Standards and Technology. https://nvlpubs.nist.gov/nistpubs/SpecialPublications/NIST.SP.800-218.pdf (accessed 08 May 2023).

PCI (2022). PCI Data Security Standard. Payment Card Industry. https://blog.pcisecuritystandards.org/pci-dss-v4-0-resource-hub (accessed 08 May 2023).

SWIFT (2022). Customer Security Controls Framework. Society for Worldwide Interbank Financial Telecommunication. https://www.swift.com/news-events/webinars/customer-security-controls-framework (accessed 08 May 2023).

Synopsis (n.d.). How to Leverage ASOC. https://www.synopsys.com/software-integrity/resources/ebooks/manage-software-risk-with-asoc.html, https://creativecommons.org/licenses/by-sa/3.0/legalcode (accessed 08 May 2023).

5

Assessments

The journey from risk appetite to security operations is complicated and thus often plagued with loose ends that may create gaps in compliance with enterprise policy as well as industry and regulatory standards. Therefore, a CISO should have some kind of a feedback loop to provide assurance that the cybersecurity policies, processes, standards, and procedures (PPSP) actually resulted in the risk appetite reduction that policy is designed to produce. In some organizations, the assurance is achieved with a formal risk assessment led by the CRO wherein each business process owner compares their own operations to enterprise PPSPs. Because it is performed by the organization under review, this is referred to as a *Risk and Control Self Assessment* (RCSA). Organizations may also conduct or contract *regulatory and/or best practice assessments* that compare their cybersecurity program to some well-defined standards like HIPAA or NIST CSF. Another assessment methodology is a "*pentest*," an amalgam of the words "penetration" and "test." It is a test by cybersecurity professionals trained in the tactics of threat actors. They scan enterprise systems for vulnerabilities in public-facing sites and if any are found, exploit the vulnerable to gain access to internal systems; that is, to *penetrate* them. A more formal assessment is the one by independent evaluators who analyze risk in the context of PPSPs, and also collect tangible artifacts of the cybersecurity program to identify both vulnerabilities and control evidence gaps. Where these evaluators are *verifiably* independent of the enterprise, the assessment may properly be called an *audit*.

No matter what type of assessment is done, the basic idea of an assessment is to see if enterprise cyber defense is able to control the technology used to support its mission and strategy and does not let that control fall into the hands of threat actors who would damage the mission, destroy the operation, and/or misuse enterprise resources. A cybersecurity assessment is generically defined by the systemigram in Figure 5.1. The mainstay of the systemigram reads: *An assessment evaluates objectives that dictate scope that correspond to an approach that produces an opinion.*

Stepping Through Cybersecurity Risk Management: A Systems Thinking Approach, First Edition. Jennifer L. Bayuk.
© 2024 John Wiley & Sons, Inc. Published 2024 by John Wiley & Sons, Inc.
Companion website: www.wiley.com/go/STCRM

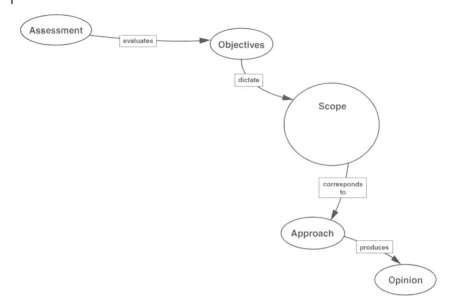

Figure 5.1 Assessment Mainstay

An assessment can last 90 seconds or be continuous. In the spectrum of the different ways one may embark on risk assessment, the 90-second assessment is at one end, an internally motivated, limited scope, time-constrained effort to avoid an active threat. At the opposite end of the spectrum is an industry or regulatory standard assessment.

I use the term *90-second* assessment for situations where an expert is put on the spot for an opinion. These occur when there is some event in the news like a ransomware attack or a new insidious malware and the CISO is asked by management, "Could that happen to us?" That question becomes an assessment objective. The objective is a statement of the thing to be proved or disproved in the course of an assessment. It is usually a question of whether or not a given systems environment meets some security objective. Phrased as an objective, the question, "Could that happen to us?" would be worded as, "The enterprise is not vulnerable to the cyberattack described in the news story." The opinion is expected to be *true, false,* or perhaps *likely true,* with some estimate of probability. For this reason, assessment objectives are often stated in terms of *assurance.* Many reviewers, especially auditors, prefer to state the objective as *providing assurance* that a system of interest is secure rather than to state an opinion that a system of interest unequivocally meets a security objective. This is because of the potential liability for falsely guaranteeing a system to be secure, especially when there are known gaps in control evidence. It also reflects the well-known fact that zero days may be lurking, so a system that seems secure today may not seem to be tomorrow.

An assessment scope is directly derived from the objective. In the 90-second example, it is the enterprise systems that use the technology identified in the news report. That said, scope sometimes changes in the course of an assessment. For example, if the technology under review is not completely known at the time the objective is set and the set of underlying technology to be reviewed turns out to be larger than originally thought, the scope expands. This situation is disparagingly referred to as "scope creep." However, as long as the objective remains the same, this situation is not an expansion of scope, it is a correction of the original misconception. If it was incorrectly described in a statement of work, it should be corrected, or the objective should be modified. Thus, the process of defining any given assessment is often a small project in itself.

It can also happen that scope seems reduced in the course of an assessment. Figure 5.2 reveals more of the assessment systemigram to show that an evaluator develops an approach for performing the assessment. It also shows that those who operate the processes in scope and/or manage its technology, or *stakeholders*, must be engaged to participate in the assessment. If stakeholders establish constraints on the approach planned by the evaluator, these may reduce the capability of the approach to fully cover scope of the review. Where this occurs, the scope does not change, just the approach. Though it may be easier to reword the approach of the assessment than to acknowledge that it may not be possible to meet the objective. Unless the objective is reworded, constraints do not affect scope per se; they affect only approach. So the opinion will generally be hedged with the admission that the

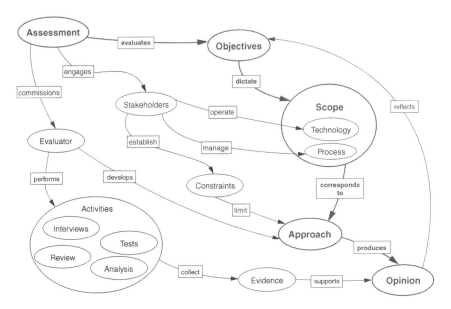

Figure 5.2 Assessment Systemigram

evaluator was unable to complete a comprehensive examination, but that generally does not prevent the assessment from being completed.

Many evaluators faced with conflicting constraints and objectives write a very detailed "statement of work" that skips the definition of scope and instead defines an approach that takes into account constraints and ignores the original objective. Clients that sign off on the "statement of work" tacitly agree that the full review objective may not be met. In this way, many people confuse approach with scope. The tendency exists because people like to define the scope as something that they *can* review rather than acknowledging that there are constraints in developing an approach that may threaten the review objective. This is especially true when time is short. Evaluator resources are not infinite. The objectives of many types of security assessments may only be met in an asymptotic progression. Professional auditors call this a "level of assurance" (AICPA 2015). However, it is always more appropriate and professional to rewrite the review objective than to confuse scope with approach.

An assessment approach comprises activities that cover the scope in a way that meets the objective of the review, given the constraints. All reviews are in some sense constrained by the time available to the evaluator to complete the review. There are usually alternative sets of activities that cover the scope and objective. The idea is to find the set hampered by the fewest constraints. In the 90-second example, the setting in which the question is asked is typically in a regularly scheduled meeting on some other topic with perhaps a dozen people in attendance. The CISO can think for a bit and glance down and make a few notes while deciding what to say, but the truth is, there are about 90 seconds within which an assessment has to occur before people get impatient. That introduces a constraint. The appropriate options are "yes," and "no." A CISO can sometimes do this because they typically have a full understanding of the scope of the potential attack surface and the extent to which controls that could deflect the specified attack are in place. Their approach is to exercise expert judgement that draws on all the patterns of attack and response with which they are experienced. However, the time constraint may result in the response, "we probably are, but my staff is running (or will run) a scenario and I will get back to you shortly." This is a hedged opinion that serves to complete the 90-second security review and replace it with an assessment based on evidence gathered using a scenario analysis approach.

There are as many types of security assessments as there are different combinations of objective, scope, constraint, approach, and result. The variables in any review are by no means limited to the examples presented herein. The spectrum on which assessments diverge varies widely within these common parameters. Figure 5.3 demonstrates just how flexible a security assessment can be. Assessments can have objectives that are business driven or technology driven. They can have

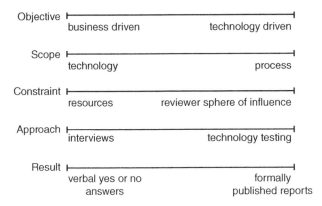

Figure 5.3 Assessment Spectrum

scope that is defined by technology or process. They can have constraints ranging from time and resources to evaluator sphere of influence. (*Evaluator sphere of influence cannot be underestimated as a constraint because the data gathering required for a typical security review often crosses organizational and even company boundaries.*) Approaches can range from interviews to technology testing. Opinions can range from verbal yes or no answers to formal published reports.

5.1   Standards Adherence

These may be self-assessments, outsourced assessments, or formal audits by internal or external auditors, a certification team, or a regulatory authority. When performed by a regulator, they facilitate oversight by regulatory bodies who are appointed by law to protect the interest of the community served by a specific industry. For example, the Federal Financial Institutions Examination Council has published *Cybersecurity Assessment Tool* (FFIEC-CAT), a set of cybersecurity control requirements that correspond to the regulations governing the US financial industry (FFIEC 2017). Similarly, the US Department of Health and Human Services, Health Insurance Portability and Accountability Act (HIPAA) has published a *Security Rule*, a list of safeguard requirements that must be followed by health care provider, health plan providers, and health care clearinghouses (NIST 800-66 2022).

In fact, most enterprises new to cybersecurity risk assessment or a CISO new to an enterprise will begin with a standards assessment. It is an easy way to gauge how the current control practices within the organization compare to requirements listed in the document. The first step is to select an industry or regulatory standard that enterprise stakeholders believe applies to them. This is why regulatory standards tend to be good candidates. The enterprise actually has to comply with regulatory standards to achieve its mission, that is, to legally stay in business. So self-assessment in comparison with industry standards may seem like an efficiency measure. However, where there is already a perceived weakness in a cybersecurity program, the standard is more likely to be NIST CSF or ISO 27001&2 because those standards provide more specific guidance on capabilities required by any cybersecurity program.

While regulatory standards reflect the opinions of cybersecurity professionals focused on a specific type of business, cybersecurity itself has become its own industry and best practices shared among industry participants have made their way into the more general set of standards bodies, those founded to ensure the smooth flow of commerce by creating specifications for interchangeable parts. International standardization is a well-established means for many technologies to become more adaptable. Cybersecurity standards have been produced for a widely diverse set of industries, including but not limited to information processing, telecommunications, textiles, packaging, energy production, shipbuilding, and financial services. Standards bodies like the US National Institute of Standards and Technology (NIST) and the International Standards Organization (ISO) have also created more general recommendations for best practices in the professional field of cybersecurity risk reduction. These and others like them may be expected to proliferate for years to come.

Recall the enterprise standard derived from industry standard guidance in Figure 4.18. It shows how an enterprise standard can map to an industry standard. We say "map" in cybersecurity rather than "match" because the connection between the two concepts is rarely if ever exact. The standard contains a requirement description and the enterprise version is a description of an actual situation that meets the requirement. Although the example shows wording designed to call attention to the language of the standard, the map from an internal standard to an external standard does not have to exactly match. If an argument can be made that some internal control maps to the requirement, and there is evidence the control is operating effectively, then the internal standard can demonstrate adherence to an external standard. Note the use of the word "adherence" rather than "compliance." Comparing one document to another does not actually demonstrate standards compliance, it just signifies that management has considered the requirements and responded with an appropriate plan. It would take an actual audit to demonstrate standards compliance to the satisfaction of a standards audit. The opinion in a standards assessment that is not an audit is either a claim of adherence, or a set of issues that the organization needs to resolve in order to claim adherence to the standard. Even where only adherence is observed, management is provided with at least some assurance that their own internal efforts to drive down cybersecurity risk compare favorably to the industry standard.

Most standards do not specify exactly what type of cybersecurity risk event a given requirement is meant to contain. Instead, they promote a vision of what good cybersecurity looks like in combination with a set of processes designed to achieve their vision. The organization adheres to the standard to the extent that they maintain practices similar to those identified in the standards. If an organization does not meet a requirement, it may be that the requirement is not applicable to their business process, or it may not be known whether it is applicable. Even if positive applicability is determined, there may be some analysis required to decide whether there is an actual issue to be addressed, and then the priority of the issue will be assessed to determine whether it should have priority with respect to resources available. As opposed to scenario analysis, where one starts with a cybersecurity risk category, and works down through the infrastructure to see to what extent the enterprise is at risk, standards risk assessment is a bottom-up approach, wherein issues are identified in standard assessments and then aligned with risks. The risks are then analyzed in the context of aggregated events and issues.

While Figure 3.2 represented the NIST standard as five NIST functions in a cycle, united by governance and meant to invoke the standard's emphasis on continuous improvement, Figure 5.4 shows the protect function in a list format (NIST CSF 2018). Each function is similarly divided into *categories*. These are processes instantiated by a cybersecurity program, referred to by the standard as groups of cybersecurity function *outcomes*.

Within each category, there are *subcategories*, a subdivision of category outcomes into technical and/or management activities (e.g., standards and procedures). Other assessment documents would refer to these subcategories as *control objectives*, or *requirements*. NIST does not because it recommends an assessment approach where the categories are used as guidance for developing individual organizational profiles, and the assessment should occur only after a business has established its profile. Presumably, an organization would use its risk appetite to customize the extent to which it targets compliance with the requirements in the

NIST CSF Version 2 Protect Categories			
Function	Function Unique Identifier	Category Unique Identifier	Category
PROTECT: Safeguards to manage the organization's cybersecurity risks are used	PR	PR.AA	Identity Management, Authentication, and Access Control
		PR.AT	Awareness and Training
		PR.DS	Data Security
		PR.PS	Platform Security
		PR.IR	Technology Infrastructure Resilience

Figure 5.4 NIST CSF Protect Categories

NIST CSF Version 2 PR.AA Subcategories and References			
Category	Subcat Unique Identifier	Requirements	References
Identity Management, Authentication, and Access Control: Access to physical and logical assets is limited to authorized users, services, and hardware and managed commensurate with the assessed risk of unauthorized access	PR.AA-01	Identities and credentials for authorized users, services, and hardware are managed by the organization	CIS Controls v8.0: 5.1, CIS Controls v8.0: 6.7 CRI Profile v2.0: PR.AA-01 · CRI Profile v2.0: PR.AA-01.01 CRI Profile v2.0: PR.AA-01.02 CSF v1.1: PR.AC-1
	PR.AA-02	Identities are proofed and bound to credentials based on the context of interactions	CRI Profile v2.0: PR.AA-02 CRI Profile v2.0: PR.AA-02.01 · CSF v1.1: PR.AC-6
	PR.AA-03	Users, services, and hardware are authenticated	SP 800-218: PO.5.2 CRI Profile v2.0: PR.AA-03 CRI Profile v2.0: PR.AA-03.01 CRI Profile v2.0: PR.AA-03.02 · CRI Profile v2.0: PR.AA-03.03 CSF v1.1: PR.AC-3 CSF v1.1: PR.AC-7
	PR.AA-04	Identity assertions are protected, conveyed, and verified	CRI Profile v2.0: PR.AA-04 CRI Profile v2.0: PR.AA-04.01
	PR.AA-05	Access permissions, entitlements, and authorizations are defined in a policy, managed, enforced, and reviewed, and incorporate the principles of least privilege and separation of duties	SP 800-218: PO.5.2 SP 800-218: PS.1.1 CIS Controls v8.0: 3.3 CIS Controls v8.0: 6.8 CRI Profile v2.0: PR.AA-05 CRI Profile v2.0: PR.AA-05.01 · CRI Profile v2.0: PR.AA-05.02 CRI Profile v2.0: PR.AA-05.03 CRI Profile v2.0: PR.AA-05.04 CSF v1.1: PR.AC-1 CSF v1.1: PR.AC-3 CSF v1.1: PR.AC-4
	PR.AA-06	Physical access to assets is managed, monitored, and enforced commensurate with risk	SP 800-218: PO.5.2 CRI Profile v2.0: PR.AA-06 CRI Profile v2.0: PR.AA-06.01 · CRI Profile v2.0: PR.AA-06.02 CSF v1.1: PR.AC-2 CSF v1.1: PR.PT-4

Note: Unlike Version 1 as described in the text, Version 2 does not cite COBIT or ISO

Figure 5.5 NIST CSF PRAC Requirements

subcategories. Each would be labeled: *Partial, Risk-Informed, Repeatable*, or *Adaptive*, and this would comprise a profile.

Figure 5.5 shows an excerpt of NIST CSF requirements corresponding to the protect function. Protect has been given the acronym "PR." Within the protect function, there are six categories, including the *Identity Management, Authentication and Access Control* category that appears in the figure. It has been given the acronym AC. Three subcategories, or requirements, are listed in the figure, and their labels are a combination of those acronyms and the order in which they appear in the document: PR.AC-1, PR-AC-2, and PR.AC-3. NIST CSF not only lists the detailed requirement but also publishes guidance in the form of similar cryptic labels that appear in other industry standards with more detailed control descriptions that, if implemented by the enterprise undergoing assessment, would be evidence of compliance with the NIST CSF requirement.

The reference standards in Figure 5.5 are listed in an alphabetical order and there is no recommendation that one will be more germane than another in evaluating any given security program. As described in Section 4.4, the Center for Internet Security (CIS) publishes technical configuration details while ISO 27001 focuses on information security management requirements. The focus of the standard identified as *COBIT* is in between. Although like ISO, it includes management standards, they are for technology generally, not specific to cybersecurity. COBIT originally was an acronym for *Control Objectives for Information Technology*, published by an organization called ISACA, which was originally an acronym for the *Information Systems Audit and Control Association*. But as the profession evolved, those full names were deemed to be just part of a larger puzzle of information and technology governance and management. Therefore, the full names were dropped from the organization's branding while the acronyms persist. The first requirement in Figure 5.5 is "Identities and credentials are issued, managed, verified, revoked, and audited for authorized devices, users and processes." It cites a COBIT requirement in that document's section called, "Deliver Service and Support" (DSS) (ISACA 2019, pp. 229–235). Within COBIT DSS, requirement #5 is "Managed Security Services" and wherein requirement #6 is "Managed Business Process Controls." This type of reference is consistent with a Joiners, Movers, Leavers (JML) process as described in Section 4.3. Evaluators for an enterprise that has developed a robust JML process would therefore routinely assess this requirement as *met.*

The opinion of an assessment based on an industry or regulator standard like NIST CSF will be based on the accumulated evaluation of each individual requirement. Figure 5.6 shows how that information is recorded for each requirement. The assessment evaluator labels each requirement according to an enterprise convention for attesting to compliance, in this case *Meets, Does not Meet, Plans to Meet,* and *Compensating Control.* They also create a record of the observations they made during the assessment, and the artifacts they collected that show whether or not there is tangible evidence that the requirement was met. Note that the evidence cited takes the same form as the industry standard control references. In the *Evidence* column of Figure 5.6, the *ISP:B.2.1* may refer to an enterprise security policy in a document *called Information Security Policy*, section *B*, subsection 2, requirement number 1, as in the policy excerpt in Figure 4.9. It would not refer to an industry standard because assessment evidence has to be local to the assessment scope. Where the requirement is not fully met, the assessment evaluator may also record a recommendation based on their experience. This is not binding on the enterprise being assessed, just an informative advice.

The requirement responses will be aggregated for reporting to stakeholders. Figure 5.7 is an excerpt from an example presentation of a cybersecurity assessment result using high level graphics from a NIST CSF assessment report. The detail in the report would typically include a list of "issues" in the form of requirements not met, accompanied by the recommendations of the evaluator that appear in the last column of Figure 5.6.

As an enterprise selects standards with which to assess their organizations, a CISO should keep in mind that an actual cybersecurity risk assessment will be primarily based on their own systems and processes, not by some set listed in the standard, however similar they may appear. There is no correct choice other than the utility of standards in assessing the degree to which an organization is exposed to cybersecurity risk, and the adequacy of the technology control environment within which the cybersecurity program operates. Moreover, the utility of an assessment opinion relies not so much on the choice of standard, but on the evaluator.

Response	Requirement	Observations	Evidence	Recommendation
ID.AM-1: Meets	Physical devices and systems within the organization are inventoried	Asset inventory is maintained via enterprise workflow wherein procurement, supplier risk management, and technology operations are tightly integrated. Contact: Physical, Phyllis	Cited_Controls: ISP:C.4: Physical Security (Policy, Protect) INFSEC:AM: Asset Management (Standard, Identify)	
ID.AM-2: Meets	Software platforms and applications within the organization are inventoried	Software inventory is maintained via technology workflow starting with procurement and maintained via the life of the software asset. Contact: Cio, The	Cited_Controls: INFSEC:AM-SW: Software Inventory (Standard, Identify)	
ID.AM-3 Compensates	Organizational communication and data flows are mapped	Although technology notifications are automated and crisis management notifications cover all staff, data flow documentation is partial and procedures sometimes must be supplemented with call lists. Contact: Opsman, Sec	Cited_Controls: ISP:A.4: Communication (Policy, Identify) IPCM:4.D: Communicate (Procedure, Respond) FCSS-CFG:IV-CO.3: Respond Procedures (Procedure, Respond) Files uploaded: CallLists.xlsx	
ID.AM-4 Planned	External information systems are catalogued	Third Party vendors are cataloged and data exchanges logged, but there is no systematic method to ensure that all Third Parties are in the catalog. Contact: Opsofficer, Chief Issue flagged.	Cited_Controls: FCSS-CFG:III.4: Third Party Service Logs (Control, Identify)	Charge accounts payable with creating a Third Party vendor record as a precondition of payment.
ID.AM-5: Not Met	Resources (e.g., hardware, devices, data, time, personnel, and software) are prioritized based on their classification, criticality, and business value	Although ranks are assigned to resources based on business criticality and information classification, resources for critical controls such as endpoint security are not prioritized accordingly. Contact: Techrisk, Tammy Issue flagged.	Cited_Controls: ISP:A.2: Information Classification (Policy, Identify) FCSS-CFG:V.2: Asset Rank (Standard, Identify)	Establish security support tiers by rank and prioritize resources for security services accordingly.
ID.AM-6: Meets	Cybersecurity roles and responsibilities for the entire workforce and third-party stakeholders (e.g. suppliers, customers, partners) are established	Security policy assigns responsibility for least privilege. Contact: Ciso, The	Cited_Controls: ISP:B.2.1: User Classification (Control, Identify) ISP:B.2.2: Departmental Responsibility (Control, Identify)	

Figure 5.6 Exemplar Assessment

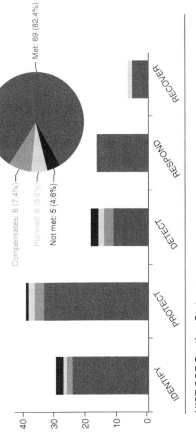

NIST CSF Assessment Results

Not Met (5)

ID.AM-5: Resources (e.g., hardware, devices, data, time, personnel, and software) are prioritized based on their classification, criticality, and business value

ID.SC-5 Response and recovery planning and testing are conducted with suppliers and third-party providers

PR.PT-2: Removable media is protected and its use restricted according to policy

DE.CM-3: Personnel activity is monitored to detect potential cybersecurity events

DE.CM-6: External service provider activity is monitored to detect potential cybersecurity events

Met: 89 (82.4%)

Compensates: 8 (7.4%)

Planned: 6 (5.6%)

Not met: 5 (4.6%)

IDENTIFY   PROTECT   DETECT   RESPOND   RECOVER

NIST-CSF Section Status:

IDENTIFY: 29 items 100% complete, 24 meet, 2 compensate, 1 plan, 2 not met, 11 controls, 3 issues

PROTECT: 39 items 100% complete, 33 meet, 3 compensate, 2 plans, 1 not met, 67 controls, and 3 issues

DETECT: 18 items 100% complete, 11 meet, 3 compensate, 2 plans, 2 not met, 10 controls, and 4 issues

RESPOND: 16 items 100% complete, 16 meet, 12 controls

RECOVER: 6 items 100% complete, 5 meet, 1 plans, 17 controls, and 1 issue

Figure 5.7 Exemplar Assessment Summary

Where all other assessment elements except assessment standard and evaluator are equal, it is the skill of the human evaluator in cybersecurity risk identification that makes one assessment opinion better than another.

5.2 Risk and Control Self Assessment

From the perspective of the CISO, the most intense assessment activity surrounds enterprise cybersecurity capability. However, from the perspective of business operations, there is still a question of whether those efforts serve the purpose of the business they were designed to support. In the professional practice of operational risk management, this question is answered by a management risk and control self-assessment (RCSA) program. That is, the same management responsible for devising strategy for achieving business mission will formally engage in an assessment of risks that may impact that mission. An RCSA program typically covers a variety of risks, cybersecurity among them. RCSA differs from a standards adherence assessment in that, rather than starting with sets of standards requirements, the starting point for the risk assessment is the businesses' own operational processes.

The objective is to provide assurance that the business process conforms to enterprise PPSPs, and that the existing PPSPs are adequate to address the risks. The risks will be articulated as event categories at some level of the enterprise cybersecurity risk hierarchy. The scope defined by the objective is the business process as well as the people and technology upon which it relies for execution. It relies on formal documentation of business process. The most basic type of control in any enterprise is business process and the fact that such documentation exists indicates that management uses a structured methodology to achieve business results, and thereby starts with review of a management control. If the process has changed since the documentation was updated, the document should be updated before the review commences. Because the evaluators are the people who define and operate the process, it is not expected that there will be either constraint on approach or scope creep.

Otherwise, however, RCSA is similar to a standards adherence assessment in that the approach is for the evaluator, in this case a representative of the process owner, to compare the scope to the requirements. In this case, the requirements are to minimize the probability of process disruption due to cybersecurity risks. Also, RCSA is similar to standards adherence assessment in that the outcome is typically a set of issues, the remediation of which, when resolved by strengthening controls, will also strengthen the process. That is, an RCSA is designed to identify points in the process that are not adequately controlled, and if exploited, will result in business process disruption. In that sense, it provides direct example of how risk assessment may be used to introduce controls that strengthen business resilience.

Assume there is a retail business that sells clothes online using an eCommerce store SaaS provider. Figure 5.8 depicts a very high-level business process workflow corresponding to an eCommerce retail clothing site. The top of the figure lists 4 distinct processes, and a few activities for each. It describes a business wherein staff photograph the clothes in-house, post the images online with prices, collect credit card information from purchasers, and ship the clothes to the address provided. The bottom of the figure shows the business systems used to support the process steps, including the outsourced eCommerce site. Although the business has outsourced the eCommerce site that is part of its process, there is still dependency on some internal technology systems to allow its product catalog to be created and published to the online site where the customers select merchandise and enter credit card data to make a purchase. There is also internal technology support for each sale to be systematically communicated to a shipping clerk.

A systematic method of assessing the risk of this (or any) business process is to lay out the steps of the process in detail, consider risks to their operation, and identify whether PPSPs cover the scope of the activities and effectively mitigate the risk to an acceptable residual level. For example, using a hierarchy such the examples in Figure 3.7, an enterprise may publish a *risk and control matrix* (RCM) to facilitate the performance of RCSAs. An RCM lists each process activity side by side with the enterprise cybersecurity risk register at some level of the hierarchy, followed by the *control objective(s)* that the process owner has determined will, if achieved, mitigate the identified risk. In the context of RCSA, the business process is placed first within the RCM, so the evaluator is not simply comparing a risk to a control objective, but a risk to a control in the context of the business process.

The RCM itself is not an assessment. Rather, it is a plan for an RCSA. Most of the work in the RCSA is examining actual controls (PPSPs) at work within the process that is the scope of the RCSA and determining if those controls sustain process managers' attempts to succeed in achieving their controls objectives. That is, in a manner similar to risk appetite statements at the executive level, process managers create qualitative statements at their own level describing what is an acceptable situation with respect to the process' capability to reduce the risk. The RCSA uses these statements as a starting point to evaluate whether the controls in place within the process (i) achieve the stated control objective identified in the RCM, and if so, (ii) whether or not it will mitigate the identified risk.

Figure 5.9 includes a few excerpts from an example of an RCM designed to be utilized in an RCSA. In it, the business process is listed in the order of the workflow in Figure 5.8. Then each process activity is tagged with a risk at level 2 of the hierarchy at the top of Figure 3.7 (i.e., *Harm to Confidentiality, Harm to Integrity, and Harm to Availability*). The process owners' control objectives are customized

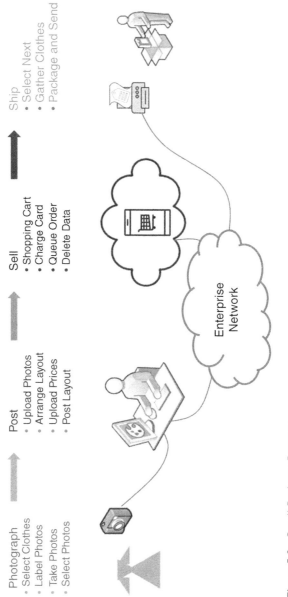

Figure 5.8 Retail Business Systems

Photograph
- Select Clothes
- Label Photos
- Take Photos
- Select Photos

Post
- Upload Photos
- Arrange Layout
- Upload Prices
- Post Layout

Sell
- Shopping Cart
- Charge Card
- Queue Order
- Delete Data

Ship
- Select Next
- Gather Clothes
- Package and Send

Enterprise Network

Process: Photograph

Activity	Risk	Control Objective
Select Clothes	PH.SC-C *Confidentiality Marketing*	Selected clothes should not be made public until posted.
	PH.SC-I *Integrity Marketing*	Selected clothes must be under supplier contract.
	PH.SC-A *Availability Marketing*	Selected clothes must be available for restock.
Label Photos	PH.LP-C *Confidentiality Marketing*	Inventory stock number tags must not contain supplier identifiers.
	PH.LP-I *Integrity Marketing*	Photos must be tagged with correct Inventory stock number.
	PH.LP-A *Availability Marketing*	Photo stock number tags must be automatically readable for immediate reconciliation with supplier inventory.

Process: Post

Activity	Risk	Control Objective
Upload Photos	PO.UP-C *Confidentiality Sales*	Selected photos must be stored in encrypted format, uploaded in and encrypted state, then decrypted on the eCommerce site.
	PO.UP-I *Integrity Sales*	Post-uploaded, stock numbers records are reviewed to ensure pricing and color information are correct.
	PO.UP-A *Availability Sales*	Photos are uploaded in such a manner that they are automatically entered into high availability configurations within the eCommerce site.

Figure 5.9 Excerpts from Retail Business Systems RCM

to address the risk inherent in the performance of the activity. The evaluator is tasked with examining each row and evaluating whether there are enough cybersecurity controls to protect the process activity from probable damage due to a cybersecurity event in each risk category. The risk column in Figure 5.9 lists the risks with the same type of cryptic references that NIST CSF used to refer to COBIT and ISO. But in this case, they refer to process step, activity, and risk. As the evaluator conducts the assessment, data is accumulated under these tags to facilitate aggregate reporting by process, risk, or both.

The assessment data accumulation is facilitated by automation that is referred to in the risk profession as "GRC." GRC was originally an acronym for *Governance, Risk and Control,* but in many organizations has morphed into *Governance, Risk and Compliance.* This transition in thinking about the control objective of the technology as compliance is understandable in that, for many assessment evaluators, the job is to determine compliance with policies, standards, and procedures rather than to evaluate risk. It is often presumed that the risk evaluation occurred during the control design process, so verification that the enterprise security architecture is correct substitutes for the determination on whether it is effective. Though this observation may seem cynical, the conflation is often justified. Business process owners and their staff cannot be expected to internalize the tenants of zero trust and apply them to their business activities. It is enough that they make a sincere effort to understand how enterprise controls can facilitate their objectives for secure business operations.

An RCSA accomplishes this. In an RCSA, business process activities are formally compared to enterprise cybersecurity PPSPs to identify whether the processes are covered, from a cybersecurity controls perspective, with the protection, detection, and response capabilities of the enterprise risk management program. Of course, this mapping would not be possible if the business did not clearly identify the system or systems in scope for each process activity. The ability to translate scope to system(s) is a critical and essential component in any assessment. When system engineers refer generically to a system, network, or application, they use the term *system of interest* to differentiate the system under scrutiny from the rest of a technology or business environment. In an RCSA, the scope must include all the technology applications and infrastructure that support the business, and the term system of interest encompasses the technology, business processes, and people operating that technology. Where the scope is articulated in terms of business process, the first step in a review for the assessor is to identify all the systems of interest that support the business process, the controls used to maintain that technology, and the extent to which the controls are verified and validated.

In this case, the person conducting the risk assessment, the *evaluator*, would be focused on cybersecurity risk. The Photograph and Layout 1 and 2 in the process would not be considered critical unless photos and price information could be compromised. If this concern was adequately addressed, the next area of focus for the evaluator would be a critical review how the activities in process step 3 are performed. The evaluator would need to understand:

- How is the information in the shopping cart calculated? Do we verify that the prices in the shopping cart are the same as what was posted?
- How is the card charged? Where is the record that the money was actually received?
- What happens to the shipping label data after it is printed? If we lose the shipping label, how will we know what was ordered?

From these descriptions of events that might negatively impact the process, the evaluator can identify controls that are intended to minimize the risks of each specific negative impact, and gain assurance that the overall process will be as effective as expected. If the expected controls are not in evidence, the evaluator may make recommendations for control improvements.

Figure 5.10 is an excerpt from a GRC report on the full mapping from an RCSA process activity to enterprise PPSPs. Note that the Evidence column in Figure 5.10 lists the controls with the same type of cryptic references that NIST CSF used to refer to COBIT and ISO. But, in this case, they refer to controls that are part of the enterprise security architecture. Note there is a recommendation column in the report. From the content, it can be inferred that the field is not required if control objectives are fully met. But in cases where controls fail to provide evidence that

Response	Requirement	Observations	Evidence	Recommendation
SE.SC-C: Meets	Shopping cart software is configured only to run if network connection is encrypted at the transport layer.	Contact: Procure.	*Cited_Controls:* CloudSEC:SaaS-10: Network Encryption (Standard, Protect)	No recommendation recorded
SE.SC-I: Not Met	Shopping cart software displays the same prices on check-out form as appear in current layout.	Although changes to the shopping cart software are reviewed when SaaS-ECom send notification of functional changes, this feature is not routinely tested. Issue flagged.	*Cited_Controls:* CloudSEC:SaaS-4: Change Control (Standard, Protect)	Consistency between price uploads and shopping cart displays should be added to the quality control testing specified in SaaS-3.
SE.SC-A: Compensates	Shopping cart software has no single point of failure and is configured for high availability.	Although these features are not specified in detail or included in testing, review performed in support of SaaS-5 resulted in the inclusion of high availability requirements in the SaaS-ECom contract. Contact: Enginir.	SaaS-ECom undergoes annual SASE SOC2 Examination. *Cited_Controls:* CloudSEC:SaaS-2: Contractual Requirements (Standard, Protect) CloudSEC:SaaS-5: Technology Control (Standard, Protect)	Review availability requirements in the vendor SASE SOC2 Examination Report and update contract to enhance availability as needed and add penalties for negative findings.
SE.CC-C: Meets	Card charge end-to-end process is encrypted and customer personally identifiable information is purged from system directly after charge completed and shipping label is created.	TLS is required by contract and a check on the version is performed in the automated quality control testing in support of SaaS-6.	*Cited_Controls:* CloudSEC:SaaS-10: Network Encryption (Standard, Protect) CloudSEC:SaaS-6: Integrity Testing (Standard, Protect)	No recommendation recorded

Figure 5.10 RCSA Progress

control objectives are met, a risk management organization conducting an enterprise-wide RCSA will typically require participants to demonstrate that they understand what needs to be done to achieve the objective, or have learned what needs to be improved as part of the RCSA process. Where there is an actual project plan that will achieve the recommendation, the "response" column may be tagged "Plans to meet" rather than "Does not meet" the objective, a significant bit of additional evidence to be considered in assessing overall process cybersecurity risk.

An RCSA also typically allows for a gray area in that the control objective may be partially met, in this case called a *compensating control*. In Figure 5.10, the evaluator observes that there is a contractual control for the Sell Process Shopping Cart activity SE-SC-A, but there is no obvious enforcement mechanism, so it is marked "Compensates" instead of "Meets." In this case, the evaluator knows that there is some self-assessment testing done by the vendor and the firm should be able to monitor those test results to gain additional assurance that high availability is in place. The evaluator indicates that the vendor undergoes a Statement on Standards for Attestation Engagements (SSAE) for a System and Organization Controls (SOC) Examination annually and the examination is a report on controls at a service organization relevant to security, availability, processing integrity, confidentiality, or privacy (AICPA 2015). So the evaluator recommends that the contract should be updated to include penalties for any availability findings in that report.

It may seem strange to call one of the outcomes of a self-assessment a "recommendation," it reflects the fact that the main result is the set of issues and what to do about the issues is not always decided before the assessment is over. So the evaluator will offer their opinion, but the actual issue remediation will be left to the judgment of those who own the process under assessment.

5.3 Pentests and Vulnscans

Every industry has some types of assessments that are unique to its mission. In real estate, there are building inspections. In electronics, there are standard tests to determine whether components are vulnerable to fire hazards. In health care, there are surgical room inspections. In cybersecurity, there are pentests. The first pentesters were called "tiger teams," an Apollo-era term for expert and innovative technical specialists, selected for their experience, energy, and imagination. They were assigned to identify and enumerate every possible source of failure in a spacecraft. Anyone familiar with the Apollo 13 mission understands the combination of seriousness and urgency that motivates the creation of such a team. In that mission, flight controllers wrote innovative technical instructions that saved the lives of three astronauts in three days, instead of the usual three months that a similar document normally took to complete (NASA 2022). The term "tiger team" was adopted by cybersecurity managers in the 1990s to recruit highly technical and creative researchers to focus on finding system vulnerabilities that could negatively impact commercial technology services. Their activities were guided by research in failure modes, effects, and criticality analysis (FMECA) wherein each system component was analyzed for potential failure and the output of these studies were failure descriptions, expected impact, and impact severity levels.

Figure 5.11 is an example of such FMECA methodology (Rausand, 2014 p. 61). It begins by listing system components. Each is individually examined to determine under what conditions it would fail, and how that failure may be detected. These are labeled component failure modes, in this case dangerous or safe (*as in the principle of fail safe*). An FMECA analysis will also assess the risk related to each failure mode, and typically include a quantitative severity measure with each failure condition. This is a key part of the analysis adopted by pentests, which assign a severity rating to each vulnerability identified in the exercise. The pentest severity rating may be an environmental customization of the Common Vulnerability Score (CVSS) assigned to a known exploited vulnerability, or it may be fully customized by the assessment team.

Note the difference between a diagnostic and a proof test in Figure 5.11. This is the difference between verification and validation. A diagnostic is an automated configuration check on the component's security, such as an operating system security agent reporting back to a SIEM on whether a device is configured according to established enterprise security standards for the device type. This is a verification that the component's security is correctly implemented. A proof test

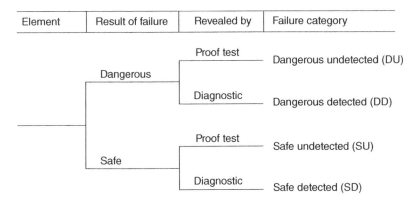

Figure 5.11   Example FMECA

is a method of testing the system while it is operating to ensure it functions as effectively as expected. This is a security validation test. While any assessment may include both correctness and effectiveness tests (perhaps calling them verification and validation or calling them diagnostics and proof), many internal assessments include only correctness (perhaps calling them verification or diagnostics). A pentest is distinguished from other assessments in that its major focus is on effectiveness, validation, and proof.

An FMECA analysis should indicate whether the component failure could bring down the whole system, that is, whether it may be a single point of failure (SPOF) or a common cause failure (CCF) failure that could contribute to a widespread system impact by causing other component failures. In both cases, one failure cause can disable an entire system. But two or more redundant subsystems must fail in a true CCF, while only one must fail at a SPOF.

To translate from the traditional FMECA analysis in the figure to a pentest, think of the description of unit as a hardware or software component of the system of interest, the description of failure as the effect of an act of vulnerability exploit, and the description of dangerous undetected failure as a step in a threat vector that, in combination with other steps, would allow damage to the confidentiality, integrity, and availability of the system.

Note that the SPOF specification of failure description is accompanied by a detection capability. This is very similar to a vulnerability scan, part of the reconnaissance activity performed by threat actors as they study their target. When pentests first began, the pentesters had to create their own methods of probing their customer's network with custom software. These were typically archived as individual modules that over time accumulated and eventually packed into commercial vulnerability scanning software.

The late 1990s saw the development of the Security Administrator Tool for Analyzing Networks (SATAN). SATAN was one of the first vulnerability scanners created to identify network-accessible vulnerabilities, and became an essential cyber defense tool as more and more businesses became reliant on internet commerce. The SATAN code was turned into a commercial product and was soon followed by Nessus. There are now at least 20 vendors participating in this space. This includes only commercial scanning tool vendors. The number of consultants and service providers who use these tools to provide scanning as a service numbers in the thousands.

Nevertheless, threat actors still write their own scans for zero-day vulnerabilities and newly announced CVEs, as do the commercial scanning companies. It is now industry best practices to alternate among penetration tests and vulnerability scanning companies to ensure that the enterprise is able to, at least on a rotating basis, test itself against known vulnerabilities from as many different scan module collections as possible.

Another significant choice in pentest planning is its scope difference in the evaluation of the result of a penetration test to know how many applications were tested, and which ones. When management has contracted for the tests, and internal staff has participated in them, it may be more trouble than it is worth to require evidence that the applications not identified to have vulnerabilities were actually scanned. However, it is still very important to know the full scope of the test, as it may be a partial list of applications and those not on the list should still be on queue to be tested at another time.

Just as is any other control assessment, pentests have an objective, scope, constraint, approach, and result. The objective is typically to provide assurance that internet access cannot be exploited to identify dangerous failure modes in the systems in scope. The scope would typically include all enterprise internet access points unless there is a need to narrowly define the access points and applications in scope to accommodate resource constraints. Mapping the objective to the scope is not trivial so guidelines should be set to govern any gray areas that emerge in the course of the assessment. In addition to resource constraints, there may be constraints imposed by stakeholders that inhibit the ability of a pentester to execute tests.

For example, stakeholders may not want people scanning internet access points during business hours when a spike in activity caused by a vulnerability scan may reduce the network performance of a business application. At that point, the testers must adopt an approach comprised of activities that cover the scope in a way that meets the objective of the assessment given the constraint. Constraints may thus lower the level of assurance in the result, and the result will typically be hedged to acknowledge the constraint. That is, the conclusion of the report may admit that a full pentest assessment could not be completed, but the tests performed, in combination with defender diagnostics and vulnerability assessments, provide pretty good assurance that enterprise cyber defense is healthy. That is, the result of the assessment is always the communication of whether the assessment objective was met even if it was only partially met.

Another relevant aspect of a pentest is the extent to which it embraces the didactic relationship between threat actor and cyber defender. When the cyber defense team is aware of and included in the test, they are distinguished from the pentest team with the adjectives red and blue. The red team is testing, the blue team in defending. Where one or more team member observes and/or participates on both cyber test and defense teams simultaneously, this is called a purple team (blend of red and blue). Like sportscasters providing play by play commentary, they heighten awareness of the extent to which the red team has penetrated enterprise cyber defenses. This maximizes real-time awareness of cyberattack in progress and influences cyber defense teams to innovate rather

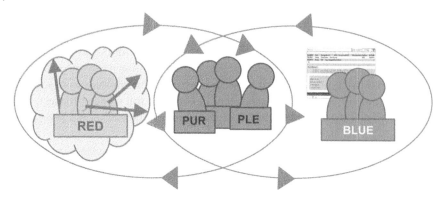

Figure 5.12 Pentest Team Dynamic

than rely on existing defenses. Just as pentests that include a blue team may be expected to learn more about a purple team will have a broader view of the activities that lead to a "fail dangerous" test outcome. A key benefit of including purple teams in a pentest assessment is that the severity rating of each finding may be expected to be a joint exercise, leveraging both internal and external views of operational impact. Another benefit is efficiency in bringing the cyber defenders up to speed on the threat vectors that lead to dangerous findings. Because they will have witnessed what it looked like from their monitoring systems, they should be able to identify what improvements need to be made to create the visibility into the vectors more quickly, and what configuration changes need to be made to thwart it.

There are many ways to organize red, blue, and purple teams to maximize the control improvements gleaned from the pentesting process. A typical interaction is illustrated in Figure 5.12. In the figure, skilled pentesters form the red team and are located in a network location external to enterprise resources. Cyber defenders form the blue team and they stay in their primary work locations, focusing at first on day-to-day monitoring activities. The purple team is positioned to observe both teams in action. The Venn diagram shows how the members of the purple team overlap with both the red and blue teams. The arrows show how the information flows back and forth between all three teams as the test progresses.

In many cybersecurity programs, pentests are performed intermittently (e.g., annually). Where pentests are a persistent part of the security program, it provides a source of continuous control improvement. Although the main outcome of a pentest is a list of software vulnerabilities, where blue and purple teams participate, the findings may include other ineffective defenses as well. All issues are typically prioritized for remediation just as is any other risk or control assessment.

5.4   Audits

The audit is the most rigorous assessment because auditors must collect evidence supporting positive as well as negative findings with respect to an organization's controls. Many publications refer to "independent audit," but that phrase is redundant. While an assessment may not be independent of the domain that is being assessed, the word *audit* is reserved for independent assessments. The audit is also the hardest type of assessment to complete, given the prerequisite that the evaluator is independent of the enterprise. By definition, the auditor is an outsider yet also responsible for evidence-based fact checking of nearly everything they are told by the stakeholders in scope. Even if it were not for enterprise regulatory requirements to ensure independence, a professional code of ethics prevents certified technology auditors from being personally responsible for any information technology security management within the scope of their audit domain (ISACA 2023; IAA 2023). That is, while enterprise risk managers may report directly to the process owners of the processes they assess, even internal enterprise auditors are subject to Institute of Internal Auditors standards for the professional practice of internal auditing which defines auditing as an *independent* assessment function and requires that even internal auditors be independent of the activities they audit as a condition of their ongoing certification.

In the above discussion of RCSA, it was observed that business process owners cannot be expected to internalize the tenants of zero trust and apply them to their business activities. It is enough that they make a sincere effort to understand how enterprise controls can facilitate their objectives for secure business operations. An audit is the way to check if those process owners actually did successfully achieve their control objectives. Moreover, auditors are not constrained to pass assessments based on PPSP or regulatory compliance, but are also empowered to opine on whether risk is adequately reduced to an acceptable residual level, given risk appetite.

Auditors typically employ automated systems that make it easy for them to make sure all relevant testing requirements are identified and that sufficient evidence is collected to prove or disprove that a requirement it met. The term "workpapers" refers to an auditor's playbook, as well as all the corresponding observations and evidence gathered in the course of completing an assessment. The term is adopted from the financial audit profession, as claims of monetary value determined by financial auditors must always be backed by solid proof of transaction integrity.

Unlike the case of RCSA, the business process steps are not laid out in the audit plan. In this case, the audit is based on NIST CSF. A business process is typically the scope of the review, and if an RCSA exists, it may be part of the evidence that the NIST CSF control objective is met. A cybersecurity auditor focuses more heavily on

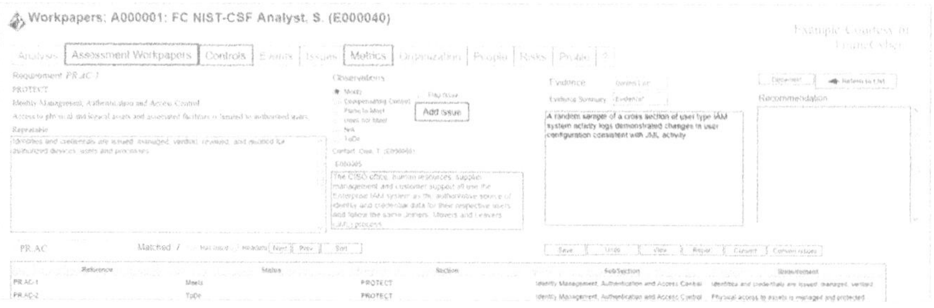

Figure 5.13   Audit Workpapers

the systems themselves and the extent to which the systems are capable of enforcing any business control. Unlike an RCSA, there is no assumption that enterprise security architecture is effective. The assumption is that enterprise security architecture is *not* effective *unless* enough evidence can be gathered to prove that it is effective.

Figure 5.13 displays a field set of information gathered by an auditor in the course of evidence collection as it appears in a GRC tool. In the leftmost column of the screen is the assessment requirement. It is displayed in the context of the hierarchy in the document, which also shows of appearance in the document in the table below. The requirement selected from the table is displayed in the left column and the auditor's opinion on whether the requirement is met is signified by the choice of a radio button in the second column. The auditor will need to identify the person in the organization who is the most authoritative source on how this requirement is met, in this case it is an IAM requirement, and the accountable person is the CISO. The list of individuals with security roles and responsibilities will have been stored in the system to make it easy for the auditor to correctly identify the appropriate contact and drop the contact record into the workpaper screen.

Where the controls themselves are stored in the same system, they can often be selected from tables and dragged into the fields of the workpaper screen. This is what allows the type of cross-reference by code evidence that appears in the RCSA example in Figure 5.10. Although it may be enough evidence for an RCSA that someone is accountable for meeting each control objective and there is a corresponding documented control, it is not enough to pass an audit. An auditor is required to *test* the control to verify that it is operating effectively. That test must be customized for the specific requirement under review. For example, an auditor assigned to review the control objectives in NIST subcategories would typically start by interviewing the contact and obtaining documentation of the PPSPs relevant to the requirement, the process, and the systems in scope. The documentation should reflect the systems security architecture that enforces the control, making it possible for the audit to design a technology test to see if the documented architecture is implemented correctly and operated effectively (i.e., verify the controls are correctly built and validate that the controls are working). The result of the control test, positive or negative, serves as evidence that the requirement is met or is not met.

These tests may take the form of a direct examination of system configuration, an analysis of network traffic in comparison with authorized data flow, an automated vulnerability scan, or a comparison of user entitlements with *joiner, mover, leaver* status. Evidence of the test result must be included in audit workpapers. Note the workpaper data entry screen has a label "Evidence." The label has an asterisk, indicating that some evidence has been uploaded. The screen's "View" button shows the auditor at a glance the full set of evidence collected in support of the assessment of this control. In this case, the evidence is in the form of a comparison between IAM system activity logs and HR and supplier management's records on the dates of JML activity. The auditor has included a note that a comparison was made between these samples, and this implies that the JML records were randomly selected from each user population and the IAM records were found to be consistent with that activity. Of course, the evidence should also include the basis upon which the sample is agreed to be statistically valid. Figure 5.14 provides an example view. Such a bird's eye view of management attention to a single control objective is hard to accomplish with traditional documentation methods, wherein each document type is solely contained in a separate repository, and documents are cross referenced only at the document level.

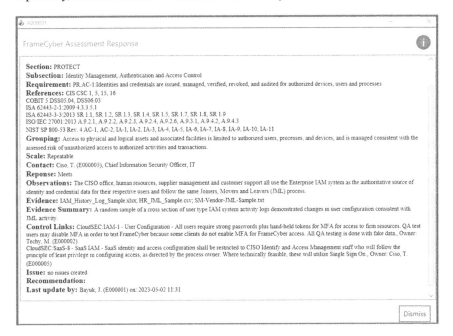

Figure 5.14 Example GRC Evidence Summary

So far, we have focused on audit's independent performance of control assessment. While independent auditors are repeatedly engaged to perform comparisons of enterprise controls with industry and regulatory standards, they are also formally engaged to create the audit program itself (Bayuk 2005). The entity engaging the auditor may be the executive management but also could itself be more independent such as the Board of Directors or a Regulator. The scope of the review will be designated by that entity. It may be an enterprise cybersecurity program, a business organization or process, a systems security architecture review, and/or any other topic of management oversight or concern.

A cybersecurity auditor will weigh the pros and cons of various alternative audit activities against three kinds of risk: *inherent*, *control*, and *detection*. Inherent risk is derived from the level of complexity of the activity under review as well as its *materiality* with respect to organizational objectives. Materiality means the extent to which potential losses due to negatively impacting cybersecurity events could result in the inability to execute business mission. Control risk is the probability that internal controls are inadequate to reduce the risk to an acceptable residual level. Detection risk is the probability that the audit process fails to identify policy violations according to plan. Inherent cybersecurity risk is always high, so auditors tend to assume that and focus mostly on control and detection. They will start with a preliminary data-gathering process, typically reviewing technology management committee presentations and interviewing cybersecurity management to understand the strengths and weaknesses of the technology control environment. They will do research into the technology upon which the controls are highly dependent. They may solicit information from the user community to gauge their experience with system security issues. This research, in combination with their own expertise and experience, allows them to customize a set of control verification and validation tests that will allow them to assess control and detection risk.

Where there are well-documented procedures for complying with documented system security architecture standards, an auditor is easily able to design verification tests to see if each procedure is consistently followed. For example, follow the procedure and check the resulting configuration against the standard. It is also easy to design validation tests to check whether the standard architecture achieves the desired result with respect to very specific expectations. For example, monitoring network traffic to see if all customer data flow is encrypted. Where such documentation is not available, the auditor must rely on validation tests to see if the system's security architecture is actually thwarting threats. That could entail observing activity in the operations center for long hours and observing control execution first-hand. Even if it seems the architecture is suitable for purpose, the auditor will likely document a finding on a high probability of detection risk and recommend documenting standards and procedures.

It is ironic that perhaps the greatest need for procedure comes not from the organization performing it but from the outsider whose job is to verify that it is in place. An external assessor or auditor cannot verify that people are operating a control in a repeatable manner with the same desired outcome unless they are provided with the steps of which the procedure is composed. So wherever they are available, auditors will carefully examine procedures and verify that they accomplished the expected outcome. After verifying that the procedures are being followed and also validating the control, they can provide a high level of assurance that the control is in place.

In contrast, some technology controls can be verified in a highly automated manner. A vulnerability scan verification may be made using activity records that provide evidence that all applications in inventory were scanned periodically using an industry standard scanner and that the results were remediated in a timely manner. Its validation can be performed by pointing the enterprise's vulnerability scanning process at known vulnerable sites (some provided by security professionals just for this purpose) and checking whether the scanner correctly identified all the known vulnerabilities on the test site. But even these types of tests are subject to statistical rigor. That is, systems selected for testing must be a statistically valid data sample from the full population of the systems to test. This requires enumeration of the full population and application of an algorithm to randomly identify test targets.

Although workpapers will include all audit evidence and be archived for inspection (even auditors get audited), the main outcome of an audit is a formal report summarizing activities performed, issues identified, recommendations, and conclusions in a manner consumable by a nontechnical layperson. Figure 5.15 provides an abbreviated example.

5.5 Spot Checks

In an enterprise engaged in the professional practice of risk management, input to the cybersecurity risk assessment process will include not only issues identified in standards assessments, but significant events and issues identified via other means. There may be bug bounty programs where an enterprise pays hackers for finding vulnerabilities in their software. There may be customer complaints of data exposure that result in security incident investigations. There may be law enforcement organizations contacting the legal department to advise the enterprise that their trade secrets have been published on the dark web. All of this input is relevant to the assessment of cybersecurity risk. The contribution of information supplied from any source is necessarily a subset of the picture an enterprise will use to estimate the probability that it will fall (or has fallen) victim to cyberattack.

Date: XXX XX, XX

Organization: Technology

Objectives: To determine the adequacy of control procedures and the use of best practices for ECommerce internet systems environment to verify cybersecurity risk to be below enterprise risk appetite

Executive Summary: The current ECommerce internet service offering was implemented in November of last year. The implementation of this system was the responsibility of the ECommerce business unit, though it also provides information to customers of the Consulting and Marketing business units. The system is operated at or above industry standard control practices, with one exception, noted below. Based upon the overall control environment and management's commitment to address systems vulnerabilities immediately upon identification, the overall assessment for the Internet Service offering is satisfactory.

Significant Findings and Recommendations:

The Ecommerce application allows users to access the database via a database login and password that is embedded in the compiled code accessed by the web server to retrieve customer data. It is possible for an operating system user to execute this code and use the login and password and access the database directly. Operating system users are not authorized to view this data. Such direct access even by authorized users would bypass application access controls that prevent users from viewing customer data in aggregate.

Our contracts with customers include confidentiality clauses which any disclosure of customer data would breach. If this vulnerability is considered a breach of confidentiality, SoftServe may incur serious liabilities.

This situation occurred because commercial development tools used to create the Internet software hid the database interaction from the application architects. They designed security into the application without awareness of the underlying architecture of the product. The effect is that users who are familiar with the development tool may easily identify configuration files that contain database access passwords.

We recommend that the database access mechanism provided by the commercial development tool be replaced by a privilege management that contains the encrypted database login and password. Moreover, we recommend that this database and password be changed on a daily basis, and that Internet users who authenticate to the application will then receive this database access code only after authentication.

Figure 5.15 Mini Audit Report

Cybersecurity staff are routinely assigned to assessments that come in a variety of unexpected forms. They do not all have objective criteria; the scope is sometimes left entirely to the evaluator. In addition to the planned assessments discussed above, a security manager or CISO may be expected to provide assessments in a variety of situations, both planned and ad hoc. Where standard due diligence requirements for conducting an assigned assessment do not exist, this activity may be referred to as a "review" rather than an assessment. Some are purely opinion based on expertise and experience and others are formal comparisons between a narrowly defined technology environment and existing PPSPs. One notable example is a preproduction security policy compliance review conducted in the course of a formal application or infrastructure change control process. Another is the determination of the enterprise business process or department from which exposed enterprise trade secrets were taken.

In a situation where there is a report of a cybersecurity problem or potential cybersecurity problem, if management knows that there are control standards that should be in place to reduce the risk that such problems will occur, then it is common to seek a local opinion. That is, to engage an internal expert to review each expected control standard implementation and provide a *yes* or *no* answer for the question: "is this standard implemented?" In any field, this is called *a spot check*. Each *no* may be referred to as a *spot check finding* and may end up in an issue-tracking system regardless of whether it was a result of any formal risk governance process activity.

Assessments have become ubiquitous. Accounting firms do cybersecurity assessments as part of their oversight of financial records. Companies who sell cyber insurance do assessments to determine the risk of offering insurance. Cybersecurity incident response businesses do assessments to develop recommendations for preventing incident recurrence. Though not part of the cybersecurity risk management process, these may be long and expensive undertakings. A given enterprise may be subject to a wide variety of assessments with different scopes, objectives, and methodologies.

Assessments may also appear as spot checks but be part of a more comprehensive strategy. For example, a regulatory cybersecurity assessment may be conducted for a banking subdivision of a company, not the entire enterprise. A penetration test team may be asked to focus only on public-facing websites that contain personally identifiable information. An internally performed NIST CSF assessment may have set an objective of process efficiency rather than risk reduction. But as long as an assessment or review provides information about its scope and purpose, the evaluator, identified issues, and the dates within which the assessment occurred, it can provide information of value to the risk assessment process. The workpapers of each assessment can independently add building blocks of assurance to support the enterprise-level risk management framework.

No matter what the form of the assessment, any identified issues should be centrally tracked, analyzed for potential impact, aligned with cybersecurity risk hierarchy, and prioritized for remediation.

References

AICPA (2015). Guide to Financial Statement Services. American Institute of Certified Public Accountants. https://us.aicpa.org/content/dam/aicpa/interestareas/ privatecompaniespracticesection/qualityservicesdelivery/keepingup/ downloadabledocuments/financial-statement-services-guide.pdf (accessed 08 May 2023).

Bayuk, J. (2005). *Stepping Through the IS Audit, A Guide for Information Systems Managers, 2nd Edition*. Information Systems Audit and Control Association.

FFIEC (2017). Cybersecurity Assessment Tool. Federal Financial Institutions Examination Council. https://www.ffiec.gov/pdf/cybersecurity/ffiec_cat_ may_2017.pdf (accessed 08 May 2023).

IAA (2023). Global Internal Auditing Code of Ethics. The Institute of Internal Auditors. https://www.theiia.org/en/content/guidance/mandatory/standards/ code-of-ethics/ (accessed 08 May 2023).

ISACA (2023). Code of professional ethics, ISACA (formerly Information Systems Audit and Control Association, Control Objectives for Information Technology). https://www.isaca.org/credentialing/code-of-professional-ethics (accessed 08 May 2023).

ISACA (2019). *COBIT 2019 Governance and Management Objectives*. ISACA, www.isaca.org, 2019.

NASA (2022). Apollo 13. National Aeronautics and Space Administration. https://www.nasa.gov/mission_pages/apollo/missions/apollo13.html (accessed 08 May 2023).

NIST-800-66 (2022). *Implementing the Health Insurance Portability and Accountability Act (HIPAA) Security Rule*, National Institute of Standards and Technology. https://nvlpubs.nist.gov/nistpubs/cswp/nist.cswp.04162018.pdf (accessed 08 May 2023).

NIST-CSF (2018). Framework for Improving Critical Infrastructure Cybersecurity, version 1.1. National Institute of Standards and Technology. https://nvlpubs.nist. gov/nistpubs/cswp/nist.cswp.04162018.pdf (accessed 15 January 2024).

Rausand, M. (2014). *Reliability of Safety-Critical Systems: Theory and Applications*, John Wiley & Sons, Incorporated.

6

Issues

In the context of operational risk, an issue is a noun. Oxford dictionary defines an issue primarily as *an important topic or problem for debate or discussion*. The example provided is *global warming*. Merriam Webster's dictionary defines an issue as *a vital or unsettled matter*, providing the example of *economic issue*. Both dictionaries have several secondary meanings. Oxford's secondary definition translates issue directly to *problem* or *difficulty*. An example is: users are experiencing *connectivity issues*. Merriam Webster's secondary definition also directly translates issue to *concern* or *problem* (e.g., issues with a *person's behavior*).

These are all in the ballpark of the way cybersecurity risk issues are viewed through the lens of a cybersecurity risk framework. However, the secondary meaning is more germane to a risk issue. A risk issue is a circumstance that provides evidence of the enterprises' vulnerability to risk. They are typically control weaknesses but may be any circumstance that indicates potential for an increase in risk. A topic for debate or discussion does not qualify as an identified difficulty or concern, and it is only when concern is undoubtably justified that an issue receives the adverb "risk." That said, a cybersecurity issue debated or discussed via scenario analysis can be the starting point for the identification of one or more cybersecurity risk issues.

The distinction between a potential concern and a highly probable event often confuses newcomers to risk when issues are discussed. It sometimes seems optional to them whether an issue should be addressed in some way that makes it less deserving of the adverb risk. They do not recognize that if an issue has been declared a risk, it is by that fact adopted by management as a situation to be remediated. This may be due to the definition of risk as a potential opportunity as well as a negative impact. But in cybersecurity, the word "risk" seldom, if ever, refers to the former.

Stepping Through Cybersecurity Risk Management: A Systems Thinking Approach, First Edition. Jennifer L. Bayuk.
© 2024 John Wiley & Sons, Inc. Published 2024 by John Wiley & Sons, Inc.
Companion website: www.wiley.com/go/STCRM

If the "risk issue" term of art was not confusing enough to a layperson familiar only with the primary definition of the word issue, there are several other definitions of the word issue that could lead them further astray. The word issue can correctly refer to an instance of a serial publication, a subset of stock shares, distribution of a license, an emergent flow, and even an offspring. Depending on the situation, these interpretations may feasibly be considered analogies for a threat, cyberattack, vulnerability, or data leak. This may be the reason why newcomers to risk management often seem slightly confused by what cybersecurity risk managers call an "issue."

At the other end of the spectrum of definitions, the term "issue" is so entirely taken for granted in risk management to be synonymous with risk that the two terms are often conflated by their cybersecurity counterparts. Through the eyes of a junior SecOps staff member, every time they are presented with an issue, it is a risk. This has had the consequence that some cybersecurity programs' risk lists look nothing like risks, but merely sets of issues that indicate probable risk. The rationale leads to issues such as known vulnerabilities being tacitly assumed to *be* a risk as opposed to a *risk indicator for a real risk*. That real risk may be fully defined in a risk register format that includes event subcategories, probability estimates, and other types of risk indicators, but it may not be visible to everyone whose work contributes to it.

6.1   Issue Identification

For example, if a penetration test reveals vulnerabilities that are currently publicly known to be exploited at similar firms, the vulnerability may inaccurately be declared a risk. The obvious remediation for the vulnerability is to install a software security *patch* provided by its vendor for that purpose. This remediates the known vulnerability, but it does not address the root cause of the underlying set of events that comprise the real risk. A risk is a set of events with a similar root cause and probability of occurrence. Eliminating one vulnerability does not address the fact that the enterprise allows publicly known vulnerabilities to exist in its systems. It is typically much harder to address a root cause than a single issue. Root causes are typically underlying systemic situations whose remediations require combinations of simultaneous changes in people, process, and technology. Common root causes are design flaws, deferred maintenance, economic pressures, schedule constraints, inadequate training, inattention to procedures, lack of planning and preparedness, communication failure, arrogance, and stifling political agendas (Abkowitz 2008, chapter 1). Mistaking an issue for a risk is not merely a communication gap but a breakdown in the logic of risk governance. In the example of publicly known vulnerability, the root cause is deferred maintenance and the remediation would be to establish a vulnerability management process to prevent the situation from happening again. This would include frequent scanning for existing publicly known vulnerabilities, systematically eliminating them, monitoring publications that announce new vulnerabilities, checking to see if they exist in systems, and if found, eliminating them.

Consider how the CISO equation may be used to identify a risk issue. Start with a situation wherein a vulnerability is identified in a routine vulnerability scan. Going back to Figure 3.4, the CISO equation tells us that a vulnerability by itself does not imply probability that a cybersecurity event will occur that causes damage. There must be an exploit available and there must be a threat that is not prevented. Moreover, the exploit must be capable of causing damage significant enough to impact the enterprise.

Whether it is performed in a scenario workshop, or independently by an auditor or a cybersecurity risk analyst, the process of researching exploits, mapping to enterprise systems, assessing preventive controls, and estimating damage is all part of cybersecurity risk analysis. Risk issues are a product of such risk analysis. The process of applying the adjective "cybersecurity risk" to "issue" is typically highly controlled and thoroughly reviewed from a due diligence perspective. The diligence should ensure that significant risks are thoroughly considered and also manage bias. (For example, personal preferences for specific technology control vendors do not unduly influence the estimated probability of a risk treated by one of those products.) It is only when the analysis of the circumstances surrounding an issue (a topic for discussion) is complete that the situation is declared to be evidence of risk (an *actual* problem). The description of the situation becomes a *risk issue*. By that fact, it is added to an issue-tracking list. The inclusion of the issue on the list does not mean it automatically gets high priority for remediation, but it does mean its priority should be formally assigned and its remediation tracked. It has been identified as significant. The general idea of an issue-tracking system is that the things on the list have management's agreement that they should be remediated in priority order, as time and resources allow.

Simply put, an issue is a cybersecurity risk issue if it provides evidence that an event in a cybersecurity risk category is more probable than if the issue did not exist. A simple example is a system vulnerability that is known to be part of a common threat vector (e.g., the log4j vulnerability discussed in Chapter 2). Let us say a vulnerability assessment reveals that several servers have this vulnerability. The vulnerability was consistently exploited and therefore has appeared in the CISA Known Exploited Vulnerabilities Catalog ever since it was published CISA-KEV (2023). The presence of such a highly effective exploit in that catalog plus the existence of the vulnerability in an internet-facing server makes the probability that the enterprise will succumb to cyberattack much higher than if the vulnerability did not exist. Also assume that the vulnerability has already been exploited at organizations similar to the enterprise. So even if the probability cannot be stated with numeric precision, the situation, which is the issue that the internet-facing log4j vulnerability exists, should be given the enterprise's highest priority (e.g., critical). With just this information, a cybersecurity risk analyst would be justified in opening a risk issue and assigning an issue owner, who would typically be the manager of the application team in charge of the web server.

However, it is not to be expected that the issue owner will automatically consider the risk issue a priority, so in addition to making the case for a probable cyberattack, a cyber risk analyst should research the vulnerability at the lowest possible level of technical detail to identify technical methods of interrupting corresponding threat vector(s). In the log4j case, the vulnerability can be exploited by crafting a string that looks like a harmless variable to the Java interpreter, but actually returns code that will be incorporated into the runtime environment of, and executed by, the targeted web server. Figure 6.1 is an example threat vector in a log4j attack. It shows how a hacker can exploit the website's functionality to add its own internet-connected database to the list of trusted code sources to the website's code library and thereby expand the reach of log4j's ability to execute code to any malicious software ("malware") that is compatible with the target system. In the threat vector of Figure 6.1, step 1 is to find a web server data entry field that will be resolved by the web server's logging process. The login field is a good guess because most servers will log both successful and failed access attempts. That happens in step 2. In step 3, the hacker presents another variable to be resolved that calls the malicious code loaded in step 2. In this case, the malicious code sends the hacker the web server's configuration and code base. The hacker analyzes that data to create a customized database hack. This is placed into another variable and executed by the server. The data from the database is then sent back to the hacker server.

Although the diagram in Figure 6.1 is not a detailed technical analysis, it provides enough detail about how the attack works to inform a technology team

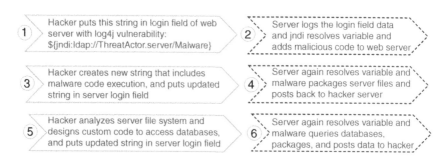

Figure 6.1 Sketch Threat Vector Basis for Risk Issue

charged with building a remediation plan. The first step can be thwarted in at least three ways. The first is to block all outbound network connections from the web servers so the webserver cannot access the hacker site. The second is to make sure all input fields are scanned for brackets and automatically parse any data fields that contain them, and reject any that matched the pattern of a jdni command. The third is to upgrade the jndi log code to a version in which the vulnerability is patched and ensure all earlier vulnerable jndi code is removed from the web server (along with appropriate detection procedures to ensure this is not the case). All of these measures are examples of good cybersecurity hygiene. The first option is the quickest and easiest to implement, but if there was some other reason the web-server needed outbound access, it may interfere with web server functionality, so it would require some research and planning. The second option would have less impact on operations, but may require some time and testing as the web server is likely to have hundreds of data fields. The third option seems the safest, running only the risk of unexpected log functionality from a hastily tested new release. The cybersecurity risk analyst would discuss these options with the issue owner and help decide what would be the best short- and long-term approach to issue remediation. Then the analyst would help the application team create a plan to implement at least one remediation in the short term, and all three in the long term. Note the short-term plan addresses the proximate cause, the current vulnerability, while the long-term plan is designed to reduce the risk of a common root cause, that is, currently unknown vulnerabilities exploited similar systemic weaknesses.

Although there may have been debate on whether to label a situation as a cybersecurity risk issue, and the matter of whether the issue is related to control decisions may be undetermined at the time an issue is identified, the fact that an enterprise does label a situation as a cybersecurity risk issue is itself evidence of the existence of a matter to be considered when analyzing cybersecurity risk. It is demonstrably related to causes of events somewhere in the risk hierarchy, even if the full set of those events are not well understood. So although "issue" seems like a vague term, it has crystal clear significance when it is modified by the term "risk."

6.2 Classification

Even a small firm may have dozens of cybersecurity risk issues to address. The importance of maintaining current information on those issues and tracking them to completion cannot be understated. The priority labels are meant to convey urgency, such as: *critical, significant, important*. The choice is made by estimating the likelihood of the issue being exploited by a threat actor, and the expected frequency and impact of such events. Presumably, no issues that are not raised to the level of importance would merit formal risk tracking, though some organizations will include a category that conveys no urgency, such as *Notable*. Where included in an issue-tracking system, this category is less like a risk issue priority and more like an *opportunity for improvement* category used to track an idea for something like a nice-to-have efficiency control.

Issue classification requires an organized data set that allows for quick status reporting. Issues are typically classified not only by priority but by type, status, source, and organization. Figure 6.2 displays an example issue recorded in a tracking system with dropdown selections for those classifications. Although the categories are commonly customized, in general terms, the type of issue will refer to the technology landscape, in this case, internal, cloud, or third party. The status will include draft, open, and closed. The source will indicate how the organization became aware of the issue. Common sources are internal and external audit because it is their job to identify risk issues. But sources may also include regulators, customers, and internal or outsourced assessments. Where an issue is discovered within the CISO organization, the source will often appear as "self-identified" to distinguish it from sources external to the security program.

The top of each dropdown selection in Figure 6.2 is the default value for the field that will be set if a choice is not made at the time it is created. This value shows that issue type and priority should remain obviously "Not set" unless specifically identified by the cybersecurity analyst. The status will be "Draft" to keep it from appearing on reports until data entry is completed. If a standard source is not selected, it will be considered "Other," presumably a small set. The organization will typically be the department within the enterprise to which remediation activity is assigned, and the contact will be the person in that organization responsible for remediation implementation. However, the responsibility may remain with the CISO by default unless formally assigned elsewhere. Where remediation requires several departments to collaborate in sequence such as design, development, and deployment, the organization may be specified at a higher level in the enterprise personnel hierarchy and the contact may change over the lifespan of the issue.

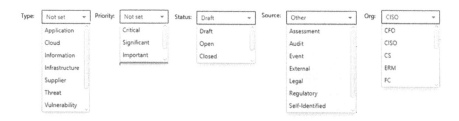

Figure 6.2 Example Cybersecurity Issue Classification

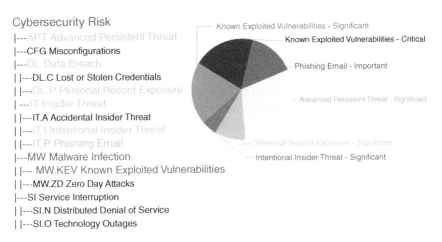

Cybersecurity Risk
|---APT Advanced Persistent Threat
|---CFG Misconfigurations
|---DL Data Breach
| |---DL.C Lost or Stolen Credentials
| |---DL.P Personal Record Exposure
| ---IT Insider Threat
| |---IT.A Accidental Insider Threat
| |---IT.I Intentional Insider Threat
| |---IT.P Phishing Email
|---MW Malware Infection
| |--- MW.KEV Known Exploited Vulnerabilities
| |---MW.ZD Zero Day Attacks
|---SI Service Interruption
| |---SI.N Distributed Denial of Service
| |---SI.O Technology Outages

Known Exploited Vulnerabilities - Significant
Known Exploited Vulnerabilities - Critical
Phishing Email - Important
Advanced Persistent Threat - Significant
Personal Record Exposure - Significant
Intentional Insider Threat - Significant

Figure 6.3 Example Cybersecurity Risk Issue Report

Where a risk-tracking system is integrated with a risk hierarchy, these classifications allow for quick search and reporting of risk issues by risk, as well as at-a-glance status reporting of overall risk remediation status. Figure 6.3 is an example of how labeling each issue with a risk category or subcategory can be informative. Cybersecurity professionals often use a stoplight analogy to show the relative priority of issues to be addressed in each event category, as in this illustration. The pie chart at the right of the figure uses an ordinal stoplight range of color for the slices and labels of types of important, significant, and critical cybersecurity risk issues. The left side of the figure is the cybersecurity risk hierarchy that lists event categories and under them, indented subcategories. Where risk issues counted in the pie chart match a cybersecurity risk category or one of its subcategories, those that match are enlarged in the left side of the figure.

The risk hierarchy also ordinally represents the important, significant, and critical severity measures with font size. Categories and subcategories for which there have been no actual incidents are the smallest. Those with important incidents are slightly larger. Those with significant incidents are slightly larger than those, and the categories with critical incidents have the largest font. Note that where two types of risk subcategories map to events of different levels of severity, the highest level of severity bubbles up to the higher level category. The top level cybersecurity risk inherits the highest priority of its categories. Note this is not a direct measure of risk because risk is measured in probability, it is merely an informative map that can be used in combination with other risk indicators to use when estimating the probability of a risk.

6.3   Criteria and Remediation

In addition to the classifications, a cybersecurity risk issue-tracking record can provide insightful information by including a *criteria*, that is, a formal demonstration of why a situation presented by an issue is not acceptable, given risk appetite. It may refer to an objective statement or an obvious risk. The statement may be a legal or regulatory requirement, an enterprise cybersecurity policy or standard, a known exploited vulnerability, an external event, and/or result of research or experience in the technology domain under scrutiny. Where issues are identified by assessments, the statement will include the assessment requirement(s) that is not fully met. Whatever the criteria, it should drive the choice of issue classification that determines its priority for remediation. Without it, there will be no urgency in addressing the issue.

Issue criteria also provide the basis for a remediation target. The goal of remediation is to change the situation described as the issue to conform to the criteria upon which the issue is based. The remediation plan should not only change the situation but ensure that the change is independently observable. Issue criteria thereby also provide a factual basis for a decision on when the issue may be considered closed. As long as the criteria remains a valid reason to declare the issue, the issue should remain open.

As previously observed, for issues based on vulnerabilities, remediation of a single vulnerability does not address the root cause of events associated with an issue. Therefore, it is important to associate an issue with a risk that has at least a partial definition in the enterprise risk hierarchy. This link identifies the set of events whose root cause should be measurably less probable once the issue is remediated. Figure 6.4 illustrates the relationship between these data fields in a manner that provides information on the issue as a whole.

Where issues are based on assessment requirements, the assessment evaluator may have provided a recommendation for remediation. Because there are usually a wide variety of ways to address issue criteria, such assessment recommendations

Issue	Summary	Source/Criteria	Remediation
I5 Open Significant 2024-02-06	NIST-CSF requirement: ID.AM-3 Type: Infrastructure	Assessment (A000002-ID.AM-3) Criteria: Does not Meet NIST-CSF assessment requirement: Organizational communication and data flows are mapped Linked Risks: CS.APT: Advanced Persistent Threat - Activities of well-organized and funded adversaries with long-term plans to achive goals that negatively impact the firm.	Enginir, Simrin FC 2024-10-31
I2 Open Important 2024-04-12	Malware event, impact Moderate: End Point Security Desktop apt malware scanning files on all shares for PII Type: Infrastructure	Event (Event-SIRT4753) Criteria: Known exploited vulnerability to threat vector: Phishing -- breach of risk appetite for PII Linked Risks: CS.MW: Malware Infection - Execution of malicious software on a firm systems.	Opsman, Sec CISO No Target

Figure 6.4   Remediation Tracking

are typically not binding. Nevertheless, they often appear in an issue description in order for the issue owner to take advantage of the evaluator's experience in prior dealings with similar issues. Some risk organizations may specify a timeframe for remediation based on issue priority. For example, five days for critical issues, thirty days for significant issues, and sixty days for important issues. Or the timeframe may be customized based on event analysis that reveals when the issue should be remediated to avoid a higher probably of further exploits. This could be a matter of days or weeks. If the remediation is targeted at less than a few days, it already has been assigned management's highest sense of urgency, so there should be no need to declare an issue unless the target is uncontrollably passed. Issues are declared so they can be tracked.

If for some reason, an issue owner cannot meet the remediation timeframe, the situation should be escalated to the next level of management. If this happens twice, the escalation should proceed to a level above that. The remediation target dates should initially be selected with this possibility of failure in mind, that is initial target dates should ensure that the formal escalation process brings untreated risks to the attention of executive management in time to personally address them.

Of course, in order to meet target dates, the issue owner must have the knowledge and skill to figure out how to accomplish the remediation or must be able to outsource it either internally or to a third-party service. The project manager for remediation does not have to be the same person as the issue owner but if there is a formal project management system in which the remediation is tracked, this should be referred to in the issue-tracking record and automatically integrated if possible. This allows the risk-reporting system to be updated when milestones are met or missed.

Risk is not opposed to remediation, but sometimes in the lives of a cybersecurity professional, it can seem that way. It can seem that risk is a method of allowing a decision not to remediate an issue. Risk professionals understand that there are other options of treating risk that do not include remediation. These include risk transfer, commonly known as purchasing insurance to reduce monetary losses instead of actual risk. There is also risk avoidance; for example, shutting down the applications that require the use of a vulnerable web server. They also include risk acceptance, that is, do nothing and hope for the best. It is this last option wherein risk becomes a method of a decision not to remediate.

The careers of most cybersecurity professionals have encountered the requirement to "accept" the risk presented by an issue. Sometimes there is a justified concern that remediating a cybersecurity risk issue will introduce instability in a highly sensitive operation. This is often the case in manufacturing industrial control systems. Sometimes a risk acceptance may just be the result of a misunderstanding of the enterprise risk appetite. Sometimes the remediation is delayed or there is resistance due to business pressures to deploy new applications quickly.

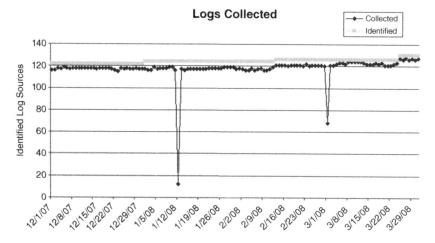

Figure 6.5 Risk versus Remediation

In this case, there are typically system stakeholders that do not psychologically accept the need for remediation. It is therefore important to have a tone at the top that supports standards and procedures to ensure due diligence in the evaluation of risk tolerance and corresponding awareness that once a risk remediation decision is made, the remediation should go forward.

Figure 6.5 illustrates a situation that can provoke a debate on risk versus remediation. The figure shows a target metric where the scope is the status of log collection from a set of systems over a timeline. The number of log sources (i.e., systems) varies as does the count of logs collected on a daily basis from all sources. The top line refers to the number of logs expected to be collected, and the lower line measures each day's count of logs that were actually collected. The number collected almost never meets its target and there are sometimes very large unexpected variations. A risk analyst reviewing this situation may look at the large drops and search for a cause. In the first case of a large drop, it may be discovered that the log server itself was down for most of the day. This explains the low number, but it does not address the root cause of the situation. Some time passes between the large drop and a smaller one. That second situation may be explained by a network outage that occurred on that day. Again, it explains the drop without addressing the root cause. Regardless of the explanations of the drops, the daily fluctuations do not have a common explanation. It may be too exhausting to look into every one, so the risk analyst may instead check a SecOps system to see if there were any confirmed cybersecurity incidents in that timeframe. If the answer is no, then the risk analyst may conclude that minor fluctuations in log collection are not a problem.

Consider this situation in the context of a risk appetite statement to the effect that there is no tolerance for undetected cybersecurity incidents. Given that automated log analysis is the primary way that cybersecurity incidents are detected, the risk appetite puts the risk analysts' conclusion in a different light. Being unable to check all the identified log sources could mean that there is cybersecurity incident activity that is not detected according to planned security architecture. In this case, the minor fluctuations present a systemic risk issue that should be tracked to full remediation.

Where risk appetite appears flexible or lacks transparency, remediation may get stalled. So the point of presenting this example on the difference between risk analysis and remediation targets is simply so that it is understood as a situation to be recognized. It depends on the enterprise's cybersecurity risk framework whether risk acceptance or remediation should win out.

References

Abkowitz, M. (2008). *Operational Risk Management, A Case Study Approach to Effective Planning and Response*, John Wiley & Sons, Inc. 2008, Chapter 1.

CISA (2023). Known Exploited Vulnerabilities Catalog. Cybersecurity & Infrastructure Security Agency. https://www.cisa.gov/known-exploited-vulnerabilities-catalog (accessed 08 May 2023).

7

Metrics

Measurement is the process of mapping from the empirical world to the formal, relational world. The measure that results characterizes an attribute of some object under scrutiny. A measure is one thing, sometimes called a primitive, that you can report on as a fact. It is the result of holding something like a yardstick against some object. Cybersecurity is not the object of measurement, nor a well-understood attribute. This means that you are not directly measuring security, you are measuring other things and using them to draw conclusions about cybersecurity.

The history of cybersecurity includes a wide variety of examples of how people use numbers to measure security processes and attributes. However, not all measures use numbers. For example, in Figure 7.1 we have a human being measured by a wall rule, and the ruler's measurement is somewhere around 5½ feet. This is a single attribute, it is height. It does not fully describe the whole human of course. If you want to describe a human, you have to give more attributes, such as *shape, color, sound, intellect.* Not all of these measures can be made with numbers, yet they are tangible attributes that help identify the person. Cybersecurity measures are like that but even less tangible. It is more like a measure of weather. You can measure temperature, pressure, and wind direction, and it can help you decide whether it is probable that your raincoat is protective enough and whether your house is high enough over the flood line, but you cannot actually fully characterize weather or cybersecurity well enough to model its identity over time. It changes too rapidly.

Industrial engineers intuitively understand that business-critical processes must be instrumented for measurement to be successfully managed. That is why pressure gauges on tanks used to measure capacity are typically customized and delivered with the tank rather than bolted on after the tank is integrated into its target environment. These measures, plus a measure of tank inventory, can be used in combination to show that the system is working as designed. Similarly,

Stepping Through Cybersecurity Risk Management: A Systems Thinking Approach, First Edition. Jennifer L. Bayuk.
© 2024 John Wiley & Sons, Inc. Published 2024 by John Wiley & Sons, Inc.
Companion website: www.wiley.com/go/STCRM

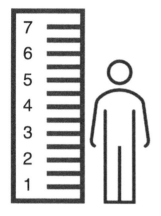

Figure 7.1 Measure

Figure 7.2 Nominal Measure

cybersecurity units of measure are tangible attributes of the cybersecurity ecosystem such as information classification, vulnerability exposure, a time to respond to an incident, and asset inventory. The term "measure" herein refers to acts of cybersecurity attribute data collection.

7.1 Measuring Cybersecurity

An example cybersecurity attribute is to specify, for each application installed on a user desktop, whether it is necessary for a business to operate. If we measure that specification with a metric, we cannot find a yardstick to put against the application and use it to automatically yield a result, like it is required or not necessary. The users of the application may not know if their business could survive without it. But once the fact has been determined, it is a measure, and the measure is one of two labels: *Not Necessary* or *Necessary*. This type of measure is *nominal*. It merely provides a name, that is it. Figure 7.2 shows an example of how a nominal measure may be recorded.

Where there is shade of grey in such measures (i.e., if there is some doubt about how necessary an application is), we may instead label each application one of a series of values. For example, *Not Necessary, Helpful, and Critical* may be used to specify that some applications are more critical than others. This allows us to specify that some applications are more necessary than others. This type of scalar measure is *ordinal*. These measurements have an order in which one thing comes after another, but nothing other than that. No numbers, just labels for what's being ordered. One application is more necessary than another. Often these measures are represented with graphics that imply a scale in color or shape, as in Figure 7.3, the cybersecurity stoplight analogy for issue priority level.

If the ordered objects in an ordinal measure were somehow measurably different from each other on the same *unit* scale, the measure created by the ordered series would be called an interval. The similarity of unit allows the scale to be numeric, measured the same way each time with a number, but no subjective assessment is required. Time and temperature have unit scales. Interval measures require both a quantity and a unit of measurement to support some ordinal ordering judgment. The interval is on a continuum with no start or stop. It just measures the units in comparison to the line on the scale. However, it is not a really

Figure 7.3 Interval Measure

scale because a scale typically has a
zero at one end and an interval does
not need one. Figure 7.4 illustrates the
interval measure of temperature. A
cybersecurity example of an interval
measure is the time it takes to respond
to a security alert, typically measured in units of minutes.

Figure 7.4 Ordinal Measure

Where there is a numeric continuum in which higher and lower values have
the same unit of measure as in interval, but there is *also* a concept of an abso-
lute zero (a concept missing in interval measures like time and temperature),
the measure is considered *ratio*. Like interval, a ratio measure also uses a
numeric scale of similar units. It differs from interval in that its scale starts
with zero, so all the measures are positive or negative. Although the word *ratio*
also refers to the division of one number by another, a numerator and denominator as in a percentage, those two numbers may also be referred to as *ratio
measures*. Figure 7.5 illustrates the concept. In cybersecurity, all ratio measures
are positive, they are counts of systems, vulnerabilities, people, logins, alerts,
among other things. A common cybersecurity ratio measure is the number of
servers in a data center.

While all cybersecurity measures are tangible attributes of the cybersecurity
ecosystem, most cybersecurity measures are not informative in isolation, but only
in combination with other measures. The term "measure" herein refers only to

Figure 7.5 Ratio Measure

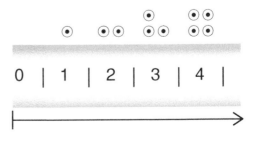

acts of cybersecurity attribute data collection, not to their individual ability to describe cybersecurity.

A readily accessible security attribute is found in security software obtained to meet a goal of system protection. But even this must be instrumented properly to produce a reliable performance measure. For example, it is common to set up a standard server-build process wherein security software such as antivirus or OS hardening agents are installed as part of a workflow. Successful completion of this step for all new and upgraded servers is often taken as a positive performance measure. It is also common for *legacy*, that is, older, machines to avoid this workflow by opting out of automated software upgrade programs or allowing software upgrade programs to run even though they will not work properly on the legacy OS. This leaves a pool of vulnerable servers below the radar of the measure. Only by careful enumeration of servers within scope and sufficient instrumentation on all servers to show what software is currently operational can you rely on performance measures to show what good performance looks like.

For example, envision a security process that has workflow to simultaneously patch any and all known high severity vulnerabilities on every machine that contains personally identifiable information. This would be designed to meet a security goal of maintaining a low-risk appetite for data breaches. It is important when operating this process to correctly identify the machines with PII, scan all of them for high severity vulnerabilities, and apply the patch to those systems. A security manager running this process should not mistake the execution of those steps for an indicator that the control works. Figure 7.6 illustrates how easy it is to make that mistake. When operating these controls, there should be corresponding changes to the systems in scope. Although it is possible to create a nominal measure that measures whether that the process of applying routine patches was completed, a

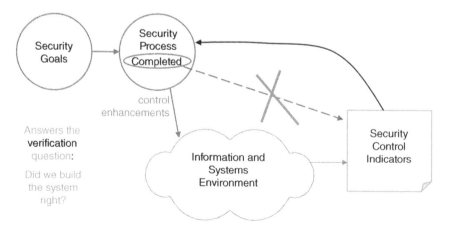

Figure 7.6 Cybersecurity Measurement Data Flow

control indicator requires a check of configuration and/or functionality of the actual system in scope. After a patching process, a rescan for the same vulnerabilities wherein none are found would be considered an indicator that the control meets its objective.

7.2 From Measures to Metrics

Metrics are based on measures and usually need to utilize more than one measure to be meaningful. When measures are combined via algorithms to provide meaningful information, metrics are produced. Cybersecurity is not a single specific attribute of a system or application being measured. Each measure must be simple enough to understand how it can be interpreted as a cybersecurity attribute. For example, measures of server counts may be of interest for a variety of reasons, such as cost of operations and staffing levels; however, when a server count measure is used to draw conclusions about security, that conclusion is what makes the measure a component of a cybersecurity metric.

When measures are combined in a manner that sheds light on security, cybersecurity metrics can create situational awareness on multiple fronts. Some of it will be good news, some of it bad news. But note the difference between good *news* and good *metrics*. Bad metrics can deceptively deliver good news. In security that is a "false negative." A false positive event is one in which the circumstance surrounding the event turns out to be harmless. A false negative is a situation in which the circumstance surrounding an event should have triggered a security alert but did not.

Good metrics can give both good and bad news that can be trusted. By good metrics, we mean metrics that are both practical and useful. We can learn from them and use them to systematically improve practices. Practical and useful metrics are easy to connect to the concept of cybersecurity. They utilize transparent data-gathering processes and support security decision-making.

It is helpful to start a cybersecurity metrics effort with a vision of what good cybersecurity looks like. Good cybersecurity (as opposed to good metrics) looks like swift and thorough cyberattack containment, mitigation, and root-cause remediation. In the absence of attacks, good cybersecurity looks like a low risk of successful attack. In the absence of an attack, a demonstration that an attack response is good requires a *verification* metric, often referred to as a target because it checks whether a control is configured and operating as designed. The target is a set of systems to which the control process or procedure is applied. The measure is a test of a configuration or function, depending on the scope of the metric. A conclusion that there is a low risk of attack requires a *validation* metric, often referred to as a *goal* metric; that is, we operate under the assumption that the goal of a cybersecurity program is to reduce the risk of a negatively impacting cyber event to an acceptable level, that is, below risk appetite. If a response test meets its target but we nevertheless succumb to cyberattack, we need to reevaluate and remediate our method of response.

This distinction between target and goal metrics may also be described as "correctness versus effectiveness" or "verification versus validation." They have also been referred to as baseline versus objective, where baseline refers to capabilities and objective refers to a planned improvement, a measure that is expected to improve as the goal for which the metric is designed may be as aspirational (Seiersen 2022, p. 7). Target, correctness, and verification metrics are based on tests of system component composition and function. With respect to security, correctness means conformance with security architecture standards. Goal, effectiveness, and validation metrics are based on measures of whether the system accomplishes its mission. In systems engineering terms, target metrics answer the question: "Was the system built right?" Goal metrics answer the question: "Was the right system built?" Using both enables a CISO to both set and receive business expectations for the cybersecurity metrics program.

Target metrics are straightforward because a CISO understands how the controls are composed and how they are expected to work. Goal metrics are more challenging because it requires adopting another's perspective on whether their goals for system security are met. These are often developed using a Goal Question Metric (GQM) approach adopted from software quality metrics, a methodology that considers what questions stakeholders like business process owners would ask to determine whether a system meets their goals for security. As they do not have the insight into technical or process design, their questions are often higher level, such as, "Are we the only ones who can see our customer's data?" These validation questions can only be answered by examining a system in operation, and creative approaches to measurement are often required to answer them.

Figure 7.7 provides an example of using an algorithm to combine information classification, vulnerability exposure, and server counts in a target metric. Continuing the example in Figure 7.6, its first measure is the number of servers in the data center. In the figure, the servers that contain personally identifiable information are labeled "PII," a nominal measure. The servers are also labeled with the highest severity level of any vulnerabilities found on the server in the most recent vulnerability scan, an ordinal measure. Although attempts to perform math on ordinal values are inherently faulty (Thomas 2019), such measures of the control environment allow you to create algorithms that read the labels and produce information you can use to see if your security program is operating as expected; that is, a verification (or lack thereof) that the control works.

Assume that there is low-risk appetite for data breaches that prompted the adoption of a control objective to systematically eradicate any and all known high severity vulnerabilities on every machine that contains PII. Say you have three

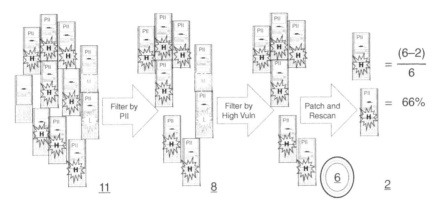

Figure 7.7   Measures + Algorithm = Metric

measures for a set of servers. One for the quantity of servers in the set (ratio). The second tests for the security attribute of "presence of PII" on a server, which assigns those servers the label "PII." The third scans all the servers for vulnerabilities and assigns them an ordinal measure corresponding to the highest severity vulnerability found on that server (one of "Low, Medium, High"). This establishes a method of listing the servers that need to have high severity vulnerabilities systematically eradicated.

The control designed to achieve the objective is a security process workflow. For example, a security program running this process should use the measures to create a list of servers to patch the vulnerabilities, then again perform the measures and recreate the list. If this process is performed effectively, the second list should have zero entries.

Figure 7.7 is an example of this metric in action. It starts by labeling and counting all the servers in the set. There are 11 servers of which 8 are labeled PII and of those, 6 have highly severe vulnerabilities. These are selected for remediation priority, and patches are applied to eliminate the vulnerability. After the patch activity, the vulnerability rescan shows 2 of the targeted servers still have highly severe vulnerabilities. This is a cybersecurity failed validation metric and a correctness metric that shows only a 66% success rate. This is a good indicator of cybersecurity risk, even though it indicates that the risk is bad.

Routine vulnerability scanning provides a practical and useful metric, which is easy to connect with the concept of security. Where servers are vulnerable and vulnerability elimination processes do not eliminate the vulnerabilities, the risk of successful cyberattack is significant. The data from which the metric is derived is obvious, it is easy to understand how the data was gathered, and so this is referred to as a "transparent" metric. Transparent metrics allow one to make conclusions about security based on knowledge of where the data comes from, what it means, and how it is used to support decisions about security.

A requirement for transparency in cybersecurity metrics program helps keep one's focus on metrics that are valid in a way that scientists call "face valid," which reflects general agreement in the layperson's opinion that a given measurement technique is suitable for its expected use. Face validity is important because people have to understand the metric in order to consider it actionable. However, because face validity is based on opinion, it is not enough to support a claim that the metric truly reflects a security attribute of a system of interest. In science and engineering, it is also preferred for measurement to be *content, criterion, or construct valid.*

Content validation implies that the full domain of content is measurable. Given the ability to count machines and provide them with cybersecurity specification measures in the form of nominal or ordinal labels as in Figure 7.7, there is content validity in that cybersecurity measure. Criterion validation implies that the correspondence between the chosen behavioral criteria and the attribute to be measured is exact. The security attributes of *highly vulnerable* may be considered criterion valid because there is a direct correspondence between system's behavioral response to a publicly known vulnerability scan and a system's ability to withstand attacks. Construct validation allows for a measure of the extent to which a set of measures are consistent with a theoretically derived hypothesis concerning the concepts being measured. Using a construct standard of validity, a theoretical model of a secure system may be used to construct a combination of content and criterion measurements that provide evidence that a given system of interest conforms to the model. An example of this is a correctly implemented systems security architecture. Whether the example metric meets this construct validity standard depends on the extent to which the servers that failed the verification test conformed to the documented security architecture or not. It is likely they did not, but the servers that passed the vulnerability scan do conform to the model. In this case, the measure could be considered construct valid.

Of course, the best designed metrics are still subject to errors in measurement, so in addition to choosing good metrics, a cybersecurity metrics program should establish criteria for measurement as well. Cybersecurity measures should be precise enough to be informative indicators of whether a system is at risk of succumbing to attack. Such measurement requirements include, but are not limited to, those listed in Figure 7.8 (Herrmann 2007). Although not all measures will subscribe to all the criteria (especially not the ordinal ones), the more criteria to which a measure may lay claim, the more information it conveys.

These criteria were first formally applied to cybersecurity in the mid-2000s. At that time, best practices in managing security included review of logs of unauthorized access attempts, authorized access at unusual hours and server process execution outside of system boot sequence. Wherever computer operating

Criteria	Description
Accurate:	data reflects the content of measurement as it was envisioned
Consistent:	measure is independent of measurer
Correct:	measure collects data according to specifications
Informative:	measurement provides information without additional context
Numeric:	measurement is precisely quantified
Replicable:	measurement repeated the same way in same environment will yield same result
Time-based:	a datetime stamp accompanies each measurement
Unit-based:	data is expressed in terms of a single recognizable quantity though may be part of a larger whole

Figure 7.8 Criteria for Cybersecurity Measures

systems had requirements for confidentiality, integrity, and availability, logs were generated. Where the operating systems could not implement the requirements, security software was "bolted on," and the security software logs had to be reviewed as well. As the logs piled up, it became impossible to review them for suspicious activity without sophisticated automation. Security Incident and Event Management (SIEM) technology could be configured to create alerts from patterns of logs, but the rule bases for those patterns were not very sophisticated. However, large budgets for SecOps were becoming the norm, so a conference of specialists in cybersecurity metrics was arranged by industry analysts, drawing dozens of volunteer program committee participants as well as sponsors. They called it Metricon (Jaquith 2004).

Metricon has since produced detailed definitions of dozens of security metrics. For example, a Metricon member shared a new method for monitoring internet routing vulnerabilities, downtime and instability, hijacking and wholesale traffic interception (Cowie 2009). Like others at Metricon, his presentation provided a concrete way to measure vulnerabilities in an extremely common computing component that was routinely left unsecured. The presenter included an observation that was a recurring theme at Metricon, "Very few people understand these risks, so they are not being measured or managed appropriately. No one is covering your back!" Figure 7.9 is an excerpt from that presentation. The figure is a good example of how Metricon participants from a wide variety of technological backgrounds educated each other on the depth and breadth of technology architecture that must be included in the scope of any effective cybersecurity monitoring program.

Over time, Metricon produced a plethora of different types of cybersecurity metrics categories, the most popular of which are listed in Figure 7.10. They span the range from threat intelligence to insider threat modeling. Of these

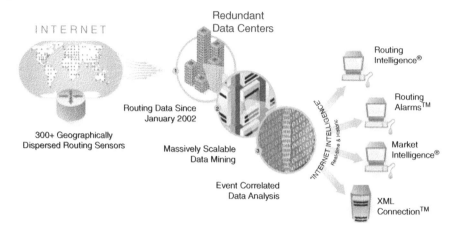

Figure 7.9 Exemplar Metricon Discussion Topic

Metric Category	Description
Adversary Skills	Metrics that estimate adversary skills levels.
Adversary Goals	Metrics gleaned from intelligence on adversary motivation and justification.
Deterministic Models	Metrics that combine measures with inference rules to present conclusions on cybersecurity.
External activity	Metrics that track threats ("internet weather patterns").
Internal activity	Metrics that chart work activity ("security staff busyness").
Monitor	Metrics that monitor performance of security processes and procedures.
Performance	Metrics that demonstrate capability to deliver system cybersecurity features.
Remediation	Metrics that show progress toward a cybersecurity control objective.
Resilience	Metrics that demonstrate system ability to recover from harmful impact.
Stochastic Models	Metrics that combine measures with probability estimates based on historical data.
Target	Metrics that combine denominator attributes to present percentage of target (e.g. device config).
Vulnerability	Metrics that show susceptibility to known threats.

Figure 7.10 Cybersecurity Metrics Categories

categories, target is by far the easiest to connect to the concept of security. Targets are typically correctness metrics, designed to show the extent to which a control is fully deployed in a given systems environment. Figure 7.7 is a target metric where the environment is defined as the set of servers, and the control is the high vulnerability elimination process. A target is based on inventory – any inventory that can be measured as a ratio. In the previous example, the inventory was the set of servers.

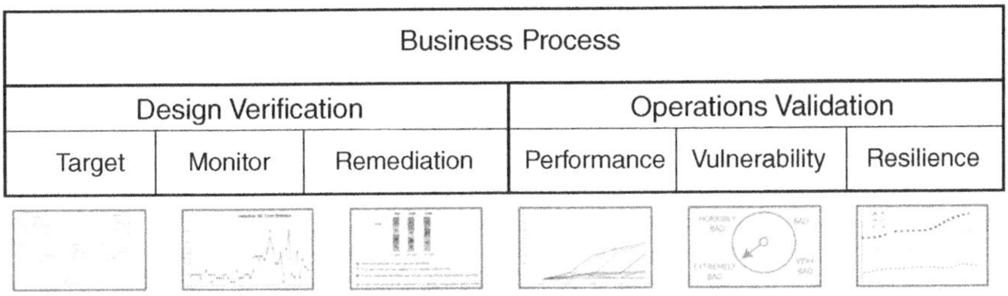

Business Process					
Design Verification			Operations Validation		
Target	Monitor	Remediation	Performance	Vulnerability	Resilience

Figure 7.11 Example Cybersecurity Dashboard

These metrics categories are useful across a range of cybersecurity domains, but some better serve for a different domain than others. In selecting metrics, it is important to understand how the utility of different types of metrics informs and supports decisions better than others. Figure 7.11 illustrates how an organization combines different categories of metrics in a dashboard approach that can provide an enterprise view or filter the data to show cybersecurity metrics corresponding to a given business process. It uses different types of visual displays to illustrate various aspects of the system lifecycle.

To produce such a wide variety of charts on a routine basis, it is helpful to have documented both the measure and metrics definitions in a repository other than a spreadsheet or similar file that will get lost with changes in staff assigned to this endeavor. Figure 7.12 shows an example of a measure definition and a metric definition that uses that measure. Note that both include algorithms and units, fields that must be used consistently in production metrics. But the measure definitions contain a field for *source*, while in its place in the metrics definition, the label is *description*. This is the main difference between a measure and a metric, the measure is the set of underlying primitives in a metrics production process. The metrics are what is presented on the dashboard. The measure record contains a field labeled *specification* because it specifies how the measure is recorded. The metric record has instead a field labeled *algorithm* because its specification is to perform calculations on its measures. That is, unless a metric is calculated external to the enterprise and delivered intact, a metric record should link to at least one measure record that provides the data that allows for metric calculation.

Another difference between the measure and metric fields displayed in Figure 7.12 is that the measure screen has a button labeled *Metrics* and the metrics screen has a button labeled *Measures*. This allows a risk analyst a quick view of what metrics the measures support and what measures are used in a metric, respectively. Although measures and metrics are separate entries in a metrics catalog, they are combined for reporting as in Figure 7.13. This allows measures to be defined once and used in multiple metrics.

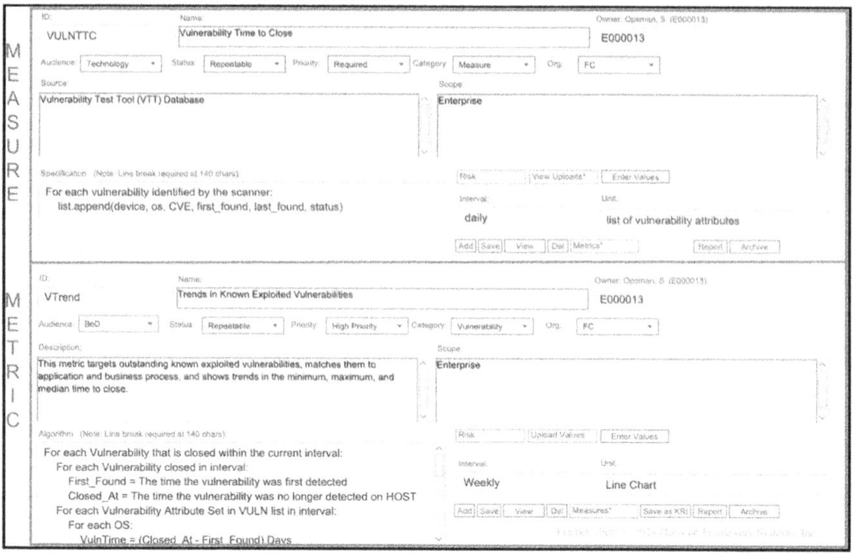

Figure 7.12 Example Measure and Metric Records

Owner	Sec Opsman (E000013)
Scope	Enterprise
Status	Repeatable
Unit	Line Chart

Algorithm:	For each Vulnerability that is closed within the current interval:
	  For each Vulnerability closed in interval:
	    First_Found = The time the vulnerability was first detected
	    Closed_At = The time the vulnerability was no longer detected on HOST
	    For each Vulnerability Attribute Set in VULN list in interval:
	      For each OS:
	        VulnTime = (Closed_At - First_Found).Days
	        OS.CLOSE_TIME_LIST.append(VulnTime)
	        if Tuple.OS = = OS:
	          if VulnTime > MAX[OS]:
	            MAX[OS] = VulnTime
	          if VulnTime < MIN[OS]:
	            MAX[OS] = VulnTime
	      For each OS:
	        Median[OS]= statistics.median_low(CLOSE_TIME_LIST)
	      For each OS:
	        Series[OS][MAX].Values.Append(MESTIME,MAX[OS])
	        Series[OS][MIN].Values.Append(MESTIME,MIN[OS])
	        Series[OS][MEDIAN].Values.Append(MESTIME,MEDIAN[OS])
	    # result is one series for each OS <MIN,MAX,MEDIAN>
	    Plot each series on a graph where the X Axis are Months and the Y Axis is Days it took to close

Interval	Weekly
Description	This metric targets outstanding known exploited vulnerabilities, matches them to application and business process, and shows trends in the minimum, maximum, and median time to close.
Measures	
Measure 1:	VULNS: Vulnerability Attributes Scope: All vulnerabilities identified by Enterprise vulnerability scanning tool.
Measure 2:	VULNTTC: Vulnerability Time to Close Scope: Enterprise
Audience	Board
Priority	High Priority

Figure 7.13 Example Metric Documentation

A metrics catalog is also helpful in the metrics planning process. It is best practice to have metrics that are leading, which means they are predictive of bad things that might happen. An example leading metric is threat intelligence that shows competitors being attacked in a manner to which the enterprise is also vulnerable. But metrics are typically lagging, that is, illustrating what happened yesterday, though the information is still valuable. An example is trends in risk issues. Or they could be concurrent, real time, such as those that immediately generate alerts to SecOps. An example is the user behavioral metrics that create alerts. There may be some metrics that are considered nice to have for which there has been an algorithm developed for which there is no current data source. A catalog is a good way to make sure the algorithm is readily available when and if the data source materializes. It also can track the status of metric development in an ordinal way, for example, from planned to partial to repeatable. Figure 7.14 is an example metric on metrics that can be produced from such a catalog.

A common use case for a target metric is to compare the effectiveness of cybersecurity control implementation across organizations. Figure 7.15 provides an example wherein the measures count the devices used by each department and also sum the number of those devices that have security attributes as measured by a variety of components in the systems security architecture. Where devices automatically copy their activity logs to a central storage unit, the presence of logs from a given device in that storage unit would be a nominal device security attribute "Activity Logs." The number of servers with that label is divided by the number of devices used by the organization to produce the percentage shown in the first bar of each organization's metric. Similar nominal security attribute measures are created to verify correctness in security implementation of the rest of the systems security architecture components in the chart to provide an at-a-glance security health check for each business department.

The "Operating System Security" measure in Figure 7.15 is typically measured with an endpoint detection tool, a name that comes from considering a device that a person uses as one end of a network connection, while the resource with which the person communicates is the other end. An endpoint security tool may provide several functions on the NIST CSF spectrum. One that prevents changes to security architecture configuration is endpoint protection. One that detects malware and/or changes to security architecture configuration is endpoint detection. One that automatically reverts changes to security architecture configuration or quarantines malware is endpoint response.

Depending on the number and type of tools used to support operating system security, each type of operating system may have multiple measures of the health checks. The top of Figure 7.16 shows the extent to which each of the operating systems used by the enterprise has endpoint security controls that span the spectrum of potential endpoint security features. The bottom of Figure 7.16

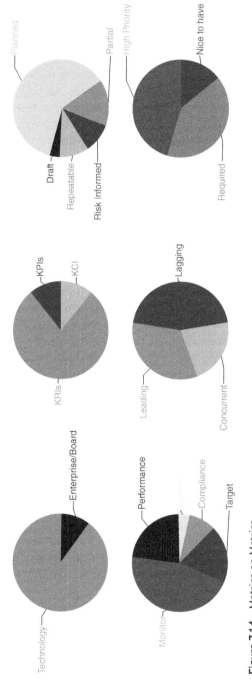

Figure 7.14 Metrics on Metrics

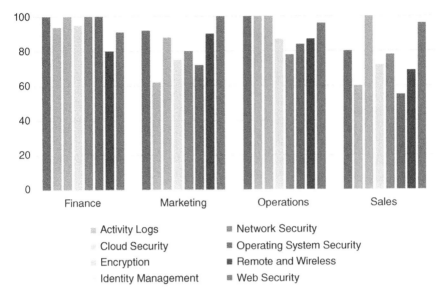

Figure 7.15 Cybersecurity Target Metric

shows the operating systems in use in the same departments listed in Figure 7.15. It is evident from this deeper level of detail underlying the operating system bars (Figure 7.15) why the department's overall operating system health check varies widely. That is, in this example enterprise, some operating systems are supported with more security features than others. This type of metric can help drive technology choices generally or identify issues in need of remediation in commonly used software. Although Figures like 7.15 are too high level to the root cause of the differences between departments, they can highlight the need for further analysis that leads to a deeper understanding of cybersecurity posture.

Complete health checks can be complicated. For example, consider a network security health metric that considers a network to be secure only if all network device operating systems are secure (Target Metric), its data flow is under strict change control, and all changes to its configuration are verified to be authorized (Monitor Metric). It may also be measured for correctness in data flow and data encryption (Deterministic Models). But like operating system security, it appears as just one of the infrastructure components that support the system security target architecture metric of Figure 7.15.

Monitor metrics are similar to targets in that they have a numeric scope of process or procedure activities but different in that they measure attributes of execution. Each activity in the process or step in the procedure is individually tested for conformance to design specification. Monitor metrics and target metrics are also interrelated because targets are achieved by people, and if people do not behave in

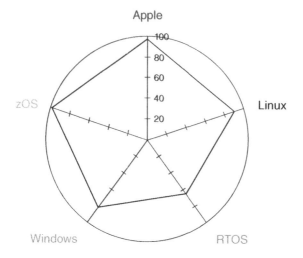

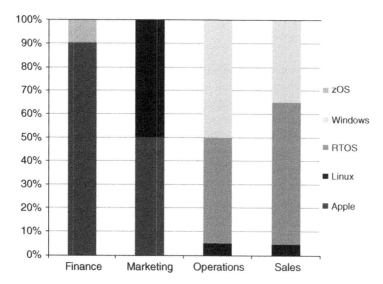

Figure 7.16 Example Cybersecurity Metrics Drilldown

a manner dictated by process, then management does not know whether targets would have been achieved had process been followed (though it can retrain or replace the people). However, if management can verify that procedure was followed, and targets are still not achieved, then this situation could mean that procedure is not working and should prompt consideration of changes in procedure. Hence in practice, target and monitor metrics are often combined.

A simple monitor metric starts with a process of procedure like the service desk password reset. The diagram on the left of Figure 7.17 is referred to as a *message sequence* diagram because it illustrates communication patterns by showing the sequence of messages passing between participants as a time sequence with the first message displayed as a horizonal line near the top. The participants in the communication are listed at the top of the diagram. The vertical line under each participant indicated that the messages represented by the horizontal lines begin or end with the participant, as indicated by an arrow. The communication it depicts is similar to that found in the least privilege example in Chapter 3, Figure 3.10 in that it includes phone interaction with supervision. The service desk asks the caller for their name and looks in the corresponding IAM user record for a two-factor mechanism with which to more strongly identify the caller using a unique Security Identification Code (SIC). The service desk sends the SIC to the user's phone. If the caller is the user, then they see the SIC on their phone and recite it. Then the service desk resets the password, sending a link to the user's phone so they can access it and reset it again to something only they know. The way the corresponding procedure is written, if any deviation from the authorized message sequence occurs, then the service desk will end the call. The way the sequence is written, for each password reset that occurred, there should be at least five records in three different systems:

1) The phone monitor log showing the reset request time and date when the service desk user was on the phone with the caller.
2) The service desk ticket showing the activities that the service desk recorded during the call.
3) The service desk log showing the password reset link sent.
4) The IAM activity log showing SIC Code sent.
5) The IAM activity log showing the user resetting their password.

All of these operations should have occurred within a few minutes of each other.

The graph at the right of Figure 7.17 shows the measure for three of the five data point events over time. Each operation within the event triggers a dot on the graph of a different color for each reset in time sequence. Where all three measures exist for each password reset within a preset timeframe (say the average call length of five minutes), they appear as a single dot on the graph. Where they do not appear as a dot, the procedure was not followed or for some reason was performed inefficiently. Where a supervisor has access to a graph like this in real time, they can use it to be alerted to an issue with a specific service desk staff member. That is what makes it a monitor metric. In this case, the actual call recording is not part of the monitor metric, but available to SecOps in case the metric indicates there is an incident to be investigated.

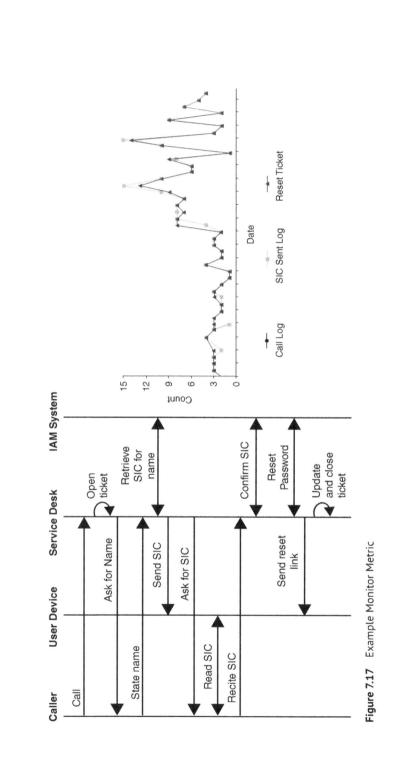

Figure 7.17 Example Monitor Metric

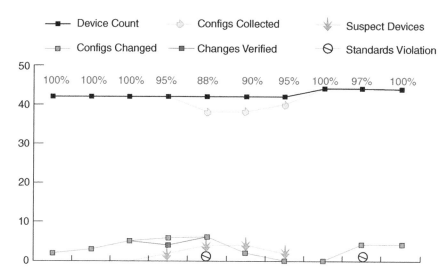

Figure 7.18 Network Device Measures

It is common for SecOps to use target and monitor metric in combination. An example of combining target and monitor metrics is displayed in Figure 7.18. This metric shows the combination in the service of firewall integrity monitoring. The measures contributing to the presentation are:

Device Count: The number of network devices in operation.

Configs Collected: The number of network devices whose configuration was retrieved in past 24 hours by network management.

Changes Detected: The number of device configurations that deviate from yesterday's configuration.

Changes Verified: The number of deviant device configurations where network operations manually confirm that deviations directly compare to authorized planned changes.

Standards Violation: The number of deviant device configurations where network operations manually confirm that deviations directly compare to authorized planned changes.

In this example, the daily metric comparison shows an occasional miss by an automated log collection process (dip in *Configs Collected* measure). It also shows that of those identified as changed, the monitor activity finds that the change fails verification (dip in *Changes Verified* measure). Both monitor attributes trigger the device to earn the label "Suspect." This may drive an overall network target metric like the one in Figure 7.18. In this case, the daily target metric denominator is the Device Count. The numerator is calculated as:

$$\text{Device Count} - \text{Configs Collected} + \text{Suspect Device} + \text{Standards Violations}$$

The *Device Count – Configs Collected* provides the number of devices that can be verified. Of those, some will be suspect or violations. So the missing configs plus those that do not match the planned change plus those that do match the planned change is the sum of deviations from the standard. Subtracting those from the device count gives you the number of healthy devices. The daily target metric is the percent of healthy devices, printed in bold above the Device Count measures in the diagram. Note that the point in time at which the metric is taken could make a significant difference in transparency of metric in an aggregate measure like the one in Figure 7.15. Where snapshots in time as shown in Figure 7.15 are taken in a time series monitor metric such as the one in Figure 7.18, the metric in the aggregate should be the least favorable number in the time interval between such snapshot reports. That is, instead of taking the average of the 10 numbers in the figure which would be 96.5%, or the last calculation of the metric, which would be 100%, the aggregate metric should be 88%, which is a more accurate reflection of the network device heath across the time interval.

Monitor metrics can also take advantage of other metrics to provide even more meticulous monitoring capability. An example is a Secure Staff metric. Where staff click on malicious email links, the incident is often dismissed as accidental. However, in combination with suspicious activity alerts such as an unauthorized USB alert from an endpoint monitoring system (Deterministic Models), these alerts can provide a pattern of insider threat. Increasingly, SecOps monitors alerts from user UBA systems that collect and store user activity patterns such as what file share they access, what time of day they normally work, and/or what data classification they are accessing (Stochastic Models). These systems can sometimes be configured to use authoritative sources to set priority for alert levels. For example, if a user is detected accessing data that fits the patterns of PII but that user is not a member of any application entitlement group that is authorized to have that access. Such alerts can trigger even higher levels of staff monitoring such as video desktop surveillance, tools that allow desktop screens to be recorded and played back at high speeds to allow SecOps a quick verification of exactly what triggers anomalous behavior alerts. Figure 7.19 is an example Secure Staff metric. If the ticks on the y axis are interpreted as activities of specific staff members, it shows the possible accidental policy violations for all users in a department within a similar job function. When a specific user is under investigation, the dotted lines provide attribution of negatively impacting activity to a specified user. In this case, the incidents identified with the *User of Interest* in the diagram are more frequent and of longer duration than those identified with peers. Even without the dotted lines, it can at a glance call attention

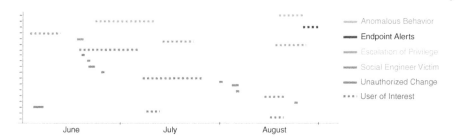

Figure 7.19 Secure Staff Monitor Metric

to potential insider threat due to unexpected frequency and duration of incidents. Even without targeting a given department, a simple Gantt chart of incident sources over time may call attention to a specific incident alert source sounding off at an unexpected frequency. Of course, to effectively utilize monitoring metrics across time there must be a centralized security incident management system that logs all incidents, not just confirmed cybersecurity attacks.

From the foregoing descriptions of metrics, it is obvious that the number and type of data sources for measures is restricted only by the imagination. However, it is important to keep in mind that only measures can provide data upon which metrics are based, and all measures have units. Units of measure can be combined to create metrics. But math can be applied only to numeric measures. If nominal or ordinal measures are expected to be combined with mathematical formulas, they must first be converted to numeric measures. If it proves difficult to make this conversion conform to a definition of unit, a repeatable rule-based deterministic measure (algorithm) may be specified.

7.3   Key Risk Indicators

Note that not all cybersecurity metrics, though they may be essential to day-to-day decision-making, convey solid information about changes in cybersecurity risk. An escalation of privilege anomaly could just be an administrator having a busy week. On the other hand, some metrics are so obviously connected to high probability of cyberattack that we call them *key* risk indicators (KRI) to distinguish them from those that may just be showing us what good cybersecurity looks like.

A metric is a *key* risk indicator only if it provides actionable information about the probability that a system will succumb to attack. For that, it is required to incorporate information about threats as well as controls. A key risk indicator should be routinely compared to risk appetite in a repeatable manner, so there is typically more effort to ensure that there are numeric measures for key risk indicators.

Control Indicator
measurement independent
of internal control
configuration and
operation is required to
assess if controls are
verified and validated.

Performance Indicator
measure the probability
of event impact on business
goals for cybersecurity
performance.

Risk Indicator
typically based on control
or performance indicators
but also may be sourced
external to the enterprise,
such as threat
intelligence.

Figure 7.20   Key Risk Indicator Types

Within the class of key risk indicators, there are target metrics and goal metrics. These will be referred to as KCI or KPIs. Figure 7.20 illustrates the concept.

Although KXIs may come from any other category of cybersecurity metric, they are typically validation as opposed to verification metrics. Control target verification metrics are a ratio composed of a numerator and a denominator that are different attributes of the same set of objects. But the metric indicates cybersecurity risk only if it is feasible that the attribute measured by the numerator indicates resilience to cyberattack. The same algorithm can look like a good news metric one day and a risk indicator the next. That is why so many publications and systems designed for executive level use employ the term "risk indicator" as opposed to "risk metric." Note that the best verification metric can only reflect whether the security was correctly built, not that it was adequate to thwart threats. For a control metric to be a risk indicator, it would have to provide evidence of inability to manage controls. Otherwise, a risk indicator needs a validation metric.

Cybersecurity practitioners often ignore this distinction and focus risk indicators directly on finding and fixing security attributes that make systems vulnerable, like CVEs. This focus results in metrics that look like Figure 7.21. In the early 2000s, the term "badness-ometer" was introduced to describe this type of security metric (McGraw 2006). A badness-ometer can only display poor security, never excellent security because it only measures if vulnerabilities exist. It can provide a nominal label of "bad," but it cannot determine that the server is definitely not vulnerable because the scanner may not test for all vulnerabilities and it cannot test for zero-day vulnerabilities. Therefore, the measure cannot correctly be used to bestow a label of "good." The graph on the bottom of Figure 7.21 is a failed validation metric because it counts vulnerabilities (bad things) in combination with a measure of time since the vulnerability was identified, and a time threshold set by management on how soon vulnerabilities should be fixed. The three measures taken at monthly intervals add up to one metric that shows what bad looks like – the security performance target was not achieved. In the target versus goal metric context, it shows that the system was not built right. There are also examples of

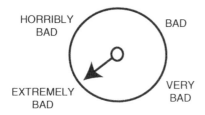

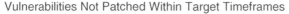

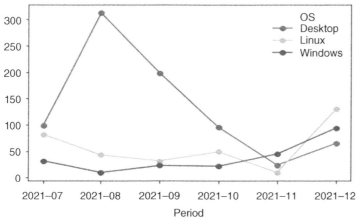

Figure 7.21 Badness-Ometer Scale and Exemplar Metric

badness-ometers that are goal metrics, such as annual monetary losses due to cyberattack (assuming your goal is not to have any). In addition to vulnerability scan metrics, these include, but are not limited to, software source code scan metrics, red team read-outs from war games, penetration test results, and audit findings. Typically badness-ometer measures fail criteria for consistency and replicability due to the changing threat and vulnerability landscape. So they should not be the sole source of KRIs.

Throughout the entire set of controls from risk appetite to procedures, and at each of the layers of control density, there are measurable cybersecurity attributes. There are technical configurations in place whether or not there are enterprise standards for them, and there are industry standards of measure if there are not (e.g., CIS). Where there are procedures, and they are typically ubiquitous, there are monitor measures that are followed. As long as there is a risk appetite that reflects enterprise mission, there are methods to determine whether it is maintained.

Controls thus viewed transparently enable the target audience to more easily grasp the point of each link in the chain in terms of the whole set of control documents, which can be both daunting and confusing to new entrants to an organization. Controls viewed holistically inspire alternatives for measurement and may be accompanied by metrics that demonstrate not only whether they are performing as designed, but whether they are effective in achieving a control objective specified at the policy or strategy level. This is an important point because the objective of a control may not be clear to someone following a procedure unless there is a direct link from the procedure to the business process and policy that it supports.

Perhaps the easiest connection to make between business risk appetite and cybersecurity controls is in the domain of web application development of software for internal use. A secure software development process will typically include code delivery handoffs between development, quality assurance testing, and production support (OWASP 2020). Each organization will have a few security procedures designed to ensure that the application meets enterprise security architecture design standards prior to it moving into development. In development, there may be a requirement for automated static and dynamic code analysis, that is to make sure there is no evidence of the most common mistakes that programmers and administrators (admins) make that leave systems vulnerable to hackers. These should reveal backdoors like hard-coded password or entitlements, or whole unauthenticated web-accessible database connections. In quality assurance, these tests will be repeated and augmented with application user role and data entitlement tests. Quality assurance procedures may include independent penetration tests and operating system security configuration health checks. In production, all of these tests will be repeated, and the application may also be independently audited. The results of control testing at each stage will be tracked and it will be obvious if a test made in development appeared to pass but the control was found lacking in quality assurance and/or production. The extent to which these tests fail in production is a key control indicator because the metrics may provide evidence of control verification and validation failure in business process software.

This key control indicator is illustrated in Figure 7.22. It compares three applications on selected criteria specific to the organization. Note all applications have been recorded as passing all development tests. If this was not the case, the application could not have proceeded to quality assurance. However, one application failed in quality assurance, so the production tests are recorded as 0%, and this is not because they failed, but because they have not yet occurred as *passing* quality assurance, which is a prerequisite for being deployed to production. Moreover, there is no pentest score in QA either, typically because a pentest is often an outsourced expense, so it will be delayed until the other tests are successful. Depending on organizational culture, it may be helpful to make these tests a DevOps competition of sorts. This makes such rigorous testing activities feel less like a chore and more like a challenge.

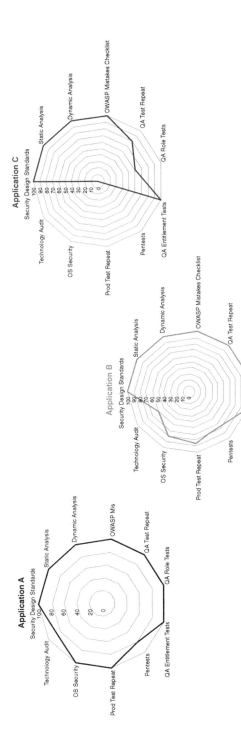

Figure 7.22 Example Key Control Indicator

In any cybersecurity program, security incident response is a hot topic. Stakeholders understand that quick and effective eradication of security incidents is a primary business goal for the cybersecurity program. However, they do not always realize that eradication is a midpoint step in a procedure that includes: Draft → Analysis → Mitigate → Contain → Eradicate → Recover → . In this realm, the stakeholder question in a GQM exercise is typically, "How long does it take to eradicate a cybersecurity attack?" But when the SecOps team tries to answer it, they end up with prerequisite questions like:

- What percentage of security tools that alert on events automatically create security incidents in the security incident management system?
- How long does it take to manually draft a security incident response ticket?
- How long does it take to analyze security incidents?
- How long does it take to contain a cybersecurity attack?

These questions are answered with Time to Respond (TTR) metrics. If these questions have not been asked at the stage level of detail before, there will likely not be measurable security incident attributes with which to answer them. Security incident response records may not have the fields to record timestamps at intermittent steps, and some incidents are closed almost immediately, so there would be no point in adding intermittent steps to all response records. Instrumentation for data collection on an actual cyberattack will exceed the level collected for every security incident. The line will likely not be obvious in the security incident response record before it is known that an attack occurred.

Although not every cybersecurity incident is a cybersecurity attack, every cybersecurity incident is a training opportunity, as well as an opportunity to demonstrate what good security looks like. Therefore, it makes sense to have a rule of thumb, such as that followed by sailors facing the first few unusually high winds and rough seas. On a sailboat, the equivalent first step in containing potential damage from adverse weather is to reduce the size of the sail, or *reef* the sail by rolling or folding part of it in. This improves the boat's stability because a very strong wind on a large sail can knock it over. The saying goes: "the time to reef is when you think of it." The cybersecurity analogy is that if you think you may need to contain cyberattack, press the "containment mode" button in the security incident management system now. Your analysis has brought you to the point where preservation is the obvious next move, whether or not you fully understand the extent of the threat.

Data on the time it takes security operations to advance through all security incident stages in each incident, whether or not it results in a successful cyberattack, is an important key performance indicator for the cybersecurity program. An example metric is the average number of minutes it takes to advance through the stages for each incident alert source, as in Figure 7.23. Where some incidents take longer to

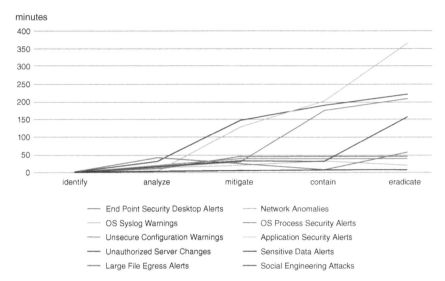

Figure 7.23 Example Key Performance Indicator

reach the mitigation stage than others, other incidents end after the analysis stage. Where a line levels out after hitting a stage, this indicates that incidents of these types rarely if ever need active mitigation and containment. Where lines continue to rise throughout all stages, these are key indicators that cyberattacks may be expected to continue from those alert sources. Having the ability to easily grasp which incident types have the highest potential to escalate together with how long it takes to reach the mitigation state sets clear priorities for SecOps telemetry improvement.

An example of a KRI that is not sourced from a KCI or a KPI is one sourced from an issue-tracking system. Where assessments and events reveal issues, where exceptions to system security architecture requirements such as endpoint protection installation are identified but cannot immediately be remediated, or in any situation wherein a cybersecurity risk issue has been declared, a process that documents the issue can be a fruitful source of cybersecurity metrics. Where the documentation includes links to the risk register and project for the planned remediation, it can be a security program performance metric. Figure 7.24 shows an issue-register snapshot of open cybersecurity risk issues. It summarizes how severe the risk is if the issue is not addressed, provides some risk context, and indicates whether remediation plans are being executed according to plan. Where these snapshots are presented as trending over time, they may provide evidence of both good and bad security program performance.

Note that one of the issue sources in Figure 7.24 is *compliance*. Compliance has a negative connotation in the cybersecurity risk community because virtually

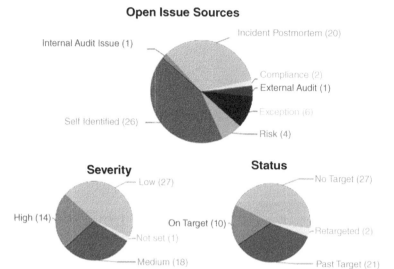

Figure 7.24 Example Key Risk Indicator

everyone with professional experience in risk assessment has witnessed a situation in which an organization demonstrated compliance with a regulatory requirement without actually securing assets. This is because regulators cannot anticipate every situation an evolving business may face, and it is sometimes possible to comply with the letter of the law rather than with its legislative intent. Where regulatory standards are treated as paper checklists rather than control objectives or specifications for risk management controls, compliance tracking can appear to be a waste of time. So it is important to think of compliance assessments not as checklist exercises, but as an exploration of the professional opinions of the standard authors, most of whom have decades of experience in cybersecurity, and are conscientiously sharing what they consider best practices for cybersecurity risk reduction. That way, compliance issues can be framed as risk reduction exercises that it would make sense for the cybersecurity program to address anyway.

That said, it makes sense for cybersecurity to avoid any declaration of a "compliance risk indicator" because *compliance risk* is itself an operational risk. Compliance risk is its own category of operational risk and is classified in some standards as belonging to a *business practices* category (BASEL 2003). Regulators tend to worry about risk presented by the companies they oversee, so most regulation includes their opinion on how to reduce cybersecurity risk, typically gleaned from observations of industry practices. This is why compliance assessments often feed issues into technology risk assessment processes.

However, while non-compliance with laws and regulations often is due to control weaknesses, the negative impact *directly* related to the business practice version of compliance risk is the consequence of simply not complying, that is, getting caught ignoring regulations, fined, executives imprisoned; these consequences do not present potential for technology disruption. Although it may be a coincident risk factor in the cybersecurity risk category, going to jail for weak controls is not usually taken into consideration by cybersecurity risk analysts. The assumption is that the enterprise will fully comply or seek regulatory reform. That cybersecurity is a coincident risk factor in assessments based on regulatory standards is how compliance risk management activities provide valuable input to cybersecurity risk management activities. That is, any instance of potential non-compliance with a cybersecurity regulation should be taken seriously, not because you might otherwise go to jail, but because the regulation highlights some cybersecurity concern that should be part of an industry standard cybersecurity program. It is enough to label the issue source as compliance simply because that is how it came to the attention to the cybersecurity program. But the issue risk event category is under cybersecurity in the enterprise risk hierarchy, not under compliance.

As the risk issue KRI example illustrates, where the X in KXI is neither C or P, it can still be R for Risk. Regardless of the number of available methods of measuring enterprise cybersecurity controls and performance, it is equally important to seek out metrics that are independent of the organization to ensure that the enterprise does not miss trends that could impact cybersecurity.

Example informative metrics that are not sourced internally include, but are not limited to:

- Trends in cybersecurity attack patterns, both overall and by industry.
- Events that have negatively impacted competitors or other industry participants – can be purchased from companies that specialize in event data by industry, such as SAS and Cyentia.
- Current Top Attack Techniques

Figure 7.25 shows an example report on trends in industry attack patterns from the Verizon Data Breach Report (Verizon 2023, p. 23). It illustrates how attack patterns have trended over time in a specific industry. Verizon publishes several such informative metric by industry and the same metric in aggregate across industries.

Figure 7.26 shows an example excerpt from an industry report published by the cybersecurity analysis firm Cyentia (Cyentia 2022, p. 16). Such event details gleaned by researchers that include incidents experienced by competitors are very useful in selecting scenarios for analysis and can also be used to enhance RCSA risk analysis, the results of which may then be used to create a cybersecurity business process performance metric.

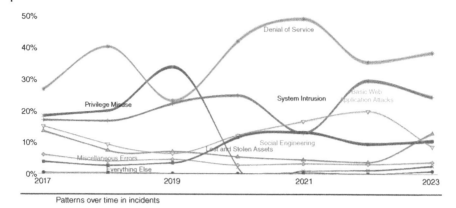

Figure 7.25 External Risk Indicators – Breaches

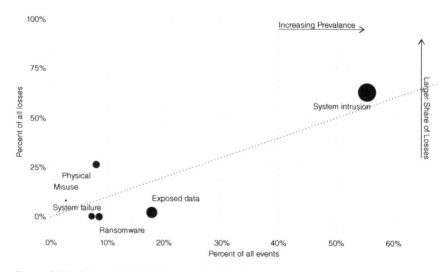

Figure 7.26 External Risk Indicators – Incident Frequency

Figure 7.27 shows MITRE's Top Ten Techniques calculator, which lets a user enter five measures of their technology environment on an ordinal scale, then calculates the attacks that environment is likely to experience, given data entered, the general state of cybersecurity controls, and an analysis of the prevalence and threat actor vectors and techniques (MITRE 2023). Trends in industry attack patterns can also help inform selection of event categories for SecOps metrics and thereby help prioritize alert telemetry changes that, in turn, reduce *time to respond* metrics.

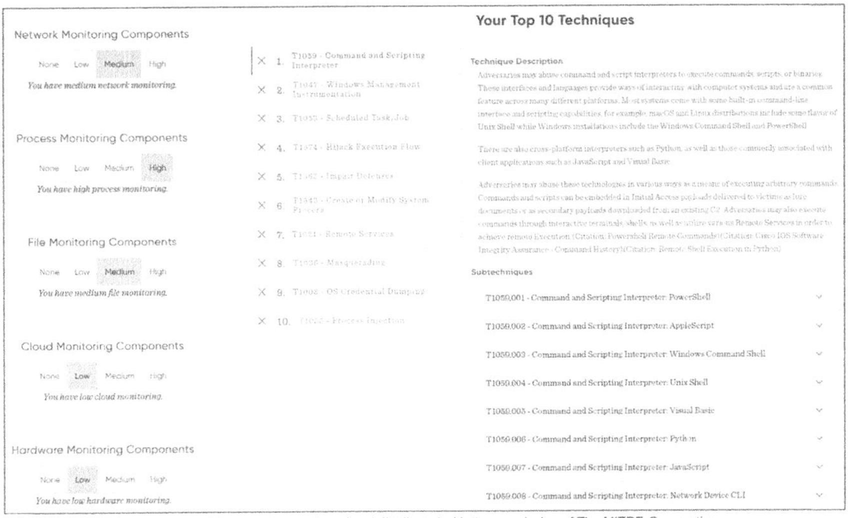

© 2023 The MITRE Corporation. This work is reproduced and distributed with the permission of The MITRE Corporation

Figure 7.27 External Risk Indicators – Threat

An overview of metrics is not complete without the caveat that the extent to which both performance and goal measures accurately reflect the cybersecurity program is a direct reflection of how well both the program and the metrics portion of the program are managed. Metrics developed in conjunction with the program can be used to monitor its maturity and if the program itself creates data rich enough to be practical and useful measures. Another important observation is that the information that the metrics provide may show that cybersecurity itself is poor. Even a well-managed program may operate under constraints that prevent it from achieving its goals. However, a CISO will not go to jail if all of the CISO's documentation, including metrics provided to external auditors and investigators, accurately reflects the status of the cybersecurity program's performance and lack of goal achievement. The internal management debate is then not whether a CISO is responsibly managing the program but reduced to why the program is constrained from delivering risk reduction to a level below risk appetite. That said, a CISO in that position should consider a career move for sanity's sake.

One source of CISO constraints may be that although the field of cybersecurity metrics has come far in the past few decades, it is not yet mature enough to have produced an industry standard list of cybersecurity metrics the way the accounting profession has generally accepted accounting principles (which took them 5,000 years to develop). However, there is consensus that business risk appetite is an appropriate guide in customizing cybersecurity policies, standards, and guidelines. As appropriate in measuring any operational risk, the goal is to find controls, events, issues, and independent sources that support the qualitative risk appetite with quantitative tolerance measures that we can trend over time to see if risk is rising or falling. Just as today's unprecedented fires and floods prompt the weather industry to revisit its assumptions on weather patterns, when cybersecurity metrics indicate risk is falling and we nevertheless succumb to cyberattack, sometimes we need to change not only our measures and metrics, but the enterprise framework we used to create them.

References

Basel (2003). Sound Practices for the Management and Supervision of Operational Risk. Basel Committee on Banking Supervision. https://www.bis.org/publ/bcbs96.htm (accessed 09 May 2023).

Cowie, J. (2009). Using Security Metrics to Motivate a Response to a Critical Vulnerability. http://www.securitymetrics.org/attachments/Metricon-4-Cowie.pdf (accessed 08 May 2023).

Cyentia (2022). Information Risk Insights Study (IRIS), Risk Retina for Nonprofits March 2022. https://www.cyentia.com/iris/ (accessed 08 May 2023).

Herrmann, D. (2007). *The Complete Guide to Security and Privacy Metrics*. Auerbach Publications.

Jaquith, A. (2004) Metricon Conference Proceedings 2004-2019. www.securitymetrics.org (accessed 08 May 2023).

McGraw, G. (2006). *Secure Software, Building Security In*. Addison-Wesley.

MITRE (2023). Top Attack Techniques, MITRE Engenuity. https://top-attack-techniques.mitre-engenuity.org/calculator (accessed 08 May 2023).

OWASP (2020). Web Security Testing Guide, version 4.2. Open Web Application Security Project® Testing Framework. https://github.com/OWASP/wstg/releases/download/v4.2/wstg-v4.2.pdf (accessed 08 May 2023).

Seiersen, R. (2022). *The Metrics Manifesto: Confronting Security with Data*. Wiley.

Thomas, M.A. (2019). Mathematization, not Measurement: A Critique of Stevens' Scales of Measurement. https://journals.librarypublishing.arizona.edu/jmmss/article/id/1465/ (accessed 08 May 2023).

Verizon (2023). Data Breach Investigations Report. https://www.verizon.com/business/resources/reports/dbir/, (accessed 21 August 2023).

8

People

8.1 Three Lines of Defense

Executive management is a stressful job. Pressure to perform comes from internal sources like the board of directors and external forces like shareholders and customers. Balancing work and family is always a time trade-off. Mid-level managers have the same pressures and even more because there are more levels of management above them, often with conflicting priorities. It is fully understood that management at all levels is likely to be constantly stressed to deliver products and services, no matter what the culture or industry. Managers also typically earned their management positions by focusing on the positive and making occasionally risky decisions that they were able to turn into opportunities. They will not always want to be faced with information about every way in which their operations could suffer from cyberattacks. They are often tempted to take shortcuts to get products out the door. In a technology environment, this means short cuts in system testing and soaking.

Although system testing is generally a well-understood process, soak time is less so. To *soak* a technology system is to start it up and let it run in an environment as close as possible to how it would be used in production. This includes simulating the user input and output over the course of a business process cycle or two. Such input might include staff and customer data entry as well as daily, weekly, and monthly data aggregation and reporting. Of course, the timespan of each cycle can be shortened, but the operations should all occur in the order planned for product use, and the system should be running for a long enough period of time for IT operations to monitor its memory, disk, and other resource usage to provide assurance that it will be stable once released for production operational use.

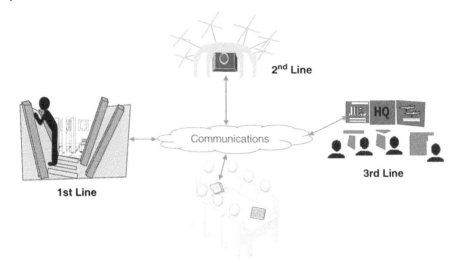

Figure 8.1 Three Lines of Defense

Soak time is often especially hard hit because if testing is unsuccessful, soak time may be the only impediment to software release. This type of pressure to cut corners is the fundamental philosophy behind the management concept of the three lines of defense illustrated in Figure 8.1. The first line of defense is business management, depicted in the figure as looking out from the trenches of a battlefield's front line with a data center in the background to protect. It is common for SecOps to use trench analogies. The first line is closest to the war, fending off adversaries as they try to blow through the barricades constructed to keep them out. First line establishes the processes and artifacts used to run the business. These include policies, technology architecture frameworks, and implementation standards.

The second line of defense is more like a quality control mechanism. Depicted in the figure as a drone, it hovers around the first line, monitoring how they are achieving business objectives. If they see the first-line struggle with a risk issue, they will research it on their behalf. While the first line of defense focuses on implementation of cybersecurity control processes, managing risks to changing assets and threat landscapes in near real time, the second line of defense focuses on trends in current and future risk. Both lines, of course, are cognizant of short-term and long-term risks. However, the objectivity and lack of urgent incident response responsibilities on the part of the second line allows them time to have a more forward-looking perspective.

As they are less pressured with day-to-day defense, the second line typically takes the lead in creating committees with key management stakeholders from the first line and together, they will construct the enterprise risk framework. The second line usually also takes the burden of organizing risk-related data and documenting the framework. Where there is a second line, there is a high probability that an RCSA program exists that the cybersecurity program can use to gain insight into how management processes work and how management thinks about and maintains control over business processes. Whether it comes from a formal RCSA program or not, access to first-line RCM strategies and corresponding documentation is essential for the second line to properly interpret first-line activities. Where an RCSA or RCM is completed by all first-line managers, the second line has an ongoing data source with which to understand first-line management's perspective on their own business processes, risks, and corresponding controls.

Where RCSAs are utilized by an enterprise, the first line may create management RCSAs to provide the second line with a starting point for monitoring activities, though in some cases, the second line will construct the RCMs to be used by the first line in their RCSA assessments. In this manner and others, the first and second lines collaborate on the enterprise risk framework including the cybersecurity risk framework. The second line also does what it can to establish general awareness of the enterprise cybersecurity risk framework and may hold formal training to ensure that the first line fully understands the risks in their scope. They will also perform risk assessments and spot checks as they see fit and make unsolicited remediation recommendations. Typically, second-line risk assessments are delivered directly to accountable line management and escalated to executive management only if they are not addressed.

Not all businesses formally specify an organization as a second line of defense, but where they do, they typically operate completely independently from the first line. The second line will typically report to a CRO that reports directly to the CEO and chairs or attends a risk committee on the board of directors if there is one. In some organizations, the second line extends beyond risk to include centralized legal and HR functions that are another type of sanity check on the behavior of the first line. The common element in formally designated second-line organizations is an independent reporting structure that allows them the flexibility of being in disagreement with the levels of first-line management below the CEO and still having their voices heard on risk and control issues.

The third line of defense is even more independent. It is charged with hands-on audits of both first- and second-line systems and operations. Publicly held companies are required to have an independent audit function, but private organizations that have large, complicated, or distributed operations typically have at least something akin to a business quality assurance group that plays the same role. Internal audit evaluates risk for all activities both the first and second lines. Their risk assessment utilizes information shared by the first and second lines, but it does not follow the exactly same process to ensure that they will be able to come to independent conclusions. The risk assessment allows audit to select specific risks that appear as moderate risk to high risk and subjects selected at-risk management activities to hands-on audits. Internal audit also opines on the execution and efficacy of the first- and second-line risk management framework (verification and validation), though it is prohibited from participating in its construction just as it is prohibited from implementing any information technology within the scope of their audit domain, that is, due to the inherent bias people have toward finding anything wrong with something they created. For certified auditors, this independence is also enforced via professional codes of ethics.

External audit has a charter similar to internal audit, but the scope of external audit may be more limited to topics of interest to external stakeholders such as the accuracy of financial statements. Both internal and external audits document an independent assessment of risk to the enterprise that is delivered directly to the highest level of management, that is, if there is board of directors, their reports will go directly to the board without the requirement for CEO approval. In a publicly held company, the board of directors is charged with due diligence with respect to minimizing risk to stockholder's investments.

Whether the highest level of enterprise accountability is with a single executive or a board of directors, the key to effective communication of cybersecurity risk to senior management is to recognize that cybersecurity risk management framework components are understood at that level, and to speak that language. If there is an operational risk management program within the organization, any new or fledgling CISO should enlist their support in arranging the placement of cybersecurity risk within the existing enterprise risk hierarchy and solicit advice on the most effective style of board communication.

It is important to understand that the CISO is the person in the first line of defense who is expected to be able to converse fluently on the topic of risk. Many CISOs came up through the ranks in security operations and rely heavily on their technology risk counterparts in the first line to incorporate their concerns into the enterprise cybersecurity risk management framework. Although they may be asked to provide status on incident response and vulnerability, they may not be tasked with board communication on risk. Nevertheless, there is a trend for this to change. With increasing frequency, guidance for boards of directors on cybersecurity risk recommends that they meet periodically with the CISO and ask hard questions about how risk is managed. It is part of board governance responsibility to make sure that management is prepared to maintain its mission in times of adversity. With increasing frequency, they are actively seeking the best plausible factual reports on cybersecurity risk produced by the first, second, and third lines to help them to grasp the enterprise's risks with a bird's eye view and enable them to recommend direction for the management of the company on that topic going forward.

Cybersecurity is a
strategic business
enabler

Encourage
systemic resilience
and collaboration

Understand the
economic drivers
and impact of
cyber risk

Cyber-resilient
organization

Incorporate
cybersecurity
expertise into board
governance

Align cyber-risk
management with
business needs

Ensure
organizational
design supports
cybersecurity

Figure 8.2   NACD Cybersecurity Principles

Figure 8.2 displays National Association of Corporate Directors (NACD) Principles for Board Governance of Cyber Risk (NACD 2021, p. 6). Note that the principle on the bottom right advises a board member to align cyber-risk management with business needs. The details explaining that principle include requiring all executives with a "chief" or equivalent in their title to report to the board on the cybersecurity implications of their activities, as well as how they use cybersecurity risk analysis to support decisions within their own domain of leadership, both generally and specifically with respect to regulatory obligations (NACD 2021, p. 9).

The principle on the bottom left of Figure 8.2 urges board members to incorporate cybersecurity expertise into board governance. CISOs can be of value to board members merely by including them in standard code of conduct level security training that is routinely offered to all enterprise staff. The detail underlying that principle includes a discussion of the pros and cons of recruiting a board member who is a cybersecurity expert versus increasing the entire board's understanding of cyber risk to a level of competence required to independently come to valid conclusions on cybersecurity risk management topics (NACD 2021, p. 11). NACD periodically publishes *Risk Oversight Handbooks* on various topics and has used this series to supplement these principles with specific questions that directors should ask about the enterprise cybersecurity risk framework (NACD 2023, pp. 69–75). With this level of international recognition of the need to cybersecurity risk issues to be widely understood, a CISO, whether in the first or second line of defense, should not be hesitant to create layman presentation materials that enable board members to appreciate any concerns they may have in their struggle to wrestle cybersecurity risk to a level below risk appetite.

The key to effective communication of cybersecurity risk to senior management is to recognize that operational risk framework components are understood at board level, and to speak that language when communicating with the board. If there is a second-line risk management program within the organization, any new or fledgling cybersecurity risk management officer should enlist their support in arranging the placement of cybersecurity risk within the enterprise risk hierarchy. Figure 8.3 is a very well-understood vision of how risk is professionally managed (COSO 2013). Developed as a model for understanding internal control as a general concept, this cube illustrates the depth of dimensions of risk management. At the top of the cube there are business control objectives of *efficient and effective operations, reliable reporting, and regulatory compliance.* Along the right side are organizational units representing the target scope of internal control efforts, that is, complete enterprise coverage. Facing front are the components of an internal control program. *Control environment* is tone at the top, which calls for ethics,

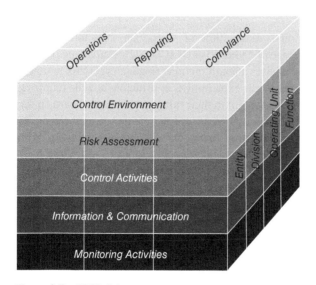

Figure 8.3 COSO Cube

integrity, and accountability. It describes how *risk assessment* should lead to *control activities* such as policies, standards, and procedures. *Information and communication* are depicted as part of the system of internal control, the sharing of reports, data, event details, external resources that are necessary for people to fulfill their roles and responsibilities. At the end, there are *monitoring activities*. Management at all levels conducts monitoring activities. Board communication about cybersecurity is an exemplar of the type of monitoring activity to which the cube refers.

Figure 8.4 is an example high-level organization chart that shows the reporting structure of the three lines. The options for CISO reports appear at the bottom of the figure. Although CISOs often report to a technology executive like a CIO, where there is a perceived conflict between the first-line technology stress and the need to focus on security, the role has been placed in the second line of defense. There is also a view that the CISO should not be involved in implementation or operations because it may introduce bias toward prior control decisions. Like independent audit, there is an expectation that a CISO can focus fully on the risk as well as the potential that controls may not adequately reduce the risk. If it were true that a control the CISO implemented did not reduce risk, then the admission would mean they had made a wrong choice with respect to past control implementation. They may want to think they work even though they might not. Hence the introduction of bias. A third option is for the CISO to peer with the CIO. This is thought to expand their voice as they would both report to the same manager, in the figure a COO. This would make it easier for them to voice disagreement

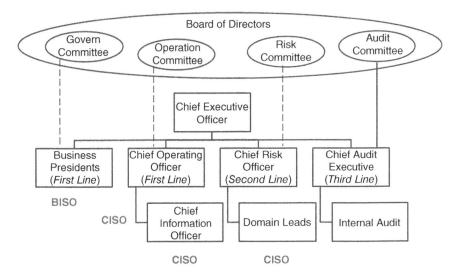

Figure 8.4 High Level Organization Chart

with the CIO while still being part of the same department processes. Another alternative is to have a CISO report directly to first-line business leaders. In the figure, this role is referred to as a Business Information Security Officer, a BISO. In very large organizations, there may be multiple BISOs and CISOs. Though one of the CISOs would typically be in charge of enterprise-wide cybersecurity policy, the others would be expected to have domain-specific knowledge in the scope of their responsibilities.

As depicted in Figure 8.1 and in the dotted lines of Figure 8.4, the Board of Directors leverages the first-line executive management and the independent opinions of the second line to gather the information they need to govern the organization. The solid line in Figure 8.3 from internal audit to the board's audit committee indicates that audit may provide unsolicited information to the board at any time. The board is expected to compare and contrast the information from all three lines of defense, as well as that provided by external auditors, to gain assurance that the information they receive from first-line management is both accurate and comprehensive. They use that information to influence management's response to risk in a manner that suits the best interests of its stakeholders and investors.

8.2   The Cybersecurity Team

The three lines of defense have very different mission and purpose but work together to govern, manage, and maintain enterprise cybersecurity. Though individually, they belong to different teams in the organization chart, collectively, they work as a team. With all these players, even when there are documented processes and RACI matrices it can be hard to figure out how it is all expected to come together. Yet experienced individuals with cybersecurity roles and responsibilities in large organizations with well-functioning cybersecurity programs do think of themselves as a team. Think of the team itself as a system of interest. Figure 8.5 shows the mainstay of a systemigram that describes that team: *The cybersecurity team thwarts threat actors who attack the technology that maintains the enterprise.*

Enterprise systems are complicated, but focusing on its people components reveals the relationships between technology roles and their interactions in support of maintaining systems security architecture, as depicted in Figure 8.6. Technology management is referred to generally, and accompanied by vendors and services upon which it relies to get the job done. Several different types of administrators are responsible for configuring different aspects of the control environment, and it is their repeatable configuration procedures that enforce enterprise's security architecture standards. IT operations monitor changes to both applications and infrastructure and resolve incidents and problems as they

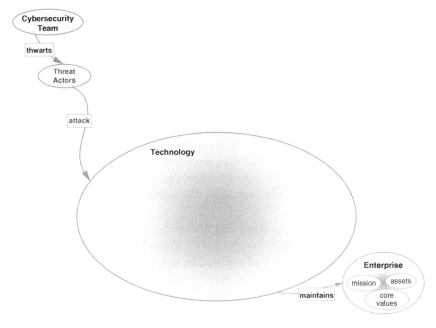

Figure 8.5 Cybersecurity People Mainstay

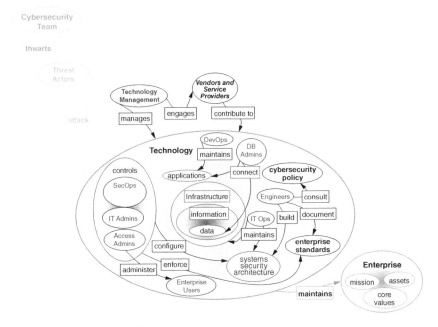

Figure 8.6 Cybersecurity System

arise, as well as manage the problem escalation process itself. Engineers typically build infrastructure including system security architecture, but application developers and database administrators also have a role in configuring data security even if it is not within the realm of direct CISO oversight. The system is presented as maintaining not just the mission and assets of the enterprise, but intangible attributes of the value of the system like reputation.

Technology people are not the only ones who directly touch enterprise technology. System security policy is a key component, and it is generally published by the CISO, who is an enterprise component, but not an essential component of the technology itself. That is, if the CISO does not show up for work, the technology is not impacted. As depicted in Figure 8.7 others that touch systems occasionally or indirectly include, but are not limited to, HR, accountants, investigators, and auditors.

HR plays a major role in specifying data flow with respect to authorized users and job functions. It is typically accountable for the accuracy of staff (employee and contract) job specifications that are used by identity and access administrators who are charged with configuring access according to the principle of least privilege. HR usually facilitates the education of all staff on Information Security responsibilities as part of onboarding wherein staff must sign that they have read

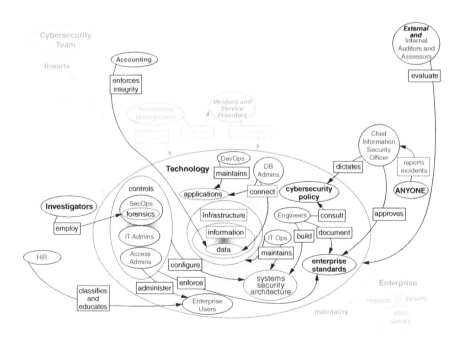

Figure 8.7 Cybersecurity System Support Team

and understood a code of conduct that includes some kind of cybersecurity responsibilities statement wherein consequences of noncompliance include dismissal. This is typically followed by requirements for periodic cybersecurity education updates. HR also may be charged with screening all individuals who perform work for the enterprise to ensure that there is no background of criminal activity or indicators of fraud.

Accountants are responsible for the accuracy of financial statements, which is no small task in large organizations where dozens of globally distributed systems may be aggregated to produce numbers on balance sheets. Those who take the responsibility seriously will identify control points in data transfers and specify programs to detect inconsistencies in data entry, reconciliations, and account balances. They will do the same for data flows that are common targets of financial fraud or asset theft.

Cybersecurity investigators may be internal or external, but in companies where data breaches are infrequent, they will typically be staffed from audit firms or licensed private investigators. Investigators will determine what evidence to preserve and execute the preservation activity, as well as analyze the data to identify and research the threat actor to support expected prosecution or civil tort cases.

Auditors and assessors may also be internal or external. Auditors in particular are required to make observations personally in order to support independent risk and control assessments. To perform this role effectively, they may have ongoing access and form a critical part of the technology control environment. Internal auditors in particular are often called upon to perform cybersecurity spot checks.

In addition to the hands-on contributions of non-technologists to the cybersecurity program, other people who are not real-time essential contributors to cybersecurity technology play behind-the-scenes roles that nevertheless are essential to total team coverage of cybersecurity risk management. These include executive management, legal, procurement, enterprise risk management, regulators, and counterparties.

Note that tone at the top exists whether you set it or not (Bayuk 2010, p. 9). It is reflected in executive behavior calculated to make people think about the things an executive really cares about. If the CEO violates cybersecurity policy by using a USB stick to take work home at night, then those in his inner circle will feel similarly empowered. If the CEO installs a videogame downloaded from the internet on his laptop, then the desktop support team who witnessed it will feel similarly empowered. So the extent to which the CEO understands and utilizes the enterprise cybersecurity risk framework, to that extent will the next level of executives take it seriously and try to use it to control the cybersecurity risk within their domain of management.

To properly support an enterprise cybersecurity risk framework, a CEO must express the mission, vision, and core values of the organization and ensure that they are agreed by the Board and executive management. A CEO must also seriously consider the possibility that the management strategy may not align with an organization's mission, vision, and core values, which would negatively affect decisions that underlie strategy selection. Mission, vision, and core values are the most important elements of the enterprise to preserve when managing risk and remaining resilience throughout negatively impacting events. That is why a risk appetite statement based on these values has the endurance required to form the basis for a cybersecurity program.

In the context of enterprise risk management, mission, vision, core values, and risk appetite are defined as (COSO 2017, pp. 3–6):

Mission: The entity's core purpose, which establishes what it wants to accomplish and why it exists.

Vision: The entity's aspirations for its future state or what the organization aims to achieve over time.

Core Values: The entity's beliefs and ideals about what is good or bad, acceptable or unacceptable, which influence the behavior of the organization.

Risk Appetite: The amount of risk, on a broad level, an entity is willing to accept in the pursuit of value.

It falls to the CEO, and the organization selected by the CEO, to devise a strategy to achieve mission and vision while preserving core values. Where a cybersecurity risk framework is part of the strategy-setting process, it should provide management with the risk information it needs to consider and decide among alternative technology strategies. The selected technology strategy should include a systems security architecture based on requirements to uphold those values. If the CEO believes in the efficacy of the cybersecurity risk framework for this purpose, everyone else is likely to embrace it as well.

Figure 8.8 shows some examples of how organizations that do not touch technology directly can be part of the team that manages cybersecurity risk. Notably, anyone, internal or external to the enterprise, plays a vital role in reporting cybersecurity incidents. They may not even be in the organization. They could be whistleblowers calling into our hotlines or reporting it on our website because they see someone on social media, for example, taking a picture of themselves in the data center eavesdropping on a network connection.

Procurement can establish and maintain procedures to correlate business requirements with procurement efforts. This should reduce the risk of unnecessary software being installed on enterprise systems. Procurement can also provide details on all vendors that handle enterprise information assets and track them by internal contact, vendor type, and function, as well as connectivity. This provides an authoritative source for network administrators to use to tell the difference between authorized and unauthorized network connections.

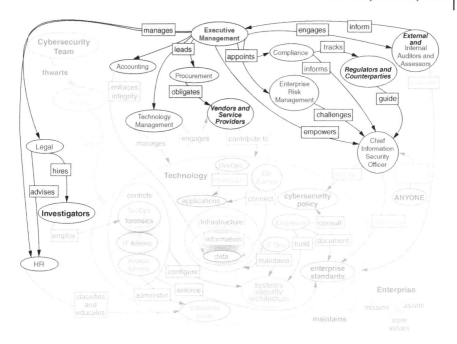

Figure 8.8 Cybersecurity Management Team

Cyber investigators are depicted as being hired by legal because typically the legal department is accountable for evidence preservation and a chain of custody. They fulfill this role by ensuring that there is adequate expertise to assist in post-cyberattack forensics activity. Legal can also help ensure that procurement has a standard set of information protection requirements to include in contracts with vendors and other third parties.

In large organizations, there is often a department dedicated to regulatory compliance, and they would help ensure that the CISO is provided with current regulations and contracts that require cybersecurity controls. The CISO can then ensure that they are digested into system security requirements.

The cybersecurity team thus serves executive management's need for enforcing risk appetite. This last connection is made in Figure 8.9. The complete systemigram demonstrates that holistically, the cybersecurity team links its individual set of processes via organizational coordination that supports the cybersecurity framework from multiple perspectives, all with a common goal of value preservation. Just as the cybersecurity risk framework as a system portrays a continuous cycle that improves enterprise's ability to thwart threat actors, its players provide continuous control reinforcement in defense of mission. Of course, in any given enterprise some cybersecurity roles and responsibilities may be labeled differently

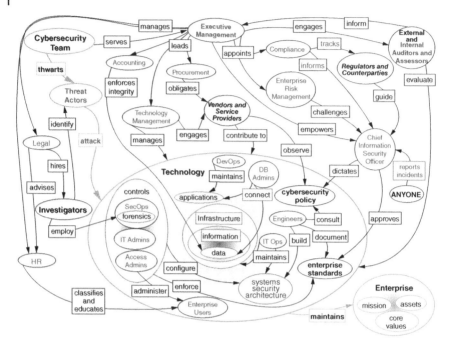

Figure 8.9 Cybersecurity Team Systemigram

or be missing altogether, the systemigram suffices to convey the broad collaboration necessary to accomplish cybersecurity goals.

8.3 Enterprise Management

Though the interactions in the cybersecurity team make intuitive sense, it still can be daunting to distribute management responsibility for cybersecurity across all of the organizations on the team. While the CIO may be accountable for the technology environment, the description of the various team players' positions makes it clear that technology staff is not the only group of people responsible for correct cybersecurity implementation. Such cross-organizational management issues are generally solved via committees that establish matrix reporting structure as in the example in Figure 8.10. The solid lines in the organization chart are direct reporting. The dotted lines indicate membership in committees identified in italics with the acronym for the officer that chairs the committee in parentheses. This indicates that the members of the committee report to the committee chair for their responsibilities with respect to the domain of the committee. The smaller dashes on the line of the right indicate a direct matrix reporting line independent of

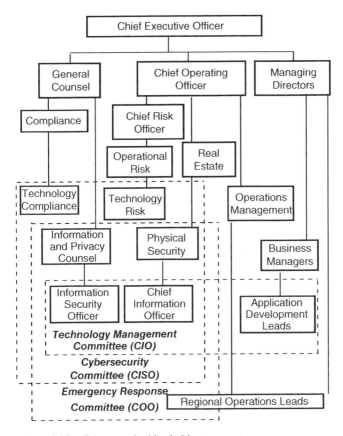

Figure 8.10 Cybersecurity Matrix Management

committee membership for regional operation leads. It is common for regional operations to represent management interests in business areas that do not have staff representation in the region.

There are three committees to which the CISO belongs and one that the CISO chairs. While on the Technology Management Committee, the CISO works under the direction of the CIO. While on the Emergency Response Committees, the CISO works under the direction of the COO. Other players may also be involved in multiple committees. The first-line members of the Cybersecurity Committee are all on the Emergency Response Committee. The CIO runs the Technology Committee and its members include technology managers that report elsewhere in the business, specifically those who develop software applications.

While chairing the Cybersecurity Committee, the CISO has access to the most senior members of technology management, legal, compliance, technology risk, and physical security. These committees are where decisions are made to collaborate on strategy and processes. It is typical to formulate plans for system features and requirements for protecting personal data and complying with regulation to notify individuals if data held by the company about them has been breached, or how to verify and process incoming requests for deleting data about an individual if the individual has requested for it to be deleted. Another common task for this committee is to support whistleblowing, a process that allows someone within the enterprise, or even outside it, to alert the enterprise there is something illegal going on within it, like information is being sold by employees. Though it may sound informal on the surface, a whistleblower may be protected by regulation. In this case, a formal whistleblower program may be run by legal because once that whistleblower makes that complaint, it needs to be investigated, which is normally outsourced because the source of reported malfeasance is not known so it could be a person in the organization who normally may conduct internal investigations (i.e., Physical Security or SecOps). The investigation also needs to be kept private so that the whistleblower does not experience retribution from the enterprise, so the CISO will typically help develop and maintain the technology required to operate it.

Often membership of the Cybersecurity Committee is dynamic. There will be a core team of obvious stakeholders, and others will be invited to join for a series of sessions in which some issue in their management domain is discussed. For example, a procurement manager will likely not be a core team member, but when it is time to examine third-party risk, procurement will be asked to come to the table. Another example is a business process owner may be invited to strategize on how to meet requirements for new data protection regulation.

Typically, this Emergency Response Committee will have business representation and the business leaders chosen to be on that committee will have the ability to reach out to a large number of people for which they may be responsible for safety, a geographical region for example. Although cyber security does not have the same type of borders as floods and fires, it often does hit regionally, as in the case where viruses spread from computer to computer in the same local area network. This type of committee does not need every single business manager to plan for such an event. These are strategy meetings and there will be projects to actually implement the processes. The committee just needs someone who is empowered to create a communications chain and be able to delegate action items and activities to wide varieties of people who can participate in solutions.

The Technology Committee will be a place where highly skilled engineers and architects can collaborate on five-year plans for innovation, as well as the more mundane business resiliency tests and other technology management responsibilities. The CISO may participate by assigning staff to test the security features of potential new acquisitions or perform technology-related merger and acquisition activities.

These are by no means a full list of committees in which a CISO may be involved. However, it should serve to convey how important matrix management is to the overall health of a cybersecurity risk management program.

8.4 Framework Element Owners

In several of the framework elements so far described, there was a concept of a designated owner or contact for a risk data record. Issues have owners, events have contacts, controls have management owners, assessments have lead evaluators, assessment requirements have control contacts, measures and metrics have owners, and risks may have owners. These assignments of people to risk management responsibilities are necessary to provide accountability for qualified contributions to the risk management process (Bayuk 2007, pp. 47–50 and 109–111). Technology today is far too complicated for one person to thoroughly understand the scope of potential risk events that may threaten an enterprise. Although risk categories may appear static at a high level, cybersecurity events that could cause damage to enterprise technology and information vary with technology itself, which is rapidly changing. There is no choice but to make the person accountable for maintaining the technology its risk owner. They should understand the potential for negative business process impact due to dependency on the technology and be primarily accountable for minimizing that risk to an acceptable level. This is what motivates the "owner" stamp on so many risk-related data records.

Owner may be a responsibility not specified by job function, but not solely by job function. Ownership is often assigned by an enterprise security process that recognizes the need for expertise to assist in the customization of some activity that is common across job functions. Like a designation of organizational process responsibility, the obligations that come with these activities are typically dictated by policy, but within a given organization, they also could be established with standards or procedures. Scenario analysis is an example of a requirement that leads a business process owner to participate in an activity that may not have not hitherto on the radar.

For example, Figure 8.11 lists a few activities in which almost any business manager may be involved. For example, asking technology to build a custom business software application. That request may end up putting them in the driver's seat for a lot of security responsibilities that no one outside of their team has enough expertise to perform. A cybersecurity process may require that the application business owner participate in or delegate participating in a security architecture review, where a security expert will look at the mission and purpose of the system and suggest security features; those features will get captured as security requirements as part of business requirement capture. The security requirements

Where a person performs this activity:	The person becomes an "owner" or "contact for the cybersecurity process for:	A sample responsibility is:
Order the development of a new business application	Security Review Participation	Security-policy-compliant systems configuration
	Security Requirements Capture	Sign off on business requirements for confidentiality, integrity, and availability
	Change Control	Acceptance testing for identification and entitlement in organization-maintained software
	Security Upgrade Management	Testing application integrity post security software fixes
Procures Commercial Off the Shelf (COTS) IT services	Security Requirements Capture	Formal requirements for security in all Requests for Product Information and Proposals
	Contract Requirements	Approval of business requirements for cybersecurity in information service provider and technology maintenance contracts

Figure 8.11 Cybersecurity Owners

would be features that would need to be implemented in the product before it could be released, and the manager who requested the application would have to formally attest that they are adequate to maintain cybersecurity risk appetite. When the software is ready for deployment, that manager would be responsible for making sure the security features were tested. A cybersecurity change control process would list that person as the control owner unless they specified a delegate, but the software will not be deployed unless the owner attests that the tests were successful.

Figure 8.11 shows similar responsibilities for people who request procurement to purchase commercial off the shelf software, for example, a customer relationship management system. The procurement department would typically manage the process by which the requirements were gathered from the authorized business users. It is very important that security requirements be part of that request for proposal process or the firm could end up buying something that they do not have the ability to secure. Technology selection plays a large role in the standard-setting process. The enterprise may require that all purchased software be compatible with its IAM solutions. The procurement manager should have a checkpoint where they make sure that they have security requirements captured and the security group may participate, but it is the business process owner who has to attest that the requirements are adequate.

Procurement will typically present the requirements to multiple vendors with similar solutions in the form of a Request for Information (RFI). In response, vendors will describe how their technology meets each requirement. Vendors who meet most of the requirements will be invited to submit a Request for Proposal (RFP). Those with the most attractive proposals will be invited to install a Proof of Concept (POC) system, a test of whether the technology meets user expectations and integrates well with enterprise systems.

Also, when it comes time to purchase something and have a contract, whether it be for software or services, security requirements would then be included in that contract. This ensures that there would be some recourse for the business if the vendors did not meet cybersecurity requirements. Note it is the procurement manager who puts all those security standards and procedures into their procurement process. The CISO facilitates a secure procurement process by lending it cybersecurity expertise.

References

Bayuk, J. (2007). *Stepping Through the InfoSec Program*. Information Systems Audit and Control Association, IT Governance Institute (ISACA ITGI).

Bayuk, J. (2010). *Enterprise Security for the Executive: Setting the Tone at the Top*. Praeger.

COSO (2013). *Internal Control – Integrated Framework: Executive Summary, Framework and Appendices, and Illustrative Tools for Assessing Effectiveness of a System of Internal Control*. Committee of Sponsoring Organizations of the Treadway Commission.

COSO (2017). *Enterprise risk management: Integrating with strategy and performance*. Committee of Sponsoring Organizations of the Treadway Commission.

NACD (2021). National Association of Corporate Directors. *Principles for Board Governance of Cyber Risk*, Insight Report. https://www.nacdonline.org/insights/publications.cfm?ItemNumber=71795 (accessed 08 May 2023).

NACD (2023). National Association of Corporate Directors. *Cyber-Risk Oversight*, Director's Handbook Series. https://www.nacdonline.org/insights/publications.cfm?ItemNumber=74777 (accessed 08 May 2023).

9

Risks

Depending on where you get your news, you may not be fully cognizant of the extent to which the world is in constant cyberwar. NotPetya was the single most significant act of cyberwar in world history and it happened in 2017. Prior to NotPetya, a ransomware attack had been launched that was named Petya. Initially, NotPetya looked similar. The main difference was that NotPetya did not have an option to pay ransom to retrieve the data it destroyed. This type of attack is referred to as a *wiper* attack because its only purpose is to render computer data storage unreadable, to wipe it out. Figure 9.1 is a timeline of the attack from the perspective of one of the hardest hit organizations, the shipping and logistics company Maersk. The source of the timeline was Maersk's former IAM Service Owner (IAM-SO), who published the story of what the event looked like from the inside (Ashton 2020). The IAM-SO was an experienced and highly skilled cybersecurity professional who specialized in identity projects. In his narrative, he expresses amazement that Maersk was not a target of the attack and yet could get hit so hard.

Maersk's shipping business ground to a halt while new laptops were purchased and manual workarounds were quickly established for formerly automated business processes. They started reimbursing customers for rerouting or storing marooned cargo and this expense alone was estimated in millions (Greenberg 2020, pp. 196–199). Maersk's chairman of the board estimated the total expense as $300 million. The full cost of the attack was estimated to be $10 billion globally, and even this figure is thought to underestimate collateral damage to the global supply chain. The attack was attributed to a threat actor nicknamed *Sandworm* by cyber threat intelligence vendors in 2014 because they found a PowerPoint wherein the threat actors had named one of their attack campaigns "arrakis02." The threat intelligence analysts were science fiction fans, as apparently was the threat actor who named the campaign. Arrakis was the name of a planet in a popular science fiction book called Dune, and Sandworm was a powerful animal

Stepping Through Cybersecurity Risk Management: A Systems Thinking Approach,
First Edition. Jennifer L. Bayuk.
© 2024 John Wiley & Sons, Inc. Published 2024 by John Wiley & Sons, Inc.
Companion website: www.wiley.com/go/STCRM

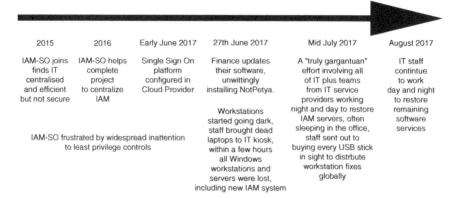

2015	2016	Early June 2017	27th June 2017	Mid July 2017	August 2017
IAM-SO joins finds IT centralised and efficient but not secure	IAM-SO helps complete project to centralize IAM	Single Sign On platform configured in Cloud Provider	Finance updates their software, unwittingly installing NotPetya.	A "truly gargantuan" effort involving all of IT plus teams from IT service providers working night and day to restore IAM servers, often sleeping in the office, staff sent out to buying every USB stick in sight to distrbute workstation fixes globally	IT staff contintue to work day and night to restore remaining software services
	IAM-SO frustrated by widespread inattention to least privilege controls		Workstations started going dark, staff brought dead laptops to IT kiosk, within a few hours all Windows workstations and servers were lost, including new IAM system		

Figure 9.1 Maersk NotPetya Timeline

species that the book's heroes engaged to drive invaders out of Arrakis. Although other Dune characters were also candidates and may have been engaged in activities more similar to those of the threat actor because in Dune, Sandworm is on the side of good versus evil, the destructive power of Dune's Sandworm made it a fitting analogy with the creator of NotPetya (Greenberg 2020, pp. 1–17).

Sandworm was eventually identified as members of Russia's General Staff Main Intelligence Directorate (GRU) Main Center for Special Technologies (GTsST) military unit 74455 (MITRE, n.d.). The group had been active since at least 2009 and members were indicted by US courts in 2020 for several attacks including NotPetya (Department of Justice 2020). In the two years before NotPetya, Sandworm had knocked out the Ukrainian electrical grid twice. Sandworm had planted the NotPetya malware in a Ukrainian tax software company used by every major Ukrainian agency and company, and it appeared to their customers to be a routine software update. Just as everyone in the US knows where they were on 9/11, everyone in Ukraine knows where they were on 27 June 2017 (Perlroth 2021, pp. xxi–xxiv).

Like many companies who are good at technology but do not believe they are a target, Maersk had a highly skilled and experienced technology team and quick access to technology vendor emergency response services. But what they did not have was a design for security architecture. Nevertheless, a security architecture existed. It included legacy operating systems with known exploited vulnerabilities. The principle of least privilege was not observed. The architecture included centralized application service accounts that were used by multiple applications worldwide and also had administrative access at the operating system level. Local administrative access was granted to users on their own desktops and laptops, so when the NotPetya hit, it was typically running with administrative privileges. There was no effective security monitoring. Luckily for Maersk, they had been experimenting with cloud services and had uploaded their user account data to a cloud a few weeks before the attack. So although all of the systems in their own offices and servers in their data centers were inoperable, they could still grant users access to cloud-based email and office software services.

The moral of the story of NotPetya is that it destroys the myth that some people with poor controls still tell themselves: "I am not a target" (Spafford et al. 2022, pp. 66–69). Now, years after NotPetya it should be clear that the first thing everyone needs to know about cybersecurity risk is that you do not have to be a target to get attacked.

9.1 Risk Categories

Some definitions of risk characterize risk events as having a possible positive impact as well as negative. Called "opportunity," it is the flip side of the probability of an event having negative impact. That is, an event, say the introduction of a new product, is expected to have a positive impact on the bottom line. However, if the product were to immediately be rejected by its target consumers, the debut event could have damaging public relations for the company that introduced it. An enterprise may have a risk appetite that dictates there must be a high probability of new product success as a prerequisite for its launch, perhaps estimated at 80%. The flip side would be a negative result, for example, if the product was the immediate target of fraud scams, it could actually lose money for the company that introduces it rather than produce expected raise in revenue. Though general guidance on enterprise risk may define it as such, assuming that any given event that could influence business objectives, either positively or negatively, the inclusion of opportunity is due to the uncertainty with respect to outcome for the enterprise with respect to *any* given event. In risk domains such as credit risk and market risk, this continuum is observable. In credit risk evaluation, where creditors do not pay back is the negative side of risk, but those who pay back is the positive side of risk, and the total is 100%. The positive outcome really is the flip side of negative outcome. Similarly, in market risk, the flip side is even more binary, a targeted consumer either purchases or does not.

However, operational risk presents a fundamentally different continuum. While market and credit risk spend their time making cases for opportunity, operational risk management spends more time estimating the probability of the negative side. This is because operational performance is itself planned in conjunction with the business mission and strategy. Even if the exact same event could have multiple cascading events impacting operations both positively and negatively, there are fewer unanticipated events of positive impact on operations. Moreover, if they do occur, the positive impact will be over and above the business plan. So it makes more sense for the risk analysts in operational risk to spend most if not all of their efforts anticipating the negative impacts and suggesting operational improvements to avoid them.

Perhaps because of this "it actually could turn out better" attitude, some risk management advice does not endorse placing events into risk categories. This is because any event categorization is inherently subjective and allows for the possibility that multiple events with differing probabilities of positive and negative outcomes can be grouped together. However, without categorization, cybersecurity risk analysts would have to take every potential event outcome individually, and there are literally thousands of possibilities.

Because cybersecurity is wholly concerned with the negative side of the risk probability equation, its risk analysts should be very careful not to place events with different probabilities into the same risk category. For example, a major global bank developed a high availability application architecture similar to the one in Figure 4.21, but did not include a recovery point objective in its requirements beyond the replicated standby database because they did not anticipate the event that brought it down (Mellor 2010). It was not a natural disaster or cyberattack, but a flaw in database code that corrupted the data in one of the databases to the point where it was unusable. Unfortunately, the corrupted data was automatically synchronized within milliseconds, with the result that the full set of high availability databases became unusable at the same time. This is a case of inadvertently classifying all negative events that could cause harm to availability in the same risk category and treating them as a single risk when in fact there was an unanticipated risk event: data integrity failure. It provides an example of why it is important to question risk categories. Though the incident was not caused by a cyberattack, it had the same effect on bank databases as NotPetya had on Maersk's Windows systems. Although the bank had much more capability for detection, problem management, and recovery than did Maersk, the incident nevertheless effectively prevented customers from accessing their bank accounts and cash machines for roughly a day. The availability recovery target was milliseconds, and the actual recovery time was measured in hours.

The categories exist to drive efficiency and effectiveness in technology control strategy. If this does not occur, of course it makes sense to revise event categories and generally question them, just as audit does in its assessment planning. Event categories should not be taken too seriously from a theoretical perspective. They were created as a practical effort to keep the job manageable. At the other extreme, there is really just one cybersecurity event category: resilience, which is the ability to withstand cyberattack. However, as events and issues get labeled with risks and controls implemented to reduce risks, there will typically be a recognizable pattern in enterprise cybersecurity risk hierarchy. Risk categories that include multiple actual loss events with long-running half-finished remediation plans will be of more concern than those with few events and validated controls.

Rather than a cybersecurity risk hierarchy appearing simply as an abstract taxonomy as it does in Figure 3.7, when there are reasoned analyses supporting risk levels, the ordinal measures will take on shades of urgency as in Figure 9.2. Note that the intensity of the border around risks at lower levels of the hierarchy moves up the hierarchy to assign the same label to the category under which it is a subcategory. In this case, the harm to confidentiality occurred due to theft of credentials via a known exploited vulnerability and resulted in monetary loss due to subsequent fraud.

The full set of such risk category records created by an enterprise is referred to as its *Risk Register*. Figure 9.3 lists data fields that are expected to be found in a risk register. In addition to name, description, and risk appetite, there is often an

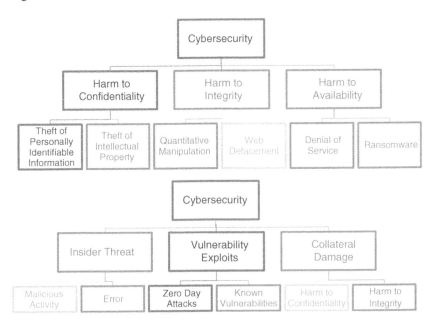

Figure 9.2 Cybersecurity Event Subcategories

Figure 9.3 Risk Register Record

ordinal measure of inherent versus residual risk and a ratio measure of probability. The ordinal measures exist in order to facilitate risk ranking (i.e., priority of treatment) even in cases where there is no data or method by which to generate a probability. Where there are both, there is typically a correspondence between the two fields, but not necessarily. Just because a risk is high probability does not necessarily give it high rank. It may be a frequent event that has no or low negative impact, and therefore may not have priority for treatment.

9.2 Risk Treatment

9.2.1 Controls

All of the above methods of understanding cybersecurity risk have pointed to the path of risk reduction, discussing how to *treat* cybersecurity risk, we have turned to various forms of controls that will *reduce* risk to acceptable levels. In various publications, risk treatment may be defined slightly differently, but typically refers to the selection of a method to modify or handle a risk. The number of methods may vary between publications as well, but normally the definition of risk treatment is making a decision on how to handle it, then executing on that decision. Controls are one method to treat risk and that method is called remediation, but enterprise risk management will often consider others. Other options for risk treatment are transfer, avoidance, and acceptance.

9.2.2 Transfer

Note that transfer does not actually mitigate the damage from a negatively impacting event, it just compensates the victim monetarily if a successful cyberattack occurs. Even the financial compensation typically does not leave the victim whole. The damage caused by the attack often lingers in the form of lost customers, employee disgruntlement, and wounded reputation for product safety and soundness. Where transfer includes compensation from a liable counterparty, this may reduce the blame assigned to enterprise negligence. However, where transfer compensation is expected to come from an insurance company, this expectation presents a risk in itself. The history of cybersecurity insurance, or *cyberinsurance*, shows a pattern of confusion with respect to customer expectations for coverage, with the consequence that claims are unexpectedly summarily denied while courts in different jurisdictions treat the same basic events and coverage arguments inconsistently.

Open peril, or *all risk*, insurance covers damage to all property in a specific scope of ownership except for items or events specifically mentioned as excluded.

This is the case in most types of home property insurance and business commercial general liability insurance. The former provides compensation to the homeowner should the home be damaged. The latter provides coverage for events wherein the covered business engages in activity that causes damage to others. In the case of home property insurance, the insured cannot be liable for the damage. That is, if you set a fire in your house, you cannot expect to be reimbursed by your insurance company. However, in the case of commercial general liability insurance, if your operations, services, or employees cause damage, you are covered, but not if someone from outside your organization causes damage to your business. That requires commercial property insurance. Open peril property insurance is available for homes, but it is harder for businesses to get them because single homes are easier to inspect and classify than business property portfolios. Businesses still purchase property insurance policies, but they are very specific about the types of assets they cover, and they generally have exclusions for negligent maintenance or categories of events.

Therefore, the companies that offer cyberinsurance have adopted an approach of trying to define the types of events that are most common and most easily remediated along with standard necessary activities that cost companies money in the aftermath of an attack. For example, PII data breaches. When PII is exposed in the course of a cyberattack, privacy laws require that the people whose data was compromised be notified so that they can be to alert to recognize fraud and take precautions like changing passwords to their bank accounts and notifying their credit card companies to send them new cards. The cost of this notification and any accompanying identity theft insurance can be very well defined. It is limited by the number of data records on people that are contained in enterprise systems. A cyberinsurance policy may also cover legal fee reimbursement in the event it is sued because of a data breach. However, that type of reimbursement will also have a prespecified limit. To limit unexpected losses, some insurers that offer cyberinsurance may cover these types of damages but exclude a more destructive cybersecurity incident like ransomware or NotPetya.

When Sony's PlayStation network was hit with a cyberattack, it had cybersecurity coverage for data breaches. Following the breach, it faced a class action suit brought by customers accusing the company of failing to protect their information. Its data breach policy covered some of its costs, but not enough to cover the potential legal fees (Wolff 2022, pp. 65–67). It filed an insurance claim under its commercial general liability policy for legal fees related to the case. Its insurance company, Zurich, denied the claim, responding that Sony's negligence did not cause the attack, the hackers caused the attack. Sony sued Zurich for refusing the coverage on the premise that its failure to protect information compromised its customer's privacy. This was ironic because Sony was using the same argument in its defense of the class action suit that Zurich used in its defense against Sony.

In the class action lawsuit, Sony claimed it was not responsible for the customer privacy breach because it had been caused by the threat actor. Sony lost both cases.

Even where destructive events such as ransomware are covered in cyberinsurance policies, insurance companies specify exclusions in an attempt to narrow the scope of covered losses. The pharmaceutical company Merck estimated that NotPetya caused damage to the enterprise totaling over $1 billion. The food processor Mondelez International estimated that NotPetya caused damage to the enterprise totaling over $100 million. Both companies had property insurance policies that covered physical loss or damage to electronic data, programs, and software with no exclusions for cyberattacks. To both companies, it seemed like they were very wise to have purchased the policy and promptly filed claims. However, to Ace American and Zurich, the insurance companies that sold Merck and Mondelez their property insurance policies, NotPetya was an act of war, a situation that was specifically excluded from coverage. Both companies sued their insurers, claiming that the US was not at war and neither were Russia and Ukraine at the time.

Figure 9.4 is an excerpt from court filings that reproduced the Ace American war exclusion clause. To a cybersecurity professional in the first line of defense, NotPetya was certainly loss or damage caused by hostile warlike action in time of peace by a government maintaining and using military forces, which is clearly the intention of the exclusion. However, the plaintiffs won both cases by claiming that hostile and warlike actions were violent and there was no violence evident in the cyberattack. Though this may seem like a good argument for cybersecurity risk transfer, insurance industry expert analysts have instead predicted that available

i. **Hostile/Warlike Action Exclusion Language**

A. 1) Loss or damage caused by hostile or warlike action in time of peace or war, including action in hindering, combating, or defending against an actual, impending, or expected attack:

> a) by any government or sovereign power (de jure or de facto) or by any authority maintaining or using military, naval or air forces;
>
> b) or by military, naval, or air forces;
>
> c) or by an agent of such government, power, authority or forces;

This policy does not insure against loss or damage caused by or resulting from Exclusions A., B., or C., regardless of any other cause or event contributing concurrently or in any other sequence to the losss.

Figure 9.4 War Exclusion Clause

insurance coverage for cybersecurity risks will become increasingly expensive and limited largely due to such unexpected court rulings (Wolff 2022, p. 225).

9.2.3 Avoidance

Avoidance is very difficult. Unless you are living off the land in the wilderness, it is impossible to maintain life as we know it without internet connectivity, banking services, mobile phones, and a host of other technologies. Even consumers are constantly under pressure to put more and more of our information online with rewards programs and other incentives. Most people have started to recognize that cloud service providers do a better job of maintaining our information than we do. We can only hope for more regulation that would make them all a safer alternative. That said, avoidance is still an option on a case-by-case basis. Unless the enterprise is in the technology business, it is prudent to let new technologies soak for a year or two before risking a business operation on them. Unless you employ cybersecurity experts to review and select all your technology security configuration options, it is prudent to use vendor recommended security features. Unless you are comfortable losing intellectual property, do not bring it with you when you travel to China (Bayuk 2022). Unless you are in the business of resilience, do not build your data center in a war zone. These are face valid choices that businesses make every day. Threat intelligence is not just useful to a security operations center, but at the highest levels of strategic business decision-making.

9.2.4 Acceptance

Consideration of risk acceptance as an alternative "treatment" should technically be skipped because it is a decision not to take action with respect to a risk, and the decision itself does not qualify as a treatment. However, it is a fact that many companies have formal policies that give executives the right to accept cybersecurity risk within their domain of operational authority. The idea behind this practice is that the executive is also responsible for the potential opportunity to be derived from accepting a risk that may have negative consequences. Where this practice exists, it is often referred to as "getting an exception" to implementing a cybersecurity control. The control could be a policy requirement like least privilege, a process documentation requirement, a technology configuration required by a standard, or a waiver of procedure. Essentially, it is weakening a building block in the structure of the risk management program. Though these exception processes are often assumed to be infrequently used, in some places they are the norm and businesses run up cybersecurity exceptions numbering in the hundreds or thousands.

The domain of vulnerability management provides a good example of this risk decision. Consider a business process such as the eCommerce store SaaS provider discussed in Section 5.2. Suppose that the SaaS provider has the log4j vulnerability on its web servers, and the SecOps team at the company has detected it with a routine vulnerability scan and advised the SaaS provider DevOps group that it needs to be fixed. The DevOps group assembles a project plan that involves reserving time for the quality assurance test team to perform a complete functionality test. The plan includes delaying the planned release of a new shopping cart feature that allows people to search for clothes of the same color as what is already in their cart. DevOps presents the plan to the business process owner, and the reaction is, "Is this really necessary? Is there a way we can simply ignore this, at least for now?" The DevOps team replies that the CISO does have an exception process whereby an executive can accept the risk of non-compliance with a standard. The executive directs them to go get the paperwork. Unfortunately, this has been a recurring theme in cybersecurity risk management since the 1900s.

However, when faced with a risk of a cybersecurity vulnerability for which there is a control treatment readily available, the opportunity to introduce a shopping cart feature is not the flip side of the risk the executive is taking. The executive is facing two different risks and making a choice to treat one and not the other. The untreated risk is cyberattack accomplished through vulnerability exploit. The treated risk is delay in the shopping cart feature. At least where there is a SSDLC available to improve software security while maintaining application functionality, the opportunity provided from development and deployment activities is not the activity at risk. It is not a judgment that the first risk does not need to be treated, though this possibility was the reasoning behind having an opt-out for cybersecurity standards in the first place. If cybersecurity risk is impacted due to long testing lifecycles, this risk should be treated as one that negatively impacts the cybersecurity program itself as opposed to any more specific risk subcategory such as *Known Exploited Vulnerabilities* because fear of application deployment delay could motivate bypass of a wide variety of cybersecurity controls, such as sharing an application service account across all applications in the enterprise rather than creating individual credentials for each application.

Different organizations have different methods of publishing exceptions. Some enter these exceptions into an issue tracking system, classifying them under a type or source label of *Exception*. Where this occurs, the executive who accepted the risk becomes the *exception owner*, and there is typically a requirement for periodic review and reacceptance for all risks within the scope of their review. Due to its storage in an issue tracking system, the exception record would then be tracked as if it were a planned issue remediation, and typically assigned a remediation target date agreed to by a cybersecurity risk analyst in the process. Although this process can be a very effective method of ensuring that the risk related to the exception is actively monitored, in situations like that of allowing a log4j vulnerability, it can

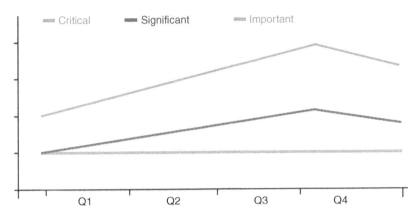

Figure 9.5   Risk Issue Trend Example

mask the fact that there is little to no expectation that remediation will ever occur. In many cases, the risk issue is presented to the exception owner on or before the target remediation date, and the exception owner routinely reapproves the exception. Unfortunately, if the issue metrics presented at the executive level are trends in risk issues as in Figure 9.5, the downward trend in lower priority risk issues in combination with a consistently low number of critical risk issues may be mistaken for an overall program quality improvement and an occasional critical risk here and there in all quarters as opposed to a program's failure to remediate a critical risk that has remained outstanding for a full year.

In organizations that link risk issues directly to risks for the purpose of reporting or have the ability to store these exceptions directly into a risk record in a risk register, a routine review of the risk register could provide assurance that exceptions do not float under the radar of audit or executive management. This of course assumes that audit and executive management are treated to periodic presentations that include information on risks for which there are known exceptions.

Continuing the example of the exception for the risk of cyberattack accomplished through vulnerability exploit, as in the case of the potential shopping cart delay, Figure 9.6 is an example excerpt from a risk report for the subcategory that corresponds to the exception, namely *Known Exploited Vulnerabilities*. The excerpt includes information that is standard in risk registers such as links to event, issues, controls, and metrics associated with this risk. The *Acceptance* section at the top of the record includes the log4j vulnerability exception, a description of scope to which it applies, the executive owner of the exception, and some information on compensating controls. Such data granularity enables aggregate reporting of risk acceptances for a specific organization that are separate from aggregated risk issue reporting.

Description	Execution of malicious software via known exploited vulnerabilities.
Appetite	The firm has no appetite for known exploited vulnerabilities in critical systems.
Acceptance:	2
Acceptance 1:	Tracking: A security update to mail servers rendered the interface to our phishing screening solution inoperable. In choosing between the two controls, it was decided to wait for a solution from the phishing vendor rather that back out the mail server security update. Owner: CIO (IT) Compensating control: Have escalated to the highest levels of phishing vendor management and have been assured a solution is forthcoming. CISO agrees. Created: 2023-09-30 22:16:25 Last update: 2023-09-20 22: 16:25
Acceptance 2:	Exception: Application eCommerce has known exploited Log4j vulnerablity on publicly accessible webserver. This allows an intruder command level access to the operating system underlying the application. Made by Char Baez (IN-Sales) Compensating Control: All outbound traffic from the application will be limited to know data flow endpoints and content-inspected to detect unauthorized exfiltration in near real time. Should exfiltration be identified, a security incident will be automatically created and outbound connections will be terminated until the incident is remediated. Advised by: CISO disagrees. Created: 2023-04-28 22:16:25 Last update: 2023-04-28- 22:16:25
Events:	2
Event 1:	MTCSPI2 - Organization Data Breach and Ransomware Attack, Exposure/High, type=Internal, 2023-04-18, closed on 2023-04-30
	Carbon Spider conducted espionage followed by data theft and a ransomware attack on the sales department.
Event 2:	PH324 - Spear Phishing, Not set/High, type=Internal, 2023-05-14, closed on 2023-05-14
	Executives in the legal department were targeted with fake personal messaged from outside counsel. One clicked a link and resulting investigation turned up known exploited desktop vulnerability.
Issue:	I12 - Vulnerability Scanner Integration Issue, target=2023-06-09, severity=Significant, A comparison of open vulnerabilities older than 30 days showed a difference in the number of vulnerable servers identified between the Vulnerability Scanning Tool and the Security Incident Management System. This integration should be automated, so its root cause is under investigation.
	A comparison of open vulnerabilities older than 30 days showed a difference in the number of vulnerable servers identified between the Vulnerability Scanning Tool and the Security Incident Management System. This integration should be automated, so its root cause is under investigation.
Control:	ISP: A.7 - Vulnerability Management type=Technical, activity=Identify, method=Policy, frequency=Continuous
	Security Operations shall establish a process to ensure that the enterprise is protected from publicly known technology threats for which security solutions are readily available (e.g. viruses, fraud scenarios).
Key Risk Indicators:	2
KRI 1:	Vulnerability_Time_ to_Close (KRI, I1), Metric: V-TTC 30 days Once a vulnerability is publicly known but not yet known to be exploited in the wild, there are nevertheless threat actors who may benefit from exploiting it, though not yet in a manner automated enough for drive by scanning. Therefore, they should be rememdiated in a time frame that corresponds to the next software development cycle.

Figure 9.6   Example Risk Report Excerpt

In 2014, a South Korean nation-state threat actor hacked into the film studio Sony Pictures entertainment, exfiltrated sensitive data, and then destroyed 70% of Sony's computers with wiper malware (Perlroth 2021, pp. 276–278). The data was then posted on the internet. It included PII, emails, HR records, and intellectual property, including but not limited to unreleased films and scripts. Cybersecurity professionals who worked at Sony headquarters were not surprised. They confidentially shared with their cybersecurity industry counterparts at other firms that they had never been able to get consensus within upper management that Sony Pictures should have certain cybersecurity controls. Somehow it made sense from a senior management perspective that, due to the special nature of doing business in Hollywood, an entire business division appeared to have received blanket cybersecurity exceptions. Moreover, the damage was not just financial and operational. It was personal. Multiple executives had to resign because of the slander they routinely conveyed via e-mail. Many CISOs publish this guideline: "Every time you send an email, consider the possibility that it may end up in the headlines." After all, even if your mailbox was secure, once the mail leaves your mailbox, anyone who gets it can share it. But Hollywood executives who were already public figures somehow had the impression that their email was completely private.

The malware planted at Sony Pictures contained 10,000 hard-coded host names for Sony devices (Strom 2018). This was possible because APT threat actors had spent months in reconnaissance inside of Sony's networks undetected. The information that quickly became publicly available about the poor state of cybersecurity controls at Sony Pictures should have obviously presented material risk to any cybersecurity risk staff who observed or participated in them. As is common after such events, a typical reaction was, "Where were the auditors?" It is increasingly common in this situation to also hear, "Where was the CISO?" It is understood that there are always shared responsibilities in corporate hierarchies as well as leadership transitions in cybersecurity, but there were cybersecurity professionals in Sony Group who knew enough about Sony Pictures to understand, if not document, its exceptions, and it was not sufficiently communicated to the level of awareness among executive management and board members that such an event was not only possible, but also highly likely.

All this said, there are also situations wherein there is no opportunity for risk transfer, controls are unavailable, and avoidance impossible. In this case, there is no other recourse for a CISO or cybersecurity risk officer than to enter a description of the situation directly into the risk register that has the same data fields as an exception, but instead is classified as *tracking*. The acceptance tracking record near the top of Figure 9.6 provides an example. It describes a situation wherein a software update has disrupted the ability of mail servers to screen email for phishing attempts. Alternative treatments in these cases always take time and leave the enterprise with the choice of temporarily living with a lower control level than desired and changing the security architecture. In this case, there are enough compensating controls to provide assurance that the risk is not critical, but it is significant enough to merit close monitoring.

9.3 Risk Appetite

The phrase, "tone at the top" has its origins in a late 1980s study of fraudulent financial reporting by commission of accountants (Treadway 1987, p. 11). The commission's final report observed that "(A)n element within the company of overriding importance in preventing fraudulent financial reporting: the tone set by top management that influences the corporate environment within which financial reporting occurs. To set the right tone, top management must identify and assess the factors that could lead to fraudulent financial reporting." After some explanation, the report makes a recommendation to establish a code of conduct, "The Commission then recommends that every public company develop and enforce a written code of corporate conduct as a tangible embodiment of the tone at the top" (Treadway 1987, p. 32). The phrase has since been adopted by corporate ethicists and auditors to generally refer to the obvious influence of management in all aspects of risk management, cybersecurity included.

Because a risk appetite statement is management's qualitative view of risk and is based on business mission and core values, it may not be obvious how it maps to cybersecurity at a category level. If there is a cybersecurity risk appetite statement but no indication in the enterprise risk appetite statement of which categories present the highest risk, it would make sense to hold a formal meeting with the author of the statement to determine if that was the author's true intention. Otherwise, the default assumption should be that cybersecurity risk in general should be avoided as much as possible, and where it cannot be avoided, remediated with multiple layers of controls.

Risks are associated with a qualitative risk appetite and quantitative tolerance measures. Where FrameCyber® is used to ensure management awareness of significant risks, it can also be used to highlight accountability for the integrity of the risk management process itself. That is, metrics should reflect not only the conclusions about risk issues described in the previous chapter on metrics, but also to verify that management is collaborating as expected to ensure the information in FrameCyber® is complete and consistent.

Risk appetite sets the tone at the top for which aspects of our mission and core values are most significant when it comes to cybersecurity. Of course, there will always be risk to the mission because there are limits on the extent to which we can control cyberspace. And that usually means we understand there will be some losses due to cyberattack. This has been a common dialogue with respect to cybersecurity. It is very typical for a corporate annual report to include a statement like the one in Figure 9.7 which declares that cyberspace is very hazardous and was published by Maersk to its investors less than six months before NotPetya. (A.P. Moller – Maersk A/S 2016, p. 30). In it, the company admits exposure to cyber security attacks that could materially affect operations to meet current and future

A.P. Moller - Maersk is exposed to **cyber security threats** that could materially affect operations and the financial condition. Cyber-attacks targeting systems or production facilities could result in severe business disruptions and significant losses, as A.P. Moller - Maersk is involved in complex and wide-ranging global services and engaged in increased digitisation of its businesses, making it highly dependent on well-functioning IT systems. The risk is managed through close monitoring and enhancements of cyber resilience and focus on business continuity management in the event that IT systems, despite their efforts, are affected.

Figure 9.7 Exemplar Annual Report Acknowledgement of Cybersecurity Risk

commitments and finances. This means that it can negatively impact the company's value and ability to meet current and future commitments. It further admits that cybersecurity attacks could result in severe business disruptions and significant losses. Later in the document, it acknowledges dependency on well-functioning IT systems and therefore is particularly monitoring *emerging risks* from a geopolitical standpoint. It claims to manage these risks using close monitoring and enhancements of cyber resilience and focus on business continuity. For this investor audience, Maersk can point to the deployment of Single Sign On in the cloud as a remediation measure for this obvious risk and claim to have averted a disaster of even greater magnitude than the one to which it befell. However, that control seems very inadequate given the fact that Maersk was operating in an emerging cyber war zone and its risk monitoring did not appear to put Sandworm on its radar. Many corporate annual statements contain similar exaggerations with respect to cybersecurity efforts. These are simply legally required warnings to investors and should not be mistaken for a true risk appetite statement that reflects tone at the top.

Corporate responsibility statements about privacy on public webpages are similar to annual report risk statements. Although they may be a prominent presence and accompanied by options to opt out of behavior tracking, it cannot be assumed that they were created at the top. The enterprise may simply consider them part of a customer experience, a function that may be performed by a marketing department. Enterprise risk appetite statements are not created solely in the service of public relations.

Measures underlying key control indicators (KCI) and key performance indicators (KPI) metrics should be as repeatable as possible to allow for comparison over time. Each measurable component of the risk category is then going to have a metrics profile associated with it, and it will correspond to the way that you want to measure your conformance with your own risk appetite. The key here is to find a way to quantify attributes of your risk appetite so that you can tell if you may be

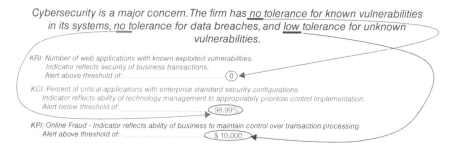

Cybersecurity is a major concern. The firm has no tolerance for known vulnerabilities
in its systems, no tolerance for data breaches, and low tolerance for unknown
vulnerabilities.

KRI: Number of web applications with known exploited vulnerabilities.
   Indicator reflects security of business transactions.
   Alert above threshold of: .... ⓪

KCI: Percent of critical applications with enterprise standard security configurations.
   Indicator reflects ability of technology management to appropriately prioritize control implementation.
   Alert below threshold of: 98.99%

KPI: Online Fraud - Indicator reflects ability of business to maintain control over transaction processing.
   Alert above threshold of: .... $ 10,000

Figure 9.8 From Risk Appetite to Key Risk Indicators

breaching it using some kind of systematic monitoring approach. However, results of assessments should also be included to ensure the risk appetite has at least one reasonably independent validation metric and these will of course change over time.

Consider the succinct risk appetite statement in Figure 4.3, Figure 9.8 is an example of that risk appetite mapped to a small set of KXIs. The phrase "no tolerance for known vulnerabilities" is mapped to application vulnerability scans. These may be aggregated from multiple scanning sources, such as network scans, operating system scans, and source code scans. The phrase "no tolerance for data breaches" is mapped to an aggregate target metric for data protection like the example in Figure 7.15. The phrase "low tolerance for unknown vulnerabilities" is mapped to an online fraud metric that may aggregate losses due to unexpected events, for example, a scam wherein a fraudster somehow changes customer postal addresses temporarily, receives their orders at some empty building, and is never found. Although these metrics may be a subset of a larger part of the enterprise cybersecurity metrics catalog, they should be informative enough to stimulate discussion at board level that may then be followed up with other metrics that answer more specific questions. Although the risk appetite is a qualitative description of the amount of risk that the enterprise is willing to accept, given its mission and core values, this map to a quantitative measure is invaluable in anticipating potential risk appetite breaches. Where risk appetite comes from tone at the top, a cybersecurity risk management team will be encouraged to find ways in which the appetite can be measured. Note that the people who may most easily identify the measures are not necessarily cybersecurity risk analysts. People working daily to support business processes are constantly analyzing risk issues because they need to maintain business operations. Someone in the role of a cybersecurity risk analyst who is not working in an operational capacity for the business every day may not be the best person to translate risk appetite into a metric because translation is fundamentally a GQM exercise and the executive who wrote the risk appetite should have the ultimate decision on which metric is used. Nevertheless, cybersecurity risk analyst participation is essential to the process to ensure that the measures have integrity and the metrics are repeatable.

Of course, the more detailed the risk appetite description, the more easily it can be mapped to metrics, and thereby the better the communication that cybersecurity program can have with the executive management that issued it. By combining information about risk appetite in a comprehensive report of risk categories, the connect between the risk appetite and risk indicator becomes more apparent. Figure 9.9 provides an example. The figure shows a cybersecurity risk called "Lost or Stolen Credentials," which is under a data loss category and so given the acronym of (CS.DL-C). A relevant section of the enterprise risk appetite statement is included in the risk record to remind risk analysts that this is the executive

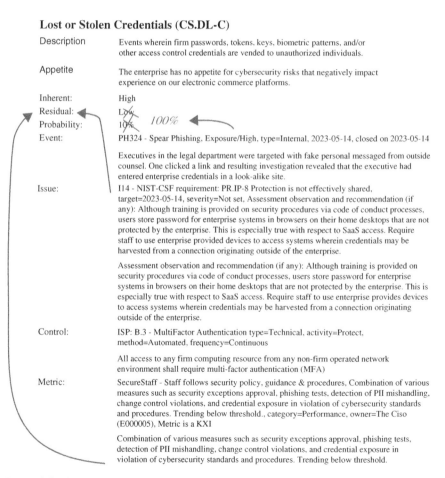

Lost or Stolen Credentials (CS.DL-C)

Description	Events wherein firm passwords, tokens, keys, biometric patterns, and/or other access control credentials are vended to unauthorized individuals.
Appetite	The enterprise has no appetite for cybersecurity risks that negatively impact experience on our electronic commerce platforms.
Inherent:	High
Residual:	Low
Probability:	10% *100%*
Event:	PH324 - Spear Phishing, Exposure/High, type=Internal, 2023-05-14, closed on 2023-05-14
	Executives in the legal department were targeted with fake personal messaged from outside counsel. One clicked a link and resulting investigation revealed that the executive had entered enterprise credentials in a look-alike site.
Issue:	I14 - NIST-CSF requirement: PR.IP-8 Protection is not effectively shared, target=2023-05-14, severity=Not set, Assessment observation and recommendation (if any): Although training is provided on security procedures via code of conduct processes, users store password for enterprise systems in browsers on their home desktops that are not protected by the enterprise. This is especially true with respect to SaaS access. Require staff to use enterprise provided devices to access systems wherein credentials may be harvested from a connection originating outside of the enterprise.
	Assessment observation and recommendation (if any): Although training is provided on security procedures via code of conduct processes, users store password for enterprise systems in browsers on their home desktops that are not protected by the enterprise. This is especially true with respect to SaaS access. Require staff to use enterprise provides devices to access systems wherein credentials may be harvested from a connection originating outside of the enterprise.
Control:	ISP: B.3 - MultiFactor Authentication type=Technical, activity=Protect, method=Automated, frequency=Continuous
	All access to any firm computing resource from any non-firm operated network environment shall require multi-factor authentication (MFA)
Metric:	SecureStaff - Staff follows security policy, guidance & procedures, Combination of various measures such as security exceptions approval, phishing tests, detection of PII mishandling, change control violations, and credential exposure in violation of cybersecurity standards and procedures. Trending below threshold., category=Performance, owner=The Ciso (E000005), Metric is a KXI
	Combination of various measures such as security exceptions approval, phishing tests, detection of PII mishandling, change control violations, and credential exposure in violation of cybersecurity standards and procedures. Trending below threshold.

Figure 9.9 Risk Subcategory Analysis

management opinion on how it should be treated. The report shows that it has not been labeled with the nominal measure "Key." Almost any category of cybersecurity risk is inherently high, and the residual risk has been labeled "Low." These ordinal labels can usually be traced to some point in time prior assessment, one in which the low label on a "high, medium, low" ordinal scale would correspond to the risk numeric probability as that is listed on the report as 10%. However, the figure shows that the risk analyst is actively connecting the other cybersecurity risk framework elements that are linked to the risk that is the subject of the report.

As if in using it in a discussion with stakeholders, the arrows in the figure show the influence of the data on the analyst's assessment of the probability measure. The figure shows that the control intended to reduce the subcategory risk is measured with a KRI that is currently below threshold. There are issues identified in a NIST CSF assessment related to the ineffectiveness of protection where responsibility for the control is shared. There is also an arrow pointing directly from the event to the analyst's change in probability. This is because, given that the event occurred, it represents a realized risk, so the analyst has crossed out the 10% estimate and replaced it with 100% to reflect that it actually happened. An event in this category would now, of course, merit a "High" residual risk on the same ordinal risk scale.

Risk reports such as those in Figure 9.9 provide examples of how individual cybersecurity risk analysts linked measures to risk, and these should be shared with the leadership who produced the risk appetite statement and discussed to determine the level at which the metrics seem face valid. Risk thresholds also need to be face valid and be accompanied with an explanation that a layperson can understand. A good example is a KRI to monitor known exploited vulnerabilities. Figure 9.10 shows that the KRI is not a fully defined metric itself but is based on a metric defined as in Figure 7.13 with a few fields added to explain why the metric is a KRI and record the agreed upon threshold. Note that this definition of a KRI using a link to an existing metric allows the base metric to be used in multiple KRIs, just as the separation of measure and metric records allows the measure record to be used in multiple metrics.

Unique ID for new Key Indicator:	Known_Exploited_Vuln	KXI Type	KRI ▾	Use Case:	Logging ▾
Source Metric Index:	VULNS-RESP			Name: Vulnerability Response Unit: Days	
Comparison		Threshold:			
>		2 days			
Explanation					

Exploits for known exploited vulnerabilities are typically automated and this brings the time at which the enterprise is targeted to a much shorter interval than if there was no known exploit.

Figure 9.10 KRI Record

If an executive agrees that the metrics and thresholds make sense given the risk appetite, reviews the risk report and associated metrics periodically, and provides the resources to maintain the metrics below threshold, then the integrity and meaning of the metric will be understood as part of tone at the top.

The executive should also be the highest point of escalation for decisions on how to respond to metrics that indicate there may be issues with the integrity of the risk management framework itself, because if the risk management framework itself is not maintained, then the metrics cannot be relied upon as well. These include, but are not limited to:

- Lack of relevant threat intelligence.
- Cybersecurity incidents that have not been assigned risk categories (and thereby escape being included in risk reporting).
- Controls that fail verification and validation metrics.
- Assessment findings of policy violations or gaps in regulatory compliance.
- Risk issues that have not been assigned risk categories.

9.4   Risk Tolerance

So far in this book, the terms risk appetite and risk tolerance may appear to have been used as if they were interchangeable. But they are not the same thing. While risk appetite is a qualitative statement that is measurable only in nominal and ordinal values, the risk tolerance measures a range of values on a scale that is numeric. The idea is to specify a point on that scale beyond which the risk appetite is undoubtedly in jeopardy of being breached; therefore, risk tolerance refers to the range of degraded performance that management deems acceptable as a demonstration that risk appetite is observed.

The terms "risk tolerance measures" and "key risk indicators" are sometimes used interchangeably. However, risk tolerance measures refer specifically to the boundaries of acceptable variations in performance related to achieving objectives, while risk indicators are metrics that help identify changes to the risks themselves. Events, controls, risks, and metrics all contribute to the risk indicator puzzle.

The subjective nature of the risk appetite discussion reveals many puzzle pieces that are important to combine to make sure that an enterprise has an accurate bird's eye view of its cybersecurity risk picture. But discussion of risk appetite is too high level to call attention to some ground truths, such as the necessity of a readily accessible asset inventory to use as a denominator for metrics. Every puzzle player knows that some puzzle pieces present bigger clues than others. Just as a puzzle enthusiast will often first focus on the outer edge, then search for other defining attributes of the puzzle, if a risk.

In cybersecurity, the edges of the big picture are analogous to the scope of enterprise technology. However technology asset inventory measures are not constrained to technology. They include attributes of technology, enterprise data, outsourced services, business processes, and people. The technology term for a repository for technology asset inventory data is a configuration management database (CMDB). It is occasionally surprising to cybersecurity staff to realize that the enterprise within which they operate, that otherwise appears strong and stable, has gaps in the CMDB that render the number, type, functionality, and location of its people, processes, and technology difficult to estimate with confidence, much less measure security attributes systematically and routinely. In some enterprises, it is possible to reliably measure attributes such as type and location, but not as reliably measure business functionality for the same set of systems. That is, there may be an infrastructure inventory that includes all devices, but no centralized records on which business applications utilize which server and network devices. This situation makes key control metrics such as the one in Figure 7.22 impossible to generate.

It is also sometimes the case that a thorough asset inventory process is managed but not utilized by all organizations within the enterprise. Oversight for the scope of cybersecurity risk tolerance is then commensurately difficult with the ability to accurately identify scope of enterprise digital asset inventory. One way that people lose track of asset inventory is that they do not apply the same security principles to a machine in a cloud as they would to one in a data center. Servers and desktops in the cloud are created with *virtual machine* technology. The hardware on which the operating system runs is shared by multiple instances of virtual machines that are started and stopped as needed. Even cybersecurity professionals attuned to the difficulties in figuring out how many and which machines are currently operational in their own data centers have difficulty applying the same measurement techniques in a supplier Platform as a Service (PaaS) cloud. Each service provider has their own method of labeling and monitoring instances of virtual machines. For example, when the virtual machines start and stop, the network address of each instance of the same machine may be different, and so automated network security scanning tools may record them as two different devices. They may not ever have a name to IP address mapping in a centralized domain name registry. Therefore, even cybersecurity measurement techniques that correctly track attributes of virtual machines in the enterprise data center may not work on a similar virtual machine spun up in a PaaS. SecOps may have a cybersecurity architecture configuration standard for each type of technology virtualized in a PaaS virtual machine as they would a virtual machine in the data center and use a security configuration scanner that will measure whether the configuration on every one of those assets meets a standard. However, they may not have a good record of exactly how many of those cloud devices exist and/or if all of them have been scanned as per the security architecture standard requirements. This type of situation motivates the need for a cybersecurity program to fully understand and apply the concept of risk tolerance.

Even PaaS virtual machines can utilize secure baselines such as those published by CIS, as well as be preconfigured with endpoint detection and response tools that report back to a central SIEM. The method of reducing uncertainty that any given virtual machine is controlled by a hostile adversary is to define what good looks like and measure deviations from that configuration. Where it is detected that a virtual machine breaches those thresholds, it should be immediately shut down and investigated. The trick is not to have 10,000 of these deviations, but to have a common process for deploying virtual machines so the anomalies detected become a manageable number. Any PaaS virtual machine that does not have this baseline should only be active while some administrators are in the process of building the baseline to be used by others. Even those machines should have some naming convention or initial configuration that allows them to be recognized as authorized. A network scanner should be able to identify the total number of instances in a PaaS as well as the numbers that deviate from standard. These measures can provide a numerator and a denominator for a risk tolerance target metric. A risk tolerance measure is typically a cybersecurity program target or goal measure trending over time, because both target and goal measures have been developed to verify and validate cybersecurity program correctness and effectiveness precisely in order to maintain risk to a level under risk appetite. Where key risk indicators cover risk categories, it is possible to measure appetite with confidence enterprise exposure to risk in a manner that at least imitates more easily quantifiable risk domains but at least is supported with fact-based evidence. Figure 9.8 provides an example translation from risk appetite to risk tolerance. Risk tolerance is also typically measured in time intervals to allow for the identification of upward or downward trends in the risk to which they correspond. For example, the presence of an unauthorized virtual machine in a PaaS environment may indicate an APT threat actor has infiltrated the PaaS and obtained credentials authorized to create virtual machine instances. Figure 9.11 presents a simple risk tolerance metric based on this example.

The key to being able to use a metric as a risk tolerance metric is to be able to demonstrate that the target is appropriately below risk appetite. It is converting a qualitative statement into a defensible number. If the metric shows a threshold crossed, it should not be tolerated because it means risk appetite is breached. Because risk appetite is management's qualitative statement on the level of risk not considered to approach capacity or otherwise conflict with enterprise mission,

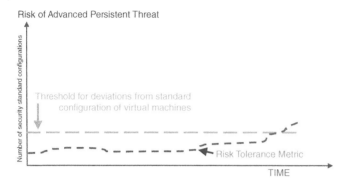

Figure 9.11 APT Risk Tolerance Metric

crossing a risk tolerance threshold implies that the enterprise has violated its mission and/or core values.

The definition of risk tolerance also implies that there is some quantifiable risk capacity. Though risk capacity may have different methods of measure based on industry, risk capacity generally refers to the maximum level of risk an enterprise can assume without being in imminent danger of collapse, the break-point for an enterprise before risk events cause results from which no recovery may be expected. Risk tolerance refers to the limit of measured degraded cybersecurity performance that management deems acceptable as a demonstration that risk appetite is observed and risk is safely below capacity. Attempts to measure conformance to risk appetite highlights attributes of actual risks and reveals the units with which risk appetite and risk capacity are measured within a risk category. Most risk capacity measures imply impact, measure units are currency, the amount of money lost when a risk event occurs. In technology risk, money is the *primary* unit of capacity measurement only in fraud cases. Risk capacity impact measures may also relate to performance against business objectives such as customers lost, reputational damage, systems downtime, or interruption in critical services. Figure 9.12 shows the relationship between risk capacity, thresholds based on risk appetite, and risk tolerance metrics.

The risk appetite threshold refers to some kind of quantitative boundary of acceptable variation in performance related to achieving some objective that will help to determine whether you are adequately controlling against adverse events in the associated risk category. Figure 9.13 shows risk tolerance metrics for two risk appetite thresholds identified in Figure 9.8, on the left is the number of web applications with known exploited vulnerabilities. On the right is the percentage of critical applications with enterprise standard security configurations. The risk tolerance metric on the left side of the figure would likely be based on a badness-ometer like that in Figure 7.21. Even one critical vulnerability would violate the

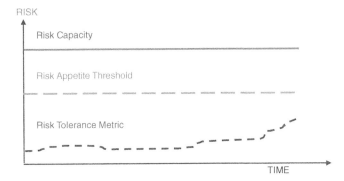

Figure 9.12 Risk Tolerance Metrics

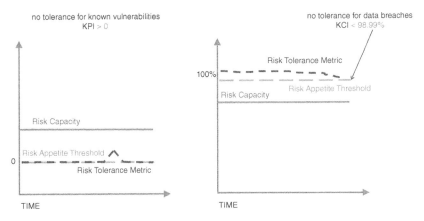

Figure 9.13 Trends in Cybersecurity Risk Tolerance

threshold because it is zero. The risk tolerance metric on the right might be based on a key control indicator such as that in Figure 7.22. The threshold is set at 98.99% so as long as the metric remains above that line, risk appetite is not breached.

It is also possible to create risk tolerance metrics using measures unrelated to a control that nevertheless provides information that a control is not working. For example, a bank can measure the number of customers that report credit card fraud as a percentage of all customers and call it a metric, then use that metric as a cybersecurity KPI. Such a *Card Theft Indicator* with a threshold of *25%* may have an explanation such as, "if over 25% of our customers experience card theft and fraud, then we will defensively reinspect our controls to ensure the root cause is not something wrong with our protection of that data."

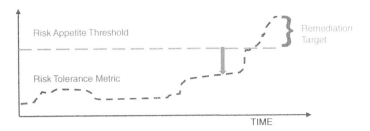

Figure 9.14 Risk Remediation Target

The most important aspect of a risk tolerance measure is the activity that should take place if it shows risk appetite is breach. In this situation, if remediation is not imminent, then a risk issue should be opened to ensure the remediation has an owner and a plan. Figure 9.14 is a simplified view of the target of risk remediation, which is to bring the tolerance measure back to below the appetite threshold. Because thresholds set a theoretical ceiling on where it seems reasonable that risk tolerance trends indicate a breach of qualitative risk appetite, when the thresholds are breached, postmortems and remediation plans provide an opportunity for systematically improving practices, including critical evaluation of methods and assumptions.

In summary, a set of good cybersecurity metrics is a tool in the toolkit of cybersecurity risk management. But an indicator of good cybersecurity management is not the same as good cybersecurity. Risk indicators should be systematically collected and discussed with management, who are empowered to effect change in whatever process, standard, or procedure that may be necessary to reduce risk to an acceptable residual level below risk appetite. Good cybersecurity metrics often reflect poor cybersecurity despite the best efforts of cybersecurity management. This is a situation similar to other fields wherein there is an uncontrollable threat (e.g., firefighting, drug counseling, and military service). Although there is a plethora of cybersecurity metrics, the key to a good metrics program is completeness with respect to performance metrics, realism with respect to goal metrics, and integrity with respect to both.

9.5   Probability Measurement

All cybersecurity risk tolerance metrics should provide some information relevant to evaluating cybersecurity risk. The metrics should be designed to be used by management to indicate whether the firm is more or less susceptible to cyberattack. If some risk measures have been designated as key, it should indicate that the probability that a determined adversary will be successful in achieving attack goals against the organization has gone measurably up or down, because the measure of the indicator is very closely tied to the estimation of the probability of successful attack. The "Key" in Key Risk Indicator is meant to focus decision-makers on the most informative metrics, as brought forth by subject matter experts who understand the details. The intent is to measure the probability of impact of successful attack on business performance, against which all other strategic endeavors are judged.

Nevertheless, the close affiliation between a risk probability and a KRI is due to the cybersecurity attributes in the environment, but they are completely different units of measure. For example, temperature and pressure are closely related, and when applied to a given system, they will both trend higher and lower at the same time. This does not mean you can measure probability with a KCI. To measure risk directly is different than using a risk indicator to measure risk tolerance. A KCI metric of 99% in the left side of Figure 9.12 means that 99% of planned controls are in place, but that does not translate into a 1% probability of cyberattack. The connection between the target percent application security configuration does not measure the likelihood of a data breach, it measures the extent to which an application has met its security performance goals. To measure a data breach, you have to measure attributes of an attack event itself that provide information on how likely this attack is to actually be successful.

There are a variety of ways one can arrive at a measure of risk probability, and Figure 9.15 lists some of the most popular approaches in cybersecurity (Axelrod 2013, pp. 108–109). Although in some enterprises, cybersecurity scenario analysis and other methods of calculating potential damage or loss substitute for risk measurement, the unit of a risk measure in other disciplines is probability.

Approach	Calculation	Strengths	Weaknesses
Ordinal	Assignment of levels of impact and likelihood, such as high, medium, low	The exercise itself can be very beneficial to the understanding of risk by various constituencies within an organization	➤ Yields a somewhat subjective view of the importance and potential impact of risk factors ➤ Subjective methods for combining risk factors ➤ Less meaningful when trying to aggregate risks across organizational units
Cardinal Scoring (i.e., numeric scores)	Assignment of scores as 1 through 10, to levels of impact and likelihood	Allows for some ability to aggregate risks by department, company, etc.	➤ Gives an unfounded sense of precision to the analysis and calculations
Probability distributions	Uses probability distributions from a set of events	Provides a more realistic view of how the estimates of the probabilities of occurrence and impact of risk factors vary	➤ Extremely difficult to get accurate probability distribution data ➤ Some do not believe that this is meaningful or doable
Objective	Attempts to remove subjectivity by asking subject-matter experts to provide estimates	Removes some the bias introduced by belonging to a group that will be directly affected by results of the analysis and/or by the impact of adverse events	➤ May not benefit from input by those who have "in the trenches" bias to overestimate ➤ Even independent subject-matter experts will likely have their own biases based on personal experience

Figure 9.15 Methods of Cybersecurity Probability Estimation

The history of risk management is all about figuring out how likely an event is to occur. While loss estimates can be a data point in determining priority for risk treatment, the measure of likelihood is in the realm of statistics. Where there is insufficient historical data available from which to calculate the probability of an event in a given category, one may estimate it based on expertise and/or experience, as in some of the examples in Figure 9.15, or dissect the event threat vector and use a measure of technical attack difficulty to assign a numeric probability to each step in the vector, and then use conditional probability to estimate the probability that the vector as a whole will become an attack.

Probability is a numeric measure of the likelihood that an event in a given risk category will occur. The risk category may be a top level risk, a category or subcategory. Probability values range from 0 to 1, where 0 indicates that the event will never occur and 1 indicates that the event will certainly occur. Probability is usually represented as a percentage, with a few decimal points, depending on the granularity of the measurement. But in cybersecurity, it is rare to see decimals in a probability because the margin of error (i.e., confidence interval) in the probability estimate is usually large enough to render decimals irrelevant.

The possible values of a probability of a given event are typically presented in terms of experiment and outcome. For example, if the experiment is a coin toss, the outcomes are either heads or tails. Assuming a fair coin, this leaves two equally possible outcomes, and the probability of both events is 50%. The number of probabilities assigned to an event will depend on the number of distinct alternative outcomes to which the event belongs. If an event is a chess game, the outcomes are win, lose, and draw, so where players are fairly matched, the outcome of all three events is 33.33%. For a cybersecurity event, it is much harder to define the experiment that includes the outcome, but not impossible. In assigning probability, there are two rules:

1) The probability assigned to each outcome must be between 0 and 1.
2) The sum of the probabilities of alternative outcomes must be 1.

Where outcomes can be specified, the probability of each may be estimated using the frequency in which they occur relative to each other. For example, let us say there is an event category called *Desktop Attack*, and it includes four subcategories: *End-user hacking, Web-delivered Malware, Phishing, and Worms*. To assign probability to each, an organization could conduct multiple pentests using each subcategory of Desktop Attack and determines the probability of a successful outcome for each. Figure 9.16 shows the outcome of the tests.

The last column of the Figure, *Probability*, assumes that desktops will be attacked using an attack in the subcategory, so the relative success frequency of the tests is also the probability. Where the probability of an attack is not 100%, some method must be used to assign a probability to the attack itself.

Desktop Attack Subcategories:	# Attempts	# Successful	Relative Success Frequency	Probability
End user hacking	130	56	0.430769231	43%
Phishing	93	32	0.344086022	34%
Web-delivered malware	122	78	0.639344262	**64%**
Worms	56	20	0.357142857	36%
Desktop Attack Category:	401	186	0.463840399	**64%**

Figure 9.16 Probability of Desktop Intrusion

The probability of an attack event may be estimated with relative frequency using threat intelligence data or industry statistics such as the Verizon Data Breach report. That is, the attack probability may be estimated based on the relative frequency of an attack type in statistics that aggregate attack type by the industry in which the enterprise operates.

The probability that a threat actor will launch an attack that is successful would then be calculated in combination with the historical outcomes in Figure 9.16. This is a conditional probability. A conditional probability calculation will still rely on the historical data collected on previous attack occurrence and outcomes. Assume that the probability desktops will be attacked is 80%. Then, given the historical data collected in Figure 9.16, the conditional probability that the attack will be successful would be calculated as:

$$\text{Probability}(\text{Desktop Attack Success} \mid \text{Desktop Attack}) = 0.8 \times 0.64 = 0.51$$

In this case, the probability of successful desktop attack is reduced to 51%. Whether the probability of a successful attack for the category is 64% or 51%, it is still a reflection of the probability of the subcategory with the highest probability of successful attack. Although this may seem to blur the distinction between subcategories, it is also understood that the pentests are simply a simulation, and any one of the subcategories may exploit the same desktop vulnerabilities as any other. This is because both attack methods and known exploits change frequently, so bubbling the highest subcategory probability to the category level is just a method of understanding that there is at least one event in the category that brings the category as described at the higher level to the highest probability of any event that is included in its description. In some cases, especially at the lower levels of a risk hierarchy, a subcategory may also be an efficiency measure in designing controls meant to address the root cause of most of the events in the category. In this case, the root cause is ineffective desktop security architecture. A desktop control standard should not need to be designed four times, rather, the same standard should protect against all four types of desktop attacks. In this case, if the probability of an attack occurrence is 80% or 100%, then the desktops using the current standard are estimated to have a 51% or 64% probability of intrusion, respectively.

Where there is no data available to estimate the probability of attack, it may be estimated using some other method, such as crowdsourcing or logical analysis based on specific knowledge of the technology in scope. Also note that, in many industries, such as banking and government, the probability of attack occurrence is well-understood to be 100%, so estimates of attack success will be sufficient to estimate the probability of a successful outcome. (This is also the basis for adopting zero trust tenets.)

Where there is no data available to estimate the probability of attack success, it may instead be possible to calculate the probability of a successful attack by estimating the probability that controls may be bypassed. This is the reasoning behind assigning strength measures to cryptography algorithms. They are rated by the number of basic computer operations such as central processing unit cycles that are required to break the cryptographic algorithm, as in decrypting a message without knowing the key. Cybersecurity control strength measured in this manner narrows the probability of successful attack by limiting it to threat actors with sophisticated and powerful computing resources as well as time to execute the attack without detection. For example, the phishing attack in Figure 9.17 has 11 steps, and only four are controlled by the attacker. They appear in solid lines and are numbered 1, 5, 8, and 10.

Assume that the probability that those steps will occur is 100%. A successful attack outcome requires at least six of the other steps to occur, numbers 2, 3, 4, 6, 7, and 9. An undetected successful attack requires a seventh step, number 11. As anyone who has ever conducted a blind phishing test to see if staff click on malicious looking links can attest, the probability that step 2 will occur

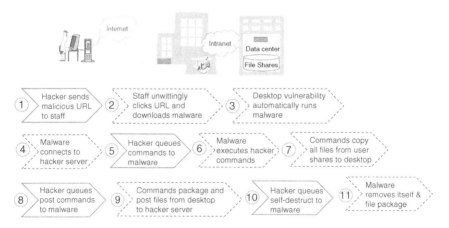

Figure 9.17 Phishing Threat Vector

(i.e., staff unwittingly click on the hacker's link) is surprisingly high. However, in the absence of zero day attacks, it is possible to harden the desktop to the point where it will not automatically run the malware delivered to the desktop by the act of clicking on the link. It is also possible to lower the probability of successful attack by limiting the activity in step 4. An outbound proxy server can automatically block the desktop's ability to connect to any server not on an enterprise's preapproved list of business partners. Of course, to bypass that control, it could still be possible for an APT threat actor to place their site on the approved list by other means, so even with the control in place, the probability of it working could be estimated at 10%. However, if step 4 is successful, the probability that steps 6 and 7 will occur is high because the hacker commands now appear on the desktop as if they were entered by an authorized user. Nevertheless, step 9 can still decrease the overall probability of a successful attack with a strong control such as blocking all outbound data uploads to sites that are not preapproved business partners. Assuming the strength estimation of the controls led an expert to assign probabilities to steps 2, 3, 4, 6, 7, and 9 as 100%, 25%, 10%, 100%, 100%, and 10%, the conditional probability that the attack vector will succeed is:

$$1 \times 0.25 \times 0.1 \times 1 \times 1 \times 0.1 = 0.0025, \text{ or } 0.25\%$$

A technology environment that did not include the controls mentioned would have a much higher probability of succumbing to the phishing attack.

Any cybersecurity event that happens internally should be considered to have a 100% probability of happening again unless the control environment changes to bring the risk to an acceptable residual level. To make sure that realized risks are captured, all cybersecurity events that produce negative consequences should be diligently recorded and its distinguishing characteristics double-checked so that it can be properly analyzed, and actions taken to ensure that its probability of recurrence is low. The same should be done for events that obviously could have resulted in realized risk, but due to some lucky twist of fate the enterprise managed to avoid the negative consequences. For example, the desktop may have been taken off the network for maintenance mid-attack before the data exfiltration and the malware discovered by desktop support. These are called "near miss" events and may also be internal or external.

Probabilities should always be assigned at the lowest level of the risk hierarchy, and just as in the ordinal risk hierarchy in Figure 6.3, the probability at the lower level should bubble up to the top, as illustrated in Figure 9.18.

Note how the discussion of appetite and tolerance above prompts the need for categories, as different metrics will be required to estimate the probability of events that cross threat and target boundaries.

Cyber: CS Cybersecurity (100%)

I---Cyber: CS.IT Insider Threat (90%)

I I---Cyber: CS.IT-A Accidental Insider Threat (20%)

I I---Cyber: CS.IT-I Intentional Insider Threat (20%)

I I---Cyber: CS.IT-P Phishing Email (90%)

I---Cyber: CS.SI Service Interruption (20%)

I I---Cyber: CS.SI-N Distributed Denial of Service (10%)

I I---Cyber:CS.SI-O Technology Outages (20%)

I---Cyber:CS.MW Malware Infection (100%)

I I---Cyber:CS.MW.ZD Zero Day Attacks (70%)

I I---Cyber:CS.MW-KEV Known Exploited Vulnerabilities (100%)

I---Cyber:CS.APT Advanced Persistent Threat (70%)

I---Cyber:CS.CFG Misconfigurations (20)

I---Cyber:CS.DL Data Leaks (80%)

   I---Cyber:CS.DL-P Loss of Personal Records (80%)

   I---Cyber:CS.DL-C Lost or Stolen Credentials (10%)

Figure 9.18 Risk Probability

References

A.P. Moller – Maersk A/S (2016). Annual Report. https://investor.maersk.com/static-files/a31c7bbc-577a-49df-9214-aef2d649a9f5 (accessed 08 May 2023).

Ashton, G. (2020). Maersk, me & notPetya (21 June 2020). https://gvnshtn.com/posts/maersk-me-notpetya/ (accessed 08 May 2023).

Axelrod, W. (2013). *Engineering Safe and Secure Software Systems*. Artech House.

Bayuk, J. (2022). Chinese Attacks on US Technology: A View from the Trenches. https://tag-cyber.com/advisory/quarterly (accessed 08 May 2023).

Department of Justice (2020). Six Russian GRU Officers Charged in Connection with Worldwide Deployment of Destructive Malware and other Disruptive Actions in Cyberspace. US Department of Justice. https://www.justice.gov/opa/pr/six-russian-gru-officers-charged-connection-worldwide-deployment-destructive-malware-and (accessed 08 May 2023).

Greenberg, A. (2020). *Sandworm, A New Era of Cyberwar and the Hunt for the Kremlin's Most Dangerous Hackers*. Anchor.

Mellor, C. (2010). Morgan Chase Blames Oracle for Online Bank Crash. https://www.theregister.com/2010/09/20/chase_oracle/ (accessed 08 May 2023).

MITRE (n.d.). Sandworm. https://attack.mitre.org/groups/G0034/ (accessed 08 May 2023).

Perlroth, N. (2021). *This Is How They Tell Me the World Ends: The Cyberweapons Arms Race*. Bloomsbury.

Spafford, G., Metcalf, L. and Dykstra, J. (2022). *Cybersecurity Myths and Misconceptions, Avoiding the Hazards and Pitfalls that Derail US*. Addison-Wesley.

Strom, D. (2018). The Sony Hacker Indictment: 5 lessons for IT Security, CSO Online (25 September 2018). https://www.csoonline.com/article/3305144/the-sony-hacker-indictment-5-lessons-for-it-security.html (accessed 08 May 2023).

Treadway, J. (1987). "Report of the National Commission on Fraudulent Reporting," National Commission on Fraudulent Financial Reporting, October 1987, https://www.sechistorical.org/collection/papers/1980/1987_1001_TreadwayFraudulent.pdf (accessed 15 January 2024).

Wolff, J. (2022). *Cyberinsurance Policy Rethinking Risk in Age of Ransomware, Computer Fraud, Data Breaches, and Cyberattacks*. MIT Press.

10

Analysis

10.1 Reports and Studies

The reports that appear in figures have so far been standard reports that may be generated automatically, depending on the capabilities of the information security management system or governance, risk, and control system used by the enterprise. There are also standard reports that are manually generated. It is not unusual for a CRO to ask all business units to produce the same information in the same format for easy assimilation by the risk and audit staff. This is usually a standard in financial reporting. It is especially common in large global organizations where different business units use different systems to manage risk and financial data, respectively. While some business process owners will be able to produce the report automatically, others may have to use a template and fill in the blanks.

What is common about reports is that these are developed in anticipation of the need for system stakeholders to review and understand cybersecurity risks within their scope of responsibility. Ideally, they are provided proactively for easy retrieval, when needed, to make decisions with respect to cybersecurity risk. Because they contain sensitive information, there may be a designated individual in each department charged with accessing and sharing reports or sections of reports with others who may not need ongoing access to all department risk information (e.g., an event contact or issue owner). There will typically be at least one report that is the main source of information on each framework element (i.e., threat, event, control, assessment, issue, metric, people, and risk) and an associated metric or two to facilitate an at-a-glance view of the full set of records for each framework element. These are often trend reports such as a report wherein the issue by source example in Figure 7.24 was instead presented as monthly or quarterly changes in issue sources and status over time.

Stepping Through Cybersecurity Risk Management: A Systems Thinking Approach, First Edition. Jennifer L. Bayuk.
© 2024 John Wiley & Sons, Inc. Published 2024 by John Wiley & Sons, Inc.
Companion website: www.wiley.com/go/STCRM

Studies differ from reports in that they are research efforts. If an executive asks a risk analyst a question to better understand a situation before making a decision, and there is a standard report that answers the question, the risk analyst can just pull it out and show it to the executive. If there is not, then the situation calls for a study. For example, an executive reviewing the SecOps TTR metric in Figure 7.23 may ask the question, "Why does it take so long to close application security incidents compared to all the others?" Recall that the metric in Figure 7.23 displayed the average time spent in each stage of response. To answer the question, the analyst would need more detail.

While the average, or mean, is the sum of the time it takes to reach a stage in all tickets of a given type divided by the number of tickets in that type, the median is calculated by ordering the time it takes to reach each stage in each ticket from low to high, then dividing the number of tickets in half and displaying the time it took to reach the stage as the value in the middle of the list. If the median is lower than the average, this indicates that fewer tickets are open for longer timeframes than displayed in the average. This is commonly interpreted as skewing the average to a higher level while masking the anomaly of the longest time of the open incidents. The analyst begins by regenerating the metric to compare the median with the average TTR and finds that the average is skewed. The analyst concludes that a few tickets may be outliers and proceeds to compare the activities in them to the others of the same type. There are three application incident response tickets that lasted for several hours longer than others.

The analyst then reviews the worklogs of these three tickets and others but finds no significant difference in the work. However, the review also reveals that many more of the application security incidents reach the mitigate stage just a few minutes after being in the analyze stage, a much shorter analysis timeframe in comparison with other event types. The worklogs show a pattern of SecOps escalation to the DevOps team as soon as they reach the analyze stage, and an escalation to mitigate a few minutes later, while in other event types there are notes in the worklog describing outcome of analysis. The analyst speculates that the relative priority of an application related incident may motivate the quick escalation. This can be confirmed by querying a sample of SecOps security incident response tickets in other categories to see what activities seem to be taking the longest amount of time. The analyst makes the queries, which show that application security incidents are escalated faster than other types of incidents.

Note that the analyst may be following a study process or procedure that requires the manager in charge of an area under study to be consulted, and regardless of whether this is the case, would likely decide to interview SecOps to find out why the application security incidents receive special treatment with respect to analysis and escalation. The manager of SecOps is not surprised to be asked to take a meeting with risk and may refer the analyst to a staff member who is more familiar with the details of the incidents in the scope of the analyst's questions. In this example, the interview reveals that there was a critical known exploited vulnerability announcement in the midst of working on a few application security tickets and all the application servers had to be restarted. This was a concern because they were being investigated for user behavioral anomalies that were still in the mitigate stage. So they moved the stage to contain, isolated the servers sequentially, and took full forensics backup including all the *volatile* data, so named because it resides only temporarily in random access memory and would be lost when the system restarted. Normally, this would be done only if the incident had been declared a cyberattack, but they did not know whether that was the case and it had taken more than double the time it normally does to close the incidents. No actual attack was diagnosed, and it was later determined that the users whose behavior caused the alerts were actually the administrators verifying the extent to which the known vulnerability was active on those servers.

In the course of the conversation with SecOps, the analyst asks about the quick escalation of application security tickets in general, just to confirm the assumption that the decision to escalate is based on priority. Instead, the response is that DevOps almost never responds to a SecOps call for help, so they do not bother to wait for an expert to confirm whether the incident requires mitigation, but instead they execute mitigation and containment procedures routinely for all application security tickets. This information enables the analyst to finish the study. The outcome of the study is depicted in Figure 10.1, which isolates the application

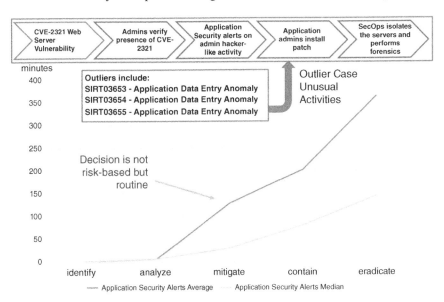

Figure 10.1 Example Study Outcome

incident average time to close from the SecOps metric in Figure 7.23 and adds the median. It is then annotated with an explanation of the three outlier incidents and to call attention to the routine mitigate and containment activities.

This was a comparatively trivial example of a study compared to the answers of some of the complicated questions that metrics can prompt. In approaching any study, a risk analyst first needs to determine where there is information available to help answer the question. In the example of Figure 10.1, it was in the form of security incident response tickets. In other studies, it may be in the form of database records of framework elements such as the threat actor depicted in Figure 2.5 or the event depicted in Figure 3.25. It may be in the form of technology inventory records that are used as the denominator in cybersecurity coverage metrics or business records that include information about application security. It may also have to be sourced externally, such as threat intelligence data feeds, metrics from independent sources, or news media.

In addition to answering questions, studies can also be aids in determining the probability that a risk event may occur with a given organization. The steps taken to produce a study presentation can be specifications for a standard report that will allow future risk analysts to repeat the same study in response to similar questions that may be posed on the future. Guidelines for study reuse are similar to measure and metrics definitions described Section 7.2 and include, but are not limited to:

- Scope of the data anticipated to be required to complete the study.
- Start and end dates for the date range for data inclusion.
- Time interval expected be relevant for data groupings and subtotals.
- Filters for framework element categories and nominal or ordinal labels to include in the study.
- Level of detail extracted from framework element records linked from the main object of study.
- Enterprise measure data sources that must be queried directly to provide information required to complete the study.

That is, if these parameters are defined once, even if under intense pressure to provide a study in a minimum amount of time, the parameters can be preserved in an information security management system to automate the same analysis should it be needed again in the future. This may not be desired for every study (of course, some will be more informative than others), so it makes sense to ask the executive receiver of the study to ask whether preserving it may seem like a good idea before expending the effort.

The sheer variety of potential data sources available for study makes it a problem for cybersecurity professionals to obtain access to the information they need to conduct their risk analysis. This is also a familiar story for an internal auditor, who

The holder of this card, <Internal Auditor Name Here>, is under the direct supervision of the enterprise Internal Audit department, whose mission is to enhance and protect enterprise mission, assets, and core values by providing risk-based and objective assurance, advice, and insight. This person is entitled to ask you any question and immediately receive an honest answer. This person is entitled to ask you to produce any information that you use in the course of conducting business, whether it be in electronic data, on paper, in third party repositories subscribed to by the enterprise, or otherwise available to you due to your position of employment herein.

Signature of the CEO
Name of the CEO
Chief Executive Officer
Enterprise

Those wishing to verify these instructions should contact the Human Resource, Legal, or Compliance representative assigned to their department.

Figure 10.2 Example Audit Identification Card

is dependent on the cooperation of an auditee to gather enough evidence to complete an assessment. In the audit case, cooperation is typically ensured by management mandate. In situations where auditors report issues with gaining access to information used to perform assessments, a typical management response is to issue "Audit Identification Cards" such as the one depicted in Figure 10.2.

Such a card would typically have a photo of the auditor on the other side, some information about the auditor's place in the organizational structure, and contact information for both the auditor and the auditor's supervisor. Although such blanket approvals for information requests are not typically extended to risk analysts, where this also occurs, formally or informally, it makes their job much easier than it otherwise would be.

Studies are not limited to reproducible reports but can use any type of media or credible observation to assist in the communication of risk. The trick is to focus on the answer to the study questions and ensure that all relevant information available within the enterprise is supplied in the service of formulating an answer. For example, a frequent topic of debate in risk remediation is whether to use a security tool to remediate an application security vulnerability or to change the application code itself to eliminate it. In the case of a vulnerability like log4j, it is possible to use a web application firewall (WAFW) to intercept all user input, screen it for patterns that have curly brackets that could be resolved into malicious commands by the java log4j vulnerable code, and terminate the network connection if any are found. An executive will sometimes question why we need yet another security tool, while a DevOps team may have priorities for its time so prefer to purchase the tool rather than change their code. Rather than bring data to answer the question, a risk analyst may instead bring some diagrams like the

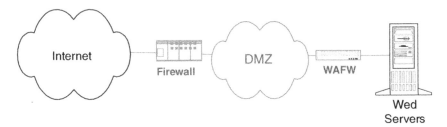

Figure 10.3 WAFW Discussion aid

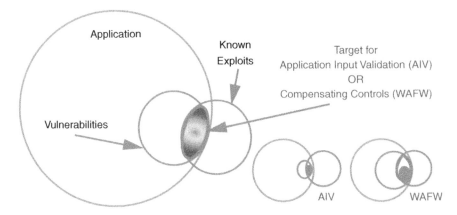

Figure 10.4 Primary versus Compensating Controls

ones in Figures 10.3 and 10.4. Figure 10.3 is a simplification of the place of a WAFW in the network, to aid in the explanation of what it does and how it works. For example, the discussion would include introduction of the fact that the WAFW itself is programmable, and its correct configuration and operation is key to gaining expected control improvement.

Figure 10.4 contains three diagrams. The first diagram shows a circle labeled *Application* and a smaller circle within it labeled Vulnerabilities. The *Vulnerabilities* circle overlaps with another circle labeled *Known Exploits*. It illustrates that application vulnerabilities are part of the application and there are likely more vulnerabilities than those that we understand are known to be exploited, as well as that some of the vulnerabilities in this application are known to be exploited. Those that are known to be exploited are labeled *Target for Application Input Validation (AIV) or Compensating Controls (WAFW)*. AIV is a method to enforce correct syntax of input fields (e.g., SSN, date, email) and also correctness of their values in the application context (e.g., monetary values within expected range, names restricted to letters and dashes). If it is part of the code of the software itself, then that feature of a WAFW would not be required to close the known exploited vulnerabilities. Hence, the figure presents them as alternatives for removing the vulnerabilities.

The second diagram illustrates that the alternative of AIV would make the vulnerability circle smaller because if the application had a method of checking all fields for valid input, then it would be overall less vulnerable to any type of input spoofing attack because the attack surface to which it is vulnerable is significantly reduced. The area of overlap with known exploits is colored in to show that this solution would fully remediate the application vulnerability issue.

The third diagram in the figure aids in the explanation of the extent to which a WAFW can protect against a vulnerability by screening input for malicious patterns. It purposely leaves part of the attack surface not colored to show that even with a WAFW, the code that does not provide application input validation is still likely to have some vulnerability exposure. This is because it is difficult to ensure that every possible pattern of exploit is part of a pattern screened by the WAFW. Moreover, as zero-day vulnerabilities are revealed, SecOps would have to write WAFW patterns very quickly and such coding under stress is prone to error.

10.2   Safety Analogies

Another effective executive cybersecurity communication analogy is to compare software architecture to civil engineering. For example, it is helpful to convey cybersecurity issues in layman's terms that make analogies with civil engineering. In the example of Figure 10.5, a bridge has the following engineering and safety problems:

1) The steel, cabling, and concrete used to construct the bridge are riddled with structural flaws.
2) Engineers have concluded that the bridge could fall down if these flawed components are not patched quickly.
3) The surface of the bridge is seriously impaired, and the required refinishing sometimes weakens the overall structure.
4) Bridge operators utilize a notification system that provides real-time information about any bridges that might be falling down. (Amoroso, 2007, p. 112)

It does not take much imagination to understand that not identifying and fixing vulnerabilities can have serious impact on safety. The structural flaws are both legacy software and zero-day vulnerabilities. The refinishing that weakens the overall structure is analogous to the constant software updates meant to improve code quality but these often introduce new vulnerabilities. The notification system is the Known Exploited Vulnerabilities Catalog (CISA n.d.). Moreover, the amount of software that is embedded in physical systems like bridges render

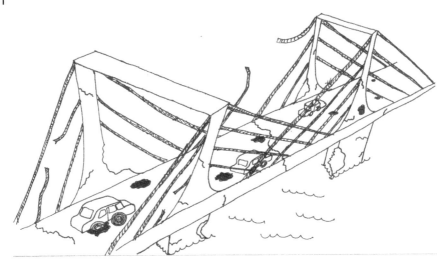

Figure 10.5 Cybersecurity Civil Engineering Analogy

even bridges susceptible to software failures. Although the analogy holds true between infrastructure projects like bridges and software projects, such as automating electronic grid operation, the analogy does not extend to the principles and practices of infrastructure engineers and software engineers.

The problem of software impacting safety first arose in the 1960s, when it became obvious to the layman that more and more aspects of physical infrastructure were reliant on software, including advanced weapon systems. In recognition of that there was a need for engineering principles to ensure safe software development; the NATO Science Committee sponsored two Software Engineering Conferences to try to influence the development of safe software by establishing an engineering approach to software creation. A conference attendee reported that the phrase "software engineering" was "deliberately chosen as being provocative, in implying the need for software manufacture to be based on the types of theoretical foundations and practical disciplines that are traditional in the established branches of engineering" (Randell 1979, pp. 1–2). His summary includes reference to topics like *Software as a Commodity, Programming Languages, and Modularity and Structuring*. Attendees discussed the issue of whether it was feasible to use a high-level language for systems programming. While they praised the development of COBOL because it allowed business people to develop their own programs without requiring prior computing experience, the controversy stemmed partially from the fact that unless a programmer was directly interacting with the hardware (the method by which a software compiler translated high-level software functions into operating system commands) may be obscured from the software engineer's view. Note that in 1968 the term "structured programming" had yet to be coined. The conference summary was written in 1979, and the author lamented that methods to apply engineering discipline to software had been forthcoming as expected, that he cannot attest to any progress in turning the phrase "software engineering" from an expression of a requirement to a description of an actual engineering discipline. He ends with a quote from the British historian Geoffrey Elton: "the future is dark, the present burdensome" (Randell 1979, p. 10).

Although the Institute for Electrical Engineering and the Association of Computing Machinery eventually adopted ethical standards at the turn of the century, the only consequences of violating them are to lose your membership in those industry associations. These are weak quality controls in comparison to actual engineering disciplines where lack of professional certification precludes consideration for contracts. Similarly, in the legal profession misconduct even with respect to ethical rules can result in disbarment.

Not much has changed since the key word in the analogy 1968 software engineering conference. As a contemporary software industry observer put it, "*Engineer* is an aspirational title in software development. Traditional engineers are regulated, certified, and subject to apprenticeship and continuing education. Engineering claims an explicit responsibility to public safety and reliability, even if it doesn't always deliver" (Bogost 2015). This observation is followed by, "Facebook has wisely retired its one-time internal-development philosophy, '*move fast and break* things,' but no business reliant on civil or structural engineering would ever have adopted such a motto in the first place" (Bogost 2015).

In recognition of the need to have some kind of professional training in cybersecurity, the US Federal government established a certification requirement for job classifications that included cybersecurity. However appropriate it may be to have such requirements, the professional certifications adopted do not aspire to the level of engineering. The training is basic, the experience is simply the ability to maintain cybersecurity in a job title attested to by a currently certified cybersecurity professional. There is no burden on the mentor to educate the individual and no burden on the certificate applicant to be an apprentice to a certified member. There is simply a certification exam on basic technologies like firewalls and basic operational concepts like the difference between policy and procedure. There is no requirement for knowledge of software development or secure coding. This will not advance the state of software security. These requirements are analogous to what you would need to know if you had a job to operate a drawbridge.

A CXO accountable for the bridge who knew about its safety flaws would be criminally negligent not to fix it. But many companies routinely run on vulnerable software every day. The "notification" system is analogous to a security monitoring measure that will alert them when it finally falls.

The key word in the bridge analogy is "patch." Everyone knows civil infrastructure needs to be patched occasionally to remain resilient. In computer science, this type of fix is also called a patch. In the context of computer science, the word "patch" has its roots in the days when computers were programmed with cables plugged into electronic circuits the size of conference room walls. Patches were the cables that altered the course of electronic processing by physically changing the path of code execution. Computer patches are now bits of software that replace the faulty ones. Due to a wide variety of constantly changing technical glitches, patches have to be downloaded from the software vendor all the time in order to keep the software working properly. They are not just issued to fix vulnerabilities that are exploited by criminals. Most patches are to protect against vulnerabilities that make systems malfunction without being attacked at all, like leaky memory and structural design flaws.

10.3 Decision Support

First line management is not eager for bad news. There is a cybersecurity joke about the CISO who reports to the CIO. The CISO walks into the CIO's office and begins a conversation with the words, "You are not going to like this but... ." The CIO stops the CISO with the palm of a hand, "If I am not going to like it, then why are you telling me?" That is the punch line. No matter who the players in such a dialog, the real answer to the boss' question is always, "Because you need to make a decision." The punch line is funny to a group of CISOs who have had that experience because they have been there, and it is an awkward situation that can best be diffused with laughter. No matter how dire a situation, if a risk analyst, or a CISO wearing the risk analyst hat at the moment, can anticipate the questions a decision-maker would want to ask before making a decision on how to reduce risk, that person can create a study that answers those questions. With such a tool in hand, the conversation can begin with the words, "I brought something I think we need to discuss... ." Instead of an introduction to a catastrophe for which there is no known solution, the door opens to a conversation about the information at risk and potential options for taking action that would have an impact on the potential for minimizing negative impact.

Good analysis anticipates the questions of people who have to make decisions. Rather than walk into the room with bad news, a cybersecurity professional should walk into the room with bad news *and* plans for at least two studies the outcome of which will enable the executive to make a choice between three alternative risk treatments. Where there is not time and resources to bring this type of presentation, the first risk treatment should be that to remediate the lack of resources for risk management itself to be able to conduct studies.

For example, in the case of the study presented in Figure 10.1, there are several decisions that could have been included in the presentation. It is clear from the presentation that three application security incidents that skewed the metric was an unusual event and not likely to happen again, but also clear that unnecessary containment escalations are routinely made due to DevOps inattention to SecOps requests for assistance. The analyst may advise the executive that other IT operations and administrative teams responsible for responding to SecOps requests for assistance have "on-call" procedures whereby one of them has to carry a shared cell-phone and each member of the groups has time slots during the week where they are the ones responsible for answering the phone should there be a call or message from SecOps. The on-call team member who is on call cannot be relieved of the responsibility unless the phone is passed to another member of the group. The executive decides to mandate by policy that any and all technology teams in a SecOps escalation path adopt a similar approach to ensuing they are available when SecOps requires assistance in diagnosing a security incident.

Studies focus on different aspects of cybersecurity program components will of course have different decision alternatives. While the example study outcome in Figure 10.1 recommends a decision with respect to procedure, in the case of the WAFW study presented in Figure 10.4, the suggested decision is with respect to technology alternatives wherein alternative A is to direct the developers to build input validation into the software application and alternative B to install a WAFW. The decision would be better supported if the analyst could bring an estimate of the cost and level of effort required to purchase, install, and operate a WAFW as well as an estimate of the level of effort it would take the developers to build application input verification into the code. The analyst would also point out that it is considered cybersecurity industry best practice to, using colloquialisms known well in the field, that is, *build security in* rather than *bolt-on* products to secure unsafe code.

In any collaborative decision model, where the problem is structured as a series of decisions and events, the certainty level of events is affected by decisions. For decisions related to enhancing or maintaining cybersecurity, an enterprise cybersecurity framework helps connect those dots. Events and assessments identify issues, and issues can come from anywhere. Issues inform management about the consequences of inherent, or uncontrolled, cybersecurity risk. Controls drive down the inherent risk of cybersecurity events to residual risk below appetite. Measures and metrics indicate whether the enterprise is successful in thwarting attacks events and maintaining controls. As illustrated in Figure 10.6, this is cybersecurity risk management in a nutshell.

The enterprise can challenge the decisions that are made by the organization because they can use indicators and probabilities identified by activities within the cybersecurity risk framework. Trends in the metrics and probabilities can be used for board level oversight. We start and end with the same picture. It is complicated, but it is not complex. In Figure 10.6, the relationships between all the concepts that are necessary to understand cybersecurity risk management

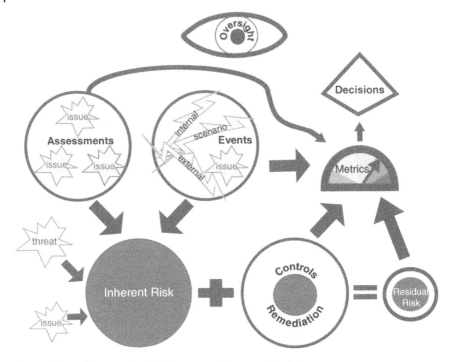

Figure 10.6 Cybersecurity Risk Framework Supports Decisions

frameworks are clear. As the inventor and engineer Charles Kettering put it, "A problem well stated is a problem half-solved."

10.4   Conclusion

As a cybersecurity professional, it is important to realize that situational awareness in the context of known avoidable or treatable cybersecurity risks is your front yard. If you cannot get management to issue a risk appetite statement and support your work, you should consider looking for another job (especially because if the enterprise does succumb to cyberattack, then you may be out of a job anyway). Luckily for the profession, there are literally tens of thousands of openings.

There is a famous case from over a decade ago now where a very prestigious cyber security consulting company was itself hacked, its website defaced, and the information on the security reviews it had done for its clients were taken by the threat actor (Wikipedia n.d.). It was highly embarrassing of course. It was hard to reconcile the fact that they provided critical cybersecurity services to major institutions while failing to protect their customers' highly confidential information. This should be a lesson to all cybersecurity professionals. Have you heard of the company HBGary? Not if you joined the profession in the past decade. It was very prestigious cyber security company back then and its employees found valuable employment due to their high level of cybersecurity knowledge and skill, but the name HBGary no longer has any name recognition in the cybersecurity community other than as a lesson that we who work in the profession all need to internalize. We should endeavor to ensure that our professional interaction with the internet is as controlled as possible and limited to creating the reputation that we would like to have and maintain for decades to come.

And it is not just organizations for whom we work that we should be concerned about. We need situational awareness at home as well. The world is embroiled in cyberwar and even those who have not formally declared it are still on the front lines. Identity theft and online fraud schemes created a decade ago are still as profitable for cybercriminals as when first created. Every member of the profession who is observed connecting their phone to any available wireless hotspot just to watch a movie while traveling provides support for those who ignore this risk.

The technology industry has even become implicit in such cybercrime. If you search for Ticketmaster in a browser, the search engine often lists three Ticketmaster look-alike sites first before presenting the real one. Unfortunately, those who do not notice the fraud and shop on the sites end up paying exorbitant fees for their ticket purchases. Though perfectly legal, this is a subtle form of fraud that chips away at our intolerance for such deception. The burden is on each individual to protect themselves, and if cybersecurity professionals cannot figure this out, the world will quickly become less and less safe for everyone.

The cyberinsurance industry is not going to step in. It has chosen the path of avoidance via exclusions. Governments seem more intent on weaponizing cybersecurity than making the internet safe. In the early days of automotive vehicles before highways were devised, traffic accidents were frequent. In the early days of commercial air traffic, plane safety features were decided by the manufacturers. There is now a saying at the FAA, that is, *behind every rule there is a crash*. Then as now, safety regulation is the only obvious solution.

In the meantime, even though all the puzzle pieces may not be well understood, it is possible to step back and see and appreciate the big picture of cybersecurity risk from the enterprise-wide point of view. A cybersecurity risk management framework allows an enterprise to organize documentation on cybersecurity risk in the form of risk appetite and tolerance metrics. Because there is an agreed upon set of risks to monitor and they are documented, the enterprises can use documentation to support a shared understanding of how the measures and metrics portray cybersecurity risk categories. Where measures are lacking, an enterprise can create scenarios and investigate root causes. It can record details of events that present cyber security risk directly and also highlight issues. Issues sourced from events are mostly in the form of vulnerabilities that an organization needs to remediate to prevent that event from happening, and the enterprise can also conduct assessments using policies and standards to further identify issues. Moreover, an enterprise engaged in an effort to exercise due diligence in managing cybersecurity risk need not tackle it alone. There are industry standards and regulations that provide recommendations how to reduce cybersecurity risk. An enterprise can use these recommendations in assessments to further identify risk issues and create remediation plans to decrease cybersecurity risk. The only thing an enterprise must do alone is establish a cybersecurity risk management framework and support it with tone at the top.

References

Amoroso, E. (2007). *Cyber Security*. Silicon Press.

Bogost, I. (2015). Stop calling yourselves engineers. *The Atlantic*. https://www.theatlantic.com/technology/archive/2015/11/programmers-should-not-call-themselves-engineers/414271/.

CISA (n.d.). Known Exploited Vulnerabilities Catalog. https://www.cisa.gov/known-exploited-vulnerabilities-catalog (accessed 08 May 2023).

Randell, B. (1979). Software engineering: As it was in 1968. *Computing Laboratory Technical Report Series*, Computing Laboratory, University of Newcastle upon Tyne, pp. 1–10, http://www.cs.ncl.ac.uk/publications/trs/papers/138.pdf (accessed 08 May 2023).

Wikipedia (n.d.). HPGary. https://en.wikipedia.org/wiki/HBGary (accessed 08 May 2023).

Appendix

Exercises in FrameCyber

Chapter 1   Framework Elements

A   True/False Questions

1   Is it true or false that an enterprise cybersecurity framework can establish how technology supports business objectives' design flaws?

2   Is it true or false that risk issues are always identified via assessments?

3   Is it true or false that standards and regulations measure cybersecurity risk?

4   Is it true or false that an event that has occurred brings the probability of an event in its risk category to 100%?

5   Is it true or false that risk managers rely on business managers for information required to evaluate cybersecurity risk?

B   Multiple Choice

1   What is the difference between a risk issue and a risk register?
   A   A risk issue is a preliminary draft of an entry in a risk register.
   B   A risk issue is monitored with metrics, but risks are not.
   C   A risk issue presents evidence that is helpful in evaluating risk, a risk register lists the risks themselves.
   D   There is no difference, they are the same thing.

Stepping Through Cybersecurity Risk Management: A Systems Thinking Approach,
First Edition. Jennifer L. Bayuk.
© 2024 John Wiley & Sons, Inc. Published 2024 by John Wiley & Sons, Inc.
Companion website: www.wiley.com/go/STCRM

2   In what sense do standards and regulations measure cybersecurity risk?

    A Standards and regulations provide comprehensive yardsticks by which to measure cybersecurity risk.

    B Standards and regulations present control requirements that reduce risk.

    C Standards and regulations can be used to identify potential cybersecurity risk issues.

    D Standards and regulations are of minimal utility in measuring cybersecurity risk.

3   Why might an enterprise maintain a threat catalog?

    A Because most standards and regulations have requirements to track threat actors.

    B Because organizations do not have any way to thwart cyberattacks.

    C Because controls should be specifically designed for each threat actor.

    D Because knowledge about cybersecurity threat actors can help thwart attacks.

4   Which of these questions about cybersecurity risk concerns the enterprise cybersecurity risk framework as opposed to a specified risk or risk category?

    A Does the cybersecurity risk management program fully address third-party risk?

    B Do cybersecurity management activities cover the full range of technology upon which the enterprise depends?

    C Is the enterprise vulnerable to ransomware attacks?

    D Are all cybersecurity controls in regulatory standards included in the enterprise risk register?

5   Which of these framework elements is a suitable risk treatment?

    A Controls

    B Issues

    C Events

    D Assessments

C   Essay

Consider the framework overview in Chapter 1 and provide some examples of how it helps an enterprise make decisions on cybersecurity.

Chapter 2 Threats

A True/False Questions

1 Is it true or false that threat actors must create a vulnerability to accomplish a successful cybersecurity attack?

2 Is it true or false that only insiders who are highly technical can successfully execute insider attacks?

3 Is it true or false that information gleaned in cybersecurity threat research is used to simulate cybersecurity attacks?

4 Is it true or false that threat actors create software packages that allow others to mimic their exploits?

5 Is it true or false that the ability to execute arbitrary commands on a target system is a prerequisite for successful cyberattacks?

B Multiple Choice

1 Which of these attributes of cyber threat actors is a criterion for admission to an enterprise threat catalog?
  A Threat actor resources include vulnerability scanning platforms.
  B Threat actor skills cover all popular operating systems.
  C Threat actors have successfully attacked competitors.
  D Threat actors have published their exploit methods.

2 Why is sharing information about cyber threat actors easy?
  A Because news stories on cybercrime always contain details on threat actors.
  B Because there are industry standards for threat actor data formats.
  C Because cyber threat actors boast about their successes on social media.
  D Because companies who are attacked publish the results of their investigations.

3 Which of the following is not essential to cybersecurity situational awareness?

  A Understanding threat actor adversaries.

  B Identifying system and network vulnerabilities.

  C Monitoring correctness of control implementation.

  D Sharing incident details with public relations.

4 Which of these threat actor types are the main customers for zero-day threats?

  A Lone wolves

  B Organized crime

  C Nation states

  D Competitors

5 Which of the following statements about attack vectors is most accurate?

  A Attack vectors are solely composed of threat actor activity.

  B Attack vectors of reconnaissance activities result in data leakage.

  C Attack vectors are threat actor skill requirements.

  D Different organizations often present the same attack differently.

C Essay

Which is a more dangerous threat actor tactic: (a) *systematic continuous targeted espionage* or (b) *drive-by compromise?* Use some examples of successful cyberattacks to support your reasoning.

Chapter 3 Events

A True/False Questions

1 Is it true or false that a successful cyberattack has an uncertainty factor of 0, and inversely, a certainty factor, or probability, of 100%?

2 Is it true or false that cybersecurity situational awareness is the process of collecting and disseminating threat actor feeds?

3 Is it true or false that an event can belong to multiple risk categories?

4 Is it true or false that cybersecurity incident response is typically performed by the multiple job roles that do not report to the chief information security officer?

5 Is it true or false that all successful cyberattacks negatively impact the attacker's target?

B   Multiple Choice

1 Which of the following is not a requirement of an exercise in cybersecurity scenario analysis?
   A Assigning a stand-in for an executive decision-maker.
   B Selecting a scenario that stakeholders believe is plausible.
   C Engaging internal subject matter experts.
   D Counteracting bias among participants.

2 Which of these circumstances is likely the root cause of a cybersecurity risk event?
   A Successful cyberattack
   B Inadequate patching
   C Known vulnerability
   D Nation-state hostilities

3 What is the main focus of a cyber forensics investigation?
   A Incident identification
   B Threat mitigation
   C Postmortem analysis
   D Evidence preservation

4 Which of the following security principles, if strictly enforced, is the best method of preventing a non-administrator insider threat actor from obtaining administrative access?
   A Deperimeterization
   B Least privilege
   C Segregation of duties
   D Separation of privilege

5 Which of the following is not essential to cybersecurity situational awareness?
   A Understanding threat actor adversaries.
   B Identifying system and network vulnerabilities.
   C Monitoring correctness of control implementation.
   D Sharing incident details with public relations.

C Essay

Event response procedures include escalation to a variety of different technology and business teams. Some event response procedures have timer thresholds for escalation, and some do not. What is an escalation timer threshold in the context of event response and under what circumstances does it make sense to have a timer threshold for escalation within an incident response procedure?

Chapter 4 Controls

A True/False Questions

1 Is it true or false that multiple departments other than the chief information security office implement a wide variety of cybersecurity controls?

2 Is it true or false that there are sometimes ways to bypass cybersecurity controls?

3 Is it true or false that documented security architecture provides a roadmap for technology engineers to comply with policy?

4 Is it true or false that a person identified as *Accountable* in a RACI (*Responsible, Accountable, Consulted, and Informed*) Matrix performs a specified activity?

5 Is it true or false that there is no difference between industry security standards and those published by any given enterprise?

B Multiple Choice

1 The statement "*Business applications shall be designed to segregate duties for financial transactions with third parties*" is an example of which control method?
   A Policy
   B Process
   C Standard
   D Procedure

2 Which of these statements most closely defines the security "fail safe" principle?
   A Access to a single function should require multiple security mechanisms.
   B Administrative access should require multiple security configurations.

C System design criteria should include no functionality by default.

D Security procedures followed by users should be easy to understand.

3 The statement *"Access the vulnerability console, click the arrow next to 'Status' on the left, and from the drop-down list, select 'Open'"* is an example of which control method?

A Policy

B Process

C Standard

D Procedure

4 Which of the following statements about security policy is most accurate?

A Security policy describes how controls should be implemented.

B Security policy documents management control objectives.

C Security policy is another term for security principle.

D Security policy sets tone at the top.

5 Which of the analogies for cybersecurity standards is most accurate?

A Tone at the top

B Architecture blueprints

C Coordinated workflow

D Implementation checklists

C   Essay

What is the relationship between cybersecurity risk appetite and cybersecurity policy?

Chapter 5   Assessments

A   True/False Questions

1 Is it true or false that all cybersecurity assessments follow the same general pattern?

2 Is it true or false that the scope of a cybersecurity assessment is set at the start and not allowed to change?

3 Is it true or false that a cybersecurity audit is a special type of cybersecurity assessment?

4 Is it true or false that people conducting a cybersecurity assessment must never overlap with the people performing activities within its scope?

5 Is it true or false that if an assessment objective is well-defined, then it is easy to identify its scope?

B   Multiple Choice

1 In a situation where an assessment is hindered by multiple constraints, what should the assessment evaluator do?
   A Withdraw from the project.
   B Change the scope.
   C Lower assurance in the result.
   D Ignore some constraints.

2 In which way is a pen test similar to a vulnerability scan?
   A The objective is to identify vulnerabilities.
   B The approach requires independent evaluators.
   C The scope is publicly facing networks.
   D The result is a set of attack paths.

3 Which of these attributes of systems is not analogous to verification versus validation?
   A Diagnostic versus proof
   B Form versus function
   C Built right versus right built
   D Correct versus effective

4 When an organization maps internal standards document to an external standards document and finds no gaps, what can be claimed in the result?
   A The organization's controls satisfy the external standard.
   B The organization has passed an external standard assessment.
   C The organization complies with an external standard.
   D The organization's standard adheres to the external standard.

5 What is the difference between a risk and control matrix (RCM) and a risk and control self-assessment (RCSA)?
   A RCMs are regulatory requirements for RCSAs.
   B RCSAs are the technology used to create RCMs.
   C An RCSA is an industry-standard, and an RCM is an internal one.
   D An RCM is a plan for an RCSA.

C   Essay

In conducting a cybersecurity audit, what influence should detection risk have in the formation of an audit plan?

Chapter 6   Issues

A   True/False Questions

1   Is it true or false that a cybersecurity risk register is a list of cybersecurity risk issues?

2   Is it true or false that an uncontrolled threat vector presents a cybersecurity risk issue?

3   Is it true or false that risk issues are typically classified by type, priority, and status?

4   Is it true or false that there is an industry-standard list of cybersecurity risk issue types?

5   Is it true or false that an issue owner is the de facto project manager for that issue's remediation?

B   Multiple Choice

1   For what purpose does an issue tracking system link risk issues to specific risks?
   A To provide assurance that risks are enumerated.
   B To provide the set of events associated with the risk.
   C To provide status reporting on risk remediation.
   D To provide details with respect to incident response.

2   Which of the following would not make sense as an issue criterion in a cyber-security risk issue tracking record?
   A Cybersecurity risk appetite statement
   B Cybersecurity standards violation
   C Cybersecurity scenario analysis
   D Cybersecurity budget discrepancy

3   What is the difference between risk analysis and remediation?
  A   Risk analysis is qualitative, and remediation is quantitative.
  B   Risk analysis assesses risk and remediation reduces risk.
  C   Risk analysis is theoretical, and remediation is practical.
  D   Risk analysis predicts risk and remediation identifies risk.

4   What is the difference between self-identified cybersecurity issues and cybersecurity issues identified by other criteria?
  A   Self-identified issues are of lower priority than issues identified by other sources.
  B   Self-identified issue criteria are enterprise PPSPs while other sources may refer to external documents.
  C   Self-identified issues are identified within the security program while other sources are external to the security program.
  D   Self-identified issues are not required to have target remediation dates while issues identified by other sources must set targets.

5   Which of these definitions best fits a cybersecurity risk issue?
  A   An emergent question
  B   A topic of debate
  C   A situation of concern
  D   An unsettled matter

C   Essay

What is the relationship between a cybersecurity risk issue and related cybersecurity events, assessments, and controls? Supplement your explanation with examples.

Chapter 7   Metrics

A   True/False Questions

1   Is it true or false that data sources for cybersecurity metrics should always be derived from internal operations and processes?

2   Is it true or false that cybersecurity measures and metrics do not directly measure security?

3   Is it true or false that good cybersecurity metrics can give both good and bad news?

4 Is it true or false that a theoretical model of a secure system may be constructed of cybersecurity measure components?

5 Is it true or false that nominal and ordinal measures are not numeric?

B   Multiple Choice

1 Which of these is the defining attribute of a target security metric?
 A The unit is a percentage where the denominator is a population to be secured.
 B The unit is a set of vulnerabilities found in a pen test target.
 C The unit is the number of secure systems and user configurations.
 D The unit is an attribute of vulnerabilities found in a scanning target.

2 Which metric category includes metrics that demonstrate the system's ability to recover from harmful impact?
 A Resilience
 B Target
 C Vulnerability
 D Monitor

3 Which of these metrics' attributes are least likely to be classification fields in a cybersecurity metrics catalog?
 A Leading, Lagging, Concurrent
 B Nominal, Ordinal, Interval
 C Exists, False, True
 D Planned, Partial, Repeatable

4 Which of these cybersecurity metrics can demonstrate that security is good?
 A Penetration tests
 B Vulnerability scans
 C Source code analysis
 D Configuration targets

5 How is it possible to use labels like "vulnerable" in metrics calculations?
 A Convert the labels to numbers according to a scale, e.g., "High = 1, Medium = 2, Low = 3."
 B Use a rule-based algorithm to assign the labels to a countable object and count the objects for which the label is valid.
 C Define the word "vulnerable" in terms of a True/False question and count the objects that meet the definition.
 D Use only labels that have clear cybersecurity standard meanings, e.g., "Critical, Significant, Important."

C   Essay

Provide a definition of the term "*cybersecurity metric.*" Explain why your definition is correct and why it applies only to metrics that provide information about cybersecurity and not to any management metric such as performance and productivity.

Chapter 8   People

A   True/False Questions

1   Is it true or false that human resources are typically accountable for the accuracy of staff job specifications that are used by security administrators?

2   Is it true or false that extensive technical background is required to make significant contributions to a cybersecurity program?

3   Is it true or false that accountants often identify control points in data transfers and specify programs to detect data integrity issues?

4   Is it true or false that tone at the top exists whether it is cultivated or not?

5   Is it true or false that there are often many different types of administrators responsible for maintaining cybersecurity controls?

B   Multiple Choice

1   Which of the following lists of job roles most accurately depicts increasing job responsibility for cybersecurity implementation?
   A   Enterprise Risk Management < Chief Information Security Officer < Internal Audit
   B   Internal Audit < Chief Risk Officer < Chief Information Officer
   C   Chief Information Security Officer < Chief Risk Officer < Chief Information Officer
   D   Chief Information Officer < Chief Risk Officer < Chief Information Security Officer

2   Of the following management committees in a large enterprise, which is the most likely to have the chief information security officer as a member?
   A   Governance Committee
   B   Operations Committee

C Compliance Committee
D Emergency Response Committee

3 For what primary purpose would a chief information security officer be included in a technology management committee?
A To help define security administration job functions.
B To collaborate on five-year plans for innovation.
C To assess cybersecurity features and functions of products and services.
D To coordinate business resiliency tests.

4 What job roles should be tasked with identifying and reporting cybersecurity incidents?
A All SecOps roles
B All cybersecurity roles
C All technology roles
D All job roles

5 Which enterprise job role should be primarily accountable for eliminating cybersecurity vulnerabilities in technology products and services?
A The individuals accountable for maintaining each technology product and/or service.
B The highest-level executive to whom all individuals accountable for maintaining technology products and services report.
C The director of security operations.
D The chief information security officer.

C Essay

What are cybersecurity job roles typically engaged in executing the NIST CSF detect, respond, and recover functions? In your answer, provide examples of each.

Chapter 9 Risks

A True/False Questions

1 Is it true or false that cybersecurity risk categories exist to drive efficiency and effectiveness in technology control strategy?

2 Is it true or false that key risk indicators should be capable of being understood by a non-technical layperson?

3 Is it true or false that cybersecurity risk probabilities should be assigned at the lowest level of a risk hierarchy?

4 Is it true or false that issues with the risk management framework itself, by definition, indicate cybersecurity risks?

5 Is it true or false that, when it is not feasible to avoid, accept, or control a risk, there is always the option to transfer it?

B Multiple Choice

1 Which of these statements about inherent risk is true?
   A Inherent risk is reduced via control implementation.
   B Inherent risk is remediated via assessments.
   C Inherent risk is identified via internal events.
   D Inherent risk is measured via control metrics.

2 Cybersecurity risk categories should be periodically revisited under what circumstances?
   A When all patterns of known event types are covered.
   B When the events in the categories no longer correlate to the same control strategies.
   C When threat intelligence reveals the enterprise is targeted by new threat actors.
   D When the categories include multiple actual loss events with no remediation plans.

3 Which of these management risk measures may be qualitative rather than quantitative?
   A Risk Tolerance
   B Risk Threshold
   C Risk Appetite
   D Risk Capacity

4 Where there is insufficient historical data available from which to calculate the probability of a cybersecurity risk event in a given category, is there a reasonable alternate method of estimating the probability?
   A Yes, because the probability of threat vector exploits on the enterprise can be estimated using attack difficulty.
   B Yes, because threat intelligence data can be used to reasonably estimate the probability of successful attack on the enterprise.

   C Yes, because statistics on external events can be used to reasonably estimate the probability of successful attack on the enterprise.

   D No, because threat vector pen tests on the enterprise cannot reasonably simulate attack success frequency.

5 Consider a situation where a parent risk category has three subcategories with probabilities of 30%, 55%, and 95%. What is the probability of a risk in the parent category?

   A 30%

   B 55%

   C 60%

   D 95%

C Essay

What influence should materiality have in selecting a cybersecurity risk tolerance threshold?

Chapter 10 Analysis

A True/False Questions

1 Is it true or false that a standard report must be automatically generated to be considered accurate?

2 Is it true or false that cybersecurity studies require pre-established measures and metrics?

3 Is it true or false that "engineer" is an aspirational title in software development?

4 Is it true or false that typical subjects for standard cybersecurity reports are trends in cybersecurity framework elements over time?

5 Is it true or false that intentionally inaccurate search results are a form of fraud?

B Multiple Choice

1 Which of the following best describes the difference between a report and a study?

   A A study requires statistics, a report is a listing.

   B A study breaks new ground, a report is routine.

C A study may be fictional, but a report is factual.

D A study requires multiple data sources, report uses just one.

2   Which of the following is a typical constraint in launching a cybersecurity study?

A Data accessibility

B Scope creep

C Lack of precedent

D Management approval

3   Which of the following would be a reason to establish a procedure to produce studies?

A To ensure that it will be possible to turn the study into a report when it is completed.

B To ensure that the analyst performing the study does not waste time.

C To ensure that managers are consulted on studies within their area of responsibility.

D To ensure that the study comes to a pre-established conclusion.

4   Which of the following does a professional software engineer require to practice that discipline?

A Obtain a license.

B Pass a certification exam.

C Join a professional association.

D None of the above.

5   Which of the following describes the best practice in cybersecurity risk analysis?

A Interviewing all impacted job functions.

B Anticipating management questions.

C Estimating problem resolution resources.

D Creating new metrics.

C   Essay

Consider yourself in the position of a politician concerned about cybersecurity risk to the nation and eager to pass laws that will regulate the technology industry. Compose an essay in three sections. In section 1, state the problem you are trying to solve with regulation. In section 2, draft a few paragraphs of regulation that you think will dramatically lower cybersecurity risk nationwide. In section 3, explain how you would expect the technology industry to comply with the regulation and exactly how this would decrease cybersecurity risk.

Index

a

acceptance   245–249
administrators   24, 26, 33, 55, 71, 95, 112, 113, 139, 205, 208, 226, 257
adversary/adversaries   17–19, 22, 30, 41, 44, 47, 65, 81, 218
alerts   10, 55, 69, 72, 80, 81, 102, 109, 131, 132, 187, 197, 232, 243
analogy/analogies   2, 23, 33, 174, 179, 186, 218, 275–278
analysis   2, 4, 7, 11, 40, 65, 70, 75, 78, 79, 82, 84, 85, 94, 128, 134, 162, 175, 183, 208, 241, 253
antivirus (AV)   3, 40, 188
architecture   13, 54, 63, 90, 104, 108, 112, 114, 118, 119, 121, 123–130, 166, 168, 183, 192, 197, 208
artificial intelligence (AI)   43, 137
assess/assessments   2, 8, 9, 14, 44, 143–171, 212, 219, 223, 303–304
assets   17, 19–21, 26, 35, 37, 49, 61, 63, 101, 110, 127, 186, 212, 218, 227, 243, 255–257
ATT&CK   18, 23, 41
attack vector   38, 41, 61, 265

b

Bernstein, Peter   3
biometric   55, 97
blue team   163, 164
breach   9, 35, 37, 50, 61, 68, 78, 93, 103, 119, 170, 188, 213, 227, 232, 243, 244, 251, 252
bug bounty   36, 169
business environment and internal control factors (BEICF)   6

c

catalogs   5, 18, 21–23, 25, 44, 51, 175, 195, 197, 252
categories   3, 7, 9, 10, 13, 40, 51, 53, 96, 149, 154, 178, 179, 195, 239–242
causes   51, 67, 68, 73, 81, 82, 86, 87, 162, 177, 243, 258
checklist   8, 118, 212
Chief Information Officer (CIO)   3, 67

audits

audits   11, 25, 33, 55, 84, 102, 143, 147, 148, 165–170, 207, 219, 220, 224
availability   1, 14, 23, 50, 84, 94, 101, 107, 125, 126, 128, 129, 160, 193
avoidance   181, 242, 245, 249, 281

Stepping Through Cybersecurity Risk Management: A Systems Thinking Approach, First Edition. Jennifer L. Bayuk.
© 2024 John Wiley & Sons, Inc. Published 2024 by John Wiley & Sons, Inc.
Companion website: www.wiley.com/go/STCRM

Chief Information Security Officer (CISO)
3, 23, 49, 50, 74, 75, 86, 89, 94, 96,
105, 107–109, 114, 115, 125, 146, 151,
154, 166, 170, 178, 190, 215, 220, 221,
223, 224, 226, 229, 231

classification 19, 50–56, 68, 79, 119,
177–180, 186, 190, 204, 277

cloud 2, 36, 123, 125, 127, 178, 239, 245

COBIT 117, 150, 151, 157, 158

code of conduct 57, 105, 138, 221,
227, 250

competitors 20, 29–33, 72, 78, 197, 213

complete mediation 56, 103

compliance 2, 7, 8, 90, 93, 94, 102, 105,
108, 119, 136, 137, 140, 143, 148,
157, 165, 212
  risk 94, 212, 213

comprehensive
  accountability 102, 120

confidentiality 23, 50, 53, 94, 101, 107,
126, 127, 155, 160, 162, 193

continuous improvement 3, 149

control objective 54, 55, 107, 149, 150,
155, 157, 158, 160, 165–167

correctness 128, 162, 190, 194, 197,
199, 257, 275

cost 21, 84, 85, 189, 237, 243, 279

count measure 189, 204

credentials 33, 35, 55, 60, 61, 97, 107,
109, 110, 151, 241, 257

criminal 4, 19, 29, 33–36, 43, 71, 72,
92, 227, 277

criteria 170, 180–183, 192, 193, 207, 208

critics/critical 104, 115, 125, 131, 133,
158, 177, 181, 185, 186, 247

Cyber and Infrastructure Security
  Agency (CISA) 40

cyberattacks 3, 6–8, 22, 24, 26, 36–38, 48,
50–52, 75, 94, 144, 163, 169, 174–176,
190, 206, 210, 211, 217, 240, 242

cyberwar 4, 237, 281

cyberwarfare 4

cycle 2, 48, 65, 84, 149, 217, 229, 264

d

damage 20, 25, 35, 47, 48, 50, 55, 69,
84, 92, 143, 157, 162, 175, 233,
237, 242–244

data 1–4, 9, 10, 13, 19, 20, 22, 23, 28,
29, 31–35, 56, 60, 61, 70, 71, 78, 82,
84, 92, 93, 105, 107, 115, 116, 125,
129, 131, 134, 135, 146, 157, 169,
170, 232, 233, 237, 240, 243, 249

database 1, 28, 31, 38, 57, 101, 123, 128,
129, 139, 170, 176, 208, 240, 272

decision 2, 4, 5, 11, 12, 58, 65, 73, 78,
91, 108, 112, 113, 137, 138, 181,
182, 191, 195, 217, 231, 242, 269,
271, 278–280

defense 2, 20–22, 40, 41, 44, 65, 78, 81,
143, 162, 163, 217–235

Deming 65

detection/detect 25, 47–50, 55, 65–77,
101, 134, 158, 162, 168, 197, 240

Drucker 65

e

effective/effectiveness 50, 55, 58, 63, 81,
91, 105, 128, 133, 162, 190, 240, 257

elements 233–235, 269, 272

engineer 94, 104, 277, 280

engineering 2, 5, 57, 58, 73–75, 90, 101,
104, 105, 128, 190, 192, 275–277

enterprise management 92, 104,
230–233

escalation 4, 69, 70, 77, 181, 205, 226,
270, 271, 279

espionage 4, 24, 31, 110, 137

evaluate 5, 6, 8, 10, 12, 155, 157

executive management 2, 7, 67, 70, 71,
89, 92, 104, 168, 181, 217, 219, 224,
227, 228, 247, 249, 253

exfiltrate   23, 28
exploit   9, 17, 28, 30, 36, 37, 41, 49, 50,
     73, 143, 162
external standards   116–123

f

fail safe   94–96, 100, 140, 161
fail-over procedures   1
feature   58, 97, 100, 101, 103, 197, 199
Federal Financial Institutions
     Examination Council (FFIEC)   147
forensics   3, 71, 73, 74, 76, 84, 102, 135,
     136, 140, 271
FrameCyber®   2, 5, 10, 12, 18, 250
framework   1–14, 90, 91, 173, 219, 220,
     222, 227, 228, 233–235
fraud   1, 24, 25, 32, 34, 43, 57, 60, 72,
     92, 119, 227, 239, 241, 252, 259

g

goal   20, 26, 54, 79, 100, 106, 188–190,
     206, 207, 230, 257, 260, 261
governance   10, 49, 96, 117, 125, 130, 137
government   4, 19, 22, 30, 51, 63, 78,
     90, 94, 119, 121, 244, 264, 277
guidelines   89, 90, 136–140

h

hacker   26–36, 38, 43, 44, 57, 61, 176,
     177, 243
hacktivists   19, 20, 22–23, 51
Health Insurance Portability and
     Accountability Act (HIPAA)
     119, 147
high availability   125, 128, 160, 240
history/historical   4, 36, 43, 44, 55, 56,
     109, 185, 237, 242, 262
human resources (HR)   26

i

identify   8, 13, 14, 22, 49, 81, 85, 102,
     166, 175, 279

identity and access management
     (IAM)   54, 56, 58, 65, 114
identity theft   34–35, 73, 134, 243, 281
impact   3, 8, 21, 23, 33, 44, 65, 78, 79,
     84, 85, 92, 120, 129, 173, 177,
     213, 233
implementation   2, 13, 54, 96, 97, 102,
     105, 119, 171, 197, 218, 223, 230
incident   6, 12, 24, 47, 51, 52, 65,
     67–71, 77, 135, 139, 193, 205, 214
indicators   10, 69, 80, 174, 206, 208,
     210, 212, 259, 261
industry standard   8, 19, 41, 68, 121,
     122, 148, 151, 169, 215
information security management
     system (ISMS)   5, 151, 269, 272
Information Technology Infrastructure
     Library (ITIL)   67, 69, 70, 107
infrastructure   14, 19, 73, 82, 115, 121,
     125, 129, 149, 171, 199, 224,
     226, 256
inherent risk   125, 168
insider threat   23–26, 54, 110, 193, 204
insiders   24, 25, 55, 64
insurance   4, 84, 119, 147, 171, 242–244
integrity   1, 23, 50, 53, 57, 84, 94, 107,
     119, 126, 128, 160, 162, 223,
     255, 260
internal standards   123, 148, 151
International Council on Systems
     Engineering (INCOSE)   5
International Standards Organization
     (ISO)   5, 148
investigation   3, 26, 69, 74, 75, 80, 84,
     102, 134, 204, 232
investments   14, 91, 220
IP Address   64, 95, 101, 127, 131, 256
ISACA   150

j

judgment   8, 41, 160, 186, 246, 303

k

key risk indicator   9, 205–216, 252, 255, 257

l

landscape   33, 117, 129, 178, 207, 218
leaders   224, 232
leadership   221, 249, 254
least privilege   58–61, 105, 110, 120, 121, 201, 226, 245
legal   5, 11, 56, 67, 73, 74, 77, 82, 94, 109, 114, 117–119, 135, 227, 229
lifecycle   2, 36, 41, 116, 129, 195, 246
likelihood   3, 177, 262
lines of defense   217–224
logging   9, 28, 99, 101, 176
logins   4, 31, 32, 34, 64, 95, 101, 102, 111, 170, 187
lone wolf   33
loop   65, 69, 90
losses   6, 7, 50–52, 79, 84–87, 168, 207, 243, 244

m

Media Access Control (MAC)   98
mainstay   5, 6, 17, 18, 74, 117, 143, 224, 225
malvertising   43
manager   2, 10, 11, 13, 25, 58, 60, 91, 111, 115, 161, 170, 174, 176, 188, 219, 232, 234, 270
mature   3, 7, 33, 106, 215
measurement   9, 84, 185, 186, 188, 192, 206, 208, 256, 258, 260, 262
measures   8, 10, 13, 68, 161, 185–189, 192, 195, 201, 203, 205, 251, 252, 254, 257, 260, 261, 272
media   5, 33, 273
metrics   182, 186, 189, 191, 192, 195, 197, 199, 201, 203–206, 213, 252, 259, 272, 311
military   22, 23, 65, 238, 244, 260
mission   5, 51, 65, 90, 92, 93, 101, 107, 109, 123, 125, 168, 226, 228, 250

mistakes   1, 33, 40, 105, 208
misuse   19, 34, 60, 102, 140, 143
mitigate   35, 50, 155, 242, 270–272
MITRE   18, 20, 23, 28, 40, 41, 214
models   44, 53, 63, 64, 185, 192, 193, 199, 204, 222, 279
monitoring   12, 13, 55, 71, 108, 109, 115, 116, 131, 138, 164, 168, 193, 203–205, 218, 219, 223, 239
multifactor authentication (MFA)   96, 97, 102, 110
myths   2, 239

n

nation   17, 19, 24, 30, 75
National Institute of Standards and Technology (NIST)   8, 17, 48, 69, 117, 118, 121, 149
near miss   265
networks   23, 26, 29, 35, 61, 63, 64, 85, 93, 101, 102, 118, 127, 131, 133, 199, 228

o

objectives   22, 48, 54, 128, 144–146, 154, 155, 157, 165, 190
open design   100, 103, 140
operational risk   1, 4, 6, 51, 82, 173, 212, 239, 240
oversee   5, 212
oversight   5, 11, 14, 114, 116, 147, 171, 226, 279
owner   131, 143, 155, 176, 181, 233–235, 246

p

patterns   40, 44, 55, 65, 123, 133, 240, 242, 275
Payment Card Industry Security Standards Council's Data Security Standard (PCI DSS)   120
penetration test   162, 163, 171, 174, 207, 208
pentest   143, 161–164, 208

perimeter   61, 64

personally identifiable information (PII)   14, 34, 139, 171, 188, 190

perspectives   2, 5, 7, 9, 10, 51, 75, 78, 175, 218

plan   8, 29, 44, 48, 71, 104, 119, 127, 129, 160, 232, 240, 260

policies   89, 94, 96, 102, 107, 136, 143, 218, 243, 244

policy enforcement point (PEP)   127

prevent   7, 25, 47, 48, 55–64, 73, 82, 95, 101

principals   102

priority   9, 69, 80, 94, 131, 132, 175, 191, 247

privileges   57–61, 103, 105, 120, 121, 138

probabilities   3, 6, 7, 12, 51, 60, 91, 99, 101, 174, 205, 240, 242, 260–266

procedures   1, 7, 50, 68, 69, 89, 91, 99, 130–136, 149, 168, 169, 189, 208, 224

process   2, 3, 7, 11, 13, 20, 28, 38, 44, 47, 48, 74, 77–79, 84, 89, 101, 106–114, 160, 219, 224, 226, 233, 245, 256, 269, 294

profiling   13

protection   44, 63, 72, 73, 84, 119, 121, 188, 197

psychological acceptability   99, 100

purple team   163, 164

q

quantitative   84, 161, 216, 250

r

realized risk   3, 6, 78, 254, 265

recover   48, 69, 210

recovery point objective   48, 128, 240, 315

red team   44, 163, 164, 207

reference monitor   56, 58, 94–96, 101, 102

regulation   8, 35, 117, 118, 120, 138, 212, 213, 229, 232

remediation   7, 8, 69, 80, 154, 160, 175, 177, 179, 180–182, 211, 246, 260, 273

reports   2, 11, 14, 72, 79, 110, 151, 171, 204, 213, 217, 222–224, 230, 248, 263, 269–275

reputation   17, 19, 120, 226, 242, 258, 281

requirements   8, 11, 52, 55, 94, 107, 113, 116, 117, 119–121, 128, 150, 151, 166, 180, 233, 234, 245

research   13, 20, 28, 40, 168, 175, 176, 180, 213, 227, 270

residual risk   11, 14, 242, 254, 279

resilience   114, 126, 128, 129, 155, 206, 240, 245, 251

risk analysis   2, 4, 7, 13, 94, 175, 183, 213, 272

risk and control matrix (RCM)   8, 155, 219

risk and control self assessment (RCSA)   13, 143, 154–160

risk appetite   9, 11, 89, 91–94, 102, 103, 105, 138, 143, 181, 190, 208, 216, 228, 250–255

risk categories   3, 6, 10, 51, 92, 239–242, 255, 258, 281

risk issue   8, 14, 87, 173, 174–180, 183, 213, 222, 250, 252, 260

risk register   7, 11, 155, 174, 241, 247, 249

risk treatment   242–249

root cause   7, 10, 67, 68, 73, 82, 84, 87, 174, 177, 182, 189, 199, 259, 263

s

safety   92, 232, 242, 275–278, 281

sandbox   99

scenario/scenario analysis   78, 79, 81, 84–87, 146, 149, 173, 175, 261

science   3, 192, 237, 276, 278

scope   4, 48, 71, 104, 116, 145, 146, 158, 242, 256, 269

scope creep   145, 154

security architecture   90, 104, 108, 112, 114, 117–118, 123–130, 158, 166, 168, 183, 190, 192, 197, 208, 224

security incident and event
management (SIEM) 193
security operations 3, 10, 35, 107, 114,
131, 143, 245
security principles 56, 58, 60, 96–102
segregation of duties 60, 61, 64
separation of privilege 57, 61, 64
Single sign on (SSO) 251
software 4, 20, 23, 28, 31–33, 36, 40,
104, 116, 127, 129, 169, 190, 234,
239, 276
Spafford 2, 239
spot check 169–171
standardize 4, 40
standards 7, 8, 13, 19, 40, 41, 69, 81, 89,
90, 96, 101, 107, 114–130, 149, 165
strategy 11, 49, 65, 93, 116, 135, 154,
208, 232
structured threat information
expression (STIX) 20, 26
studies 269–275
subject 10, 56, 94, 114, 117, 118, 169,
171, 254
subjective 186, 240, 261
Sun Tzu 17, 18, 65
suppliers 5, 110, 125, 167, 256
system 1, 3, 5, 7, 17, 21, 22, 24, 25, 28,
29, 33, 37, 49–51, 55–57, 67, 69, 71,
109–111, 117, 119, 123, 124, 132,
161, 162, 234, 243
systemigram 5, 17, 118, 143, 145,
229, 230

t

tactics 2, 37, 38, 41, 43, 54, 72, 117
target 1, 17, 19, 37, 38, 47, 48, 169,
180–183, 199, 206, 252, 257,
260, 265
taxonomy 19, 41, 52, 241
technology 1–4, 6, 7, 9, 13, 17, 25, 33, 38,
50, 54, 58, 68, 70, 74, 77, 104, 108, 114,
118, 119, 121, 125, 126, 174, 175, 234
terrorists 19, 44
threat 5–7, 17–44

threat actors 7, 17–33, 80, 92, 132, 162,
224, 257
threat networks 33–37, 43
threat vector 37–44, 71, 73, 75, 81, 84,
87, 129, 176, 262
thwart 2, 5, 40, 44, 47, 54, 64, 65, 73,
168, 177, 224, 229, 279
tiger team 160, 161
tolerance 9, 10, 93, 113, 182,
183, 255–260
tone at the top 89, 90, 92, 93, 110, 182,
222, 227, 250–252, 255, 282
training 65, 77, 78, 104, 130, 137, 138,
174, 210, 221, 277
transfer 23, 35, 56, 58–60, 127, 242–245
treatment 12, 53, 242–250, 278
trustworthy 23, 56, 64

u

unauthorized 1, 17, 23, 25, 26, 35, 55, 60,
61, 69, 101, 129, 130, 132, 204, 228
uncertainty 1, 17, 23, 25, 26, 35, 44, 55,
61, 69, 97, 101, 110, 130
utility 30, 151, 195

v

validation (valid/validity) 30, 44, 128,
133, 162, 168, 169, 180, 190, 192,
206, 208, 220
value 5, 79, 171, 178, 226, 228, 307
verification and validation 161, 162,
168, 208, 220
vulnerabilities 3, 6, 7, 9, 23, 28, 35–37,
40, 43, 93, 112, 113, 162, 169, 173,
174, 188, 192
vulnscans 160–164

w

workflows 12, 36, 65, 68, 70, 89, 106,
107, 110, 134, 188

z

zero day 35–37, 92, 144, 162, 265, 276
zero trust 54, 63, 73, 127, 129, 157,
165, 264

Printed and bound by CPI Group (UK) Ltd, Croydon, CR0 4YY

27/10/2024

14580270-0001